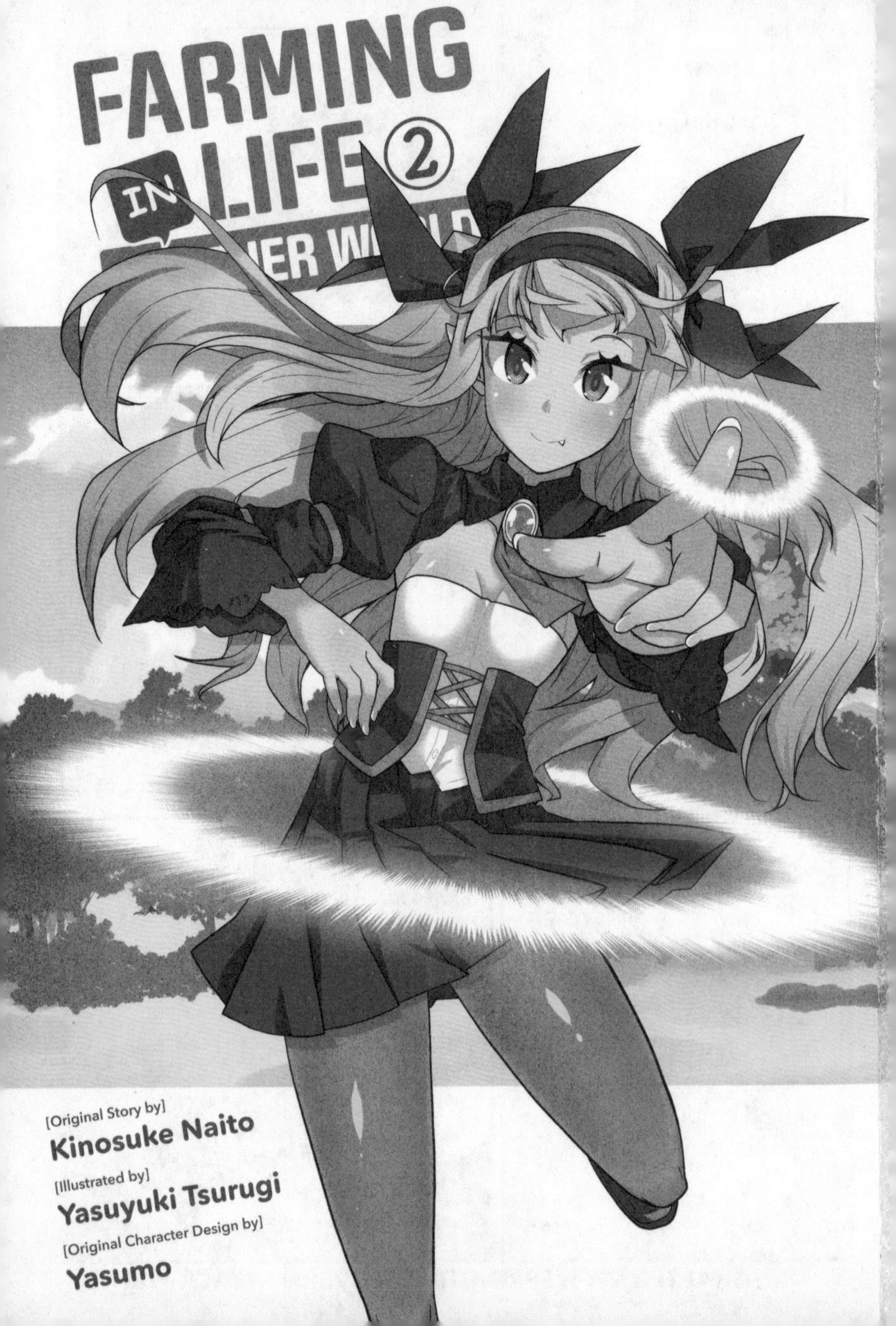

FARMING
IN LIFE 2
[Original Story by]
Kinosuke Naito
[Illustrated by]
Yasuyuki Tsurugi
[Original Character Design by]
Yasumo

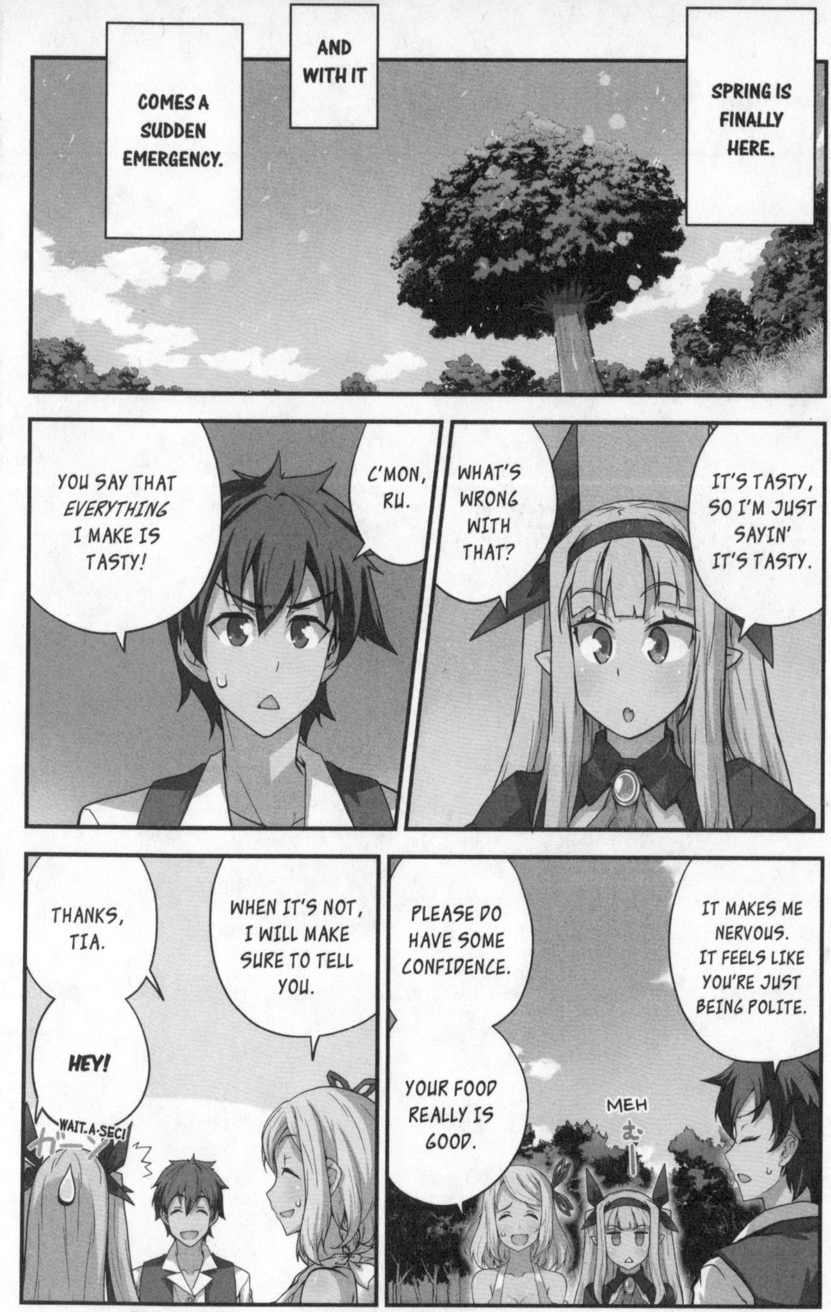
SPRING IS FINALLY HERE.
AND WITH IT
COMES A SUDDEN EMERGENCY.
IT'S TASTY, SO I'M JUST SAYIN' IT'S TASTY.
WHAT'S WRONG WITH THAT?
C'MON, RU.
YOU SAY THAT *EVERYTHING* I MAKE IS TASTY!
IT MAKES ME NERVOUS. IT FEELS LIKE YOU'RE JUST BEING POLITE.
PLEASE DO HAVE SOME CONFIDENCE.
YOUR FOOD REALLY IS GOOD.
MEH
むー
WHEN IT'S NOT, I WILL MAKE SURE TO TELL YOU.
THANKS, TIA.
HEY!
WAIT A SEC!
ガーン

CHAPTER 17: A SPRINGTIME WYVERN ATTACK PART 1

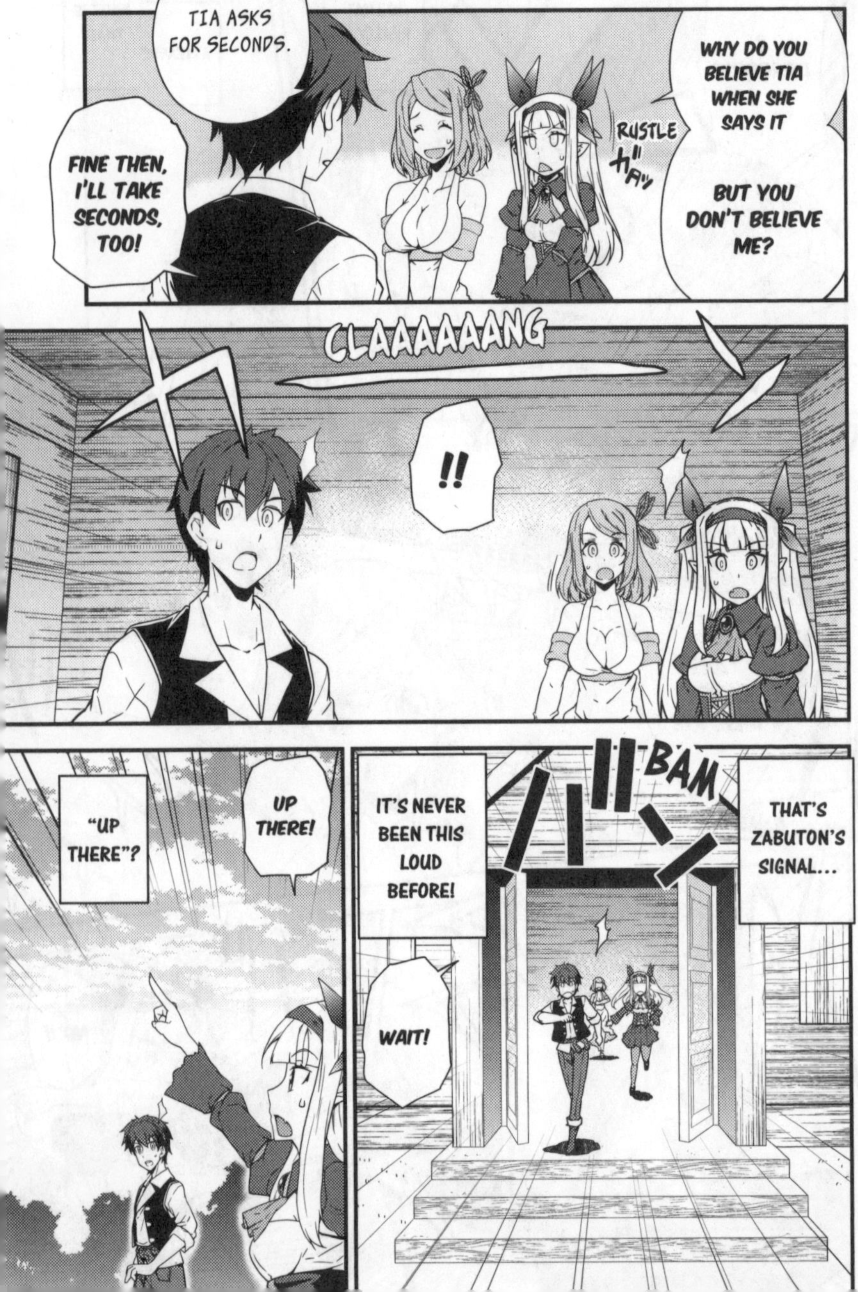

WHY DO YOU BELIEVE TIA WHEN SHE SAYS IT
BUT YOU DON'T BELIEVE ME?
TIA ASKS FOR SECONDS.
RUSTLE
ガバッ
FINE THEN, I'LL TAKE SECONDS, TOO!
CLAAAAAAANG
!!
BAM
バン
THAT'S ZABUTON'S SIGNAL...
IT'S NEVER BEEN THIS LOUD BEFORE!
WAIT!
UP THERE!
"UP THERE"?

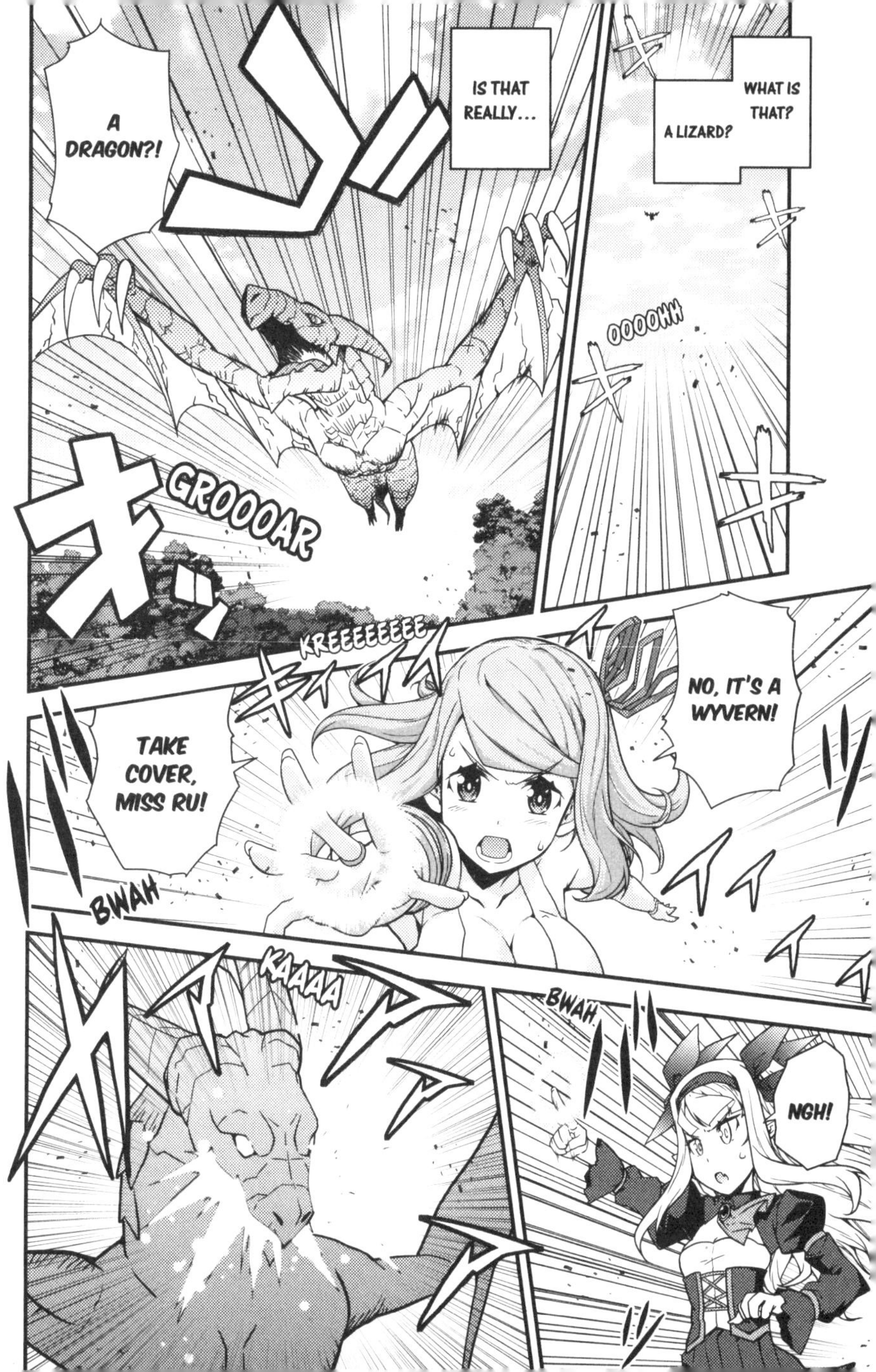
WHAT IS THAT?
A LIZARD?
OOOOHH
IS THAT REALLY…
A DRAGON?!
GROOOAR
NO, IT'S A WYVERN!
KREEEEEEEE
TAKE COVER, MISS RU!
BWAH
BWAH
NGH!
KAAAA

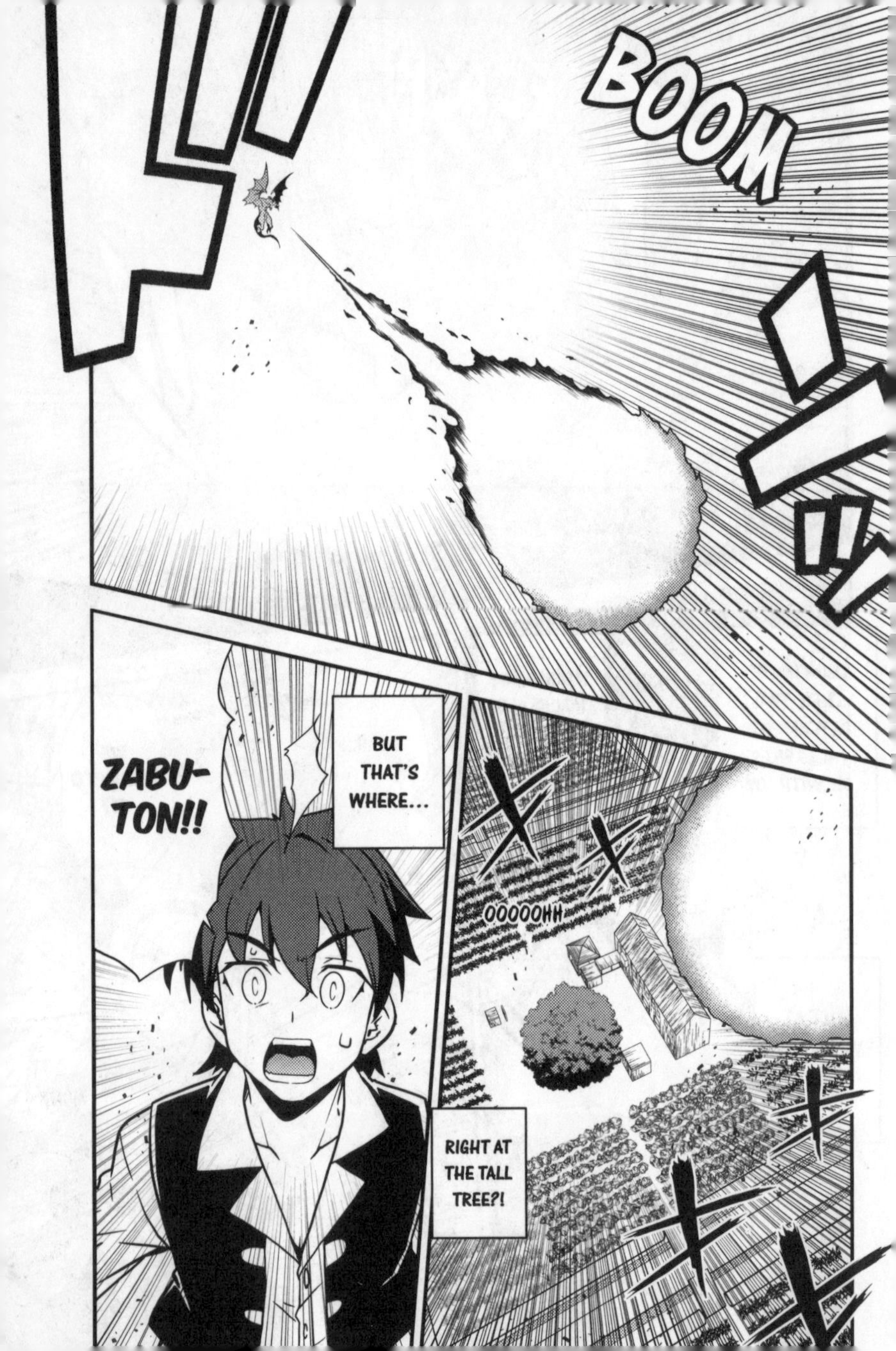
BOOM
BUT THAT'S WHERE...
ZABU-TON!!
OOOOOHH
RIGHT AT THE TALL TREE?!

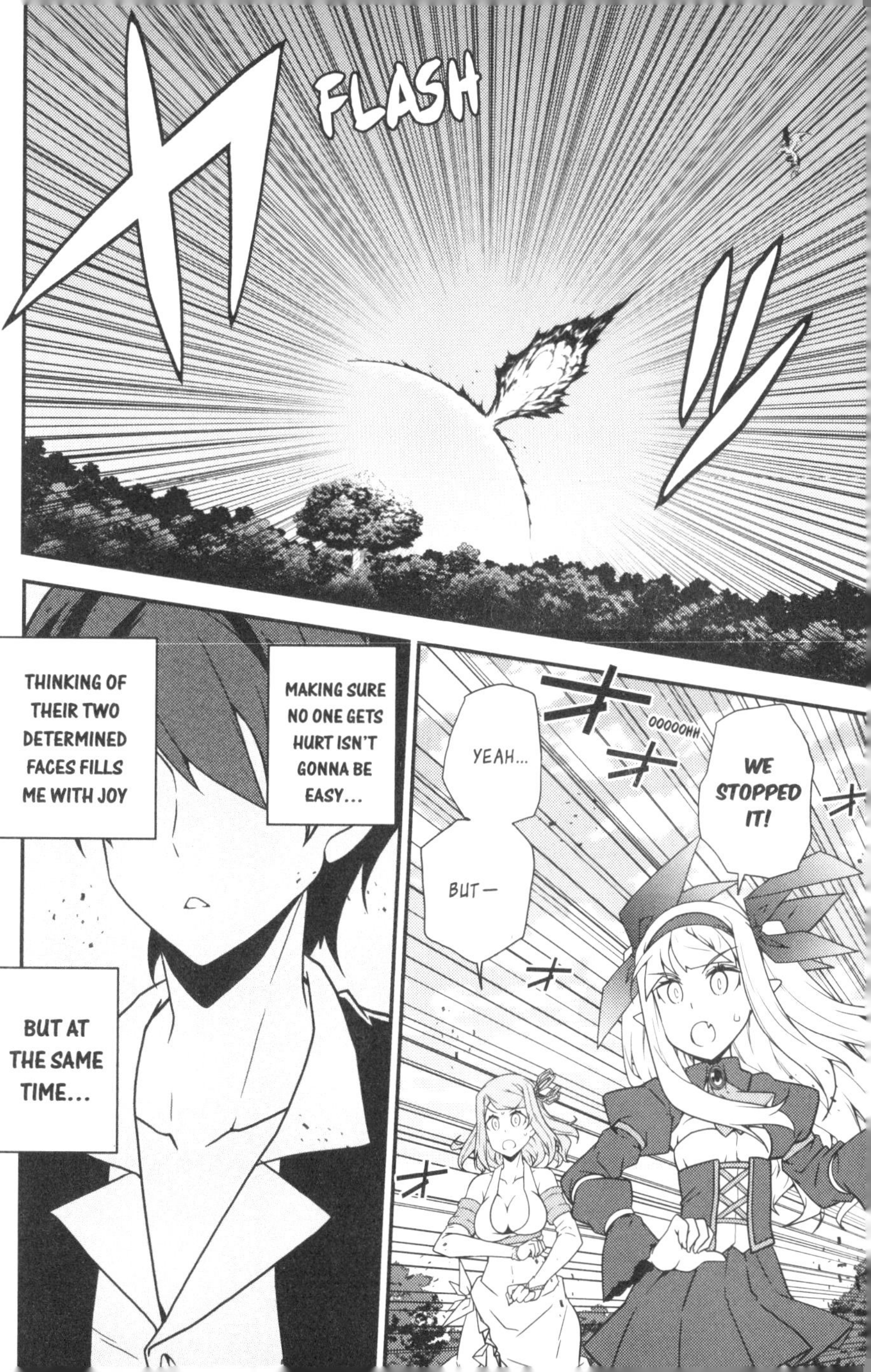
FLASH
WE STOPPED IT!
OOOOOHH
YEAH...
BUT—
MAKING SURE NO ONE GETS HURT ISN'T GONNA BE EASY...
THINKING OF THEIR TWO DETERMINED FACES FILLS ME WITH JOY
BUT AT THE SAME TIME...

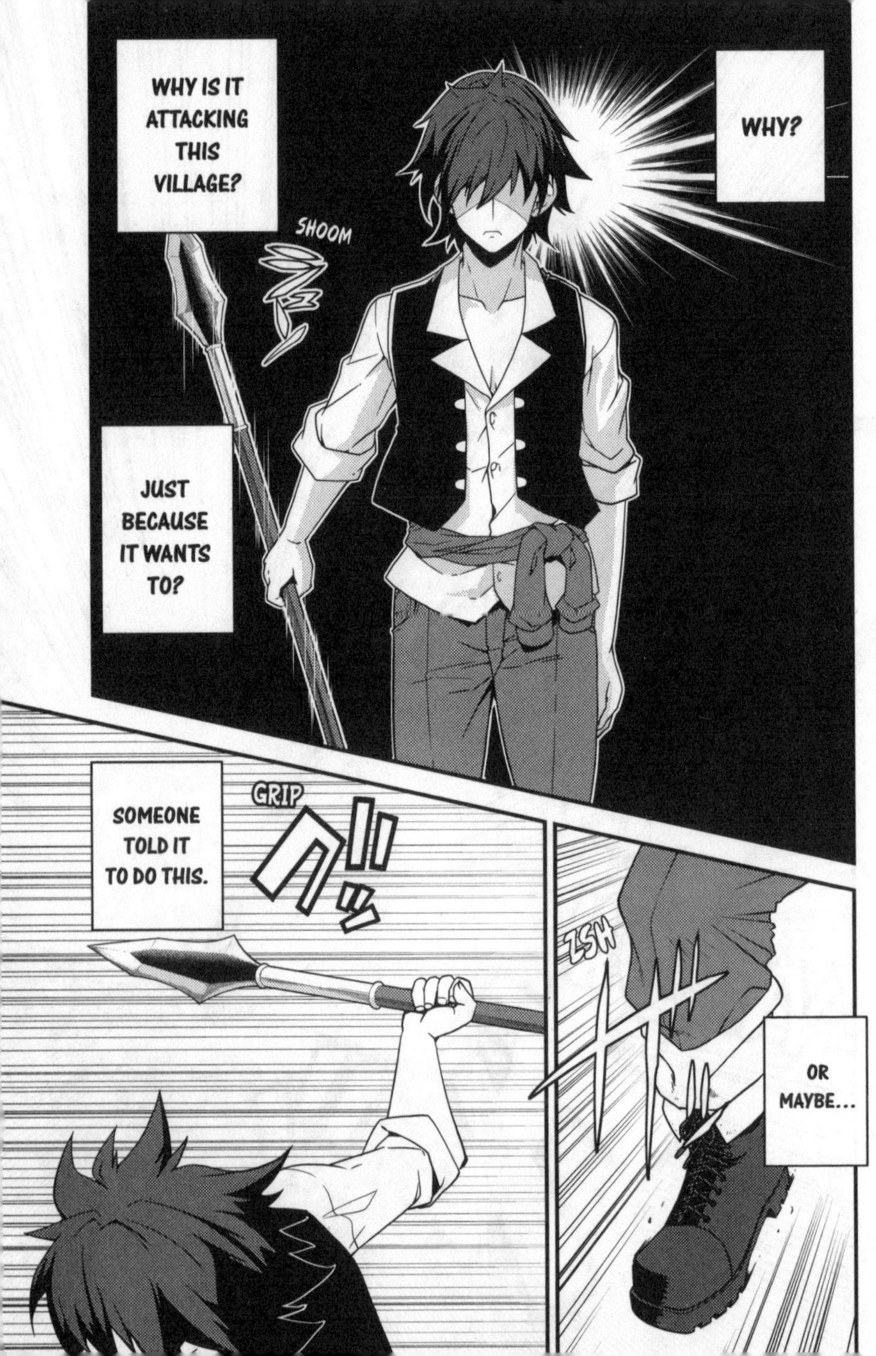
WHY?
WHY IS IT ATTACKING THIS VILLAGE?
SHOOM
JUST BECAUSE IT WANTS TO?
ZSH
OR MAYBE...
SOMEONE TOLD IT TO DO THIS.
GRIP

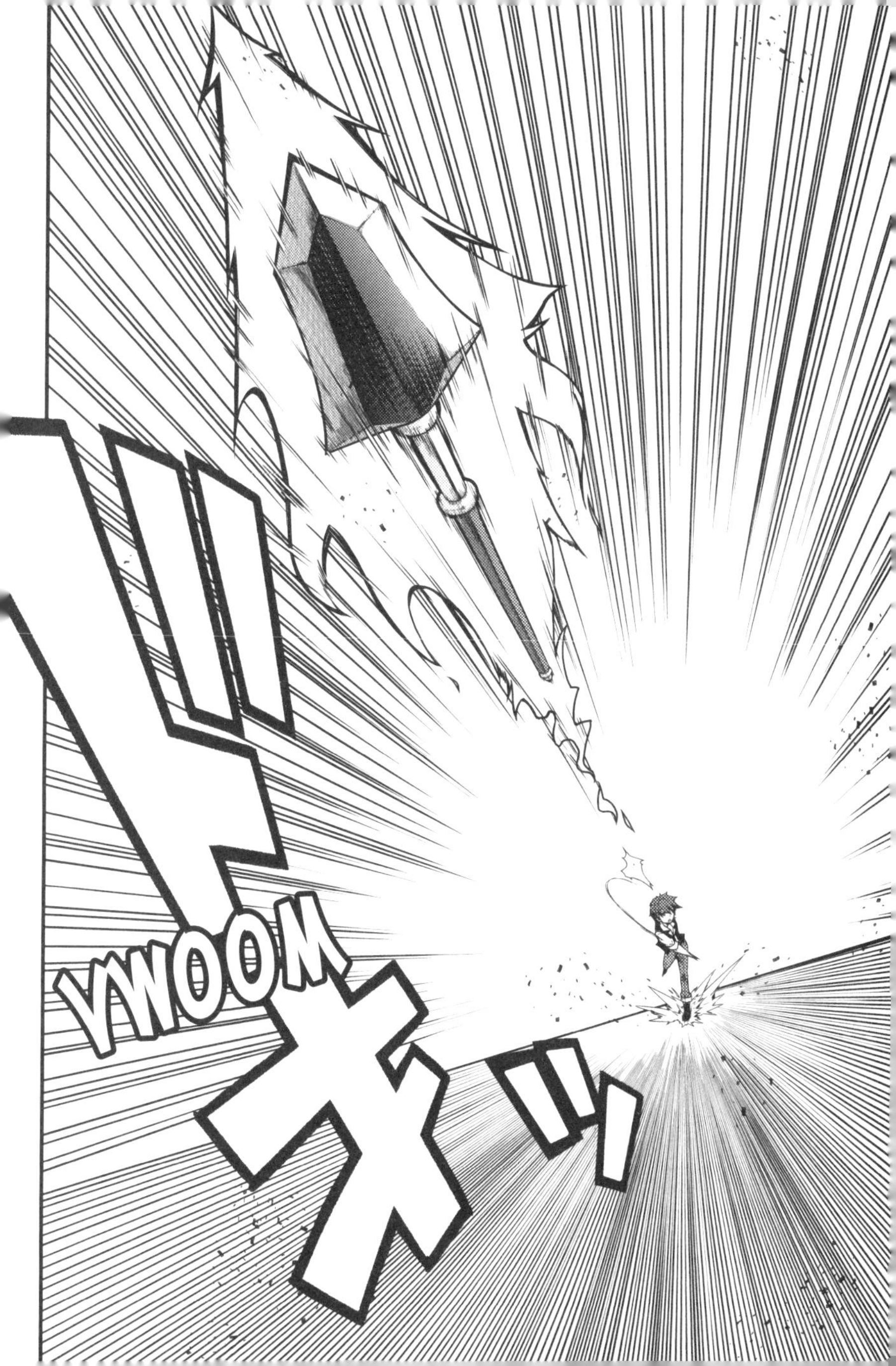
VWOOM

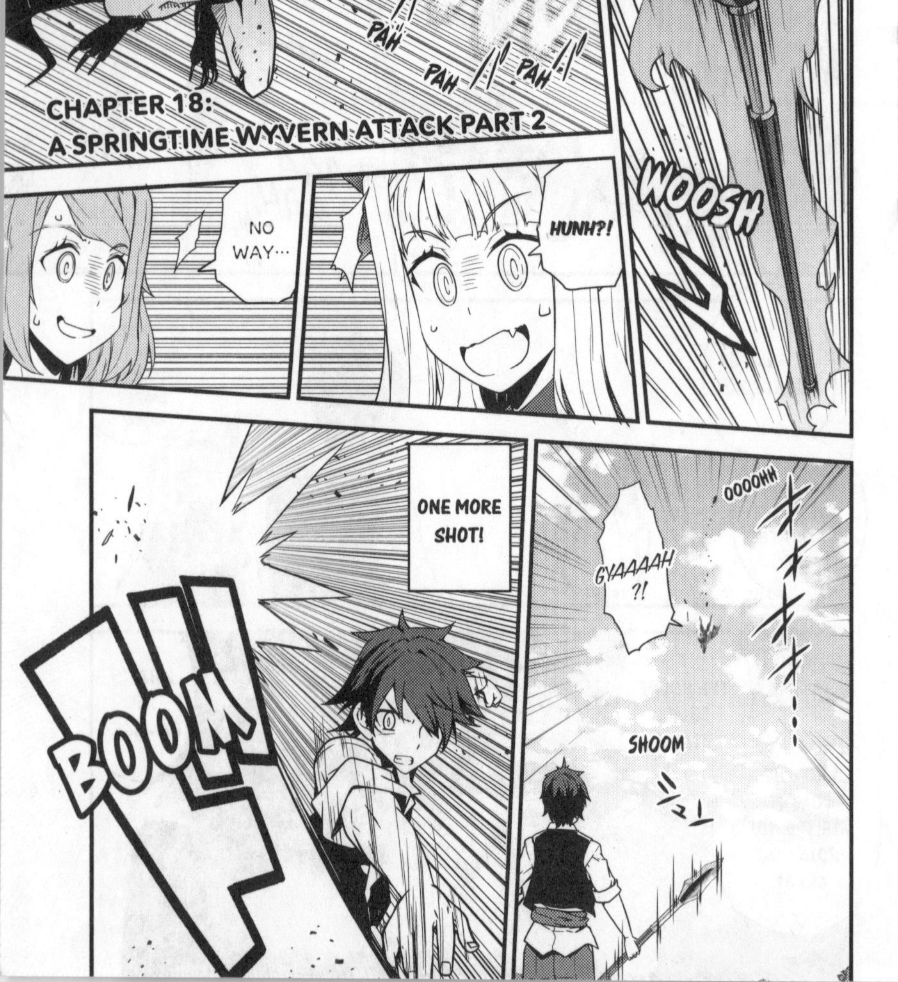
WOOSH
PAH
PAH
PAH
CHAPTER 18:
A SPRINGTIME WYVERN ATTACK PART 2
HUNH?!
NO WAY...
OOOOHH
GYAAAAH ?!
SHOOM
ONE MORE SHOT!
BOOM

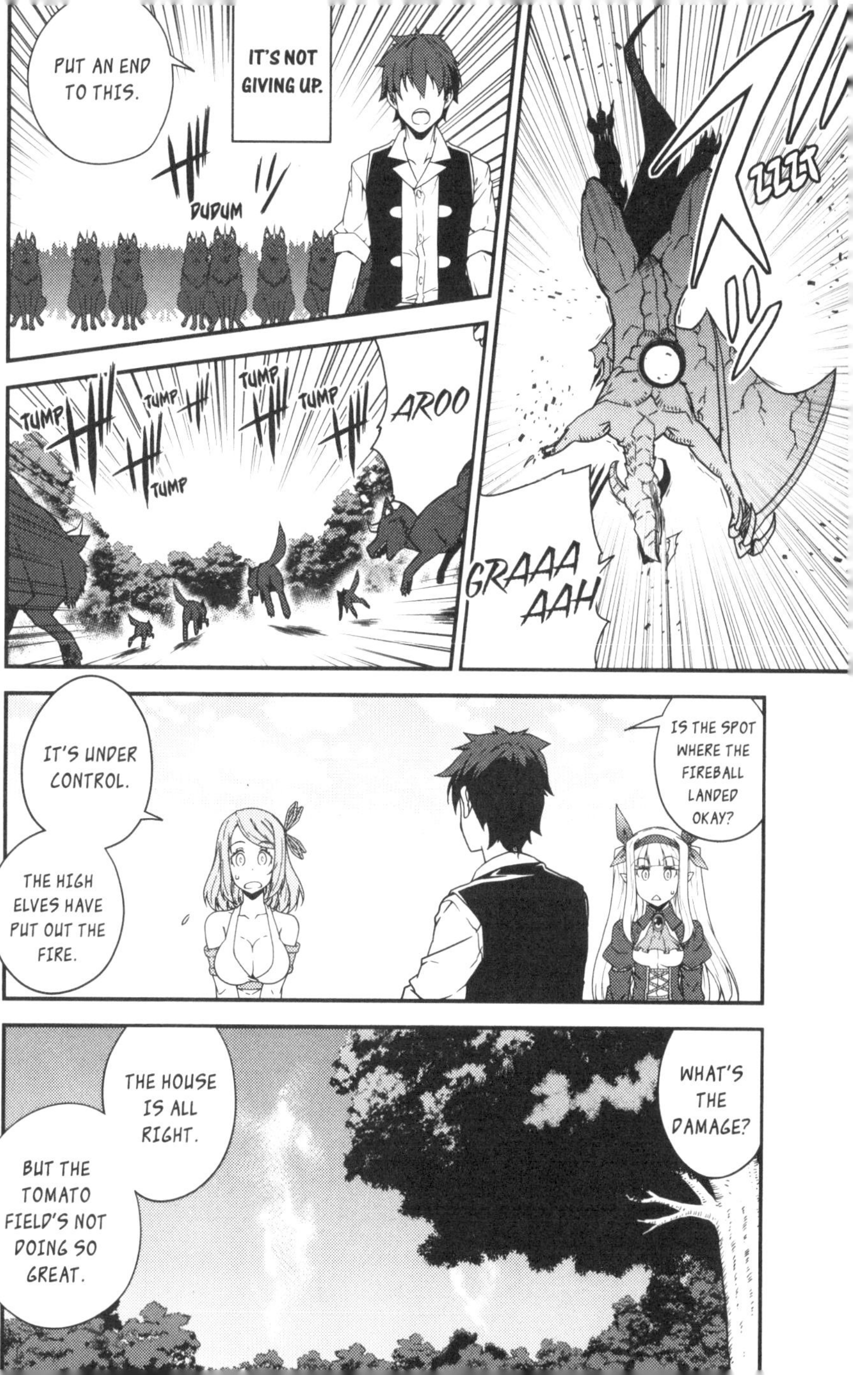
ZZZT
GRAAAAAH
IT'S NOT GIVING UP.
PUT AN END TO THIS.
DUDUM
AROO
TUMP
TUMP
TUMP
TUMP
TUMP
TUMP
IS THE SPOT WHERE THE FIREBALL LANDED OKAY?
IT'S UNDER CONTROL.
THE HIGH ELVES HAVE PUT OUT THE FIRE.
WHAT'S THE DAMAGE?
THE HOUSE IS ALL RIGHT.
BUT THE TOMATO FIELD'S NOT DOING SO GREAT.

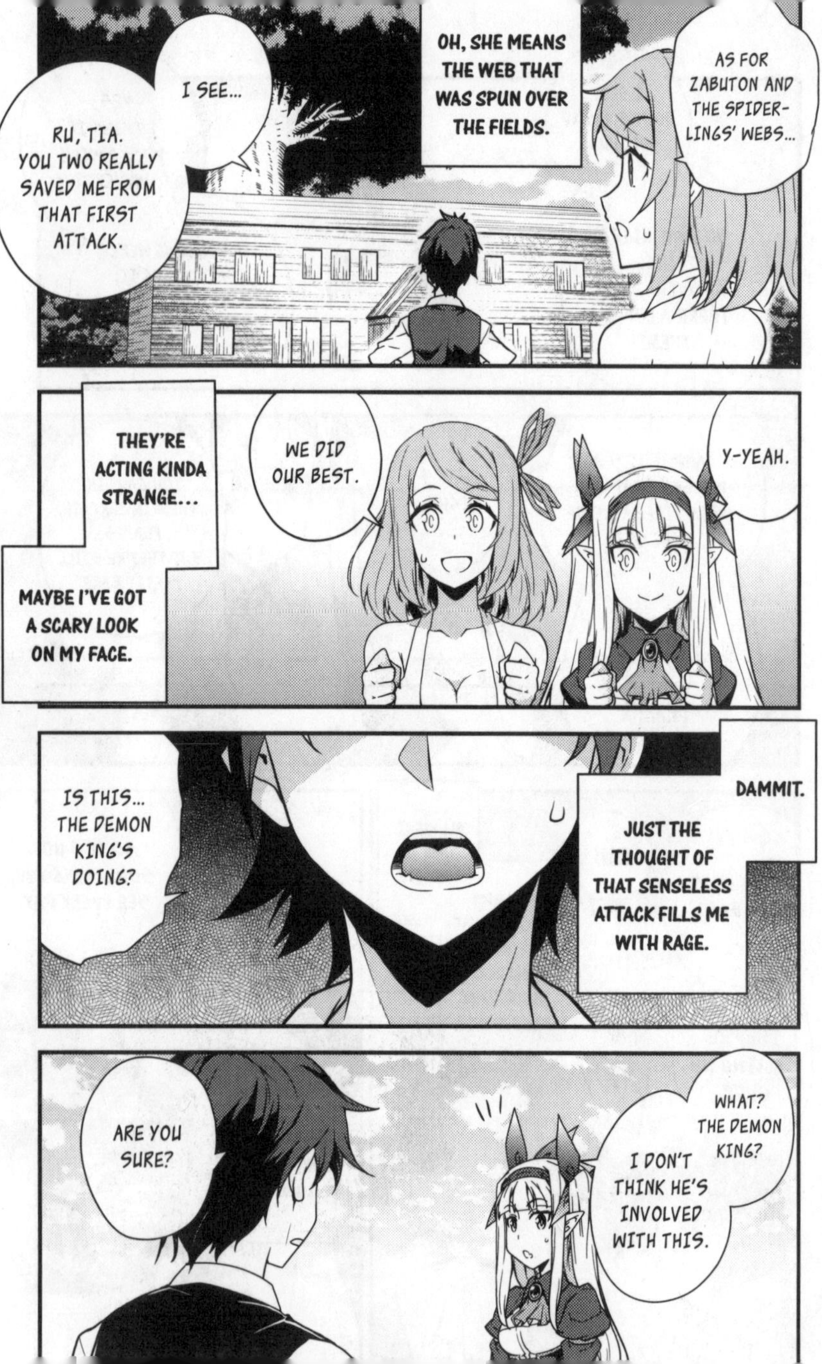
AS FOR ZABUTON AND THE SPIDER-LINGS' WEBS...
OH, SHE MEANS THE WEB THAT WAS SPUN OVER THE FIELDS.
I SEE...
RU, TIA. YOU TWO REALLY SAVED ME FROM THAT FIRST ATTACK.
Y-YEAH.
WE DID OUR BEST.
THEY'RE ACTING KINDA STRANGE...
MAYBE I'VE GOT A SCARY LOOK ON MY FACE.
DAMMIT.
JUST THE THOUGHT OF THAT SENSELESS ATTACK FILLS ME WITH RAGE.
IS THIS... THE DEMON KING'S DOING?
WHAT? THE DEMON KING?
I DON'T THINK HE'S INVOLVED WITH THIS.
ARE YOU SURE?

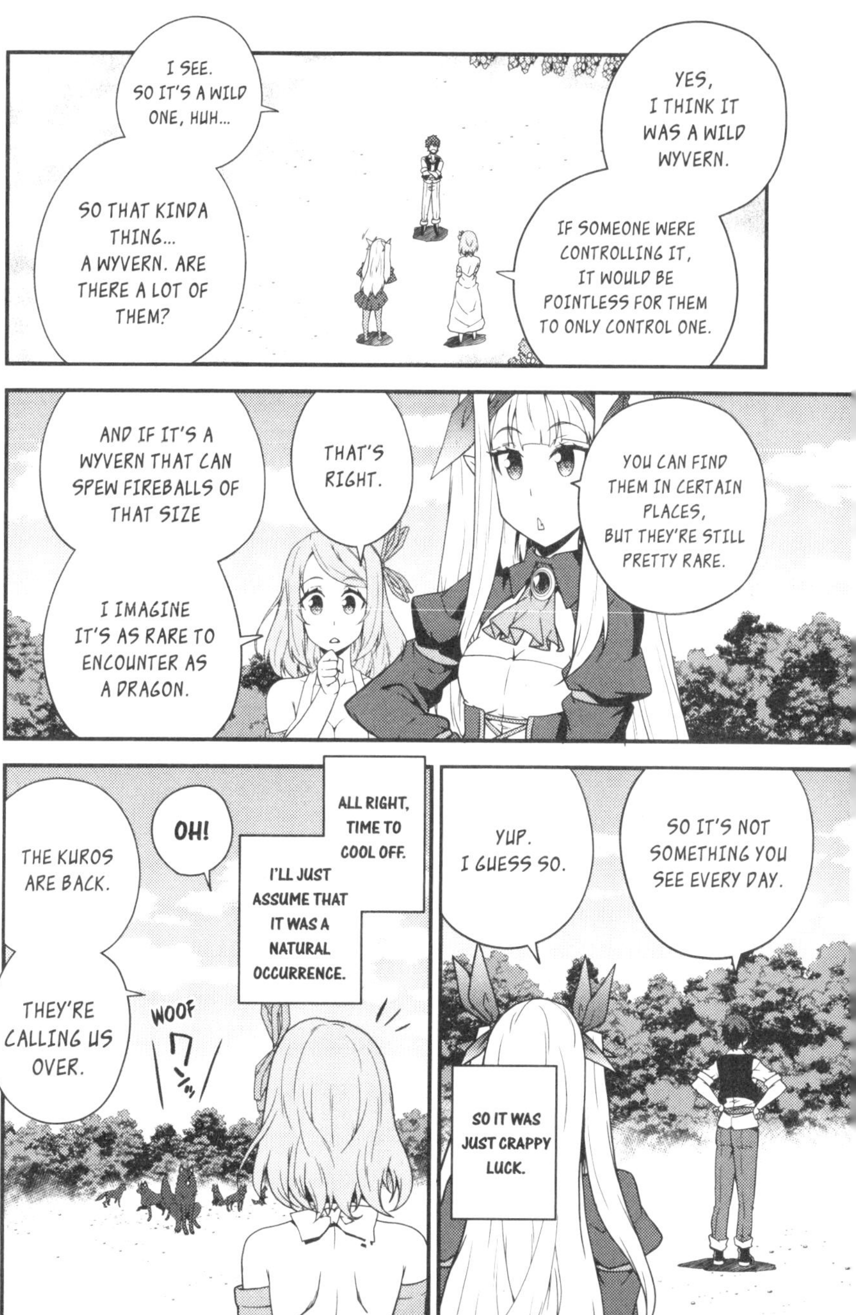
YES, I THINK IT WAS A WILD WYVERN.
IF SOMEONE WERE CONTROLLING IT, IT WOULD BE POINTLESS FOR THEM TO ONLY CONTROL ONE.
I SEE. SO IT'S A WILD ONE, HUH...
SO THAT KINDA THING... A WYVERN. ARE THERE A LOT OF THEM?
YOU CAN FIND THEM IN CERTAIN PLACES, BUT THEY'RE STILL PRETTY RARE.
THAT'S RIGHT.
AND IF IT'S A WYVERN THAT CAN SPEW FIREBALLS OF THAT SIZE
I IMAGINE IT'S AS RARE TO ENCOUNTER AS A DRAGON.
SO IT'S NOT SOMETHING YOU SEE EVERY DAY.
YUP. I GUESS SO.
SO IT WAS JUST CRAPPY LUCK.
ALL RIGHT, TIME TO COOL OFF.
I'LL JUST ASSUME THAT IT WAS A NATURAL OCCURRENCE.
OH!
THE KUROS ARE BACK.
WOOF
THEY'RE CALLING US OVER.

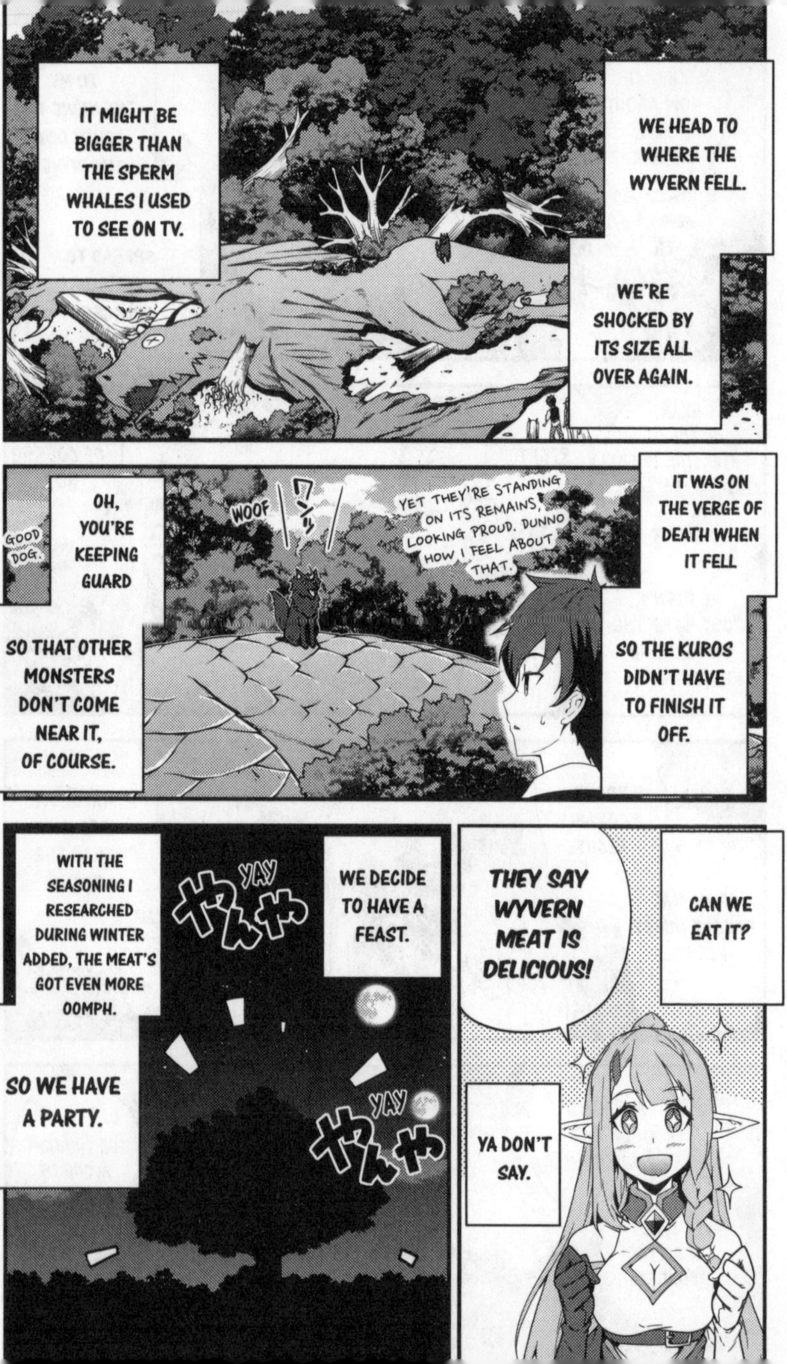
WE HEAD TO WHERE THE WYVERN FELL.
WE'RE SHOCKED BY ITS SIZE ALL OVER AGAIN.
IT MIGHT BE BIGGER THAN THE SPERM WHALES I USED TO SEE ON TV.
IT WAS ON THE VERGE OF DEATH WHEN IT FELL
SO THE KUROS DIDN'T HAVE TO FINISH IT OFF.
YET THEY'RE STANDING ON ITS REMAINS, LOOKING PROUD. DUNNO HOW I FEEL ABOUT THAT.
WOOF
ワンッ
OH, YOU'RE KEEPING GUARD
GOOD DOG.
SO THAT OTHER MONSTERS DON'T COME NEAR IT, OF COURSE.
CAN WE EAT IT?
THEY SAY WYVERN MEAT IS DELICIOUS!
YA DON'T SAY.
WE DECIDE TO HAVE A FEAST.
YAY
やんや
WITH THE SEASONING I RESEARCHED DURING WINTER ADDED, THE MEAT'S GOT EVEN MORE OOMPH.
SO WE HAVE A PARTY.
YAY
やんや

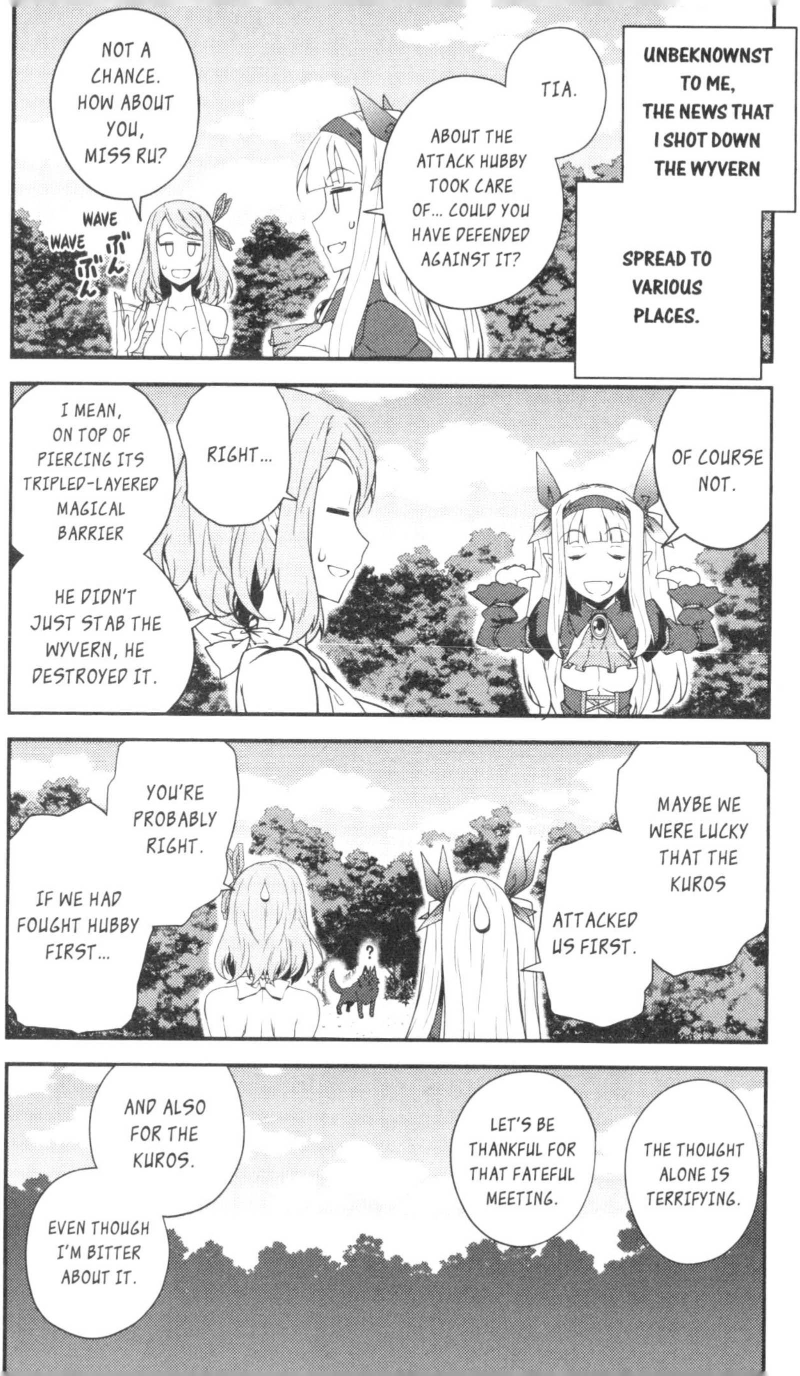
UNBEKNOWNST TO ME, THE NEWS THAT I SHOT DOWN THE WYVERN
SPREAD TO VARIOUS PLACES.
TIA.
ABOUT THE ATTACK HUBBY TOOK CARE OF... COULD YOU HAVE DEFENDED AGAINST IT?
NOT A CHANCE. HOW ABOUT YOU, MISS RU?
WAVE ぶん
WAVE ぶん
OF COURSE NOT.
RIGHT...
I MEAN, ON TOP OF PIERCING ITS TRIPLED-LAYERED MAGICAL BARRIER
HE DIDN'T JUST STAB THE WYVERN, HE DESTROYED IT.
MAYBE WE WERE LUCKY THAT THE KUROS
ATTACKED US FIRST.
YOU'RE PROBABLY RIGHT.
IF WE HAD FOUGHT HUBBY FIRST...
?
THE THOUGHT ALONE IS TERRIFYING.
LET'S BE THANKFUL FOR THAT FATEFUL MEETING.
AND ALSO FOR THE KUROS.
EVEN THOUGH I'M BITTER ABOUT IT.

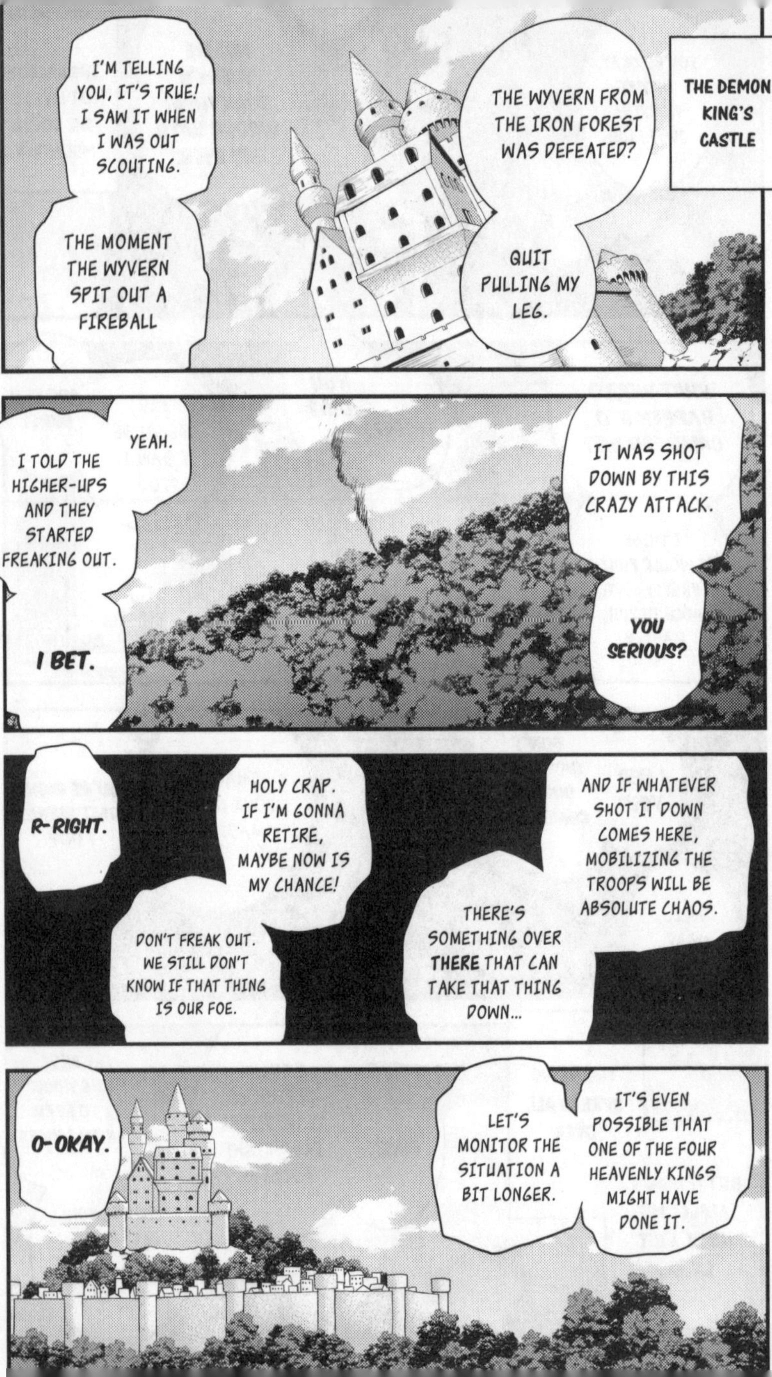
THE DEMON KING'S CASTLE
THE WYVERN FROM THE IRON FOREST WAS DEFEATED?
QUIT PULLING MY LEG.
I'M TELLING YOU, IT'S TRUE! I SAW IT WHEN I WAS OUT SCOUTING.
THE MOMENT THE WYVERN SPIT OUT A FIREBALL
IT WAS SHOT DOWN BY THIS CRAZY ATTACK.
YOU SERIOUS?
YEAH.
I TOLD THE HIGHER-UPS AND THEY STARTED FREAKING OUT.
I BET.
AND IF WHATEVER SHOT IT DOWN COMES HERE, MOBILIZING THE TROOPS WILL BE ABSOLUTE CHAOS.
THERE'S SOMETHING OVER THERE THAT CAN TAKE THAT THING DOWN...
HOLY CRAP. IF I'M GONNA RETIRE, MAYBE NOW IS MY CHANCE!
DON'T FREAK OUT. WE STILL DON'T KNOW IF THAT THING IS OUR FOE.
R-RIGHT.
IT'S EVEN POSSIBLE THAT ONE OF THE FOUR HEAVENLY KINGS MIGHT HAVE DONE IT.
LET'S MONITOR THE SITUATION A BIT LONGER.
O-OKAY.

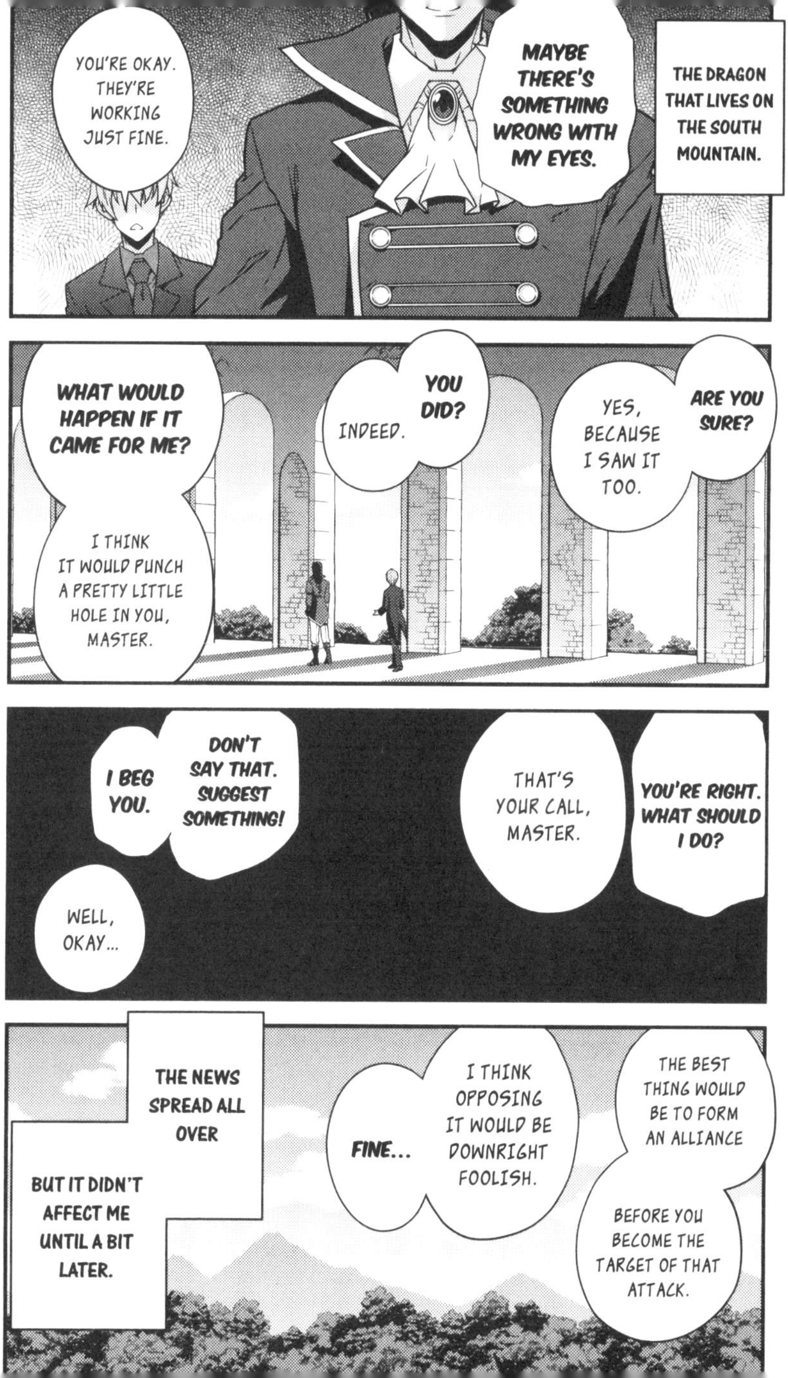
THE DRAGON THAT LIVES ON THE SOUTH MOUNTAIN.
MAYBE THERE'S SOMETHING WRONG WITH MY EYES.
YOU'RE OKAY. THEY'RE WORKING JUST FINE.
ARE YOU SURE?
YES, BECAUSE I SAW IT TOO.
YOU DID?
INDEED.
WHAT WOULD HAPPEN IF IT CAME FOR ME?
I THINK IT WOULD PUNCH A PRETTY LITTLE HOLE IN YOU, MASTER.
YOU'RE RIGHT. WHAT SHOULD I DO?
THAT'S YOUR CALL, MASTER.
DON'T SAY THAT. SUGGEST SOMETHING!
I BEG YOU.
WELL, OKAY...
THE BEST THING WOULD BE TO FORM AN ALLIANCE
BEFORE YOU BECOME THE TARGET OF THAT ATTACK.
I THINK OPPOSING IT WOULD BE DOWNRIGHT FOOLISH.
FINE...
THE NEWS SPREAD ALL OVER
BUT IT DIDN'T AFFECT ME UNTIL A BIT LATER.

CHAPTER 19: I WANT BOOZE

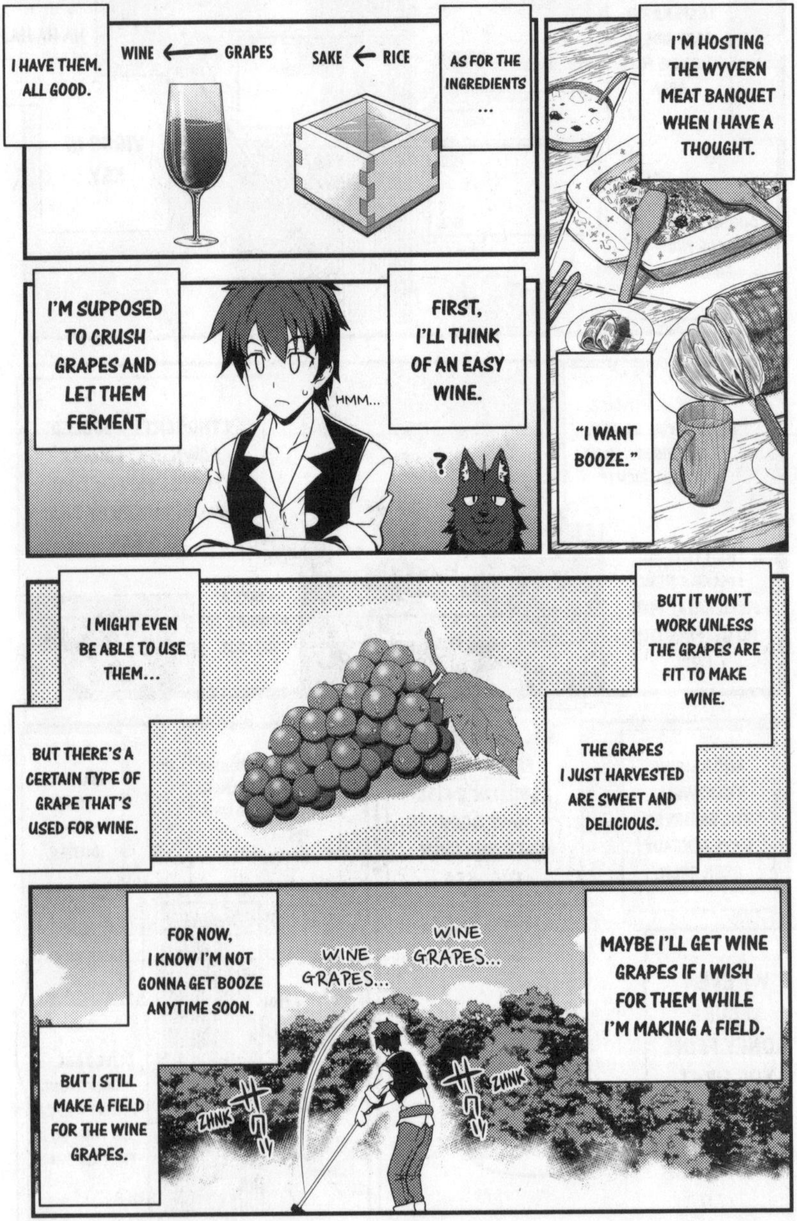

I'M HOSTING THE WYVERN MEAT BANQUET WHEN I HAVE A THOUGHT.
"I WANT BOOZE."
AS FOR THE INGREDIENTS ...
SAKE ← RICE
WINE ← GRAPES
I HAVE THEM. ALL GOOD.
FIRST, I'LL THINK OF AN EASY WINE.
?
HMM...
I'M SUPPOSED TO CRUSH GRAPES AND LET THEM FERMENT
BUT IT WON'T WORK UNLESS THE GRAPES ARE FIT TO MAKE WINE.
I MIGHT EVEN BE ABLE TO USE THEM...
THE GRAPES I JUST HARVESTED ARE SWEET AND DELICIOUS.
BUT THERE'S A CERTAIN TYPE OF GRAPE THAT'S USED FOR WINE.
MAYBE I'LL GET WINE GRAPES IF I WISH FOR THEM WHILE I'M MAKING A FIELD.
WINE GRAPES...
WINE GRAPES...
FOR NOW, I KNOW I'M NOT GONNA GET BOOZE ANYTIME SOON.
ZHNK
ZHNK
BUT I STILL MAKE A FIELD FOR THE WINE GRAPES.

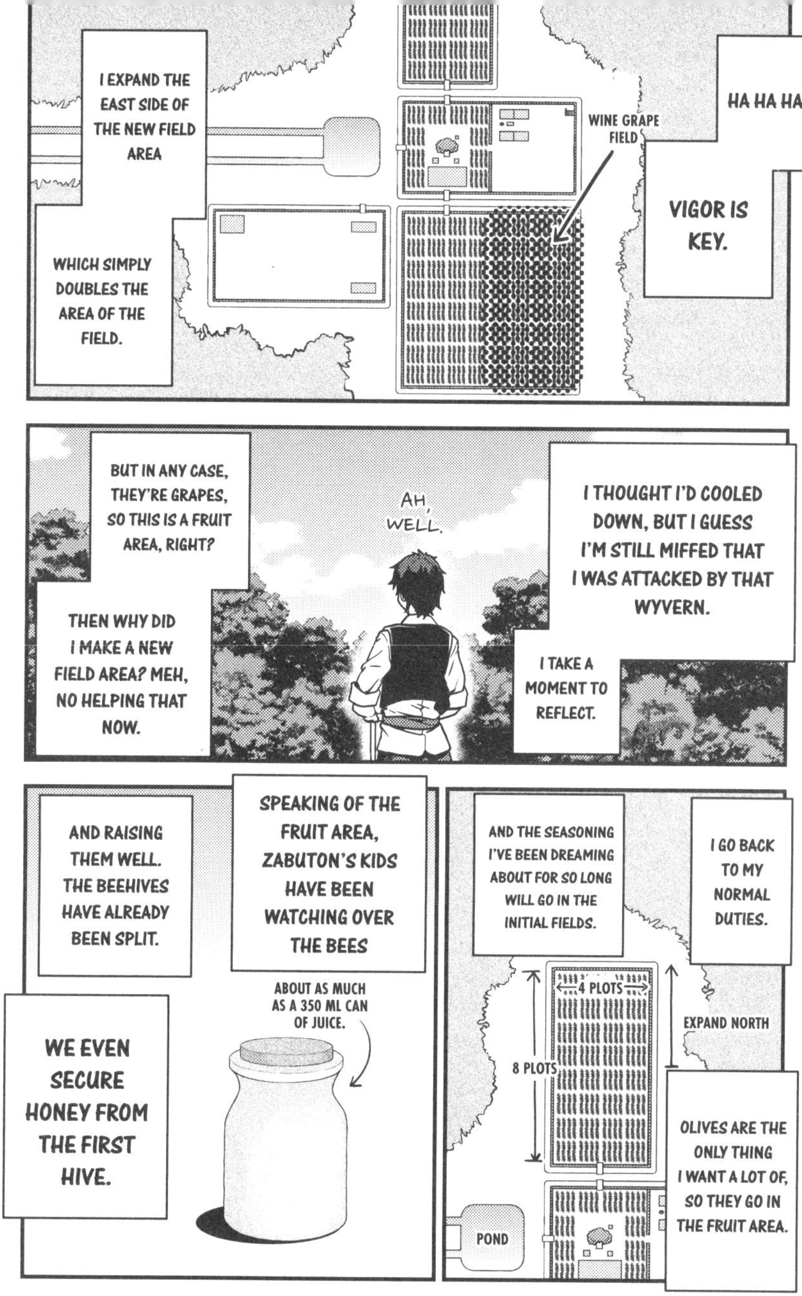
HA HA HA.
VIGOR IS KEY.
WINE GRAPE FIELD
I EXPAND THE EAST SIDE OF THE NEW FIELD AREA
WHICH SIMPLY DOUBLES THE AREA OF THE FIELD.
I THOUGHT I'D COOLED DOWN, BUT I GUESS I'M STILL MIFFED THAT I WAS ATTACKED BY THAT WYVERN.
I TAKE A MOMENT TO REFLECT.
AH, WELL.
BUT IN ANY CASE, THEY'RE GRAPES, SO THIS IS A FRUIT AREA, RIGHT?
THEN WHY DID I MAKE A NEW FIELD AREA? MEH, NO HELPING THAT NOW.
I GO BACK TO MY NORMAL DUTIES.
AND THE SEASONING I'VE BEEN DREAMING ABOUT FOR SO LONG WILL GO IN THE INITIAL FIELDS.
4 PLOTS
EXPAND NORTH
8 PLOTS
OLIVES ARE THE ONLY THING I WANT A LOT OF, SO THEY GO IN THE FRUIT AREA.
POND
SPEAKING OF THE FRUIT AREA, ZABUTON'S KIDS HAVE BEEN WATCHING OVER THE BEES
AND RAISING THEM WELL. THE BEEHIVES HAVE ALREADY BEEN SPLIT.
ABOUT AS MUCH AS A 350 ML CAN OF JUICE.
WE EVEN SECURE HONEY FROM THE FIRST HIVE.

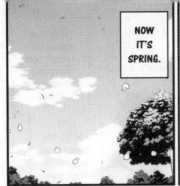

WE ALL TASTE THE HONEY WE GET, BUT WE'RE DOWN TO LESS THAN HALF IN NO TIME.
I'M JUST GLAD EVERYONE LIKES IT. NEXT TIME, WE SHOULD HAVE ENOUGH TO START COOKING WITH IT.
NOW IT'S SPRING.
AFTER I SEE ZABUTON'S KIDS OFF ON WHAT I ASSUME TO BE A SEASONAL RITE OF PASSAGE,
THE KUROS START GROWING NEW HORNS.
HOW MANY NEW ONES ARE THERE?
ACTUALLY, I CAN'T FACE THAT REALITY.
?
AFTER THIS, I GUESS THEY'LL GO LOOKING FOR MATES...
AND WELL, THINGS ARE GONNA GET CRAZY.
I IMPROVE THE RESERVOIR
1. MAKE A BANK-SIDE RESERVOIR.
RESERVOIR
2. USE A BAMBOO GATE TO PREVENT INFLUX OF WASTE/ LIVING THINGS.
AND THE DRAINAGE CHANNEL.
1. MAKE A DRAINAGE POOL.
BAMBOO GATE
RESERVOIR
2. DROP SLIMES IN TO CLEAN IT.
BATHHOUSE

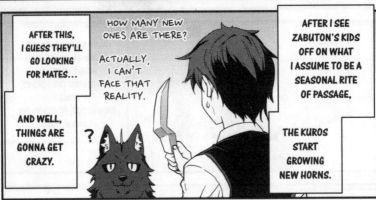

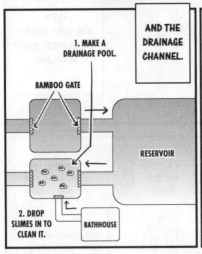

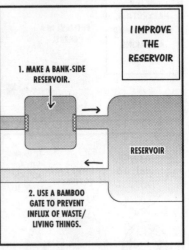

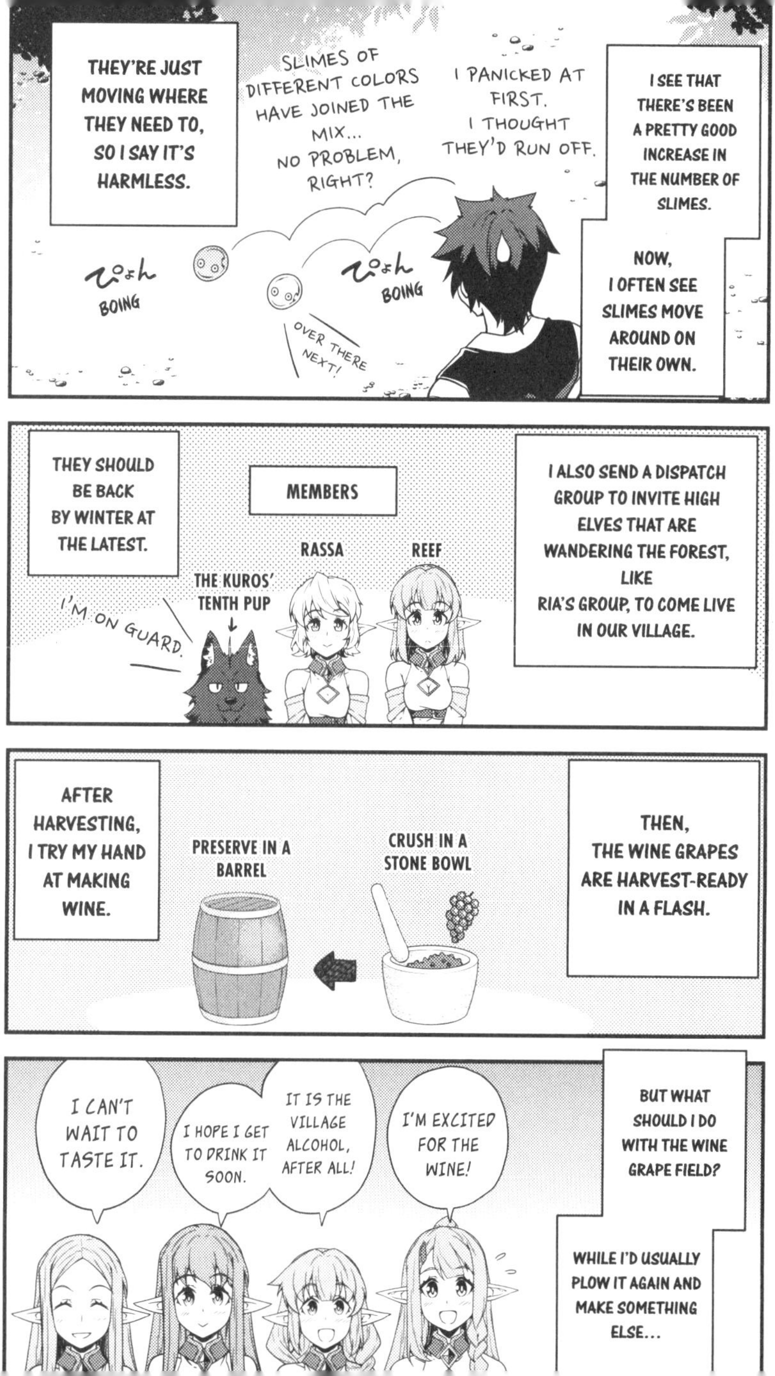
I SEE THAT THERE'S BEEN A PRETTY GOOD INCREASE IN THE NUMBER OF SLIMES.
NOW, I OFTEN SEE SLIMES MOVE AROUND ON THEIR OWN.
I PANICKED AT FIRST. I THOUGHT THEY'D RUN OFF.
SLIMES OF DIFFERENT COLORS HAVE JOINED THE MIX... NO PROBLEM, RIGHT?
ぴょん BOING
OVER THERE NEXT!
ぴょん BOING
THEY'RE JUST MOVING WHERE THEY NEED TO, SO I SAY IT'S HARMLESS.
I ALSO SEND A DISPATCH GROUP TO INVITE HIGH ELVES THAT ARE WANDERING THE FOREST, LIKE RIA'S GROUP, TO COME LIVE IN OUR VILLAGE.
MEMBERS
REEF
RASSA
THE KUROS' TENTH PUP
I'M ON GUARD.
THEY SHOULD BE BACK BY WINTER AT THE LATEST.
THEN, THE WINE GRAPES ARE HARVEST-READY IN A FLASH.
CRUSH IN A STONE BOWL
PRESERVE IN A BARREL
AFTER HARVESTING, I TRY MY HAND AT MAKING WINE.
BUT WHAT SHOULD I DO WITH THE WINE GRAPE FIELD?
WHILE I'D USUALLY PLOW IT AGAIN AND MAKE SOMETHING ELSE...
I'M EXCITED FOR THE WINE!
IT IS THE VILLAGE ALCOHOL, AFTER ALL!
I HOPE I GET TO DRINK IT SOON.
I CAN'T WAIT TO TASTE IT.

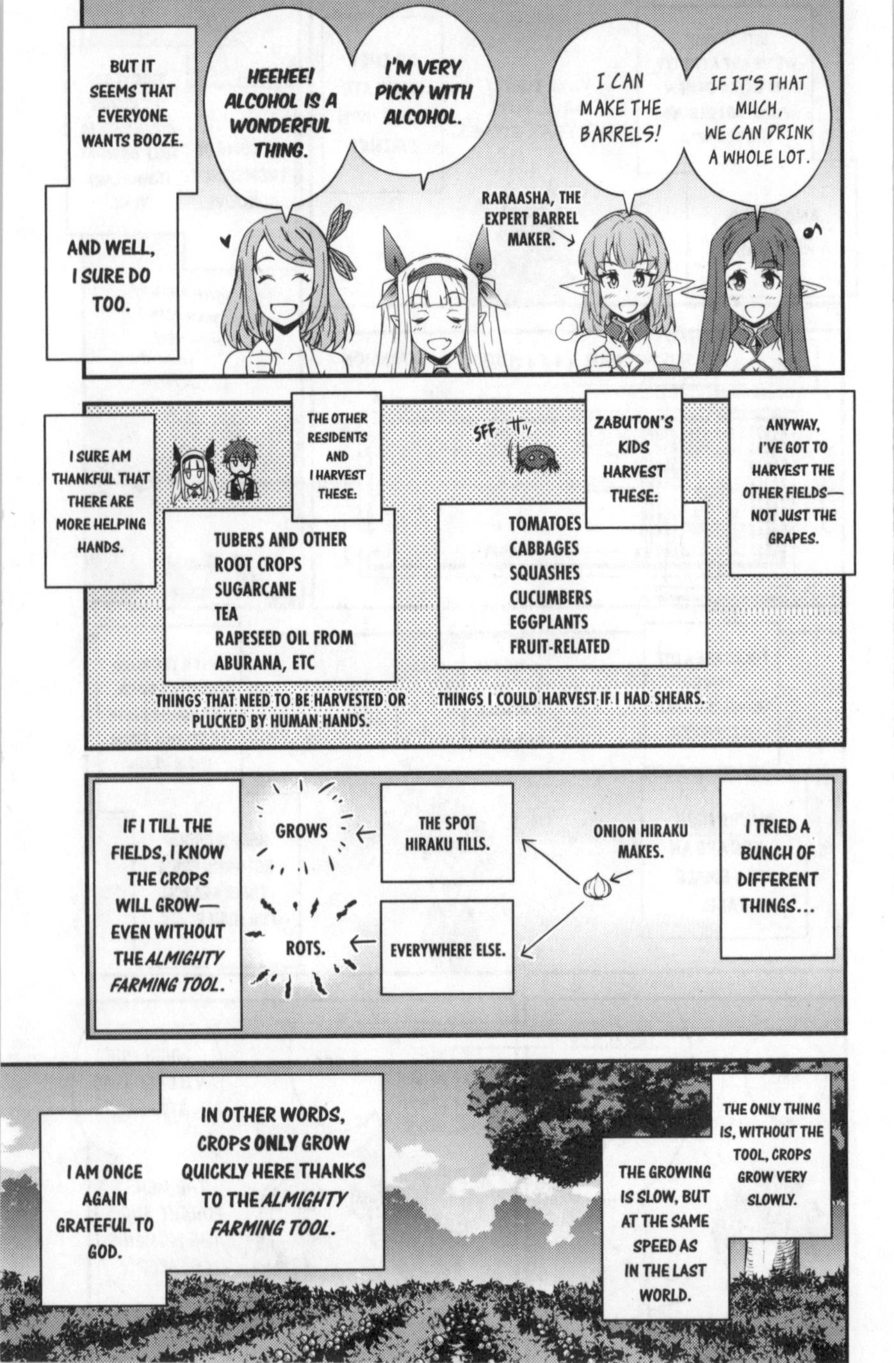
IF IT'S THAT MUCH, WE CAN DRINK A WHOLE LOT.
I CAN MAKE THE BARRELS!
RARAASHA, THE EXPERT BARREL MAKER.
I'M VERY PICKY WITH ALCOHOL.
HEEHEE! ALCOHOL IS A WONDERFUL THING.
BUT IT SEEMS THAT EVERYONE WANTS BOOZE.
AND WELL, I SURE DO TOO.
ANYWAY, I'VE GOT TO HARVEST THE OTHER FIELDS—NOT JUST THE GRAPES.
ZABUTON'S KIDS HARVEST THESE:
TOMATOES
CABBAGES
SQUASHES
CUCUMBERS
EGGPLANTS
FRUIT-RELATED
THINGS I COULD HARVEST IF I HAD SHEARS.
SFF
THE OTHER RESIDENTS AND I HARVEST THESE:
TUBERS AND OTHER ROOT CROPS
SUGARCANE
TEA
RAPESEED OIL FROM ABURANA, ETC
THINGS THAT NEED TO BE HARVESTED OR PLUCKED BY HUMAN HANDS.
I SURE AM THANKFUL THAT THERE ARE MORE HELPING HANDS.
I TRIED A BUNCH OF DIFFERENT THINGS...
ONION HIRAKU MAKES.
THE SPOT HIRAKU TILLS.
EVERYWHERE ELSE.
GROWS
ROTS.
IF I TILL THE FIELDS, I KNOW THE CROPS WILL GROW—EVEN WITHOUT THE *ALMIGHTY FARMING TOOL*.
THE ONLY THING IS, WITHOUT THE TOOL, CROPS GROW VERY SLOWLY.
THE GROWING IS SLOW, BUT AT THE SAME SPEED AS IN THE LAST WORLD.
IN OTHER WORDS, CROPS ONLY GROW QUICKLY HERE THANKS TO THE *ALMIGHTY FARMING TOOL*.
I AM ONCE AGAIN GRATEFUL TO GOD.

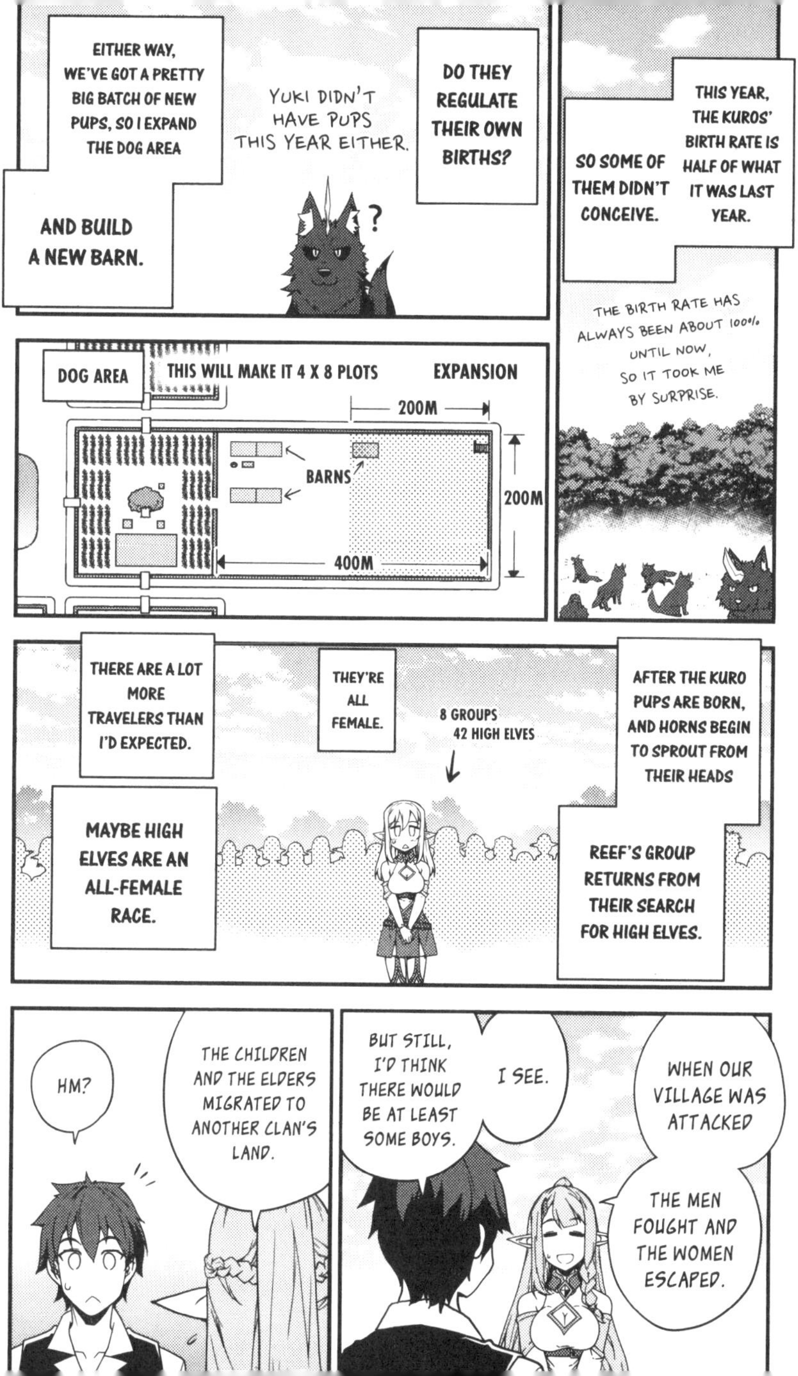
THIS YEAR, THE KUROS' BIRTH RATE IS HALF OF WHAT IT WAS LAST YEAR.
SO SOME OF THEM DIDN'T CONCEIVE.
THE BIRTH RATE HAS ALWAYS BEEN ABOUT 100% UNTIL NOW, SO IT TOOK ME BY SURPRISE.
DO THEY REGULATE THEIR OWN BIRTHS?
YUKI DIDN'T HAVE PUPS THIS YEAR EITHER.
EITHER WAY, WE'VE GOT A PRETTY BIG BATCH OF NEW PUPS, SO I EXPAND THE DOG AREA
AND BUILD A NEW BARN.
EXPANSION
THIS WILL MAKE IT 4 X 8 PLOTS
DOG AREA
200M
BARNS
200M
400M
AFTER THE KURO PUPS ARE BORN, AND HORNS BEGIN TO SPROUT FROM THEIR HEADS
REEF'S GROUP RETURNS FROM THEIR SEARCH FOR HIGH ELVES.
8 GROUPS 42 HIGH ELVES
THEY'RE ALL FEMALE.
THERE ARE A LOT MORE TRAVELERS THAN I'D EXPECTED.
MAYBE HIGH ELVES ARE AN ALL-FEMALE RACE.
WHEN OUR VILLAGE WAS ATTACKED
THE MEN FOUGHT AND THE WOMEN ESCAPED.
I SEE.
BUT STILL, I'D THINK THERE WOULD BE AT LEAST SOME BOYS.
THE CHILDREN AND THE ELDERS MIGRATED TO ANOTHER CLAN'S LAND.
HM?

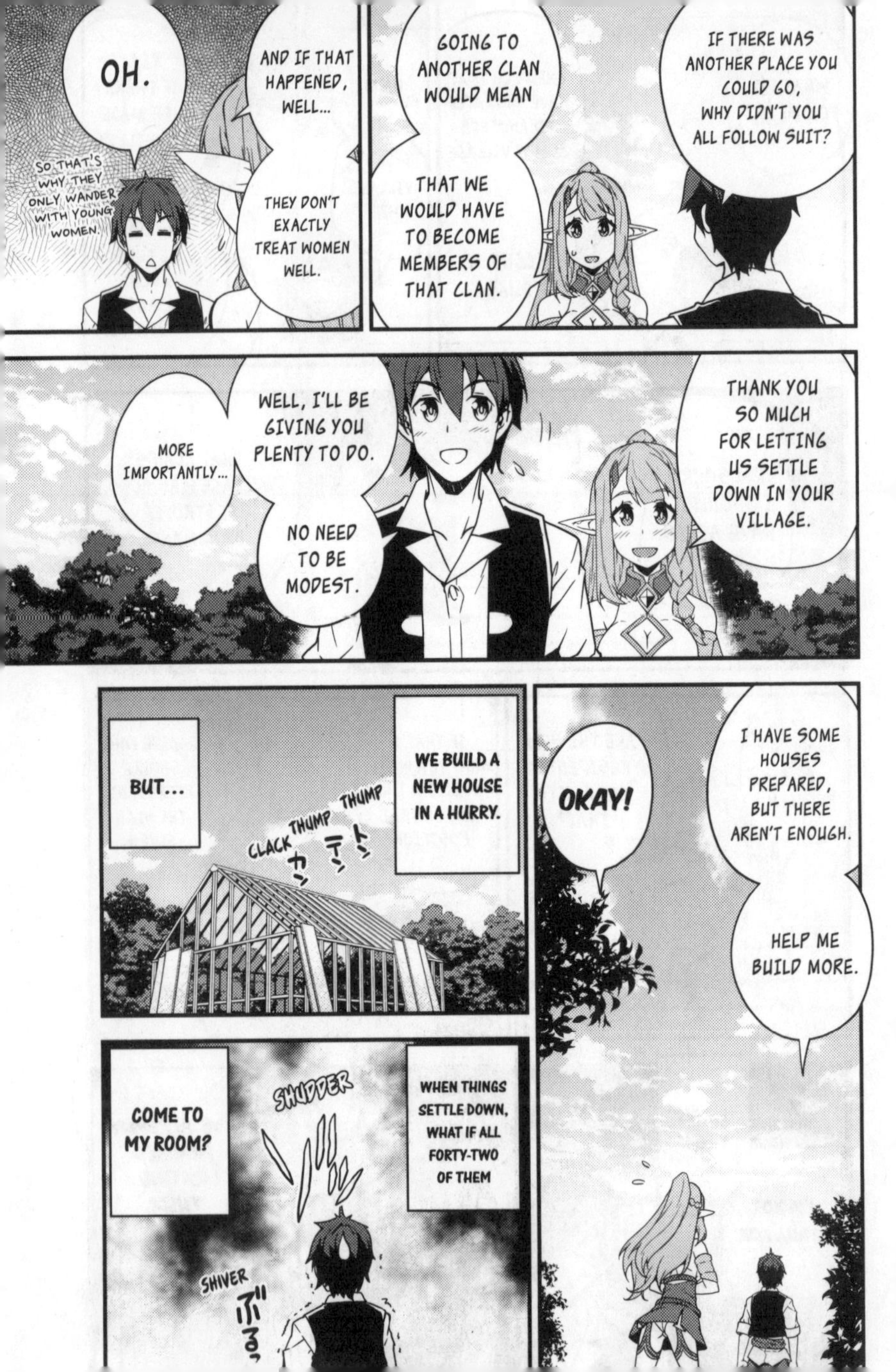
IF THERE WAS ANOTHER PLACE YOU COULD GO, WHY DIDN'T YOU ALL FOLLOW SUIT?
GOING TO ANOTHER CLAN WOULD MEAN
THAT WE WOULD HAVE TO BECOME MEMBERS OF THAT CLAN.
AND IF THAT HAPPENED, WELL...
THEY DON'T EXACTLY TREAT WOMEN WELL.
OH.
SO THAT'S WHY THEY ONLY WANDER WITH YOUNG WOMEN.
THANK YOU SO MUCH FOR LETTING US SETTLE DOWN IN YOUR VILLAGE.
WELL, I'LL BE GIVING YOU PLENTY TO DO.
NO NEED TO BE MODEST.
MORE IMPORTANTLY...
I HAVE SOME HOUSES PREPARED, BUT THERE AREN'T ENOUGH.
HELP ME BUILD MORE.
OKAY!
WE BUILD A NEW HOUSE IN A HURRY.
THUMP
THUMP
CLACK
BUT...
WHEN THINGS SETTLE DOWN, WHAT IF ALL FORTY-TWO OF THEM
SHUDDER
COME TO MY ROOM?
SHIVER

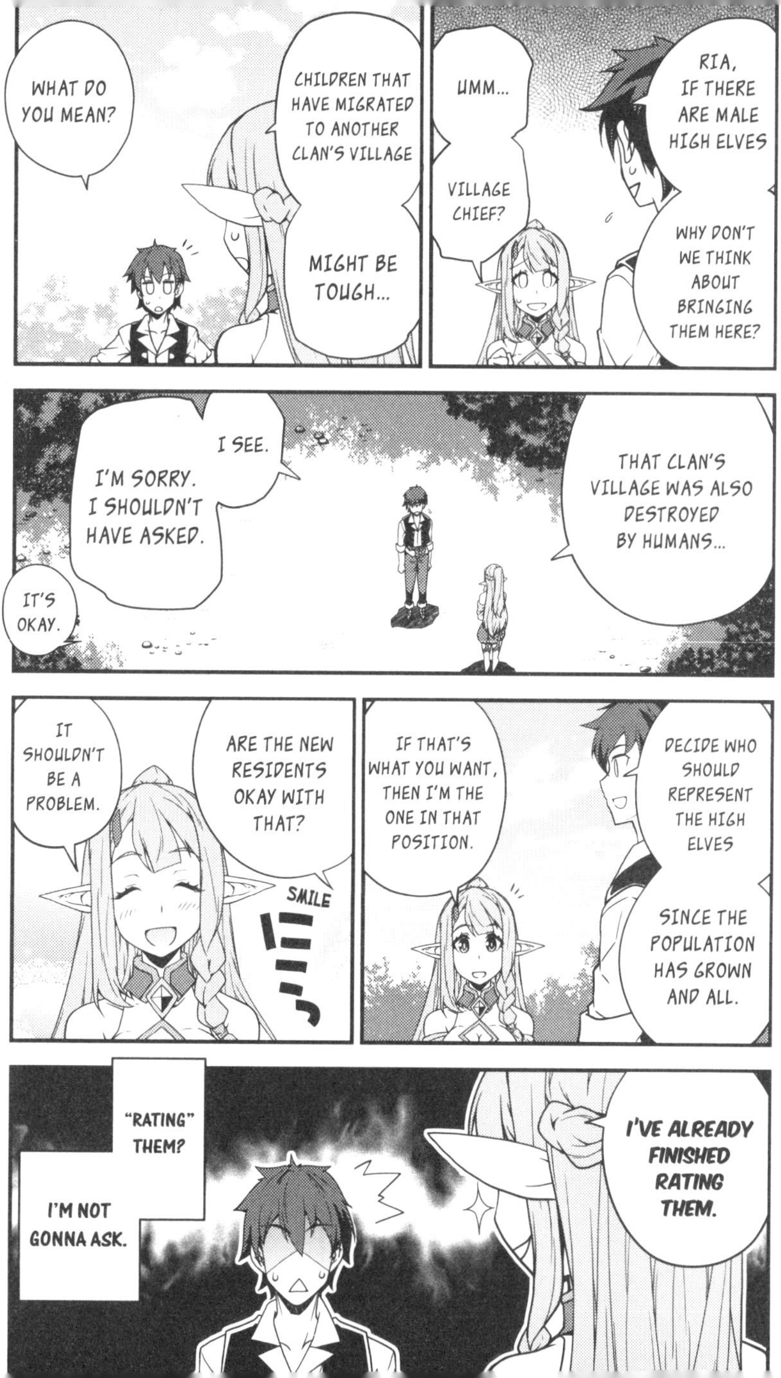
RIA, IF THERE ARE MALE HIGH ELVES
WHY DON'T WE THINK ABOUT BRINGING THEM HERE?
UMM...
VILLAGE CHIEF?
CHILDREN THAT HAVE MIGRATED TO ANOTHER CLAN'S VILLAGE
MIGHT BE TOUGH...
WHAT DO YOU MEAN?
THAT CLAN'S VILLAGE WAS ALSO DESTROYED BY HUMANS...
I SEE.
I'M SORRY. I SHOULDN'T HAVE ASKED.
IT'S OKAY.
DECIDE WHO SHOULD REPRESENT THE HIGH ELVES
SINCE THE POPULATION HAS GROWN AND ALL.
IF THAT'S WHAT YOU WANT, THEN I'M THE ONE IN THAT POSITION.
ARE THE NEW RESIDENTS OKAY WITH THAT?
IT SHOULDN'T BE A PROBLEM.
SMILE
I'VE ALREADY FINISHED RATING THEM.
"RATING" THEM?
I'M NOT GONNA ASK.

CHAPTER 20: FLORA, THE CAMBION MAIDS, AND THE COWS

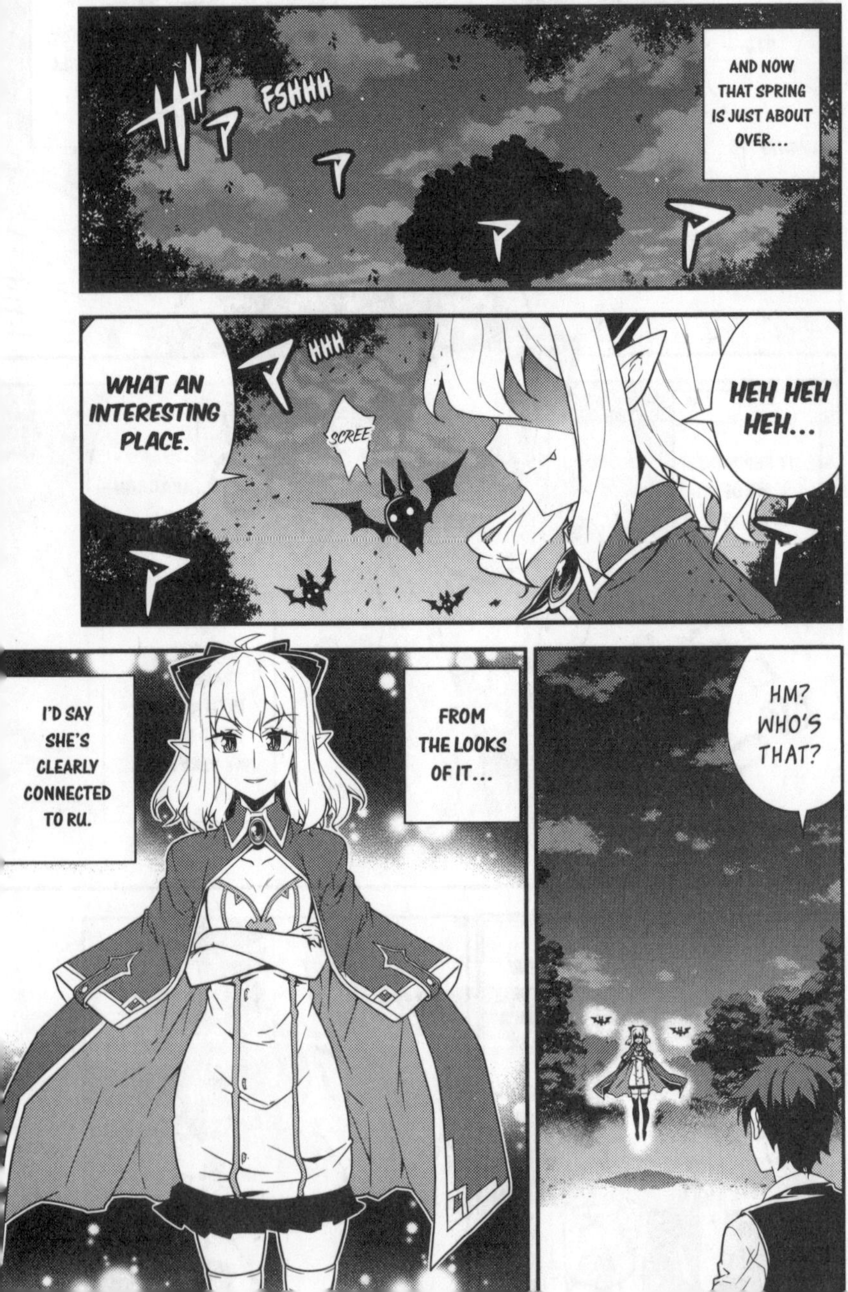
AND NOW THAT SPRING IS JUST ABOUT OVER...
FSHHH
HEH HEH HEH...
HHH
SCREE
WHAT AN INTERESTING PLACE.
HM? WHO'S THAT?
FROM THE LOOKS OF IT...
I'D SAY SHE'S CLEARLY CONNECTED TO RU.

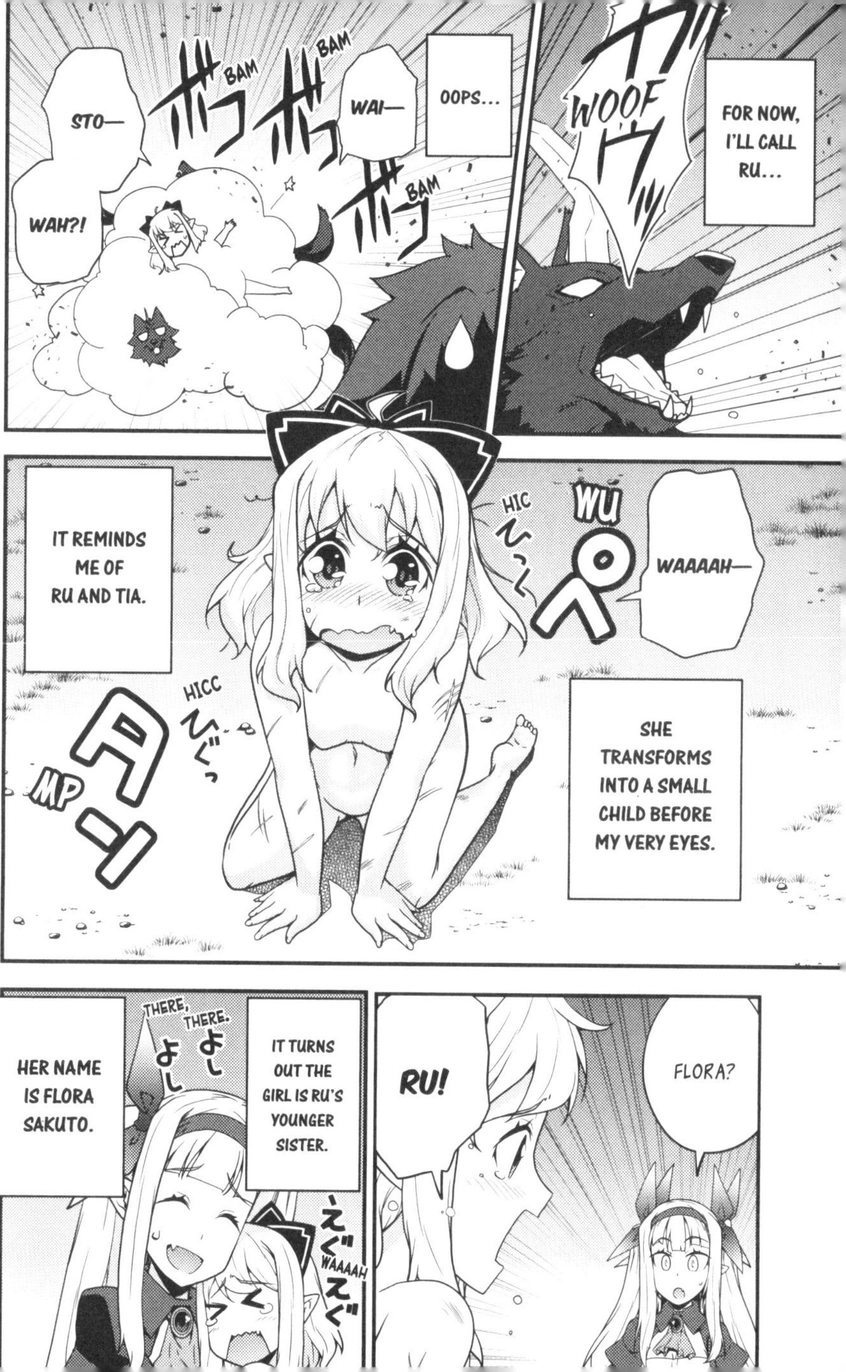

FOR NOW, I'LL CALL RU...
WOOF
OOPS...
BAM
WAI—
BAM
STO—
BAM
WAH?!
WAAAAH—
WU
HIC ひっく
IT REMINDS ME OF RU AND TIA.
SHE TRANSFORMS INTO A SMALL CHILD BEFORE MY VERY EYES.
HICC ひぐっ
MP
FLORA?
RU!
IT TURNS OUT THE GIRL IS RU'S YOUNGER SISTER.
THERE, THERE. よしよし
HER NAME IS FLORA SAKUTO.
WAAAAH えぐえぐ

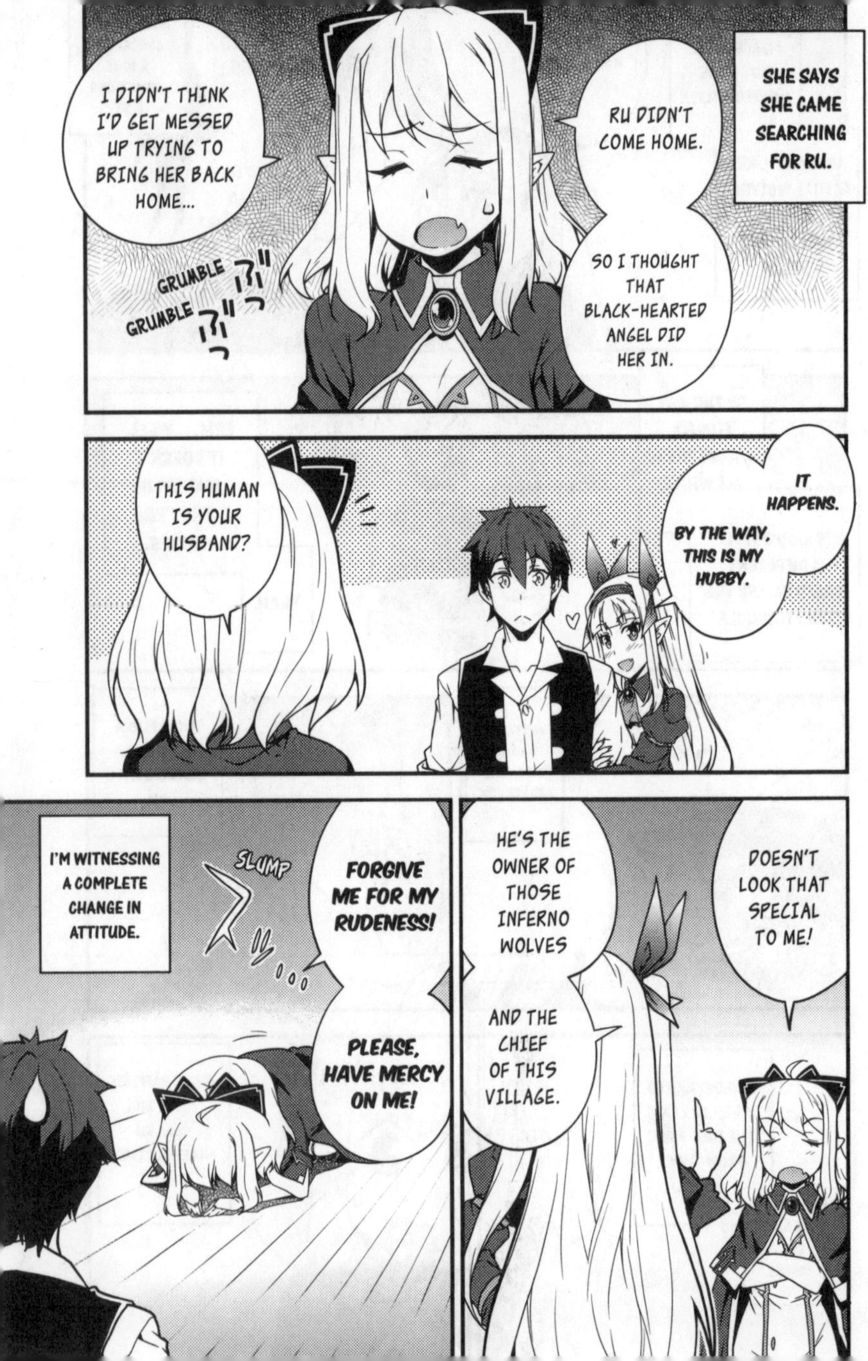
SHE SAYS SHE CAME SEARCHING FOR RU.
RU DIDN'T COME HOME.
SO I THOUGHT THAT BLACK-HEARTED ANGEL DID HER IN.
I DIDN'T THINK I'D GET MESSED UP TRYING TO BRING HER BACK HOME...
GRUMBLE
GRUMBLE
IT HAPPENS.
BY THE WAY, THIS IS MY HUBBY.
THIS HUMAN IS YOUR HUSBAND?
DOESN'T LOOK THAT SPECIAL TO ME!
HE'S THE OWNER OF THOSE INFERNO WOLVES
AND THE CHIEF OF THIS VILLAGE.
FORGIVE ME FOR MY RUDENESS!
PLEASE, HAVE MERCY ON ME!
SLUMP
I'M WITNESSING A COMPLETE CHANGE IN ATTITUDE.

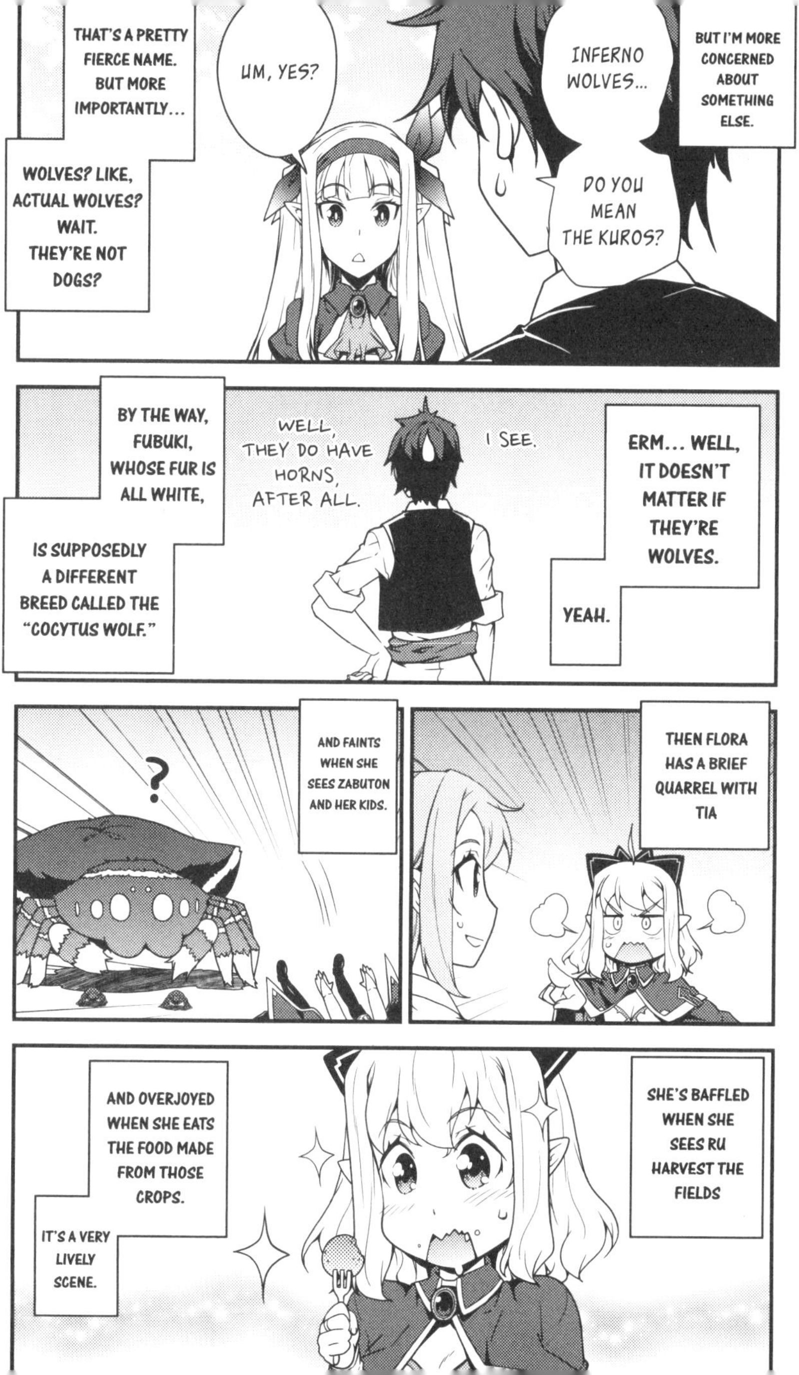
BUT I'M MORE CONCERNED ABOUT SOMETHING ELSE.
INFERNO WOLVES...
DO YOU MEAN THE KUROS?
UM, YES?
THAT'S A PRETTY FIERCE NAME. BUT MORE IMPORTANTLY...
WOLVES? LIKE, ACTUAL WOLVES? WAIT. THEY'RE NOT DOGS?
ERM... WELL, IT DOESN'T MATTER IF THEY'RE WOLVES.
YEAH.
I SEE.
WELL, THEY DO HAVE HORNS, AFTER ALL.
BY THE WAY, FUBUKI, WHOSE FUR IS ALL WHITE,
IS SUPPOSEDLY A DIFFERENT BREED CALLED THE "COCYTUS WOLF."
THEN FLORA HAS A BRIEF QUARREL WITH TIA
AND FAINTS WHEN SHE SEES ZABUTON AND HER KIDS.
?
SHE'S BAFFLED WHEN SHE SEES RU HARVEST THE FIELDS
AND OVERJOYED WHEN SHE EATS THE FOOD MADE FROM THOSE CROPS.
IT'S A VERY LIVELY SCENE.

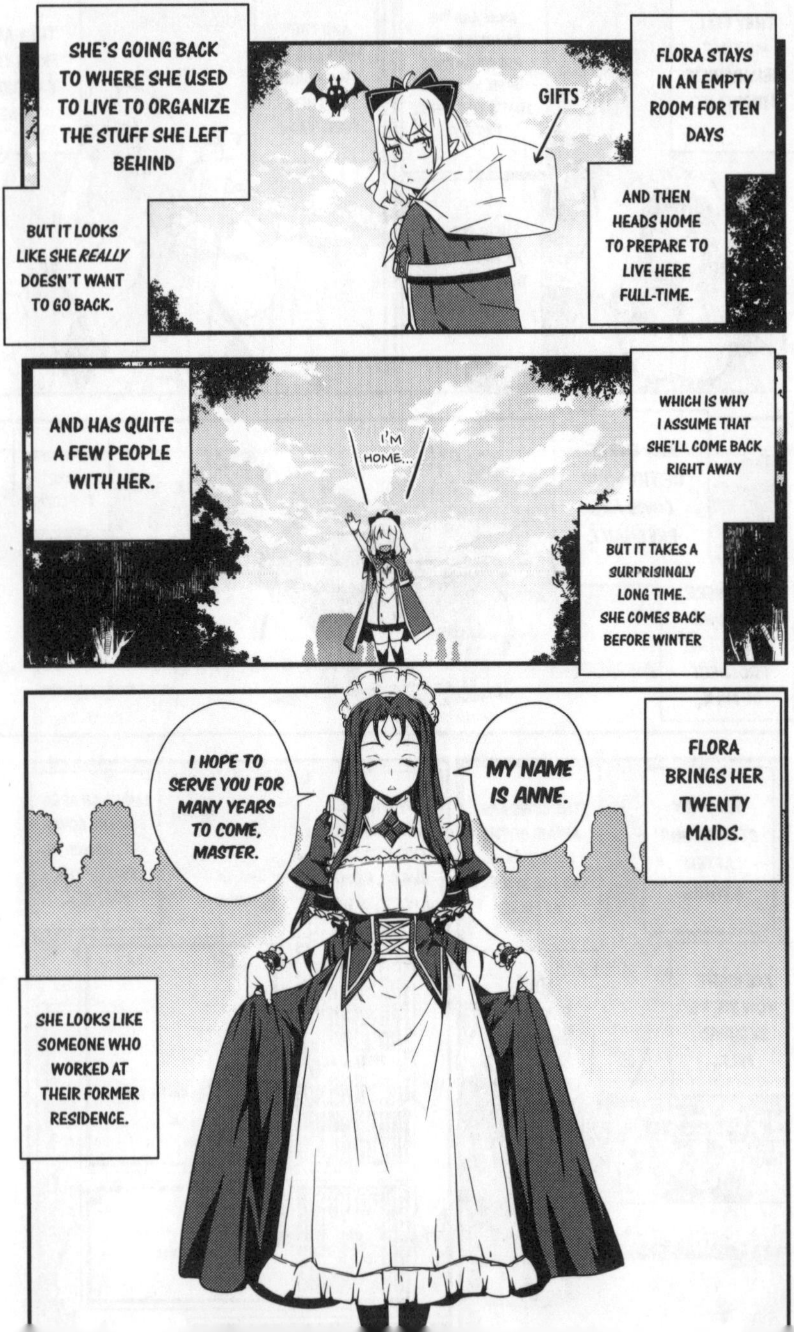
FLORA STAYS IN AN EMPTY ROOM FOR TEN DAYS
AND THEN HEADS HOME TO PREPARE TO LIVE HERE FULL-TIME.
GIFTS
SHE'S GOING BACK TO WHERE SHE USED TO LIVE TO ORGANIZE THE STUFF SHE LEFT BEHIND
BUT IT LOOKS LIKE SHE *REALLY* DOESN'T WANT TO GO BACK.
WHICH IS WHY I ASSUME THAT SHE'LL COME BACK RIGHT AWAY
BUT IT TAKES A SURPRISINGLY LONG TIME. SHE COMES BACK BEFORE WINTER
I'M HOME...
AND HAS QUITE A FEW PEOPLE WITH HER.
FLORA BRINGS HER TWENTY MAIDS.
MY NAME IS ANNE.
I HOPE TO SERVE YOU FOR MANY YEARS TO COME, MASTER.
SHE LOOKS LIKE SOMEONE WHO WORKED AT THEIR FORMER RESIDENCE.

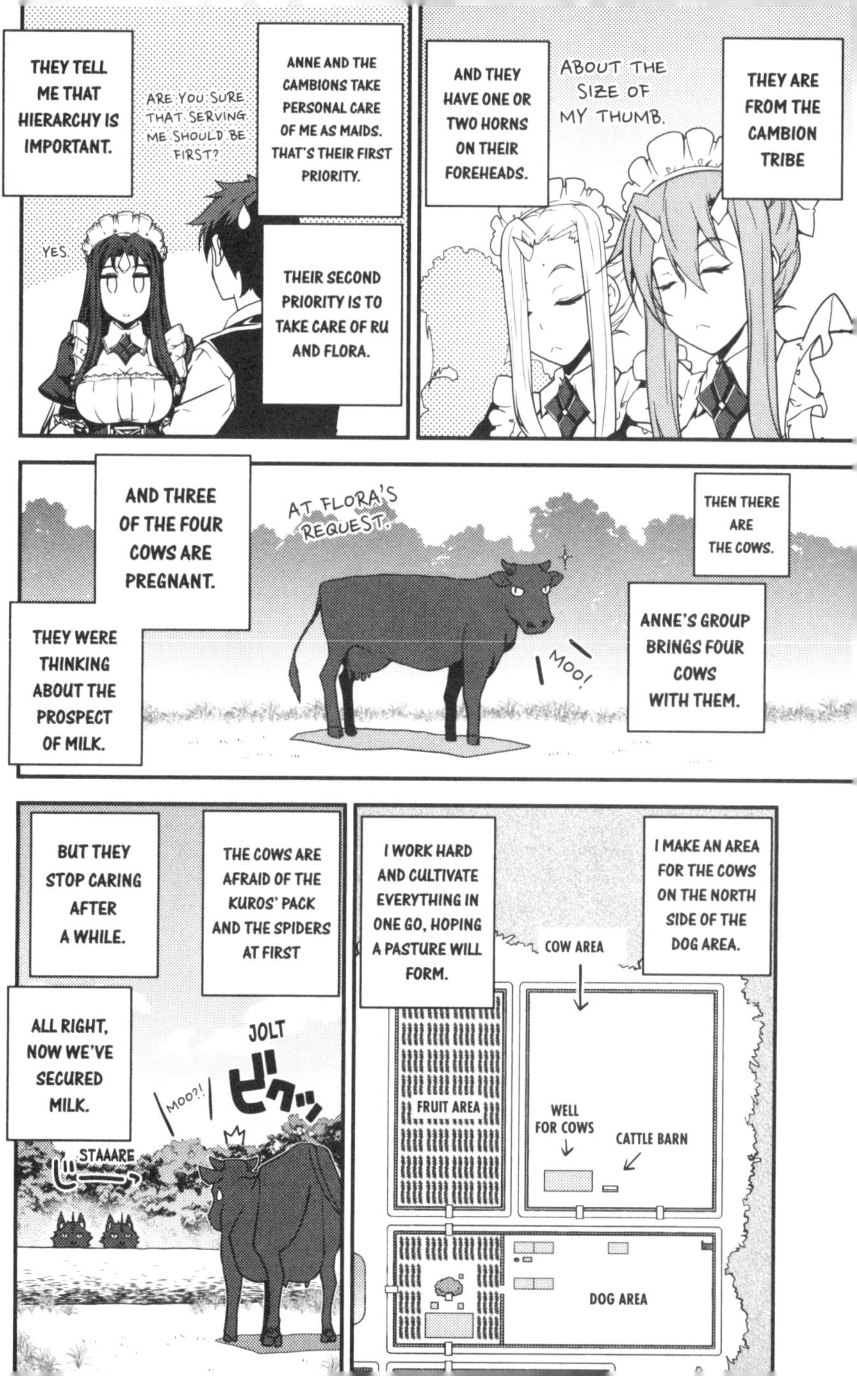
THEY ARE FROM THE CAMBION TRIBE
AND THEY HAVE ONE OR TWO HORNS ON THEIR FOREHEADS.
ABOUT THE SIZE OF MY THUMB.
ANNE AND THE CAMBIONS TAKE PERSONAL CARE OF ME AS MAIDS. THAT'S THEIR FIRST PRIORITY.
THEIR SECOND PRIORITY IS TO TAKE CARE OF RU AND FLORA.
ARE YOU SURE THAT SERVING ME SHOULD BE FIRST?
YES.
THEY TELL ME THAT HIERARCHY IS IMPORTANT.
THEN THERE ARE THE COWS.
ANNE'S GROUP BRINGS FOUR COWS WITH THEM.
MOO!
AT FLORA'S REQUEST.
AND THREE OF THE FOUR COWS ARE PREGNANT.
THEY WERE THINKING ABOUT THE PROSPECT OF MILK.
I MAKE AN AREA FOR THE COWS ON THE NORTH SIDE OF THE DOG AREA.
I WORK HARD AND CULTIVATE EVERYTHING IN ONE GO, HOPING A PASTURE WILL FORM.
COW AREA
WELL FOR COWS
CATTLE BARN
FRUIT AREA
DOG AREA
THE COWS ARE AFRAID OF THE KUROS' PACK AND THE SPIDERS AT FIRST
BUT THEY STOP CARING AFTER A WHILE.
JOLT
ビクッ
MOO?!
ALL RIGHT, NOW WE'VE SECURED MILK.
STAAARE
じーっ

CHAPTER 21: TIA LEAVES, WINTER COMES

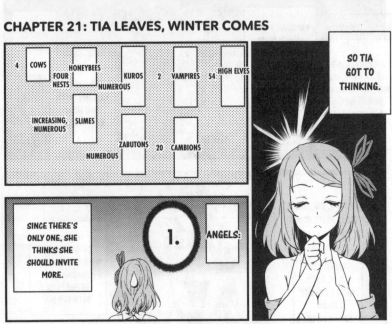

	COWS	HONEYBEES	KUROS	VAMPIRES	HIGH ELVES
4		FOUR NESTS	2	54	
		NUMEROUS			
INCREASING, NUMEROUS	SLIMES	ZABUTONS	CAMBIONS		
		NUMEROUS	20		

SO TIA GOT TO THINKING.

SINCE THERE'S ONLY ONE, SHE THINKS SHE SHOULD INVITE MORE.

ANGELS: **1.**

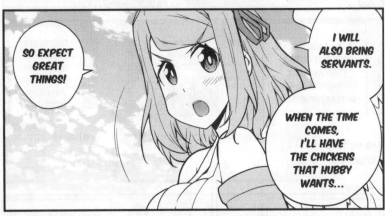

SO EXPECT GREAT THINGS!

I WILL ALSO BRING SERVANTS.

WHEN THE TIME COMES, I'LL HAVE THE CHICKENS THAT HUBBY WANTS...

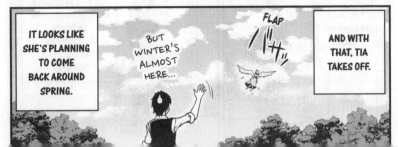

IT LOOKS LIKE SHE'S PLANNING TO COME BACK AROUND SPRING.

BUT WINTER'S ALMOST HERE...

FLAP

AND WITH THAT, TIA TAKES OFF.

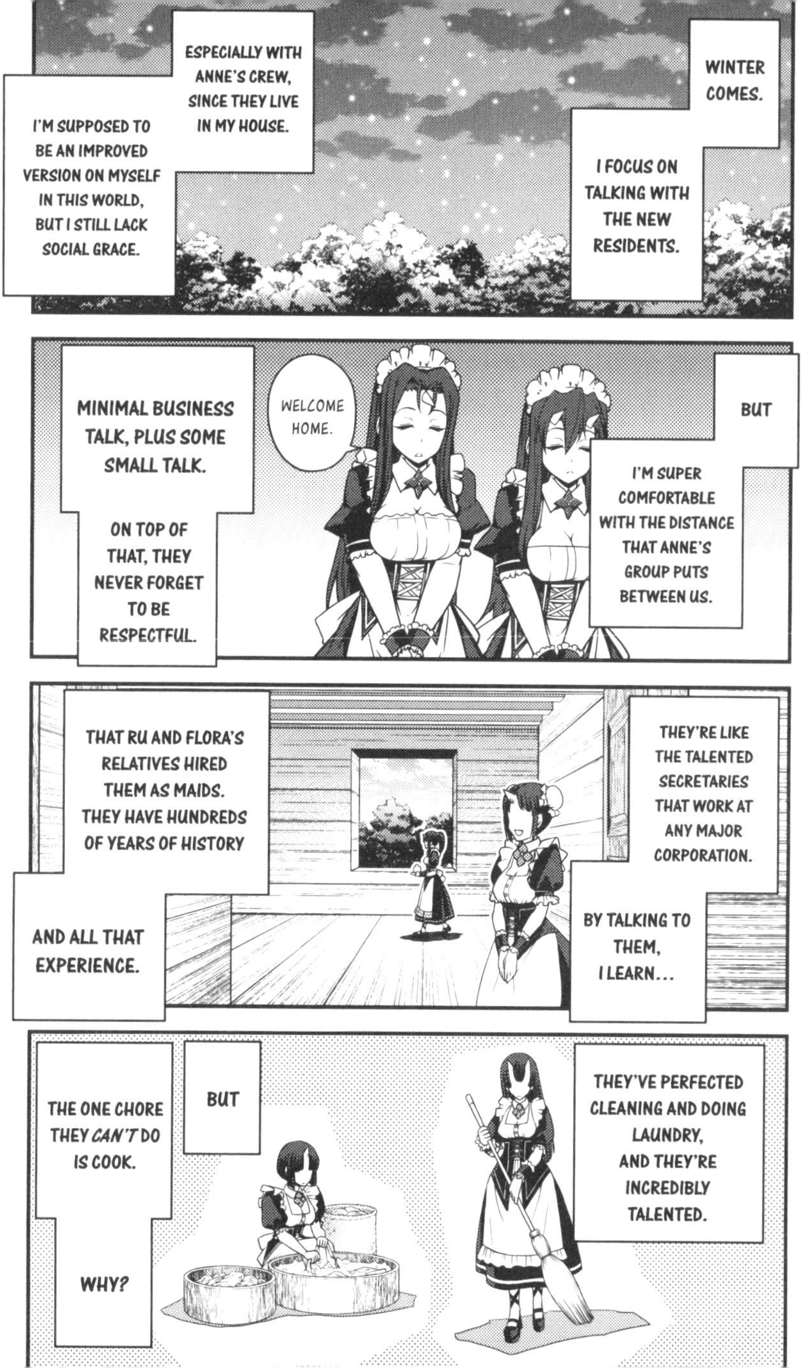
WINTER COMES.
I FOCUS ON TALKING WITH THE NEW RESIDENTS.
ESPECIALLY WITH ANNE'S CREW, SINCE THEY LIVE IN MY HOUSE.
I'M SUPPOSED TO BE AN IMPROVED VERSION ON MYSELF IN THIS WORLD, BUT I STILL LACK SOCIAL GRACE.
BUT
I'M SUPER COMFORTABLE WITH THE DISTANCE THAT ANNE'S GROUP PUTS BETWEEN US.
WELCOME HOME.
MINIMAL BUSINESS TALK, PLUS SOME SMALL TALK.
ON TOP OF THAT, THEY NEVER FORGET TO BE RESPECTFUL.
THEY'RE LIKE THE TALENTED SECRETARIES THAT WORK AT ANY MAJOR CORPORATION.
BY TALKING TO THEM, I LEARN…
THAT RU AND FLORA'S RELATIVES HIRED THEM AS MAIDS. THEY HAVE HUNDREDS OF YEARS OF HISTORY
AND ALL THAT EXPERIENCE.
THEY'VE PERFECTED CLEANING AND DOING LAUNDRY, AND THEY'RE INCREDIBLY TALENTED.
BUT
THE ONE CHORE THEY *CAN'T* DO IS COOK.
WHY?

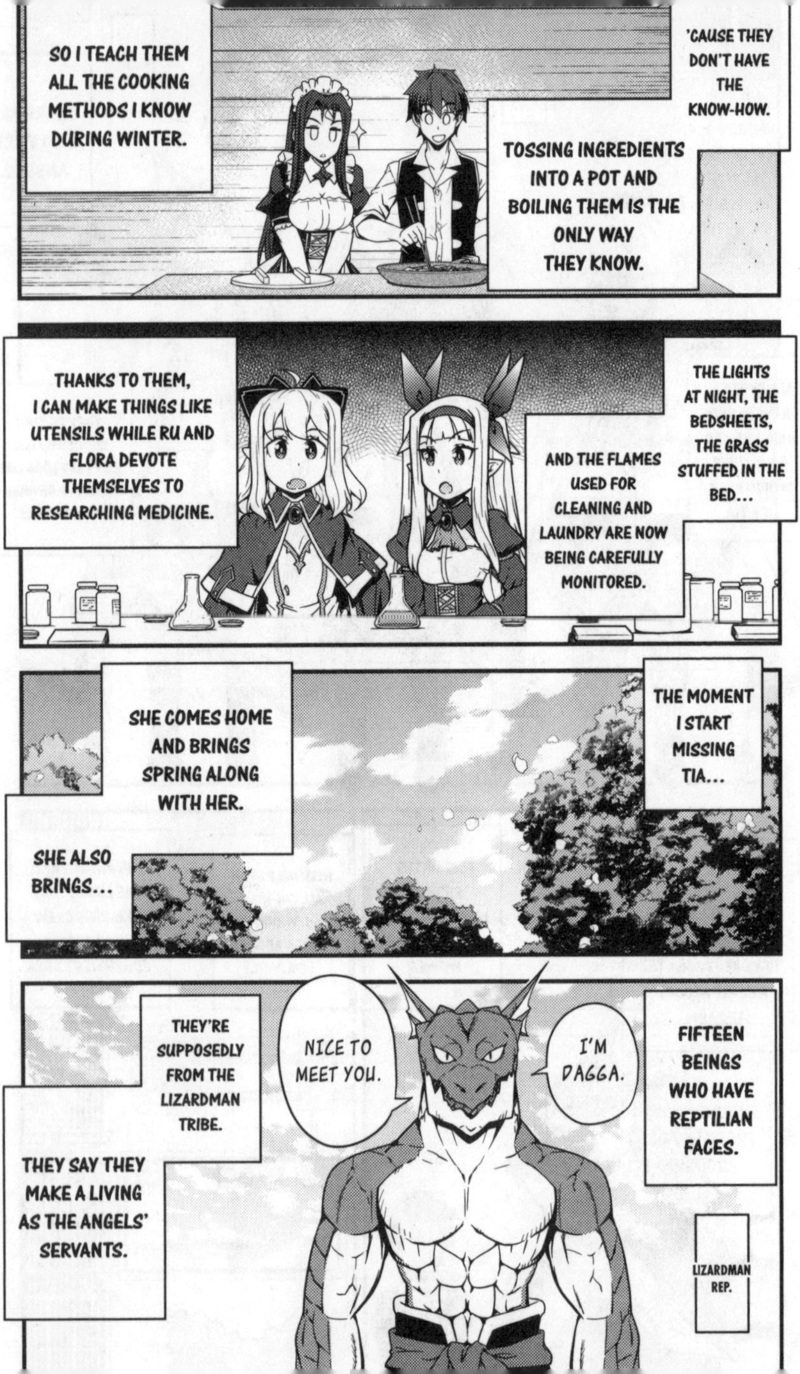

'CAUSE THEY DON'T HAVE THE KNOW-HOW.
TOSSING INGREDIENTS INTO A POT AND BOILING THEM IS THE ONLY WAY THEY KNOW.
SO I TEACH THEM ALL THE COOKING METHODS I KNOW DURING WINTER.
THE LIGHTS AT NIGHT, THE BEDSHEETS, THE GRASS STUFFED IN THE BED...
AND THE FLAMES USED FOR CLEANING AND LAUNDRY ARE NOW BEING CAREFULLY MONITORED.
THANKS TO THEM, I CAN MAKE THINGS LIKE UTENSILS WHILE RU AND FLORA DEVOTE THEMSELVES TO RESEARCHING MEDICINE.
THE MOMENT I START MISSING TIA...
SHE COMES HOME AND BRINGS SPRING ALONG WITH HER.
SHE ALSO BRINGS...
FIFTEEN BEINGS WHO HAVE REPTILIAN FACES.
I'M DAGGA.
NICE TO MEET YOU.
THEY'RE SUPPOSEDLY FROM THE LIZARDMAN TRIBE.
LIZARDMAN REP.
THEY SAY THEY MAKE A LIVING AS THE ANGELS' SERVANTS.

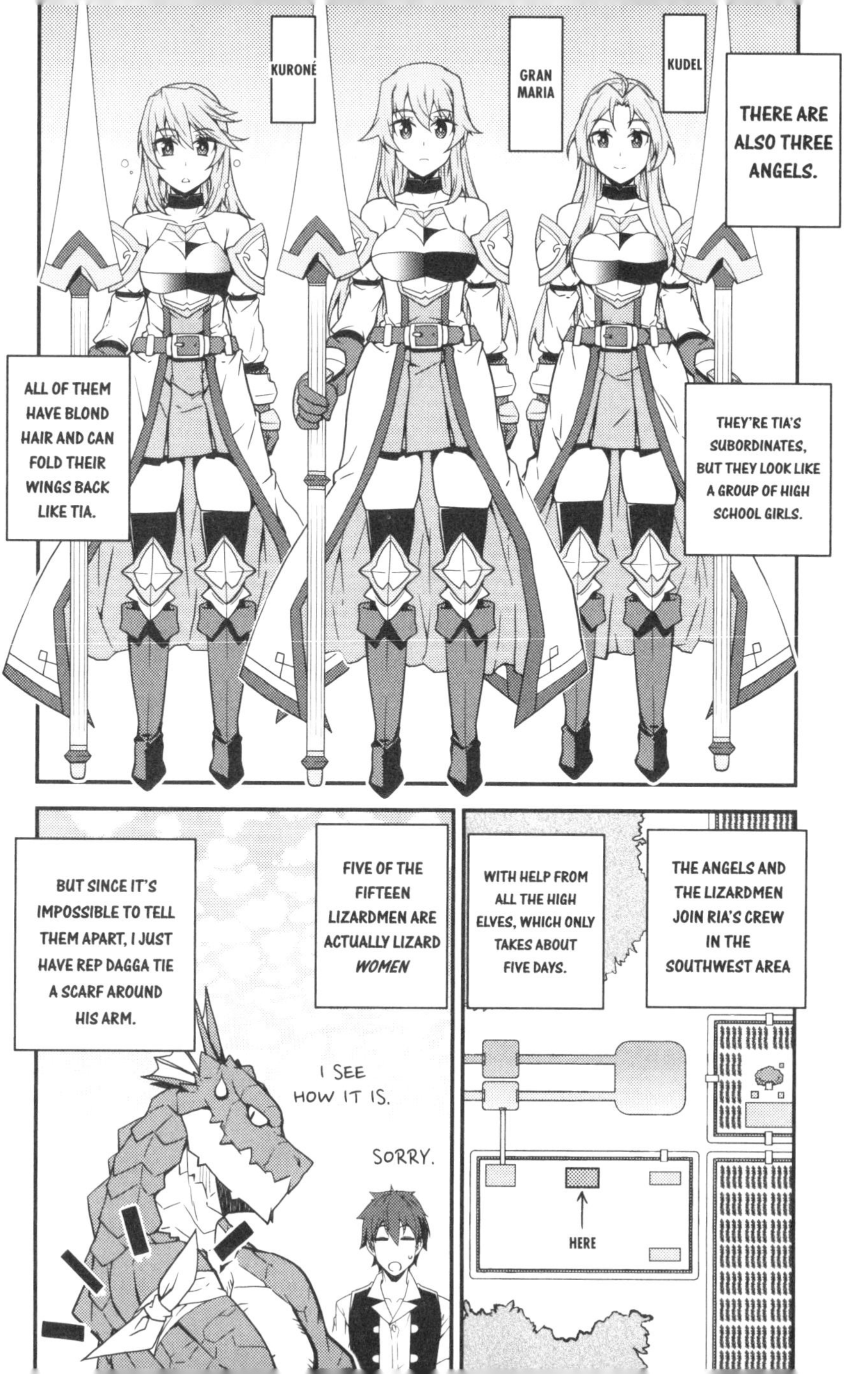
THERE ARE ALSO THREE ANGELS.
KUDEL
GRAN MARIA
KURONÉ
THEY'RE TIA'S SUBORDINATES, BUT THEY LOOK LIKE A GROUP OF HIGH SCHOOL GIRLS.
ALL OF THEM HAVE BLOND HAIR AND CAN FOLD THEIR WINGS BACK LIKE TIA.
THE ANGELS AND THE LIZARDMEN JOIN RIA'S CREW IN THE SOUTHWEST AREA
WITH HELP FROM ALL THE HIGH ELVES, WHICH ONLY TAKES ABOUT FIVE DAYS.
HERE
FIVE OF THE FIFTEEN LIZARDMEN ARE ACTUALLY LIZARD *WOMEN*
BUT SINCE IT'S IMPOSSIBLE TO TELL THEM APART, I JUST HAVE REP DAGGA TIE A SCARF AROUND HIS ARM.
I SEE HOW IT IS.
SORRY.

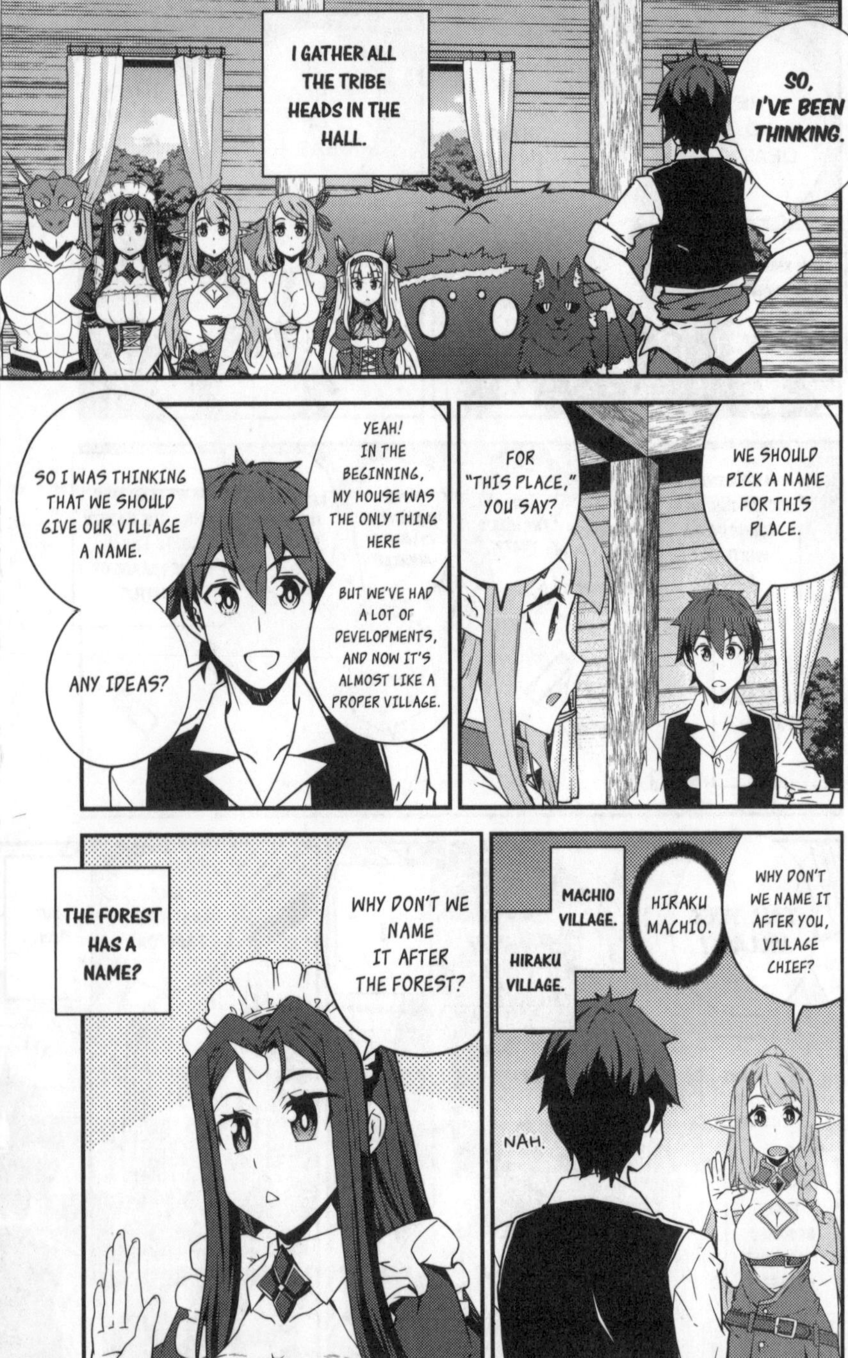
SO, I'VE BEEN THINKING.
I GATHER ALL THE TRIBE HEADS IN THE HALL.
WE SHOULD PICK A NAME FOR THIS PLACE.
FOR "THIS PLACE," YOU SAY?
YEAH! IN THE BEGINNING, MY HOUSE WAS THE ONLY THING HERE
BUT WE'VE HAD A LOT OF DEVELOPMENTS, AND NOW IT'S ALMOST LIKE A PROPER VILLAGE.
SO I WAS THINKING THAT WE SHOULD GIVE OUR VILLAGE A NAME.
ANY IDEAS?
WHY DON'T WE NAME IT AFTER YOU, VILLAGE CHIEF?
HIRAKU MACHIO.
MACHIO VILLAGE.
HIRAKU VILLAGE.
NAH.
WHY DON'T WE NAME IT AFTER THE FOREST?
THE FOREST HAS A NAME?

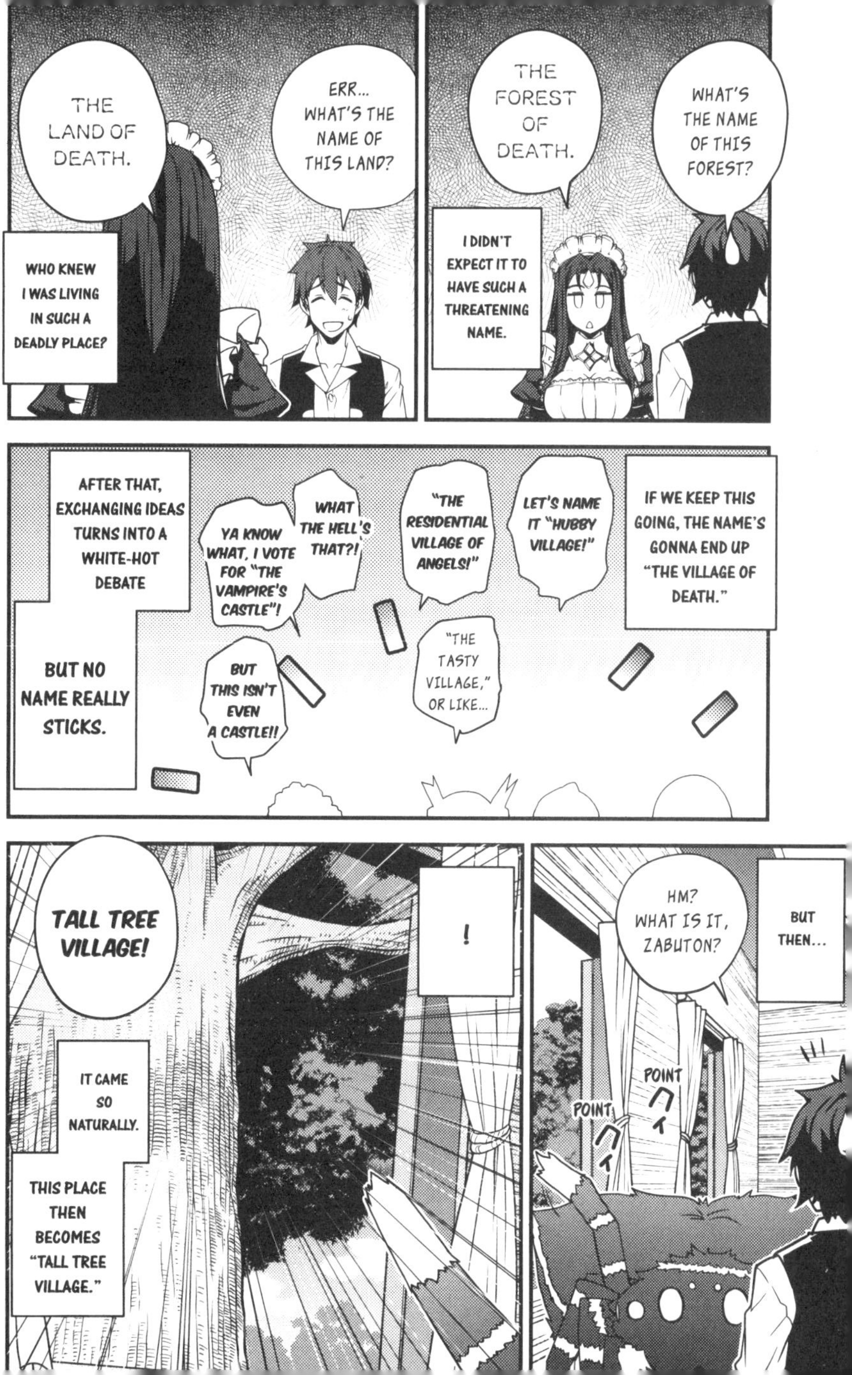
WHAT'S THE NAME OF THIS FOREST?
THE FOREST OF DEATH.
I DIDN'T EXPECT IT TO HAVE SUCH A THREATENING NAME.
ERR... WHAT'S THE NAME OF THIS LAND?
THE LAND OF DEATH.
WHO KNEW I WAS LIVING IN SUCH A DEADLY PLACE?
IF WE KEEP THIS GOING, THE NAME'S GONNA END UP "THE VILLAGE OF DEATH."
LET'S NAME IT "HUBBY VILLAGE!"
"THE RESIDENTIAL VILLAGE OF ANGELS!"
WHAT THE HELL'S THAT?!
YA KNOW WHAT, I VOTE FOR "THE VAMPIRE'S CASTLE"!
AFTER THAT, EXCHANGING IDEAS TURNS INTO A WHITE-HOT DEBATE
"THE TASTY VILLAGE," OR LIKE...
BUT THIS ISN'T EVEN A CASTLE!!
BUT NO NAME REALLY STICKS.
BUT THEN...
HM? WHAT IS IT, ZABUTON?
POINT
POINT
!
TALL TREE VILLAGE!
IT CAME SO NATURALLY.
THIS PLACE THEN BECOMES "TALL TREE VILLAGE."

CHAPTER 22: BREWED DRINKS AND THE GUEST (THE DEMON KING'S SERVANT)

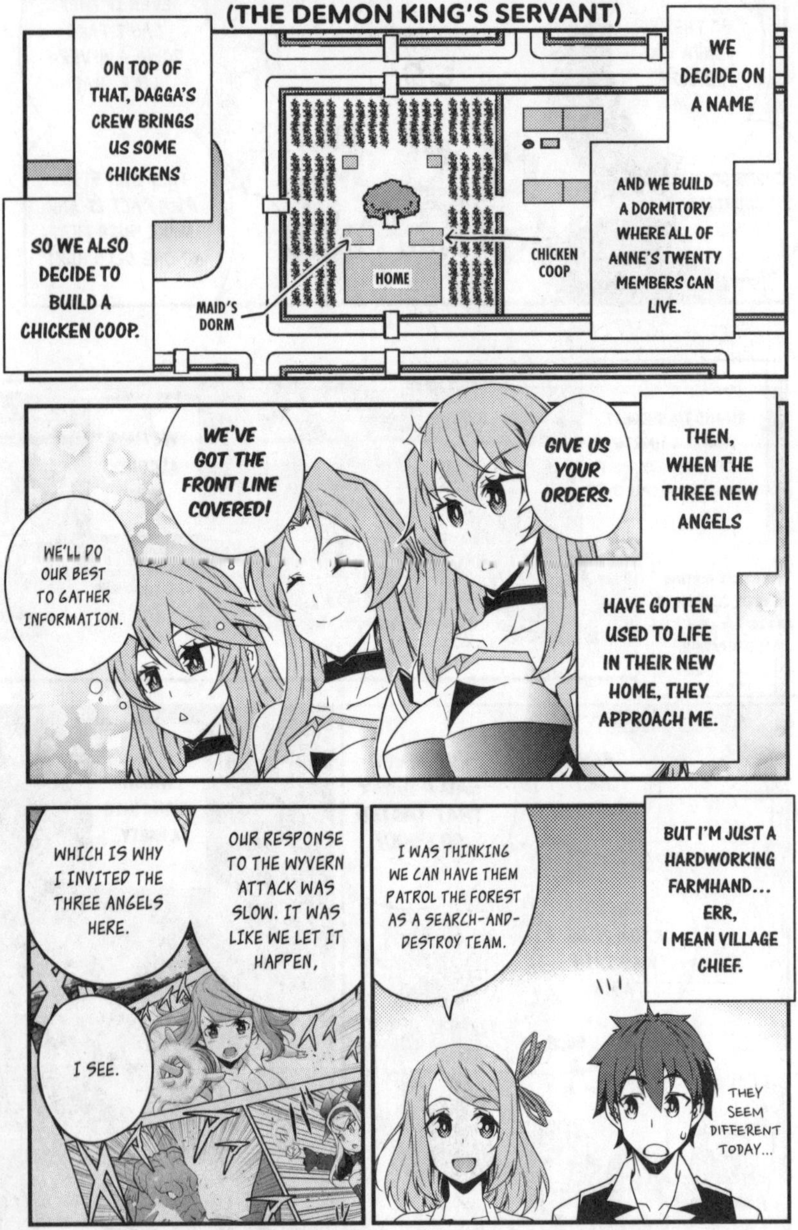
WE DECIDE ON A NAME
AND WE BUILD A DORMITORY WHERE ALL OF ANNE'S TWENTY MEMBERS CAN LIVE.
CHICKEN COOP
HOME
MAID'S DORM
ON TOP OF THAT, DAGGA'S CREW BRINGS US SOME CHICKENS
SO WE ALSO DECIDE TO BUILD A CHICKEN COOP.
THEN, WHEN THE THREE NEW ANGELS
HAVE GOTTEN USED TO LIFE IN THEIR NEW HOME, THEY APPROACH ME.
GIVE US YOUR ORDERS.
WE'VE GOT THE FRONT LINE COVERED!
WE'LL DO OUR BEST TO GATHER INFORMATION.
BUT I'M JUST A HARDWORKING FARMHAND... ERR, I MEAN VILLAGE CHIEF.
I WAS THINKING WE CAN HAVE THEM PATROL THE FOREST AS A SEARCH-AND-DESTROY TEAM.
THEY SEEM DIFFERENT TODAY...
OUR RESPONSE TO THE WYVERN ATTACK WAS SLOW. IT WAS LIKE WE LET IT HAPPEN,
WHICH IS WHY I INVITED THE THREE ANGELS HERE.
I SEE.

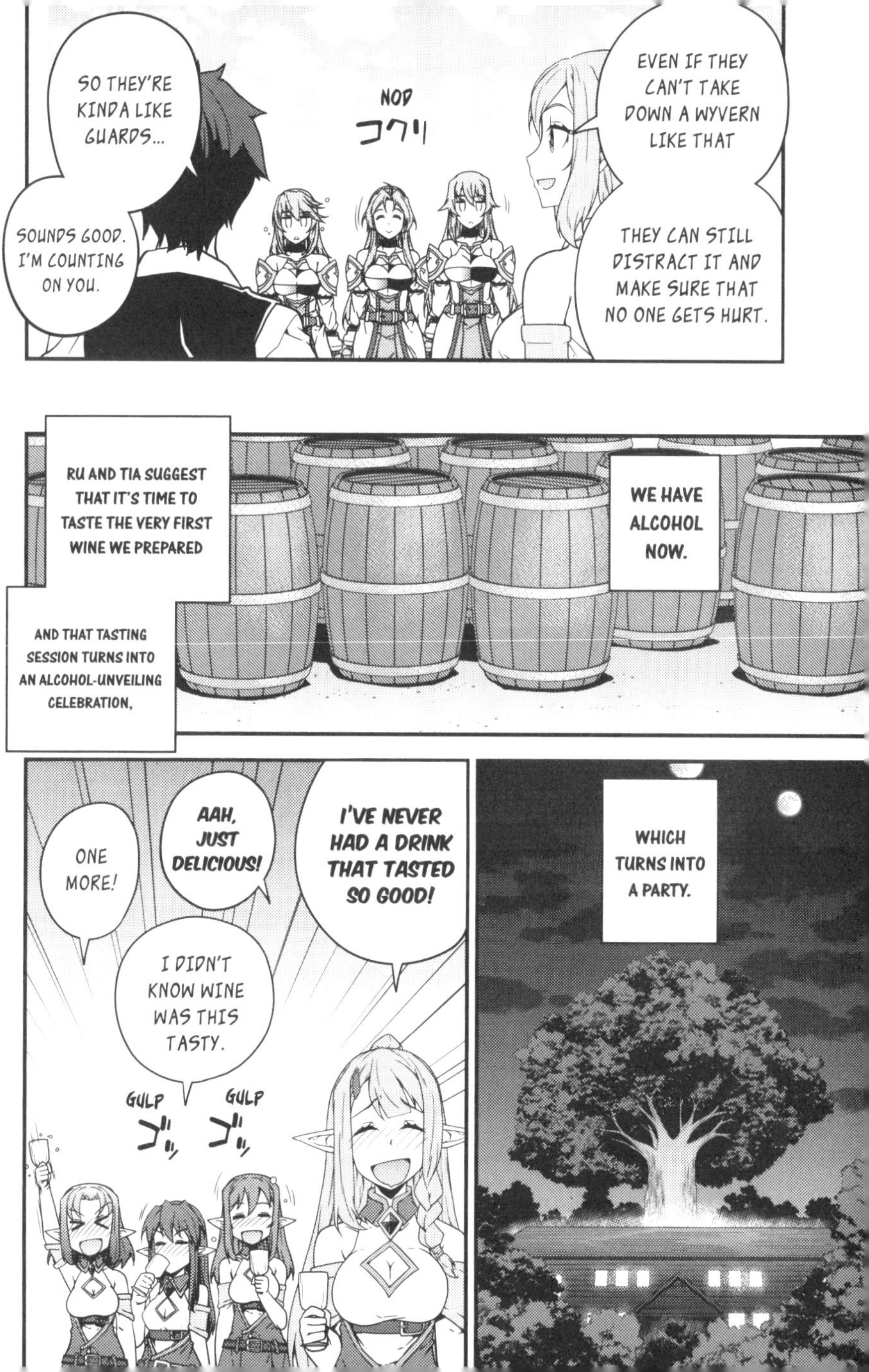
EVEN IF THEY CAN'T TAKE DOWN A WYVERN LIKE THAT
THEY CAN STILL DISTRACT IT AND MAKE SURE THAT NO ONE GETS HURT.
NOD
コクリ
SO THEY'RE KINDA LIKE GUARDS...
SOUNDS GOOD. I'M COUNTING ON YOU.
WE HAVE ALCOHOL NOW.
RU AND TIA SUGGEST THAT IT'S TIME TO TASTE THE VERY FIRST WINE WE PREPARED
AND THAT TASTING SESSION TURNS INTO AN ALCOHOL-UNVEILING CELEBRATION,
WHICH TURNS INTO A PARTY.
I'VE NEVER HAD A DRINK THAT TASTED SO GOOD!
AAH, JUST DELICIOUS!
ONE MORE!
I DIDN'T KNOW WINE WAS THIS TASTY.
GULP
ゴッ
GULP
ゴッ

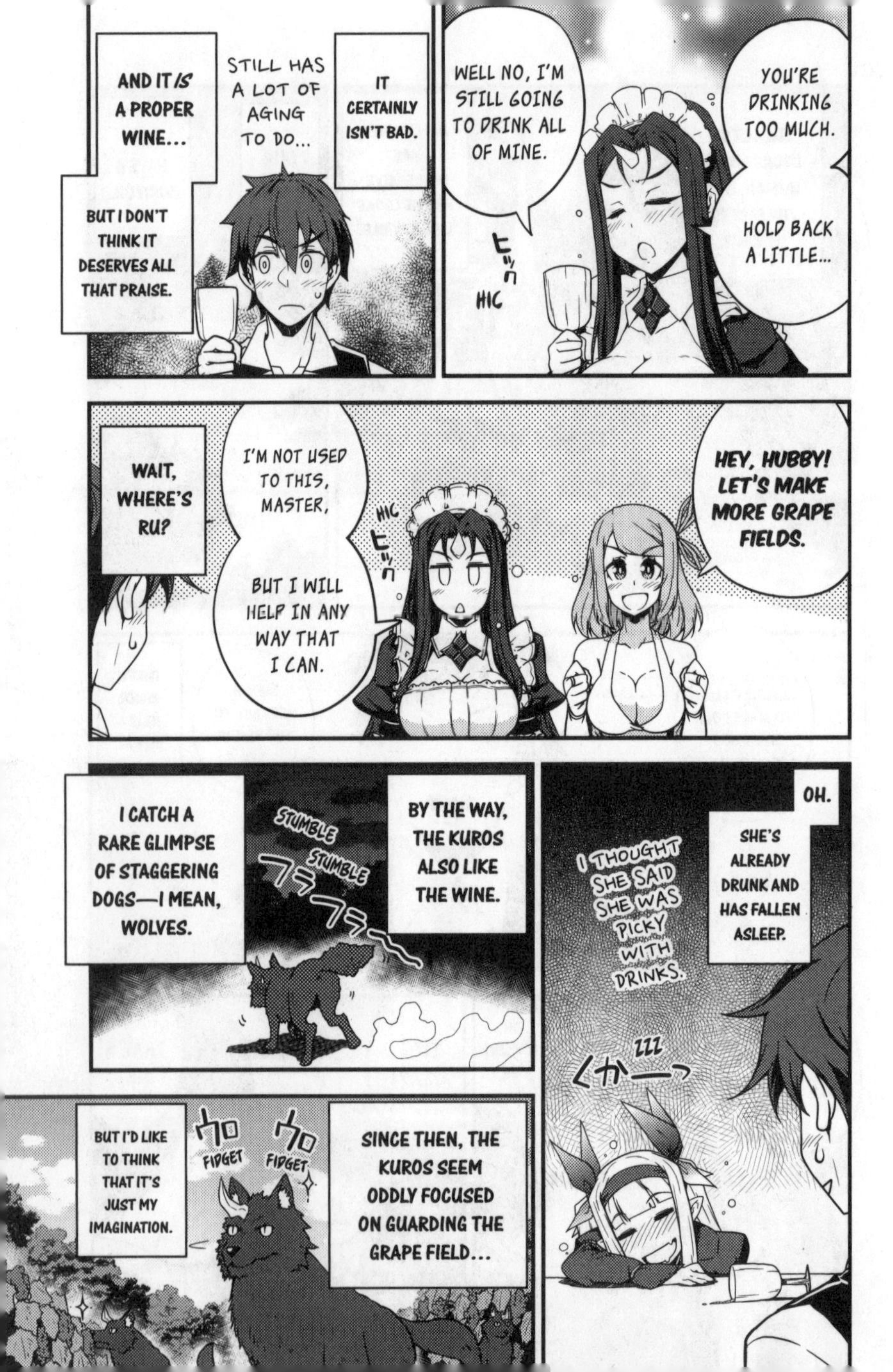
YOU'RE DRINKING TOO MUCH.
HOLD BACK A LITTLE...
WELL NO, I'M STILL GOING TO DRINK ALL OF MINE.
ヒック
HIC
IT CERTAINLY ISN'T BAD.
STILL HAS A LOT OF AGING TO DO...
AND IT *IS* A PROPER WINE...
BUT I DON'T THINK IT DESERVES ALL THAT PRAISE.
HEY, HUBBY! LET'S MAKE MORE GRAPE FIELDS.
HIC
ヒック
I'M NOT USED TO THIS, MASTER,
BUT I WILL HELP IN ANY WAY THAT I CAN.
WAIT, WHERE'S RU?
OH.
SHE'S ALREADY DRUNK AND HAS FALLEN ASLEEP.
I THOUGHT SHE SAID SHE WAS PICKY WITH DRINKS.
ZZZ
くかーっ
BY THE WAY, THE KUROS ALSO LIKE THE WINE.
STUMBLE STUMBLE
フラフラ～
I CATCH A RARE GLIMPSE OF STAGGERING DOGS—I MEAN, WOLVES.
SINCE THEN, THE KUROS SEEM ODDLY FOCUSED ON GUARDING THE GRAPE FIELD...
ウロ FIDGET ウロ FIDGET
BUT I'D LIKE TO THINK THAT IT'S JUST MY IMAGINATION.

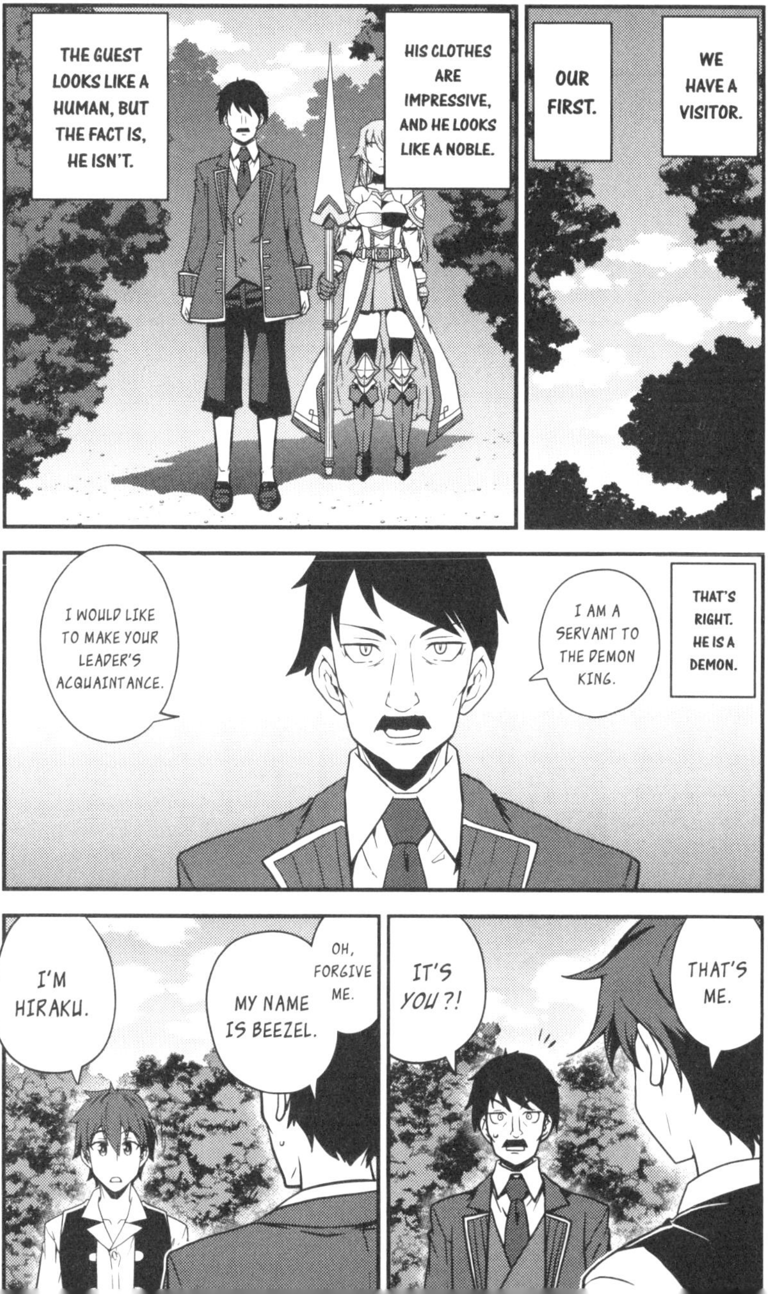
WE HAVE A VISITOR.
OUR FIRST.
HIS CLOTHES ARE IMPRESSIVE, AND HE LOOKS LIKE A NOBLE.
THE GUEST LOOKS LIKE A HUMAN, BUT THE FACT IS, HE ISN'T.
THAT'S RIGHT. HE IS A DEMON.
I AM A SERVANT TO THE DEMON KING.
I WOULD LIKE TO MAKE YOUR LEADER'S ACQUAINTANCE.
THAT'S ME.
IT'S *YOU*?!
OH, FORGIVE ME.
MY NAME IS BEEZEL.
I'M HIRAKU.

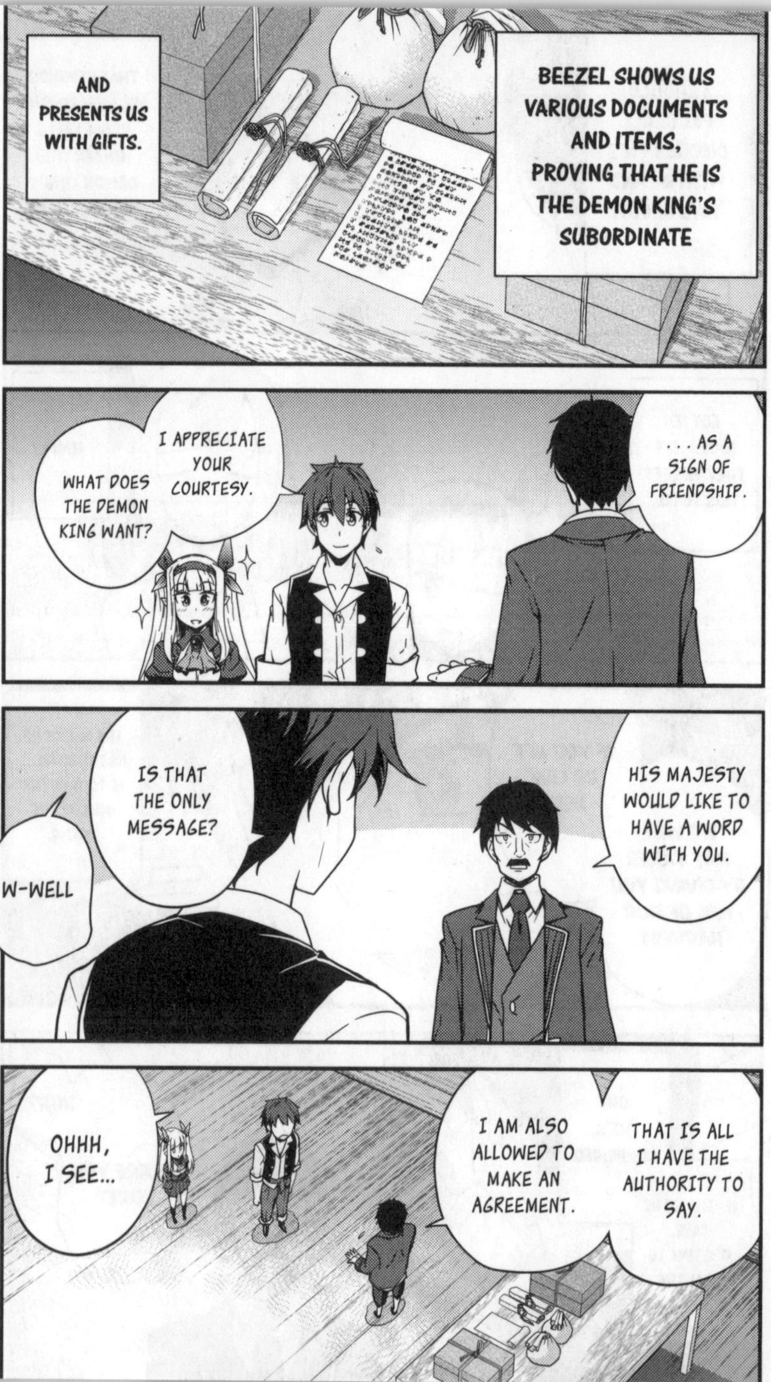
BEEZEL SHOWS US VARIOUS DOCUMENTS AND ITEMS, PROVING THAT HE IS THE DEMON KING'S SUBORDINATE
AND PRESENTS US WITH GIFTS.
. . . AS A SIGN OF FRIENDSHIP.
I APPRECIATE YOUR COURTESY.
WHAT DOES THE DEMON KING WANT?
HIS MAJESTY WOULD LIKE TO HAVE A WORD WITH YOU.
IS THAT THE ONLY MESSAGE?
W-WELL
THAT IS ALL I HAVE THE AUTHORITY TO SAY.
I AM ALSO ALLOWED TO MAKE AN AGREEMENT.
OHHH, I SEE...

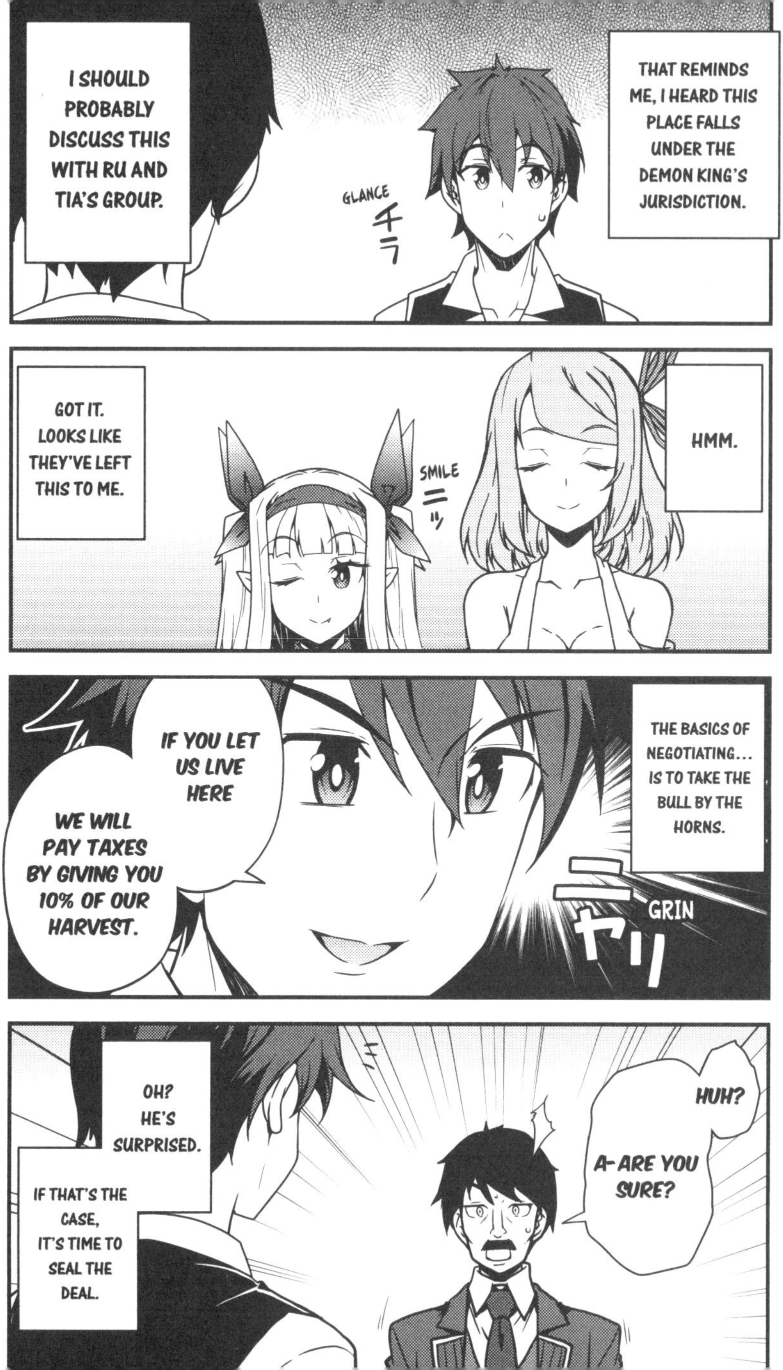

THAT REMINDS ME, I HEARD THIS PLACE FALLS UNDER THE DEMON KING'S JURISDICTION.
GLANCE
チラ
I SHOULD PROBABLY DISCUSS THIS WITH RU AND TIA'S GROUP.
HMM.
SMILE
ニッ
GOT IT. LOOKS LIKE THEY'VE LEFT THIS TO ME.
THE BASICS OF NEGOTIATING... IS TO TAKE THE BULL BY THE HORNS.
ニヤリ
GRIN
IF YOU LET US LIVE HERE
WE WILL PAY TAXES BY GIVING YOU 10% OF OUR HARVEST.
HUH?
A-ARE YOU SURE?
OH? HE'S SURPRISED.
IF THAT'S THE CASE, IT'S TIME TO SEAL THE DEAL.

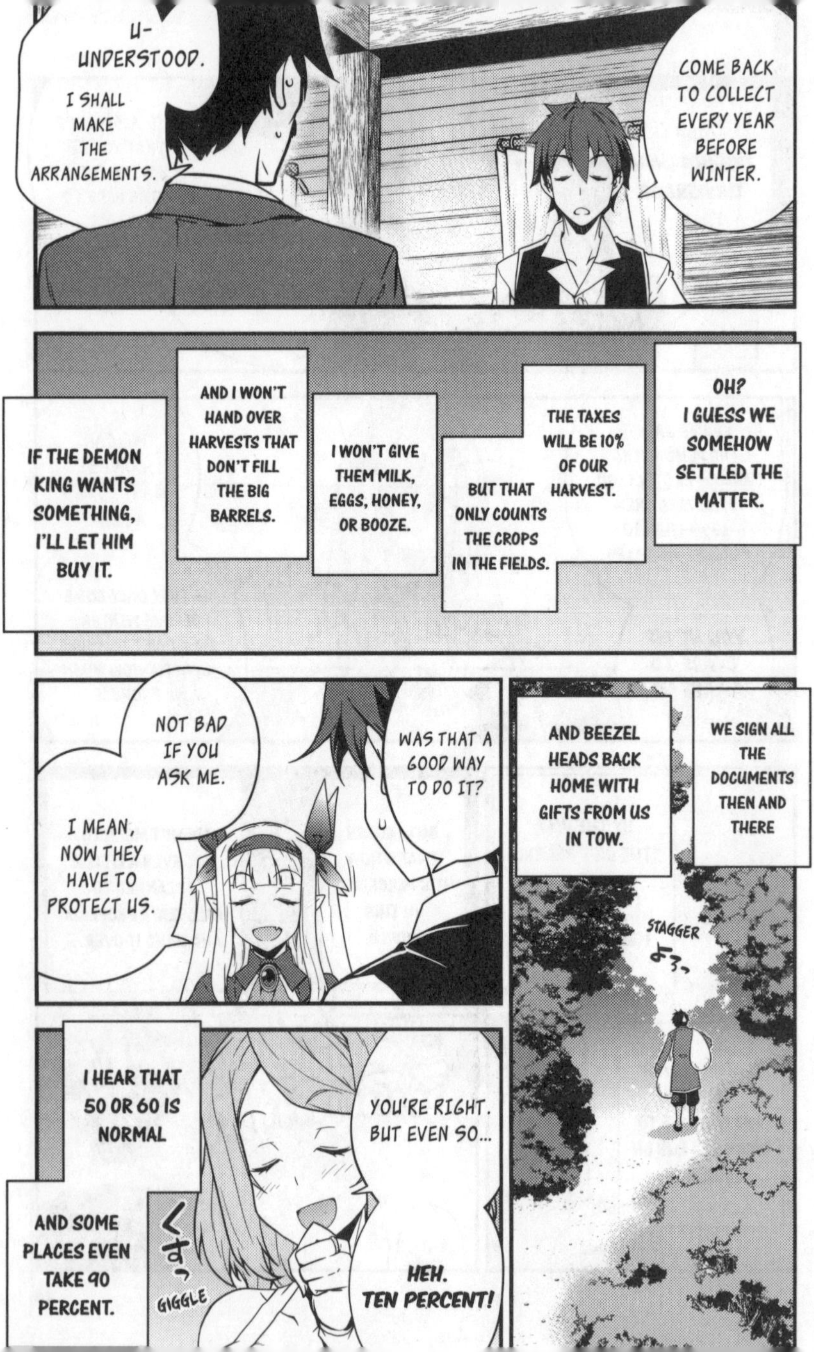
COME BACK TO COLLECT EVERY YEAR BEFORE WINTER.
U- UNDERSTOOD.
I SHALL MAKE THE ARRANGEMENTS.
OH? I GUESS WE SOMEHOW SETTLED THE MATTER.
THE TAXES WILL BE 10% OF OUR HARVEST.
BUT THAT ONLY COUNTS THE CROPS IN THE FIELDS.
I WON'T GIVE THEM MILK, EGGS, HONEY, OR BOOZE.
AND I WON'T HAND OVER HARVESTS THAT DON'T FILL THE BIG BARRELS.
IF THE DEMON KING WANTS SOMETHING, I'LL LET HIM BUY IT.
WE SIGN ALL THE DOCUMENTS THEN AND THERE
AND BEEZEL HEADS BACK HOME WITH GIFTS FROM US IN TOW.
STAGGER
よろっ
WAS THAT A GOOD WAY TO DO IT?
NOT BAD IF YOU ASK ME.
I MEAN, NOW THEY HAVE TO PROTECT US.
YOU'RE RIGHT. BUT EVEN SO...
I HEAR THAT 50 OR 60 IS NORMAL
AND SOME PLACES EVEN TAKE 90 PERCENT.
HEH. TEN PERCENT!
くすっ
GIGGLE

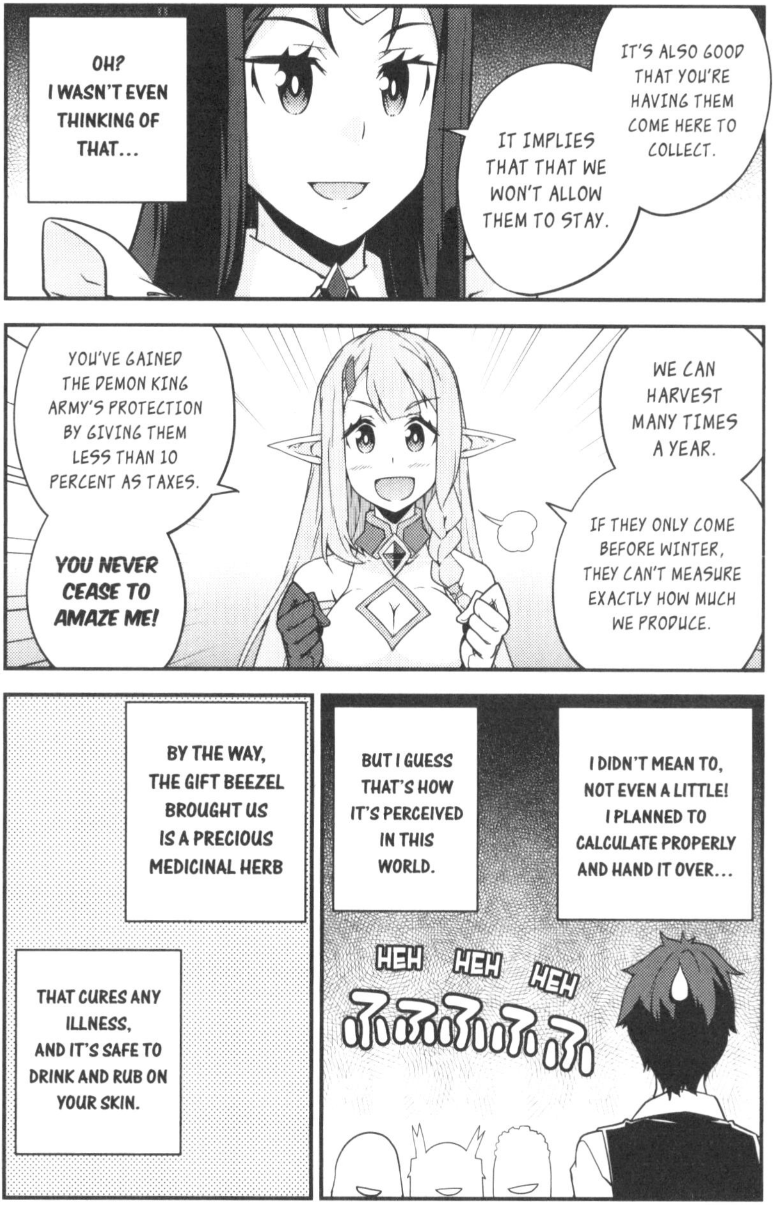
IT'S ALSO GOOD THAT YOU'RE HAVING THEM COME HERE TO COLLECT.
IT IMPLIES THAT THAT WE WON'T ALLOW THEM TO STAY.
OH? I WASN'T EVEN THINKING OF THAT...
WE CAN HARVEST MANY TIMES A YEAR.
IF THEY ONLY COME BEFORE WINTER, THEY CAN'T MEASURE EXACTLY HOW MUCH WE PRODUCE.
YOU'VE GAINED THE DEMON KING ARMY'S PROTECTION BY GIVING THEM LESS THAN 10 PERCENT AS TAXES.
YOU NEVER CEASE TO AMAZE ME!
I DIDN'T MEAN TO, NOT EVEN A LITTLE! I PLANNED TO CALCULATE PROPERLY AND HAND IT OVER...
BUT I GUESS THAT'S HOW IT'S PERCEIVED IN THIS WORLD.
HEH HEH HEH
ふふふふふ
BY THE WAY, THE GIFT BEEZEL BROUGHT US IS A PRECIOUS MEDICINAL HERB
THAT CURES ANY ILLNESS, AND IT'S SAFE TO DRINK AND RUB ON YOUR SKIN.

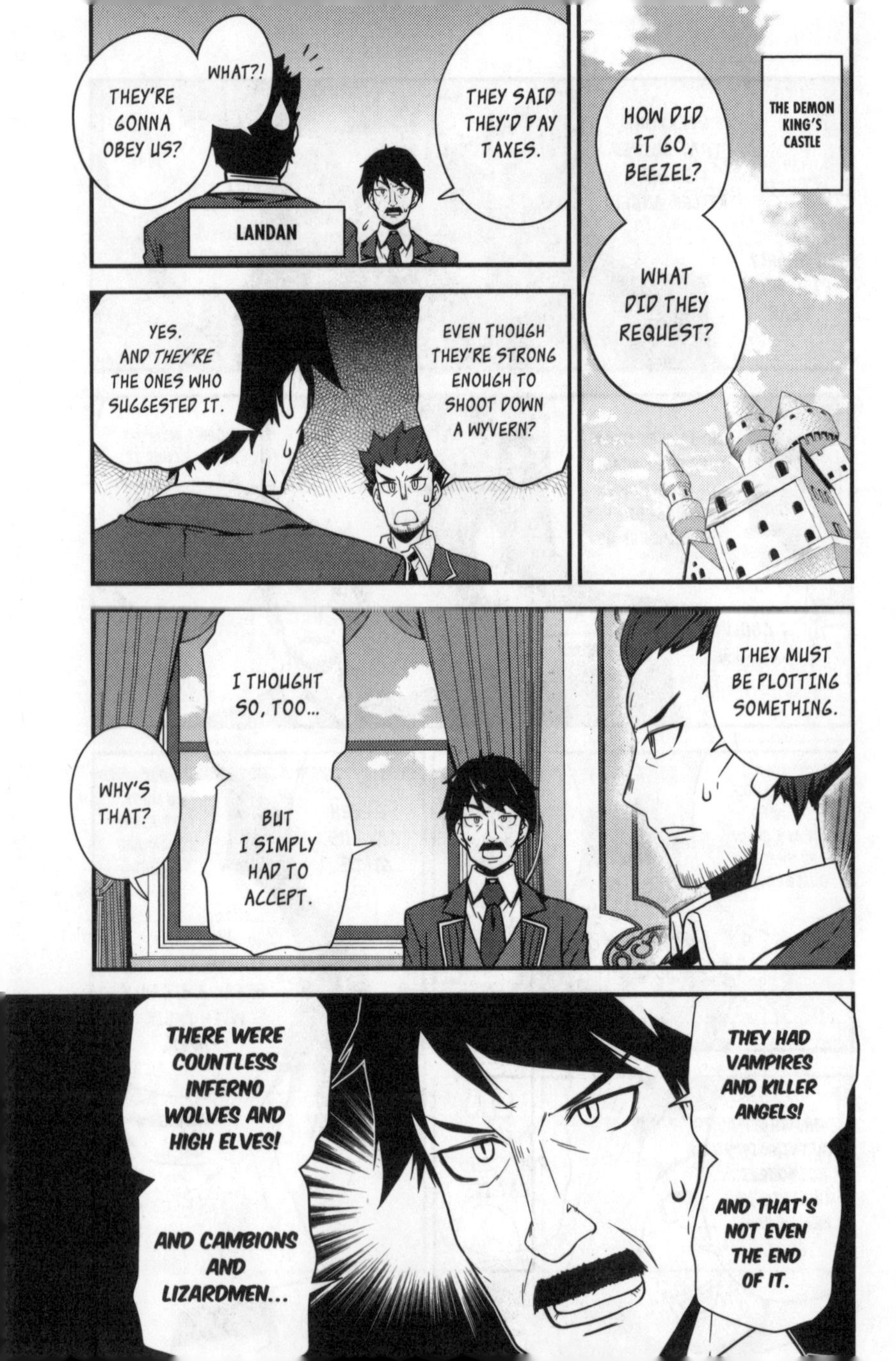
THE DEMON KING'S CASTLE
HOW DID IT GO, BEEZEL?
WHAT DID THEY REQUEST?
THEY SAID THEY'D PAY TAXES.
WHAT?!
THEY'RE GONNA OBEY US?
LANDAN
EVEN THOUGH THEY'RE STRONG ENOUGH TO SHOOT DOWN A WYVERN?
YES. AND *THEY'RE* THE ONES WHO SUGGESTED IT.
THEY MUST BE PLOTTING SOMETHING.
I THOUGHT SO, TOO...
BUT I SIMPLY HAD TO ACCEPT.
WHY'S THAT?
THEY HAD VAMPIRES AND KILLER ANGELS!
AND THAT'S NOT EVEN THE END OF IT.
THERE WERE COUNTLESS INFERNO WOLVES AND HIGH ELVES!
AND CAMBIONS AND LIZARDMEN...

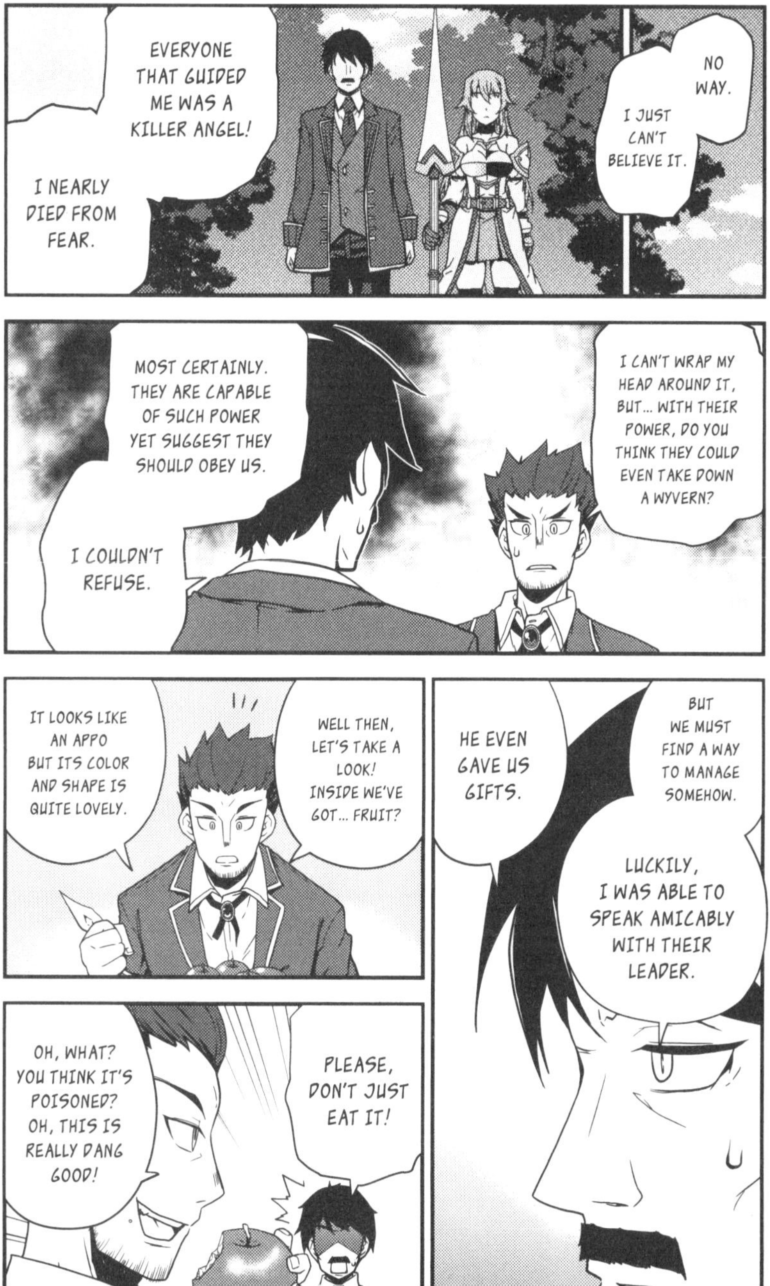
NO WAY.
I JUST CAN'T BELIEVE IT.
EVERYONE THAT GUIDED ME WAS A KILLER ANGEL!
I NEARLY DIED FROM FEAR.
I CAN'T WRAP MY HEAD AROUND IT, BUT... WITH THEIR POWER, DO YOU THINK THEY COULD EVEN TAKE DOWN A WYVERN?
MOST CERTAINLY. THEY ARE CAPABLE OF SUCH POWER YET SUGGEST THEY SHOULD OBEY US.
I COULDN'T REFUSE.
BUT WE MUST FIND A WAY TO MANAGE SOMEHOW.
HE EVEN GAVE US GIFTS.
LUCKILY, I WAS ABLE TO SPEAK AMICABLY WITH THEIR LEADER.
WELL THEN, LET'S TAKE A LOOK! INSIDE WE'VE GOT... FRUIT?
IT LOOKS LIKE AN APPO BUT ITS COLOR AND SHAPE IS QUITE LOVELY.
PLEASE, DON'T JUST EAT IT!
OH, WHAT? YOU THINK IT'S POISONED? OH, THIS IS REALLY DANG GOOD!

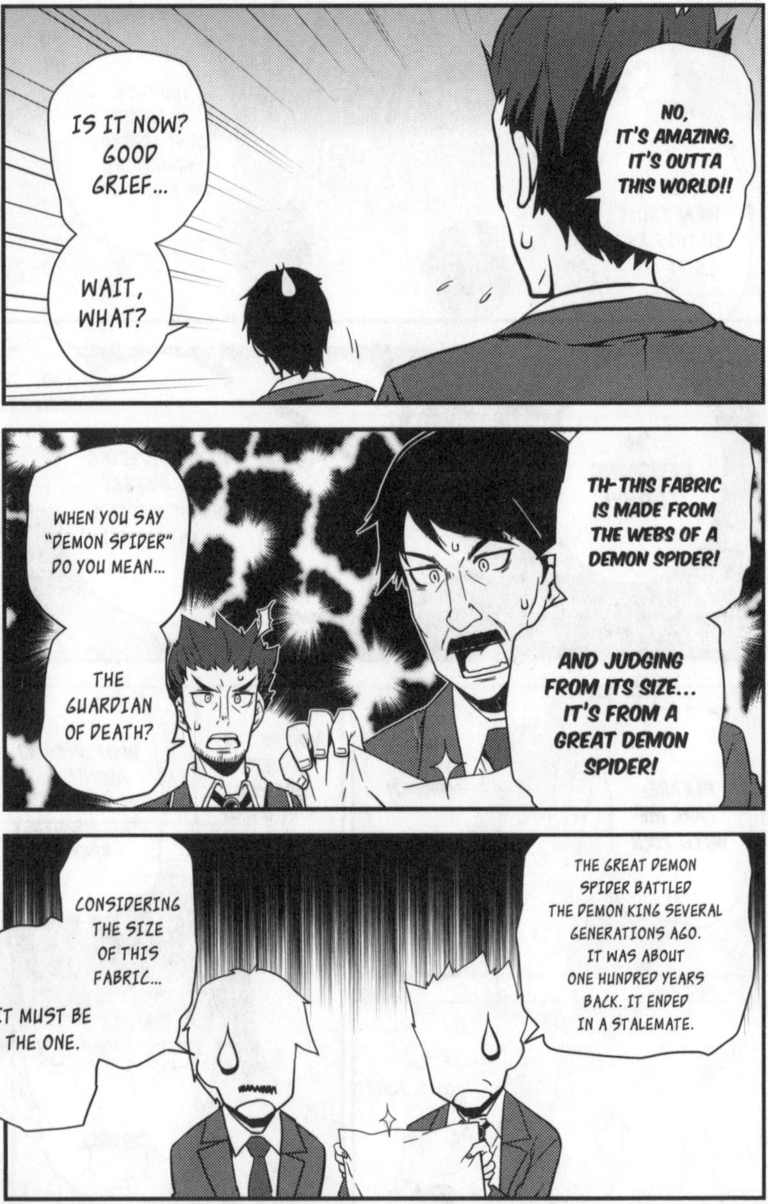
NO, IT'S AMAZING. IT'S OUTTA THIS WORLD!!
IS IT NOW? GOOD GRIEF...
WAIT, WHAT?
TH-THIS FABRIC IS MADE FROM THE WEBS OF A DEMON SPIDER!
AND JUDGING FROM ITS SIZE... IT'S FROM A GREAT DEMON SPIDER!
WHEN YOU SAY "DEMON SPIDER" DO YOU MEAN...
THE GUARDIAN OF DEATH?
THE GREAT DEMON SPIDER BATTLED THE DEMON KING SEVERAL GENERATIONS AGO. IT WAS ABOUT ONE HUNDRED YEARS BACK. IT ENDED IN A STALEMATE.
CONSIDERING THE SIZE OF THIS FABRIC...
IT MUST BE THE ONE.

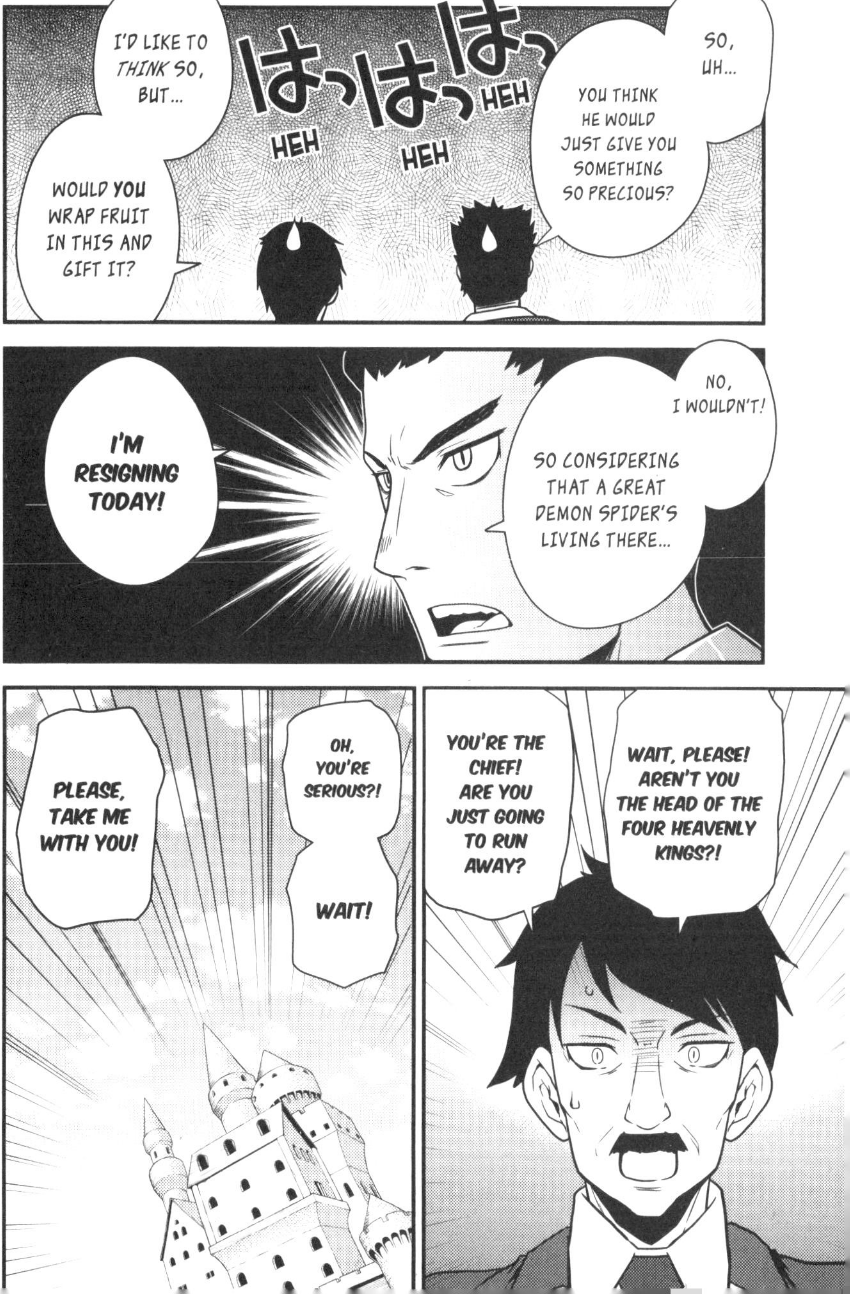
SO, UH...
YOU THINK HE WOULD JUST GIVE YOU SOMETHING SO PRECIOUS?
はっはっはっ
HEH
HEH
HEH
I'D LIKE TO *THINK* SO, BUT...
WOULD **YOU** WRAP FRUIT IN THIS AND GIFT IT?
NO, I WOULDN'T!
SO CONSIDERING THAT A GREAT DEMON SPIDER'S LIVING THERE...
I'M RESIGNING TODAY!
WAIT, PLEASE! AREN'T YOU THE HEAD OF THE FOUR HEAVENLY KINGS?!
YOU'RE THE CHIEF! ARE YOU JUST GOING TO RUN AWAY?
OH, YOU'RE SERIOUS?!
WAIT!
PLEASE, TAKE ME WITH YOU!

CHAPTER 23: DRAGON GUEST

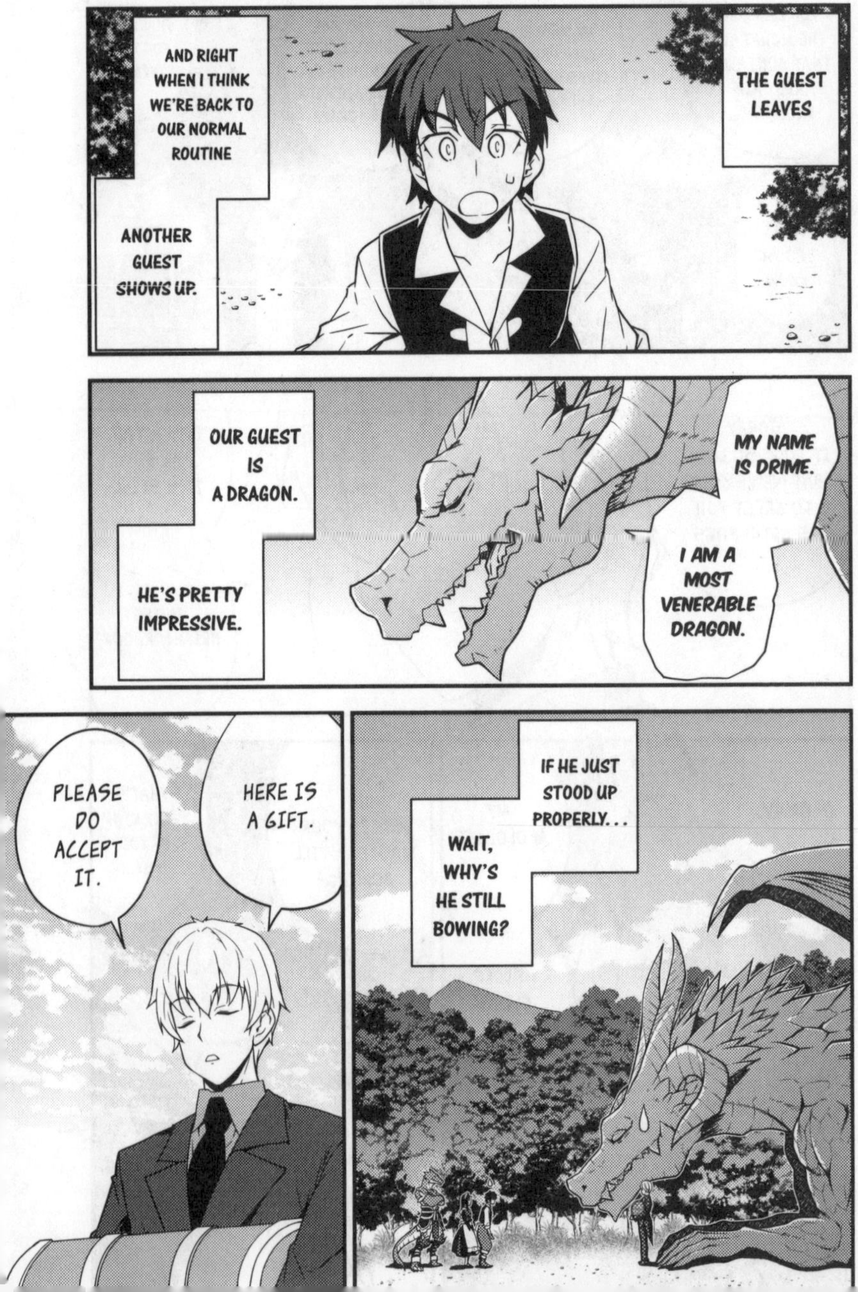
THE GUEST LEAVES
AND RIGHT WHEN I THINK WE'RE BACK TO OUR NORMAL ROUTINE
ANOTHER GUEST SHOWS UP.
MY NAME IS DRIME.
I AM A MOST VENERABLE DRAGON.
OUR GUEST IS A DRAGON.
HE'S PRETTY IMPRESSIVE.
IF HE JUST STOOD UP PROPERLY...
WAIT, WHY'S HE STILL BOWING?
HERE IS A GIFT.
PLEASE DO ACCEPT IT.

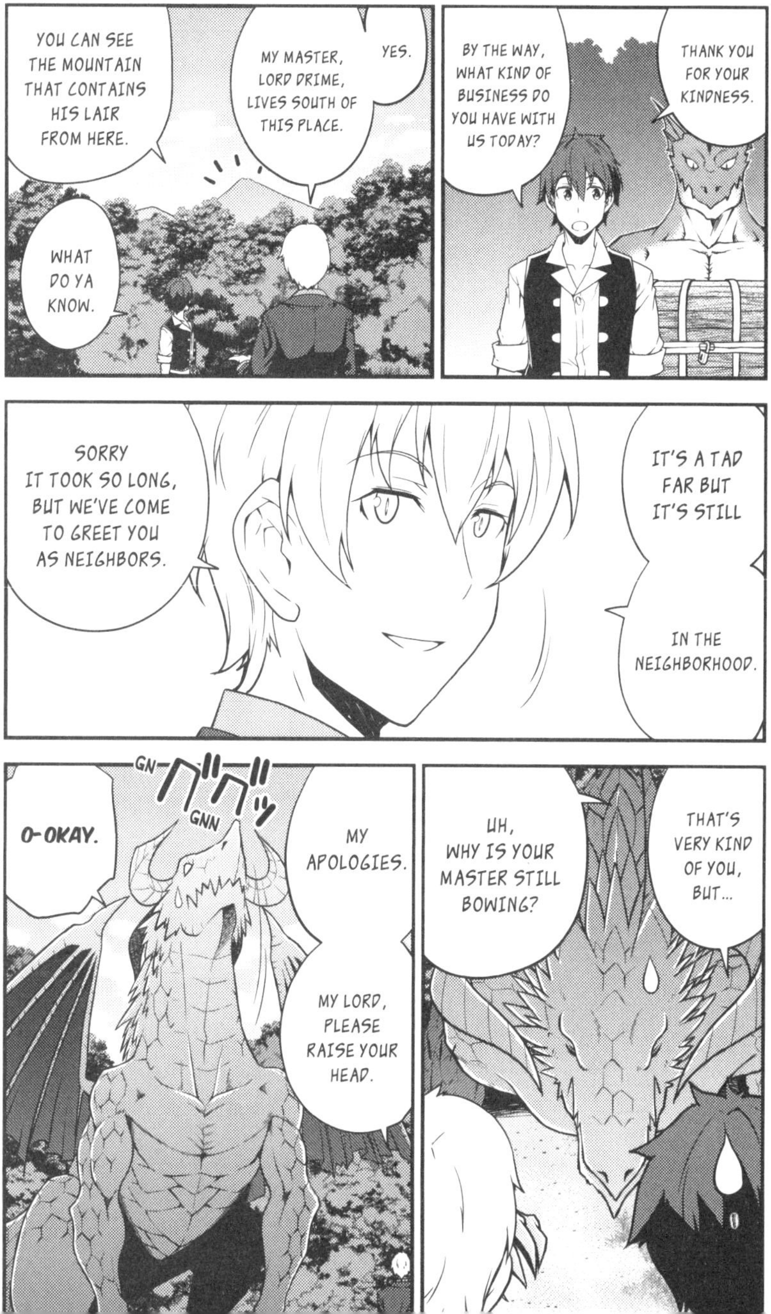
THANK YOU FOR YOUR KINDNESS.
BY THE WAY, WHAT KIND OF BUSINESS DO YOU HAVE WITH US TODAY?
YES.
MY MASTER, LORD DRIME, LIVES SOUTH OF THIS PLACE.
YOU CAN SEE THE MOUNTAIN THAT CONTAINS HIS LAIR FROM HERE.
WHAT DO YA KNOW.
IT'S A TAD FAR BUT IT'S STILL
IN THE NEIGHBORHOOD.
SORRY IT TOOK SO LONG, BUT WE'VE COME TO GREET YOU AS NEIGHBORS.
THAT'S VERY KIND OF YOU, BUT...
UH, WHY IS YOUR MASTER STILL BOWING?
MY APOLOGIES.
GN
GNN
O-OKAY.
MY LORD, PLEASE RAISE YOUR HEAD.

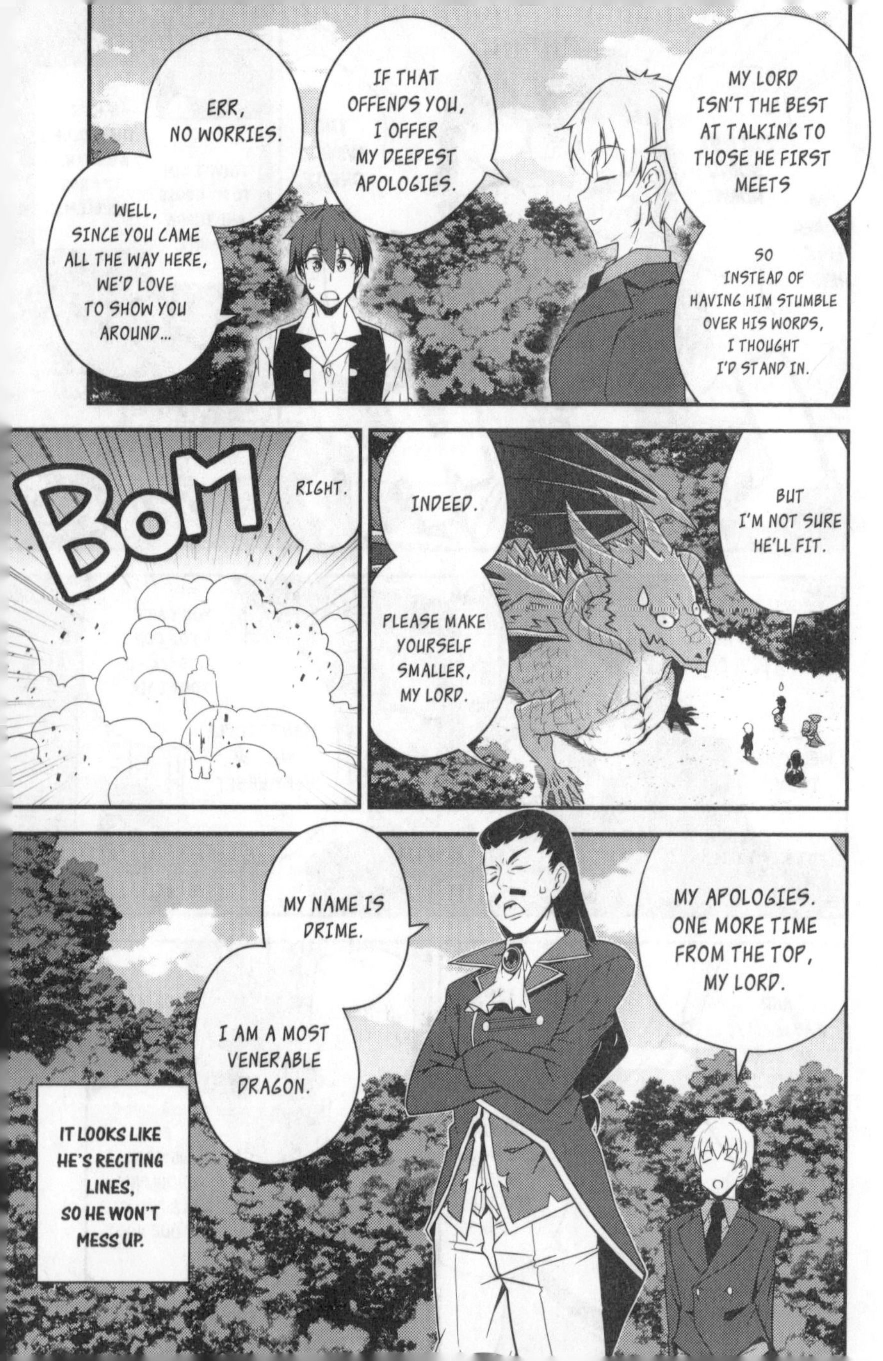
MY LORD ISN'T THE BEST AT TALKING TO THOSE HE FIRST MEETS
SO INSTEAD OF HAVING HIM STUMBLE OVER HIS WORDS, I THOUGHT I'D STAND IN.
IF THAT OFFENDS YOU, I OFFER MY DEEPEST APOLOGIES.
ERR, NO WORRIES.
WELL, SINCE YOU CAME ALL THE WAY HERE, WE'D LOVE TO SHOW YOU AROUND...
BUT I'M NOT SURE HE'LL FIT.
INDEED.
PLEASE MAKE YOURSELF SMALLER, MY LORD.
RIGHT.
BOM
MY APOLOGIES. ONE MORE TIME FROM THE TOP, MY LORD.
MY NAME IS DRIME.
I AM A MOST VENERABLE DRAGON.
IT LOOKS LIKE HE'S RECITING LINES, SO HE WON'T MESS UP.

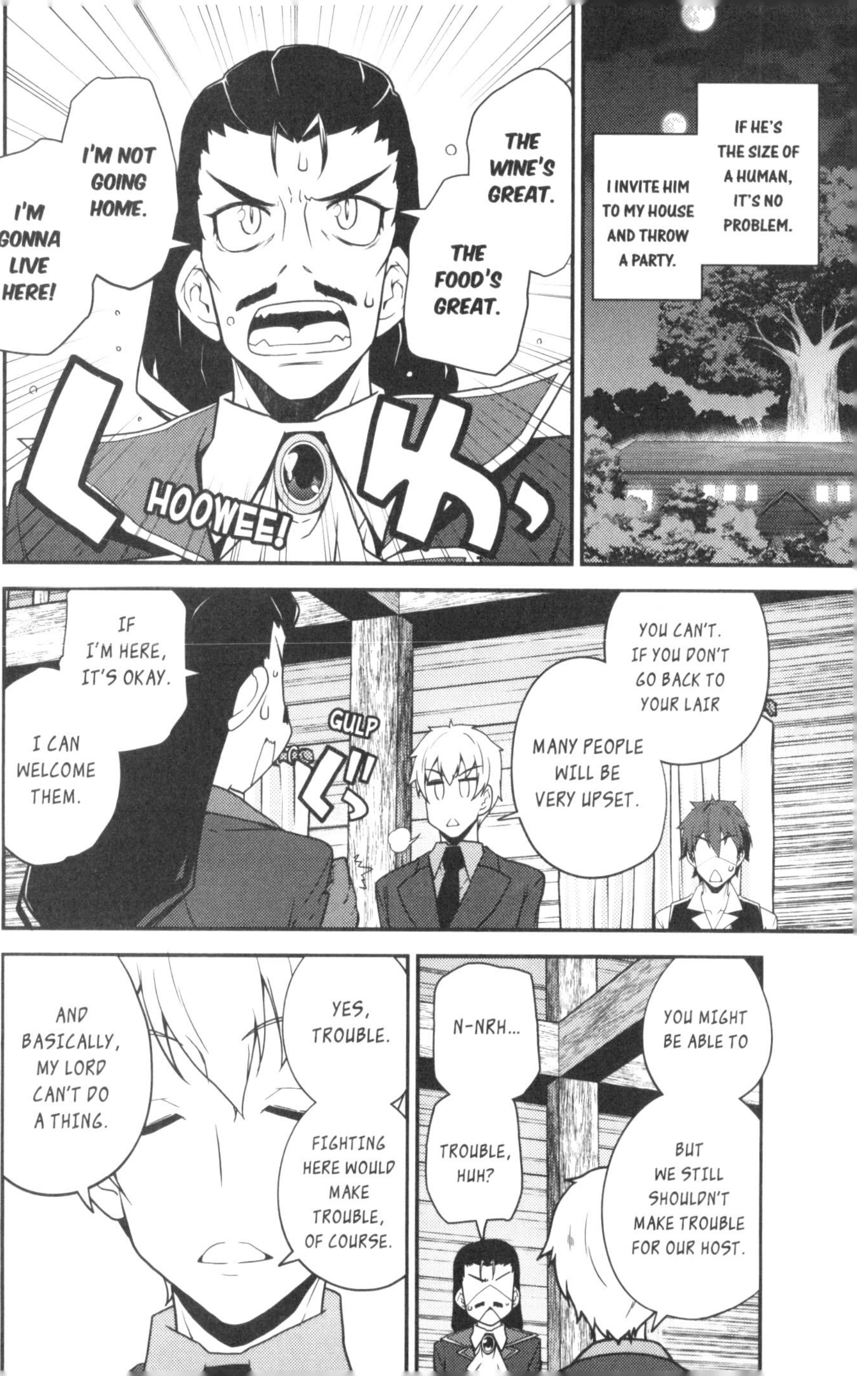
IF HE'S THE SIZE OF A HUMAN, IT'S NO PROBLEM.
I INVITE HIM TO MY HOUSE AND THROW A PARTY.
THE WINE'S GREAT.
THE FOOD'S GREAT.
I'M NOT GOING HOME.
I'M GONNA LIVE HERE!
HOOWEE!
YOU CAN'T. IF YOU DON'T GO BACK TO YOUR LAIR
MANY PEOPLE WILL BE VERY UPSET.
GULP
IF I'M HERE, IT'S OKAY.
I CAN WELCOME THEM.
YOU MIGHT BE ABLE TO
BUT WE STILL SHOULDN'T MAKE TROUBLE FOR OUR HOST.
N-NRH...
TROUBLE, HUH?
YES, TROUBLE.
FIGHTING HERE WOULD MAKE TROUBLE, OF COURSE.
AND BASICALLY, MY LORD CAN'T DO A THING.

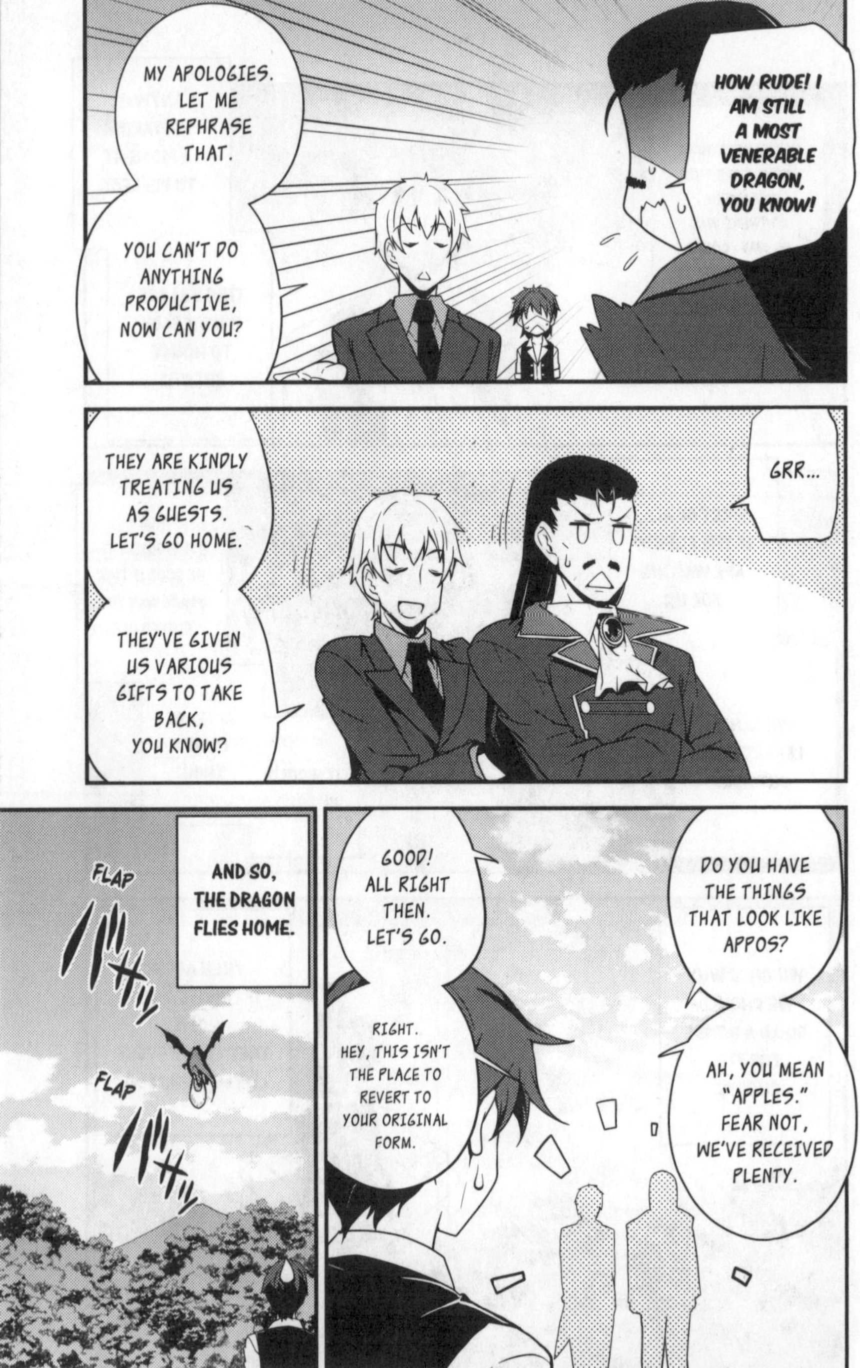
HOW RUDE! I AM STILL A MOST VENERABLE DRAGON, YOU KNOW!
MY APOLOGIES. LET ME REPHRASE THAT.
YOU CAN'T DO ANYTHING PRODUCTIVE, NOW CAN YOU?
GRR...
THEY ARE KINDLY TREATING US AS GUESTS. LET'S GO HOME.
THEY'VE GIVEN US VARIOUS GIFTS TO TAKE BACK, YOU KNOW?
DO YOU HAVE THE THINGS THAT LOOK LIKE APPOS?
AH, YOU MEAN "APPLES." FEAR NOT, WE'VE RECEIVED PLENTY.
GOOD! ALL RIGHT THEN. LET'S GO.
RIGHT. HEY, THIS ISN'T THE PLACE TO REVERT TO YOUR ORIGINAL FORM.
AND SO, THE DRAGON FLIES HOME.
FLAP
FLAP

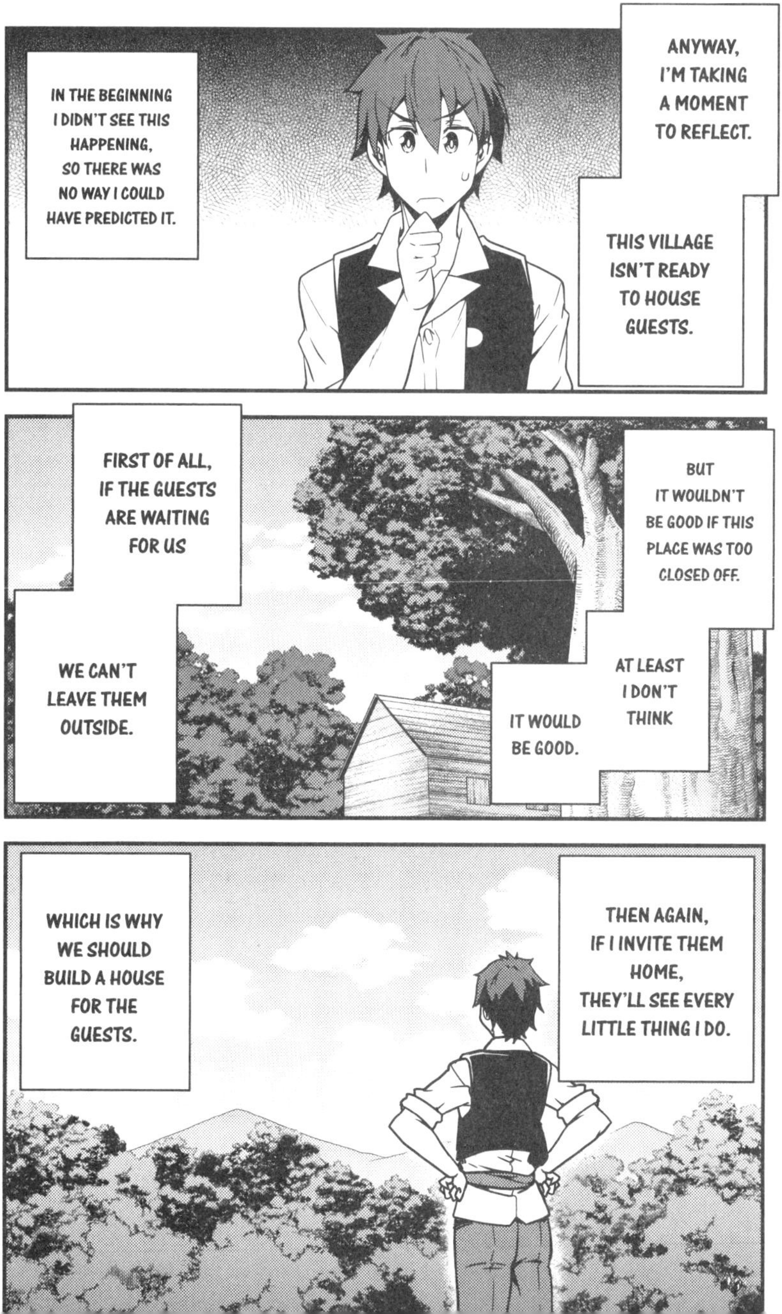
ANYWAY, I'M TAKING A MOMENT TO REFLECT.
THIS VILLAGE ISN'T READY TO HOUSE GUESTS.
IN THE BEGINNING I DIDN'T SEE THIS HAPPENING, SO THERE WAS NO WAY I COULD HAVE PREDICTED IT.
BUT IT WOULDN'T BE GOOD IF THIS PLACE WAS TOO CLOSED OFF.
AT LEAST I DON'T THINK
IT WOULD BE GOOD.
FIRST OF ALL, IF THE GUESTS ARE WAITING FOR US
WE CAN'T LEAVE THEM OUTSIDE.
THEN AGAIN, IF I INVITE THEM HOME, THEY'LL SEE EVERY LITTLE THING I DO.
WHICH IS WHY WE SHOULD BUILD A HOUSE FOR THE GUESTS.

CHAPTER 24: GUEST: BEASTKIN

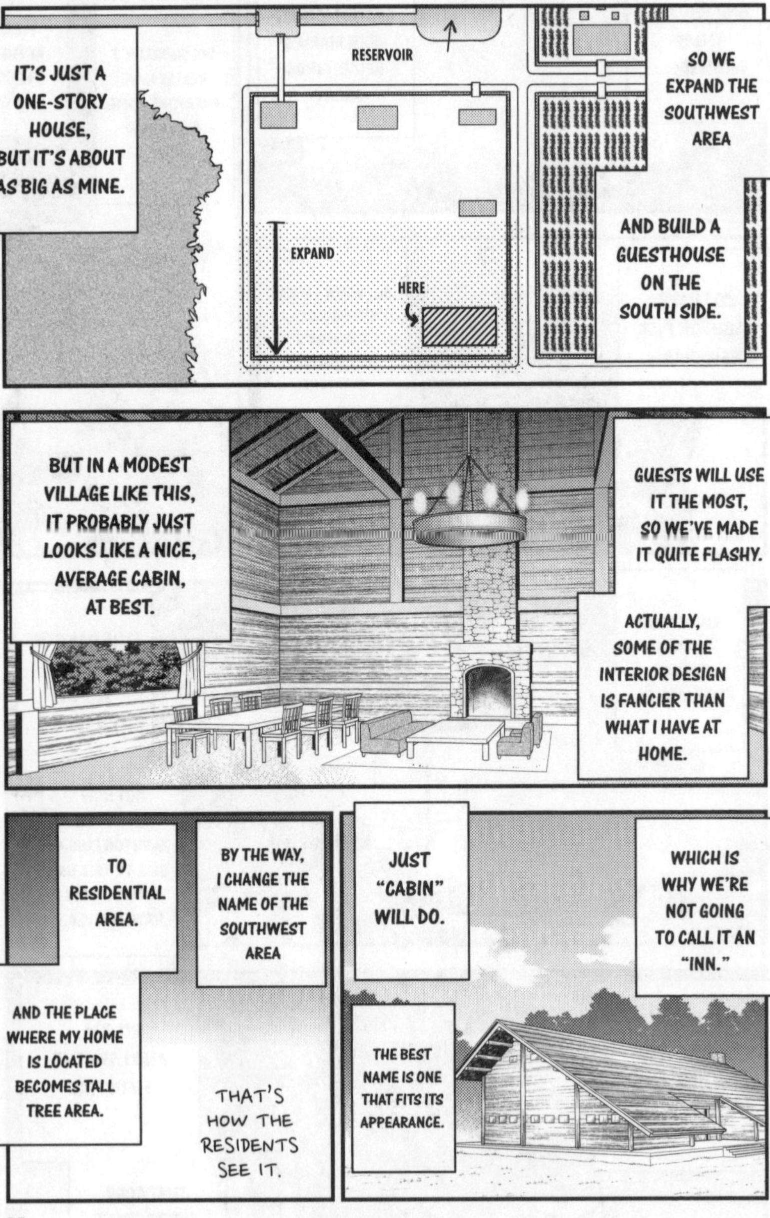
SO WE EXPAND THE SOUTHWEST AREA
AND BUILD A GUESTHOUSE ON THE SOUTH SIDE.
RESERVOIR
EXPAND
HERE
IT'S JUST A ONE-STORY HOUSE, BUT IT'S ABOUT AS BIG AS MINE.
GUESTS WILL USE IT THE MOST, SO WE'VE MADE IT QUITE FLASHY.
ACTUALLY, SOME OF THE INTERIOR DESIGN IS FANCIER THAN WHAT I HAVE AT HOME.
BUT IN A MODEST VILLAGE LIKE THIS, IT PROBABLY JUST LOOKS LIKE A NICE, AVERAGE CABIN, AT BEST.
WHICH IS WHY WE'RE NOT GOING TO CALL IT AN "INN."
JUST "CABIN" WILL DO.
THE BEST NAME IS ONE THAT FITS ITS APPEARANCE.
BY THE WAY, I CHANGE THE NAME OF THE SOUTHWEST AREA
TO RESIDENTIAL AREA.
AND THE PLACE WHERE MY HOME IS LOCATED BECOMES TALL TREE AREA.
THAT'S HOW THE RESIDENTS SEE IT.

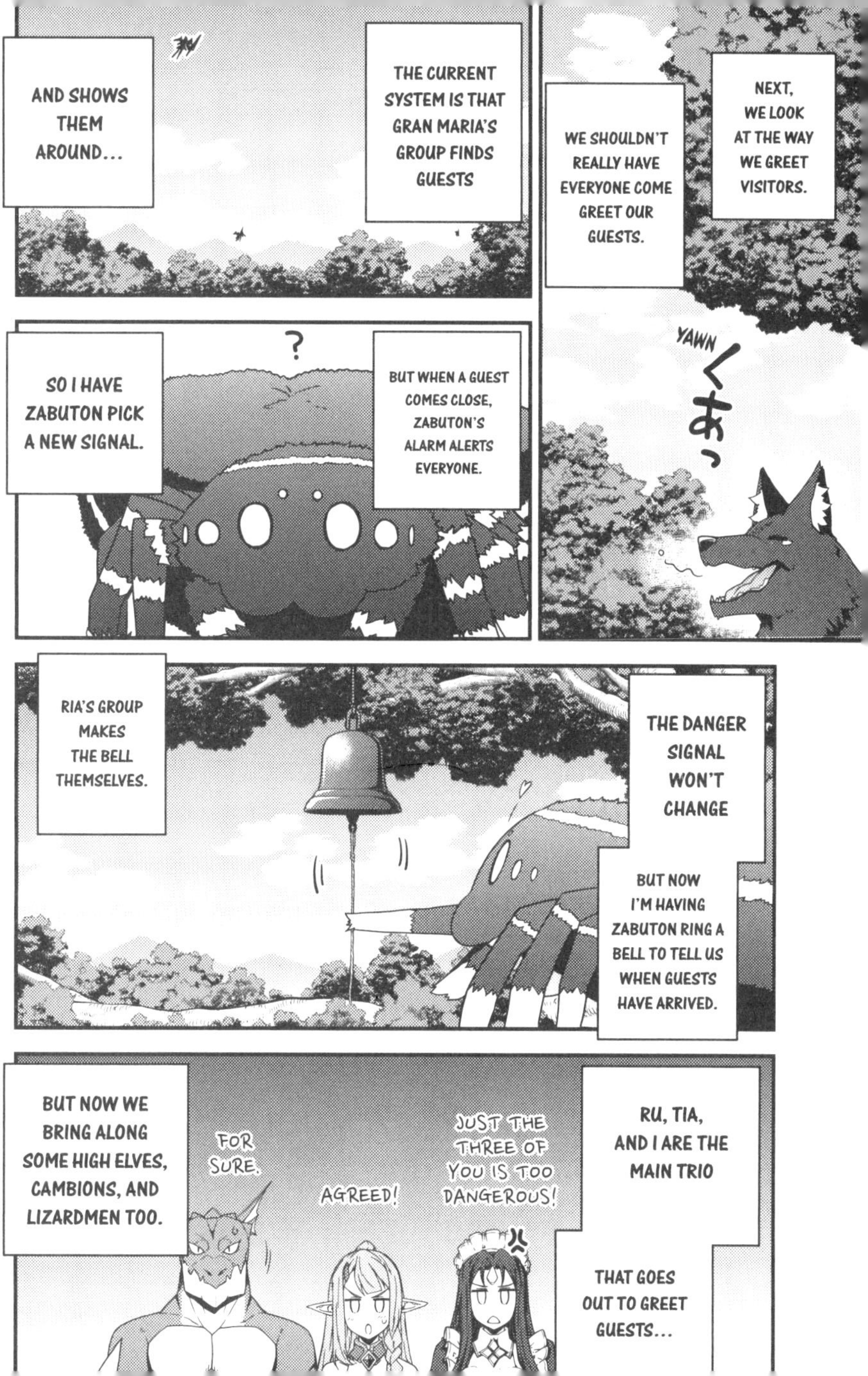
NEXT, WE LOOK AT THE WAY WE GREET VISITORS.
WE SHOULDN'T REALLY HAVE EVERYONE COME GREET OUR GUESTS.
YAWN
くあっ
THE CURRENT SYSTEM IS THAT GRAN MARIA'S GROUP FINDS GUESTS
AND SHOWS THEM AROUND...
BUT WHEN A GUEST COMES CLOSE, ZABUTON'S ALARM ALERTS EVERYONE.
?
SO I HAVE ZABUTON PICK A NEW SIGNAL.
THE DANGER SIGNAL WON'T CHANGE
BUT NOW I'M HAVING ZABUTON RING A BELL TO TELL US WHEN GUESTS HAVE ARRIVED.
RIA'S GROUP MAKES THE BELL THEMSELVES.
RU, TIA, AND I ARE THE MAIN TRIO
THAT GOES OUT TO GREET GUESTS...
JUST THE THREE OF YOU IS TOO DANGEROUS!
AGREED!
FOR SURE.
BUT NOW WE BRING ALONG SOME HIGH ELVES, CAMBIONS, AND LIZARDMEN TOO.

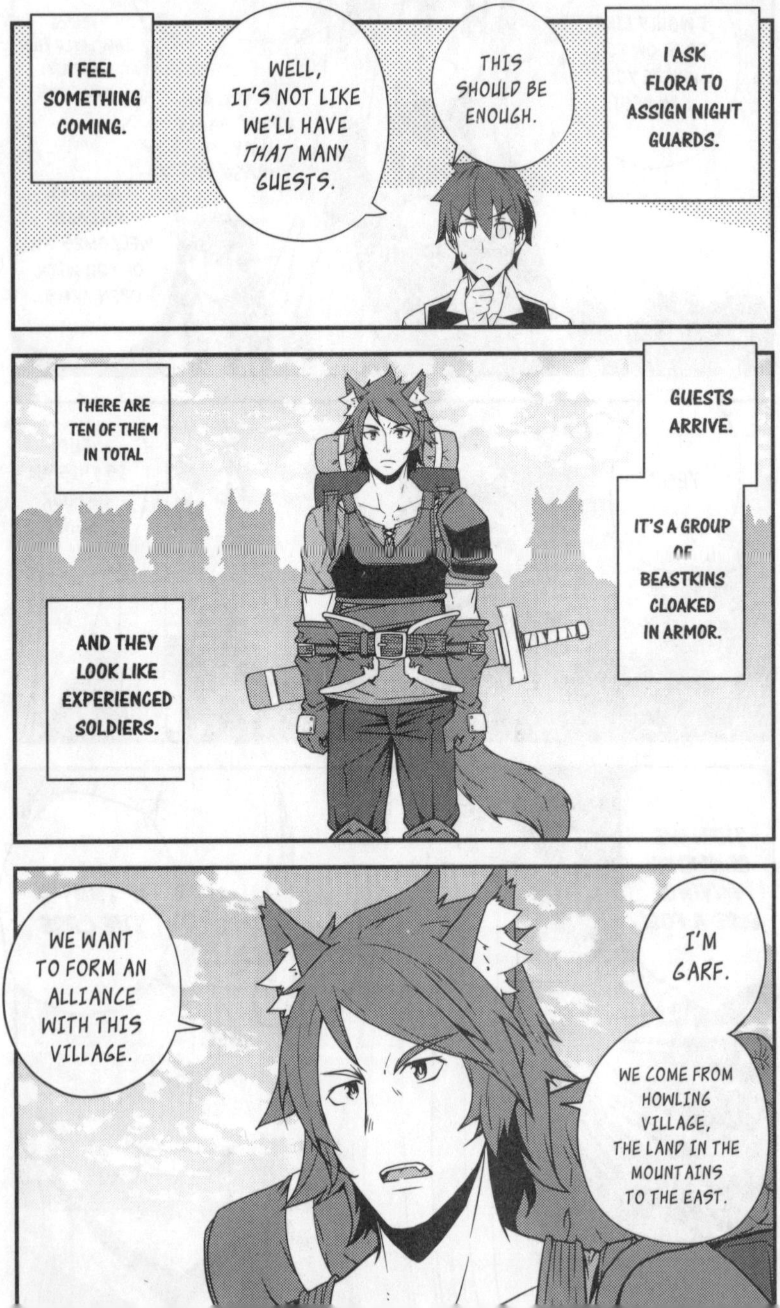
I ASK FLORA TO ASSIGN NIGHT GUARDS.
THIS SHOULD BE ENOUGH.
WELL, IT'S NOT LIKE WE'LL HAVE THAT MANY GUESTS.
I FEEL SOMETHING COMING.
GUESTS ARRIVE.
IT'S A GROUP OF BEASTKINS CLOAKED IN ARMOR.
THERE ARE TEN OF THEM IN TOTAL
AND THEY LOOK LIKE EXPERIENCED SOLDIERS.
I'M GARF.
WE COME FROM HOWLING VILLAGE, THE LAND IN THE MOUNTAINS TO THE EAST.
WE WANT TO FORM AN ALLIANCE WITH THIS VILLAGE.

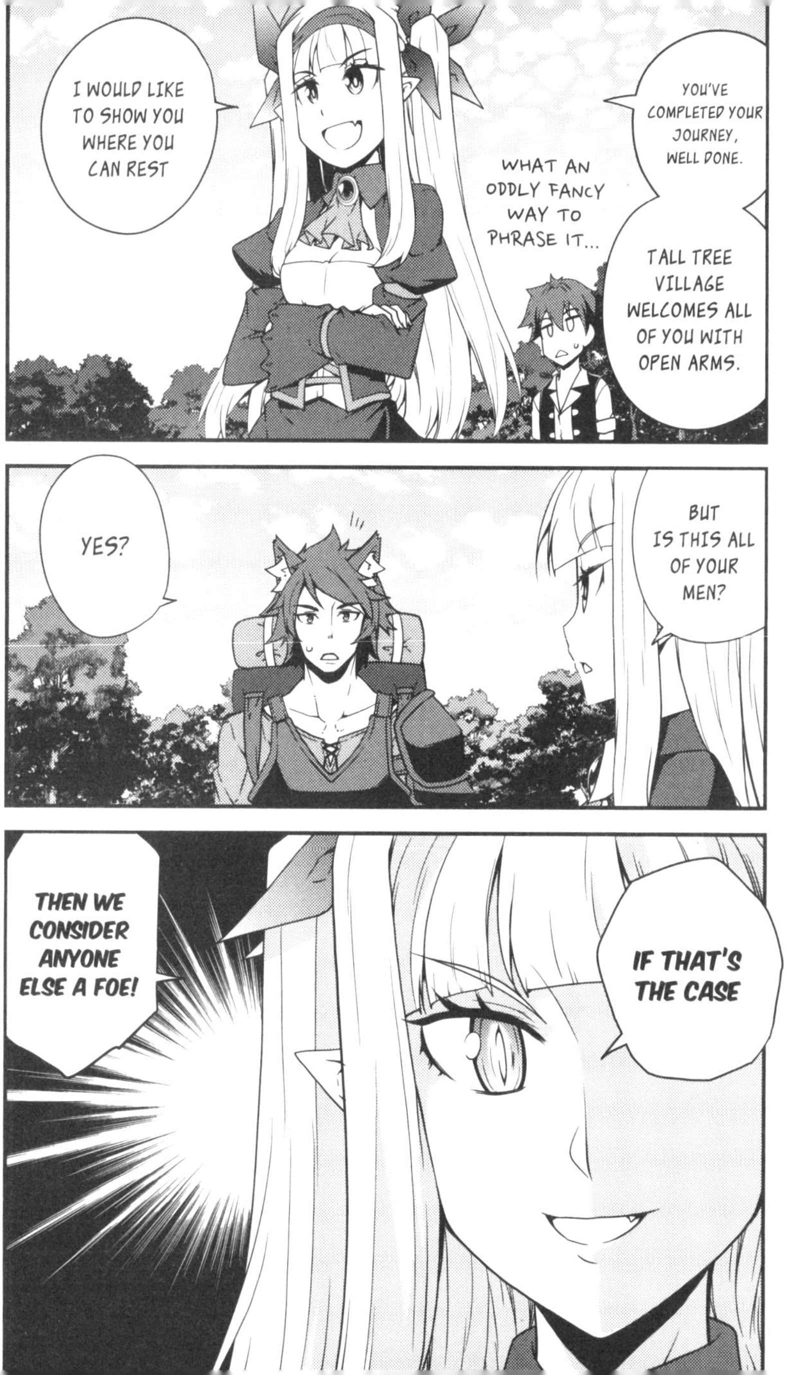
YOU'VE COMPLETED YOUR JOURNEY, WELL DONE.
TALL TREE VILLAGE WELCOMES ALL OF YOU WITH OPEN ARMS.
WHAT AN ODDLY FANCY WAY TO PHRASE IT...
I WOULD LIKE TO SHOW YOU WHERE YOU CAN REST
BUT IS THIS ALL OF YOUR MEN?
YES?
IF THAT'S THE CASE
THEN WE CONSIDER ANYONE ELSE A FOE!

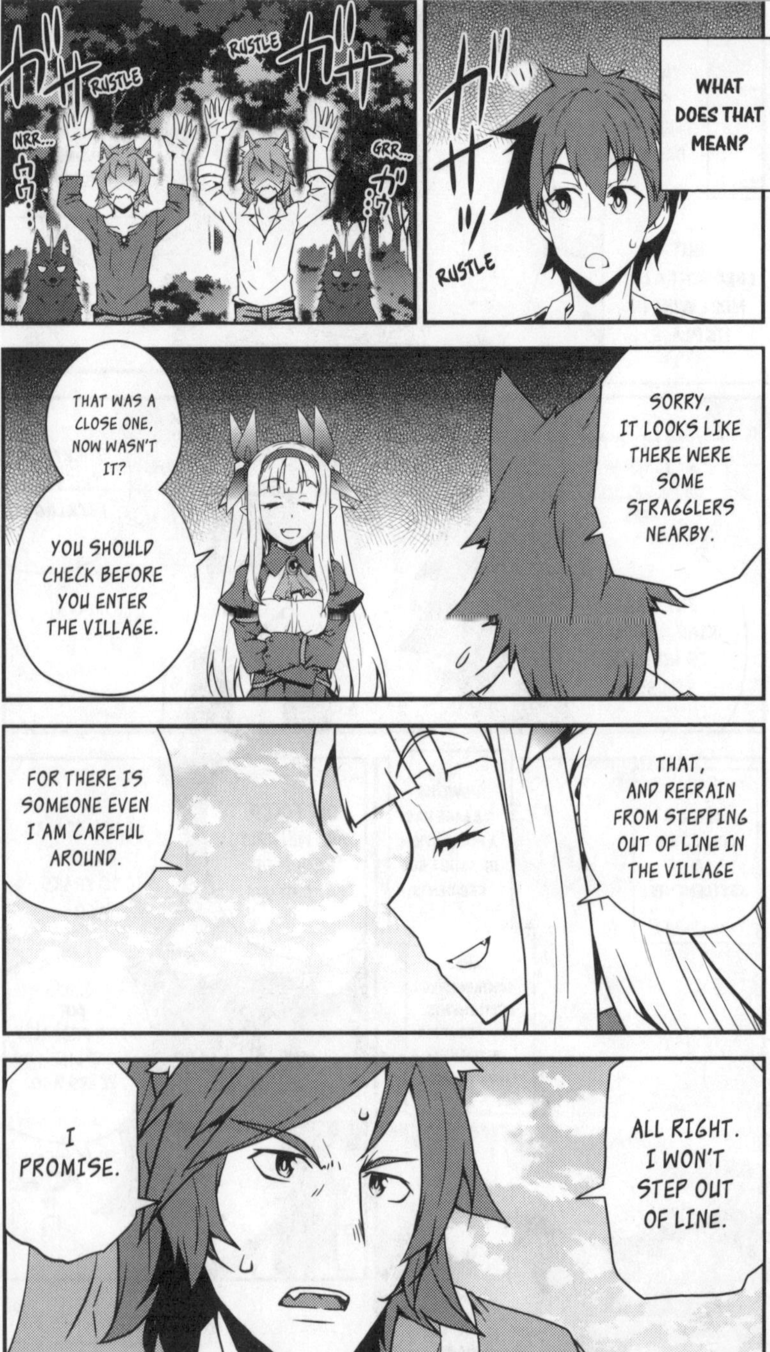
WHAT DOES THAT MEAN?
ガサ
RUSTLE
ガサ
RUSTLE
ガサ
RUSTLE
GRR...
ガウ
NRR...
ウウ...
SORRY, IT LOOKS LIKE THERE WERE SOME STRAGGLERS NEARBY.
THAT WAS A CLOSE ONE, NOW WASN'T IT?
YOU SHOULD CHECK BEFORE YOU ENTER THE VILLAGE.
THAT, AND REFRAIN FROM STEPPING OUT OF LINE IN THE VILLAGE
FOR THERE IS SOMEONE EVEN I AM CAREFUL AROUND.
ALL RIGHT. I WON'T STEP OUT OF LINE.
I PROMISE.

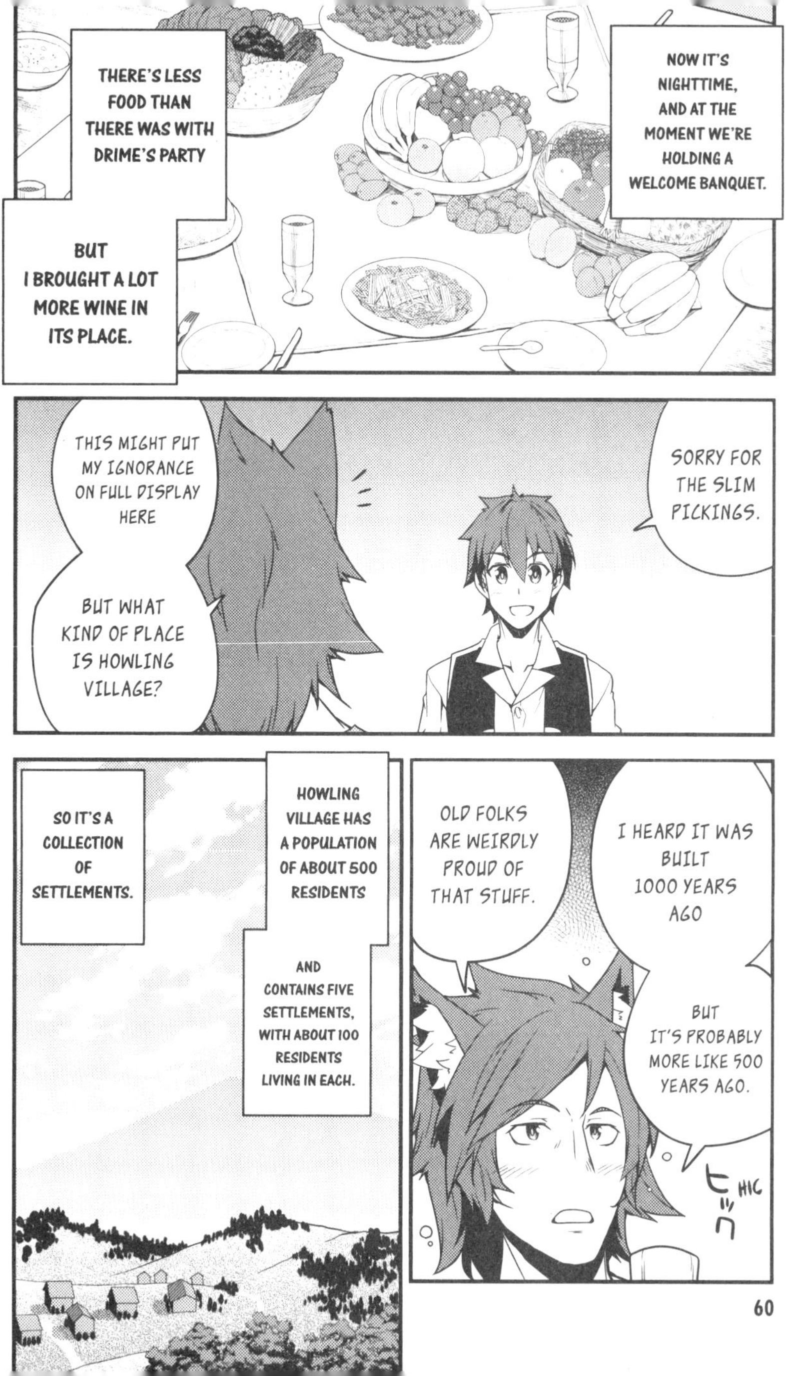
NOW IT'S NIGHTTIME, AND AT THE MOMENT WE'RE HOLDING A WELCOME BANQUET.
THERE'S LESS FOOD THAN THERE WAS WITH DRIME'S PARTY
BUT I BROUGHT A LOT MORE WINE IN ITS PLACE.
SORRY FOR THE SLIM PICKINGS.
THIS MIGHT PUT MY IGNORANCE ON FULL DISPLAY HERE
BUT WHAT KIND OF PLACE IS HOWLING VILLAGE?
I HEARD IT WAS BUILT 1000 YEARS AGO
OLD FOLKS ARE WEIRDLY PROUD OF THAT STUFF.
BUT IT'S PROBABLY MORE LIKE 500 YEARS AGO.
HIC
HOWLING VILLAGE HAS A POPULATION OF ABOUT 500 RESIDENTS
AND CONTAINS FIVE SETTLEMENTS, WITH ABOUT 100 RESIDENTS LIVING IN EACH.
SO IT'S A COLLECTION OF SETTLEMENTS.

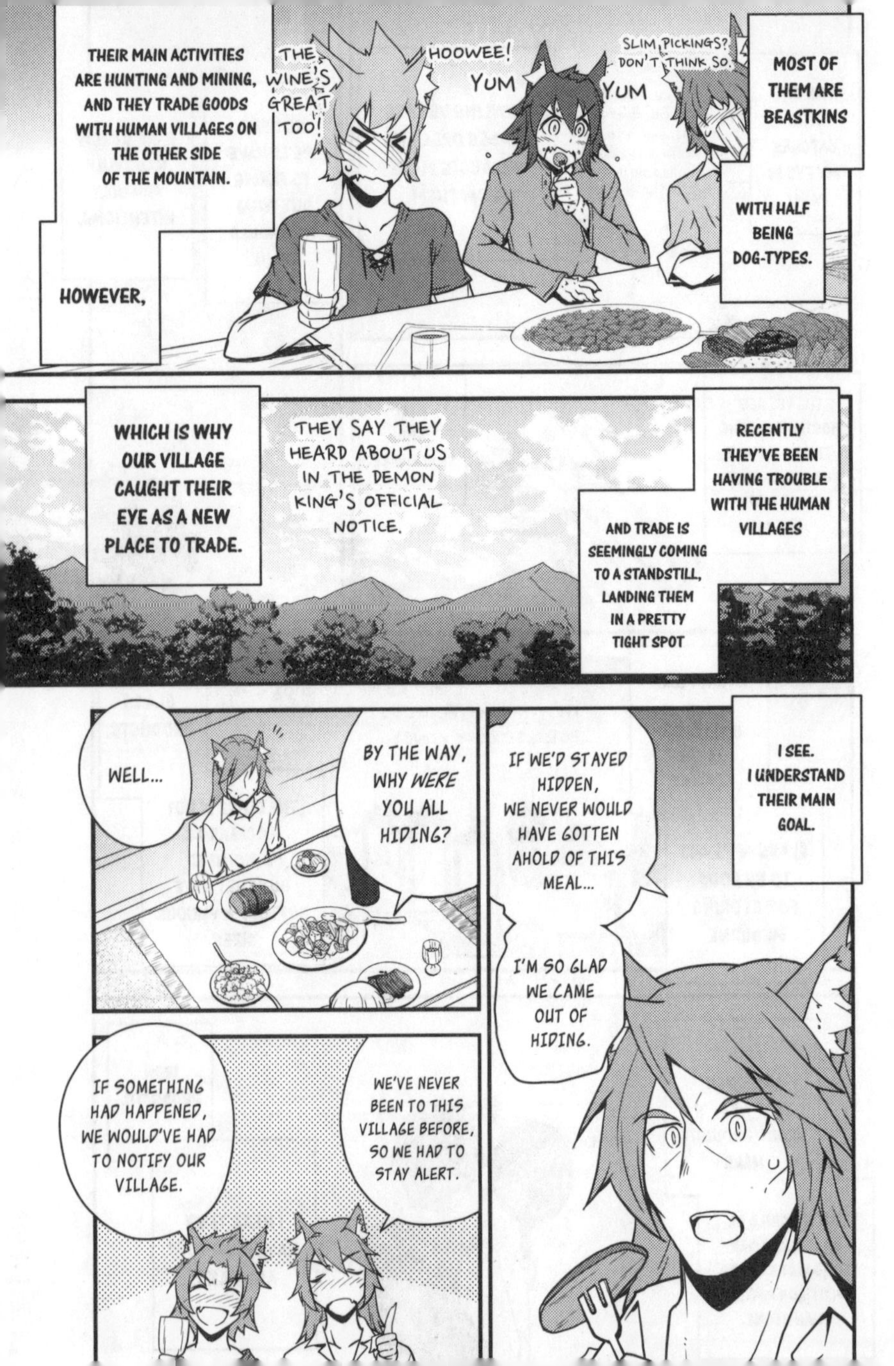
MOST OF THEM ARE BEASTKINS
WITH HALF BEING DOG-TYPES.
SLIM PICKINGS? DON'T THINK SO.
YUM
YUM
HOOWEE!
THE WINE'S GREAT TOO!
THEIR MAIN ACTIVITIES ARE HUNTING AND MINING, AND THEY TRADE GOODS WITH HUMAN VILLAGES ON THE OTHER SIDE OF THE MOUNTAIN.
HOWEVER,
RECENTLY THEY'VE BEEN HAVING TROUBLE WITH THE HUMAN VILLAGES
AND TRADE IS SEEMINGLY COMING TO A STANDSTILL, LANDING THEM IN A PRETTY TIGHT SPOT
THEY SAY THEY HEARD ABOUT US IN THE DEMON KING'S OFFICIAL NOTICE.
WHICH IS WHY OUR VILLAGE CAUGHT THEIR EYE AS A NEW PLACE TO TRADE.
I SEE. I UNDERSTAND THEIR MAIN GOAL.
IF WE'D STAYED HIDDEN, WE NEVER WOULD HAVE GOTTEN AHOLD OF THIS MEAL...
I'M SO GLAD WE CAME OUT OF HIDING.
BY THE WAY, WHY WERE YOU ALL HIDING?
WELL...
WE'VE NEVER BEEN TO THIS VILLAGE BEFORE, SO WE HAD TO STAY ALERT.
IF SOMETHING HAD HAPPENED, WE WOULD'VE HAD TO NOTIFY OUR VILLAGE.

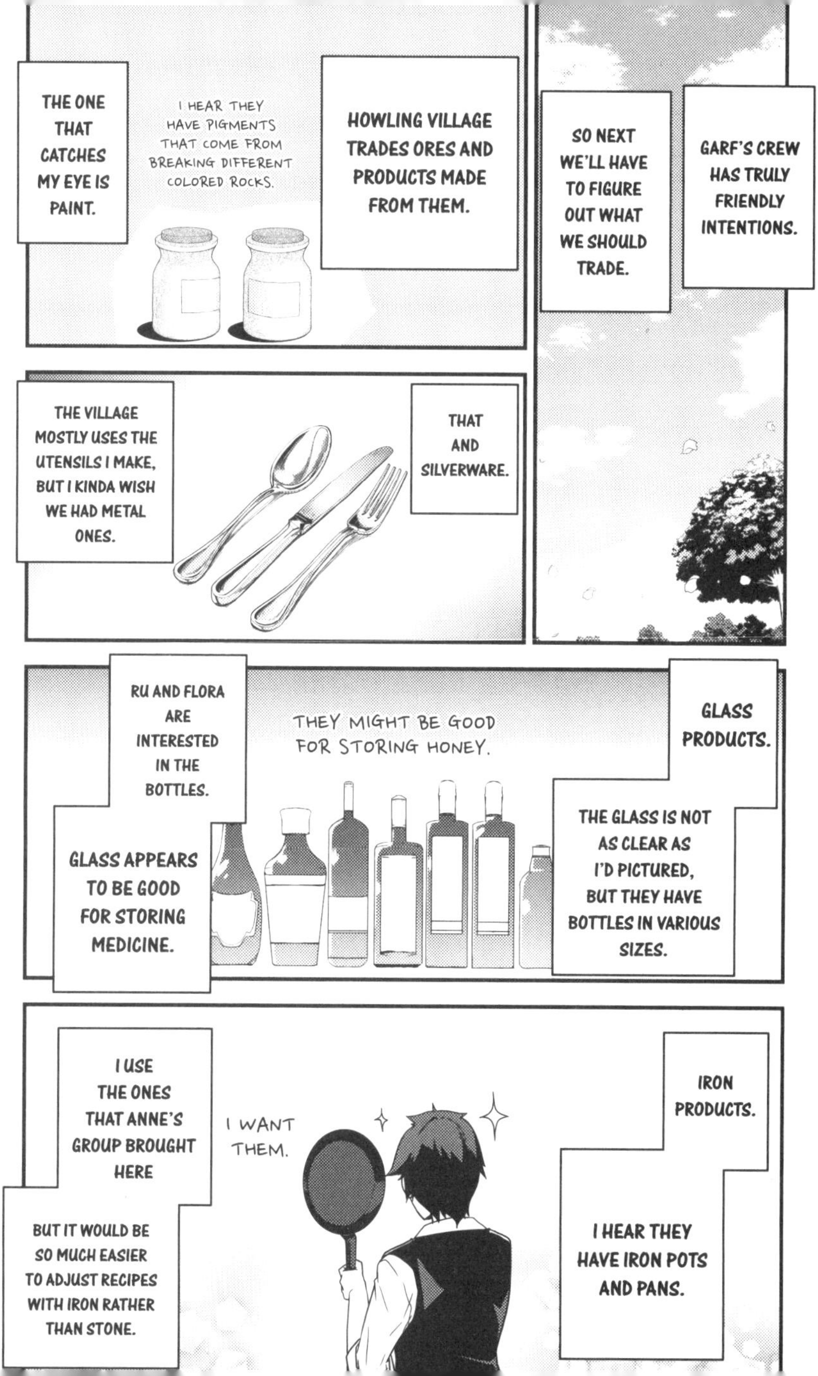

GARF'S CREW HAS TRULY FRIENDLY INTENTIONS.
SO NEXT WE'LL HAVE TO FIGURE OUT WHAT WE SHOULD TRADE.
HOWLING VILLAGE TRADES ORES AND PRODUCTS MADE FROM THEM.
I HEAR THEY HAVE PIGMENTS THAT COME FROM BREAKING DIFFERENT COLORED ROCKS.
THE ONE THAT CATCHES MY EYE IS PAINT.
THAT AND SILVERWARE.
THE VILLAGE MOSTLY USES THE UTENSILS I MAKE, BUT I KINDA WISH WE HAD METAL ONES.
GLASS PRODUCTS.
THE GLASS IS NOT AS CLEAR AS I'D PICTURED, BUT THEY HAVE BOTTLES IN VARIOUS SIZES.
THEY MIGHT BE GOOD FOR STORING HONEY.
RU AND FLORA ARE INTERESTED IN THE BOTTLES.
GLASS APPEARS TO BE GOOD FOR STORING MEDICINE.
IRON PRODUCTS.
I HEAR THEY HAVE IRON POTS AND PANS.
I WANT THEM.
I USE THE ONES THAT ANNE'S GROUP BROUGHT HERE
BUT IT WOULD BE SO MUCH EASIER TO ADJUST RECIPES WITH IRON RATHER THAN STONE.

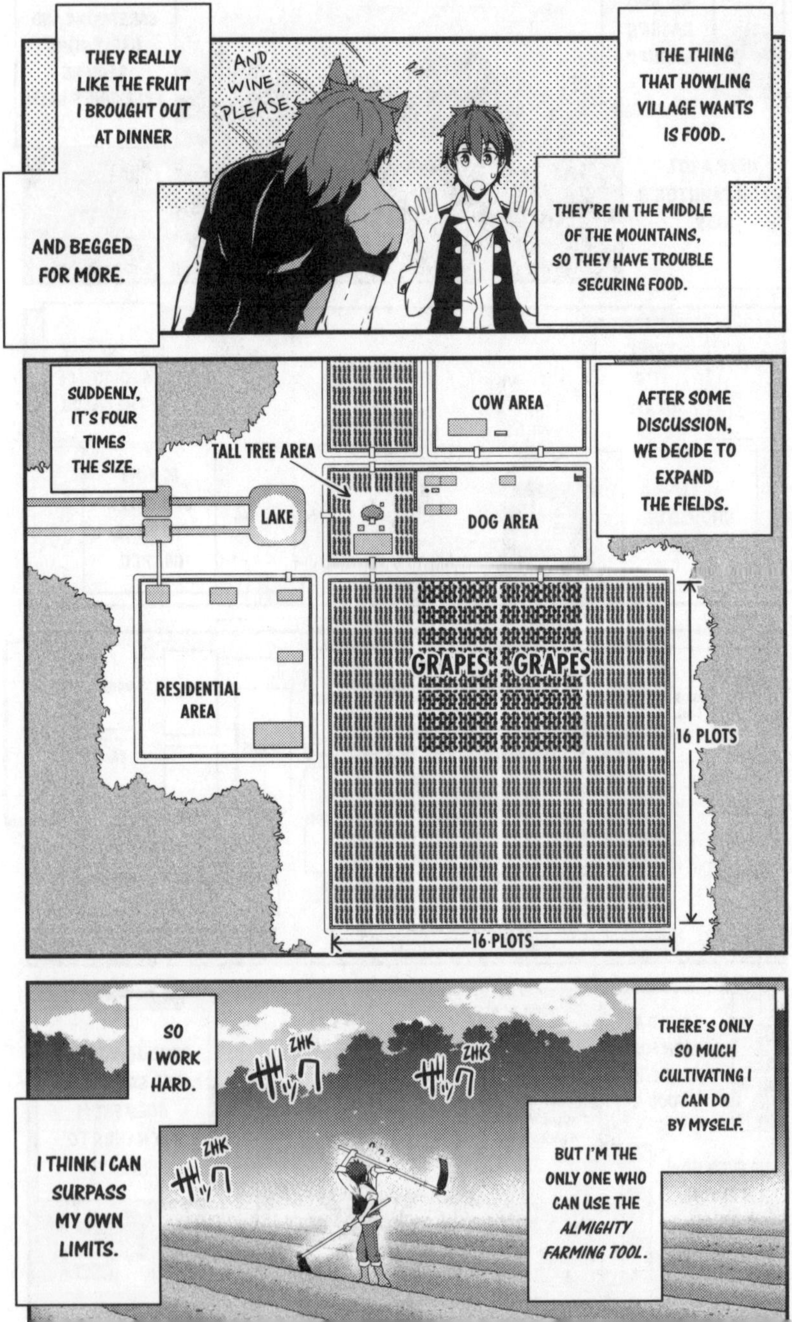
THE THING THAT HOWLING VILLAGE WANTS IS FOOD.
THEY'RE IN THE MIDDLE OF THE MOUNTAINS, SO THEY HAVE TROUBLE SECURING FOOD.
AND WINE, PLEASE
THEY REALLY LIKE THE FRUIT I BROUGHT OUT AT DINNER
AND BEGGED FOR MORE.
AFTER SOME DISCUSSION, WE DECIDE TO EXPAND THE FIELDS.
COW AREA
TALL TREE AREA
DOG AREA
LAKE
RESIDENTIAL AREA
GRAPES
GRAPES
16 PLOTS
16 PLOTS
SUDDENLY, IT'S FOUR TIMES THE SIZE.
THERE'S ONLY SO MUCH CULTIVATING I CAN DO BY MYSELF.
BUT I'M THE ONLY ONE WHO CAN USE THE *ALMIGHTY FARMING TOOL*.
ZHK
ZHK
SO I WORK HARD.
ZHK
I THINK I CAN SURPASS MY OWN LIMITS.

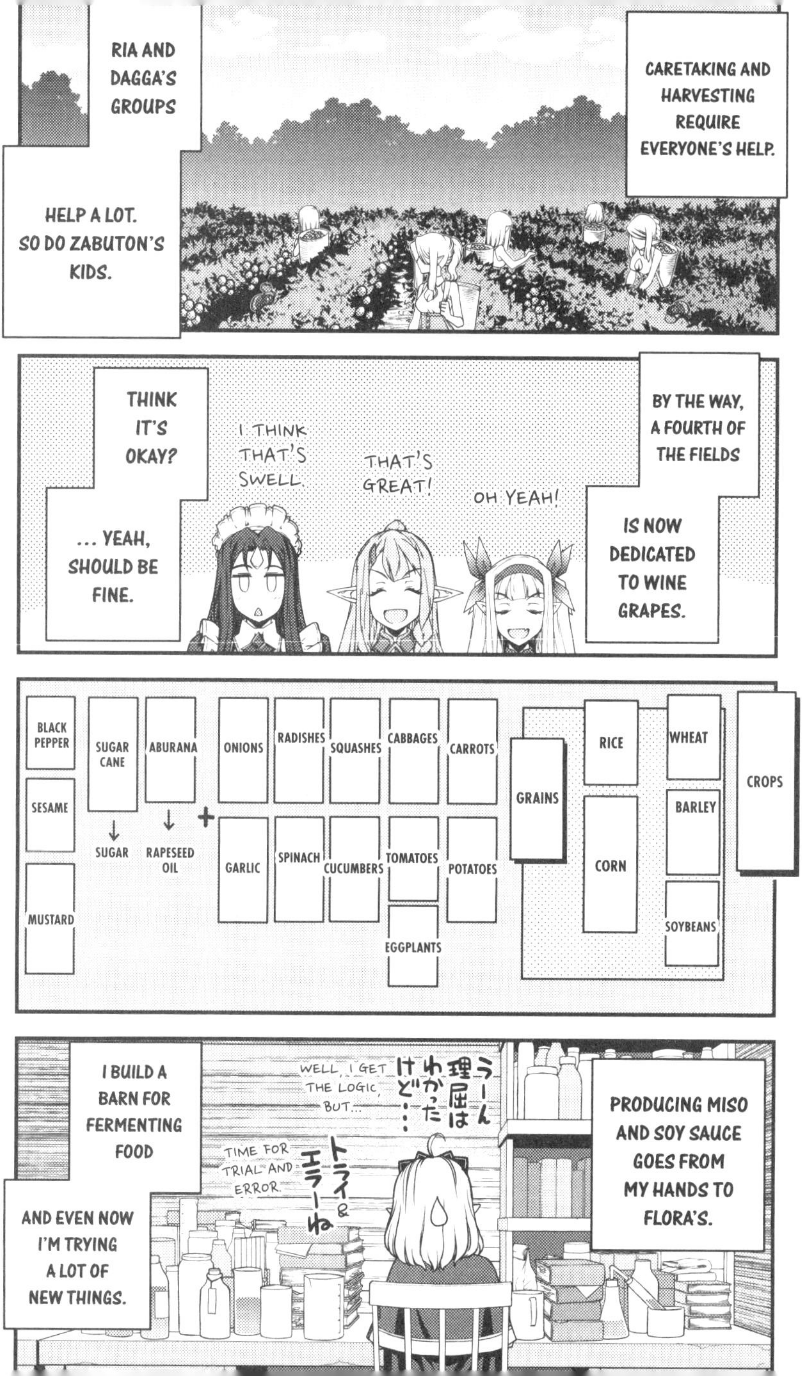

RIA AND DAGGA'S GROUPS

HELP A LOT. SO DO ZABUTON'S KIDS.

CARETAKING AND HARVESTING REQUIRE EVERYONE'S HELP.

THINK IT'S OKAY?

I THINK THAT'S SWELL.

THAT'S GREAT!

OH YEAH!

... YEAH, SHOULD BE FINE.

BY THE WAY, A FOURTH OF THE FIELDS

IS NOW DEDICATED TO WINE GRAPES.

BLACK PEPPER	SUGAR CANE	ABURANA	ONIONS	RADISHES	SQUASHES	CABBAGES	CARROTS		GRAINS	RICE	WHEAT		CROPS
SESAME	↓ SUGAR	↓ RAPESEED OIL	GARLIC	SPINACH	CUCUMBERS	TOMATOES	POTATOES			CORN	BARLEY		
MUSTARD		+				EGGPLANTS					SOYBEANS		

I BUILD A BARN FOR FERMENTING FOOD

AND EVEN NOW I'M TRYING A LOT OF NEW THINGS.

WELL, I GET THE LOGIC, BUT...

TIME FOR TRIAL AND ERROR

けど理屈はわかった：

トライ＆エラーは

PRODUCING MISO AND SOY SAUCE GOES FROM MY HANDS TO FLORA'S.

CHAPTER 25: A MARKETPLACE CALLED TRADE

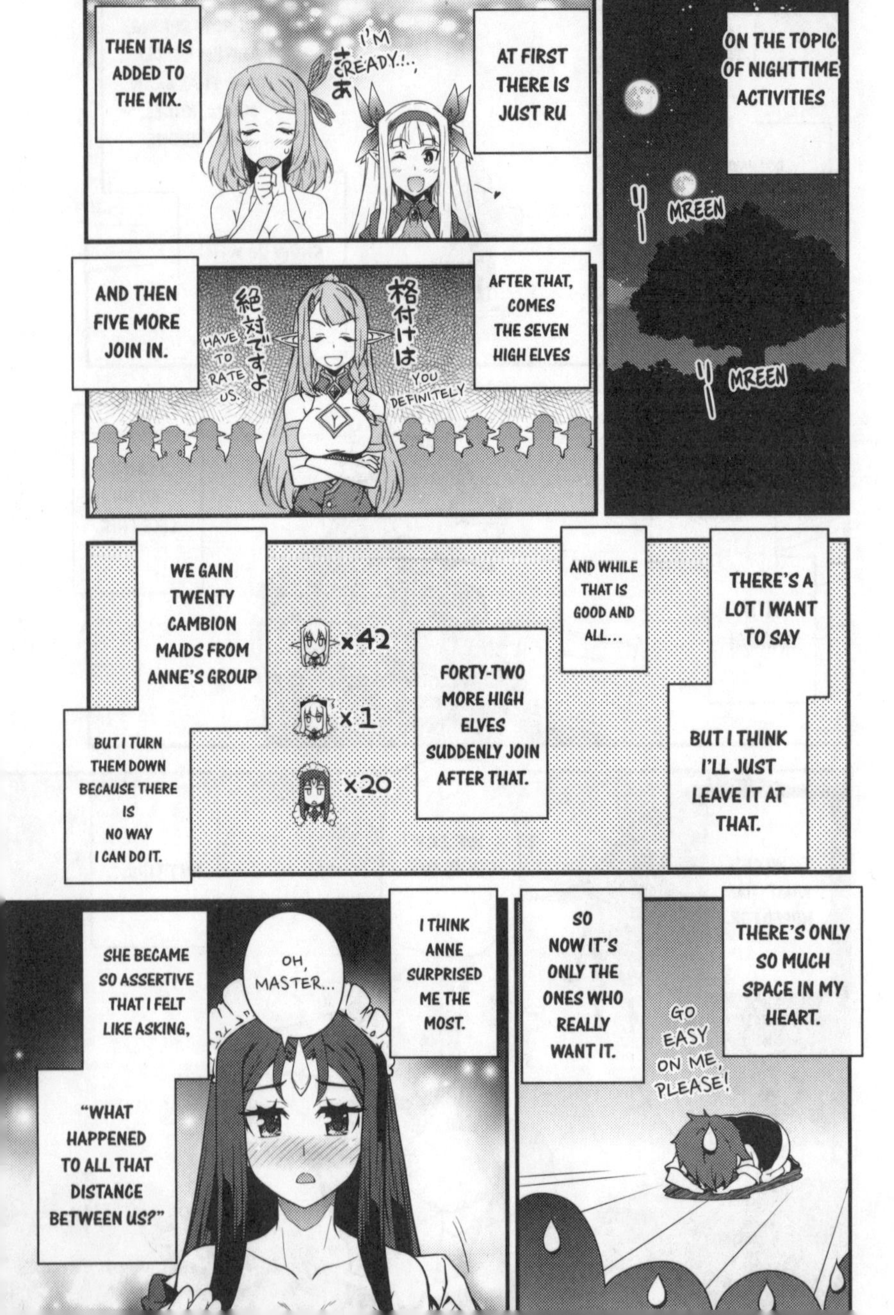
ON THE TOPIC OF NIGHTTIME ACTIVITIES
MREEN
MREEN
AT FIRST THERE IS JUST RU
あ I'M READY...!
THEN TIA IS ADDED TO THE MIX.
AFTER THAT, COMES THE SEVEN HIGH ELVES
格付けは絶対ですよ
YOU DEFINITELY HAVE TO RATE US.
AND THEN FIVE MORE JOIN IN.
THERE'S A LOT I WANT TO SAY
AND WHILE THAT IS GOOD AND ALL...
BUT I THINK I'LL JUST LEAVE IT AT THAT.
FORTY-TWO MORE HIGH ELVES SUDDENLY JOIN AFTER THAT.
×42
×1
×20
WE GAIN TWENTY CAMBION MAIDS FROM ANNE'S GROUP
BUT I TURN THEM DOWN BECAUSE THERE IS NO WAY I CAN DO IT.
THERE'S ONLY SO MUCH SPACE IN MY HEART.
SO NOW IT'S ONLY THE ONES WHO REALLY WANT IT.
GO EASY ON ME, PLEASE!
I THINK ANNE SURPRISED ME THE MOST.
OH, MASTER...
SHE BECAME SO ASSERTIVE THAT I FELT LIKE ASKING,
"WHAT HAPPENED TO ALL THAT DISTANCE BETWEEN US?"

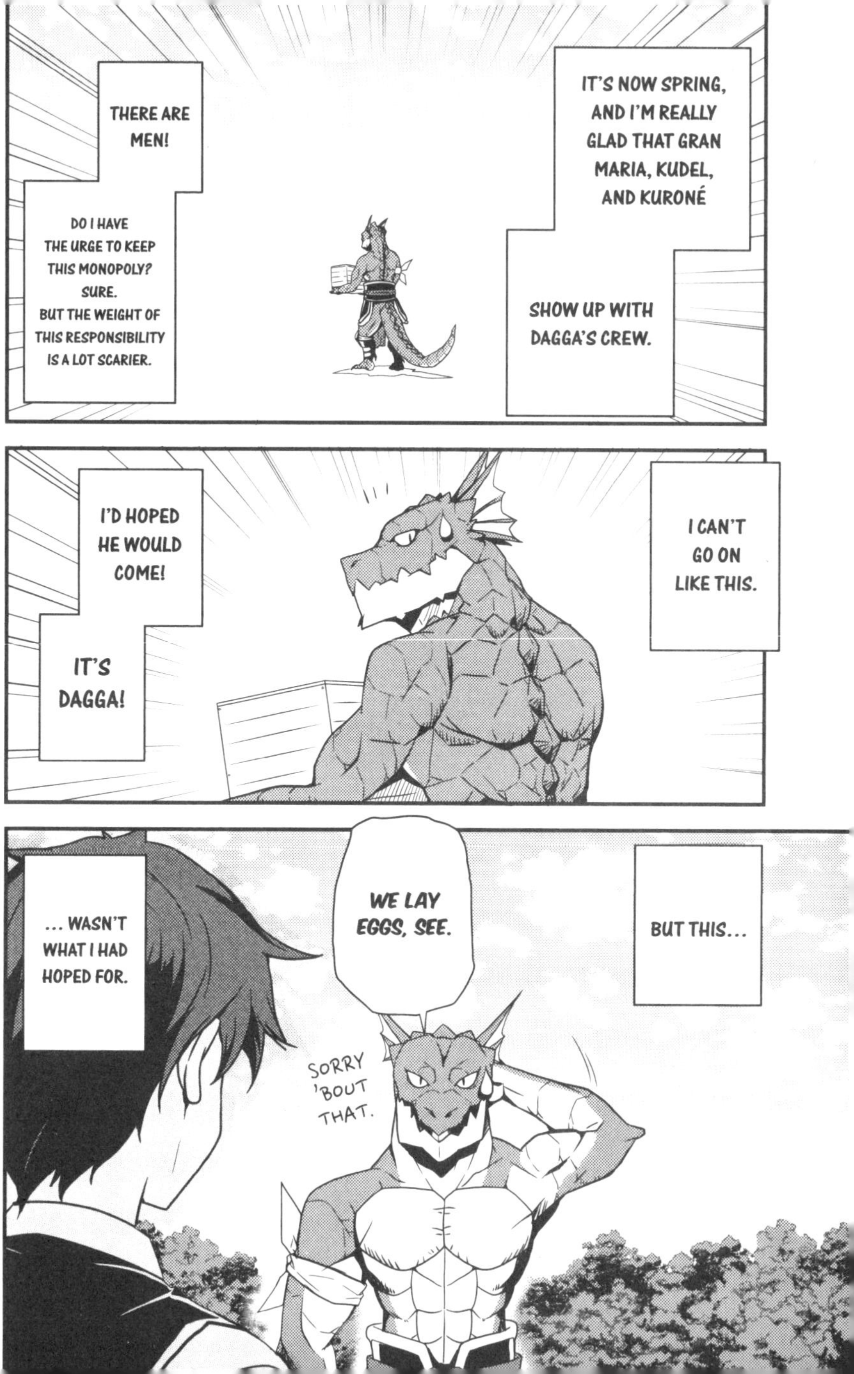
IT'S NOW SPRING, AND I'M REALLY GLAD THAT GRAN MARIA, KUDEL, AND KURONÉ
SHOW UP WITH DAGGA'S CREW.
THERE ARE MEN!
DO I HAVE THE URGE TO KEEP THIS MONOPOLY? SURE. BUT THE WEIGHT OF THIS RESPONSIBILITY IS A LOT SCARIER.
I CAN'T GO ON LIKE THIS.
I'D HOPED HE WOULD COME!
IT'S DAGGA!
BUT THIS…
WE LAY EGGS, SEE.
SORRY 'BOUT THAT.
… WASN'T WHAT I HAD HOPED FOR.

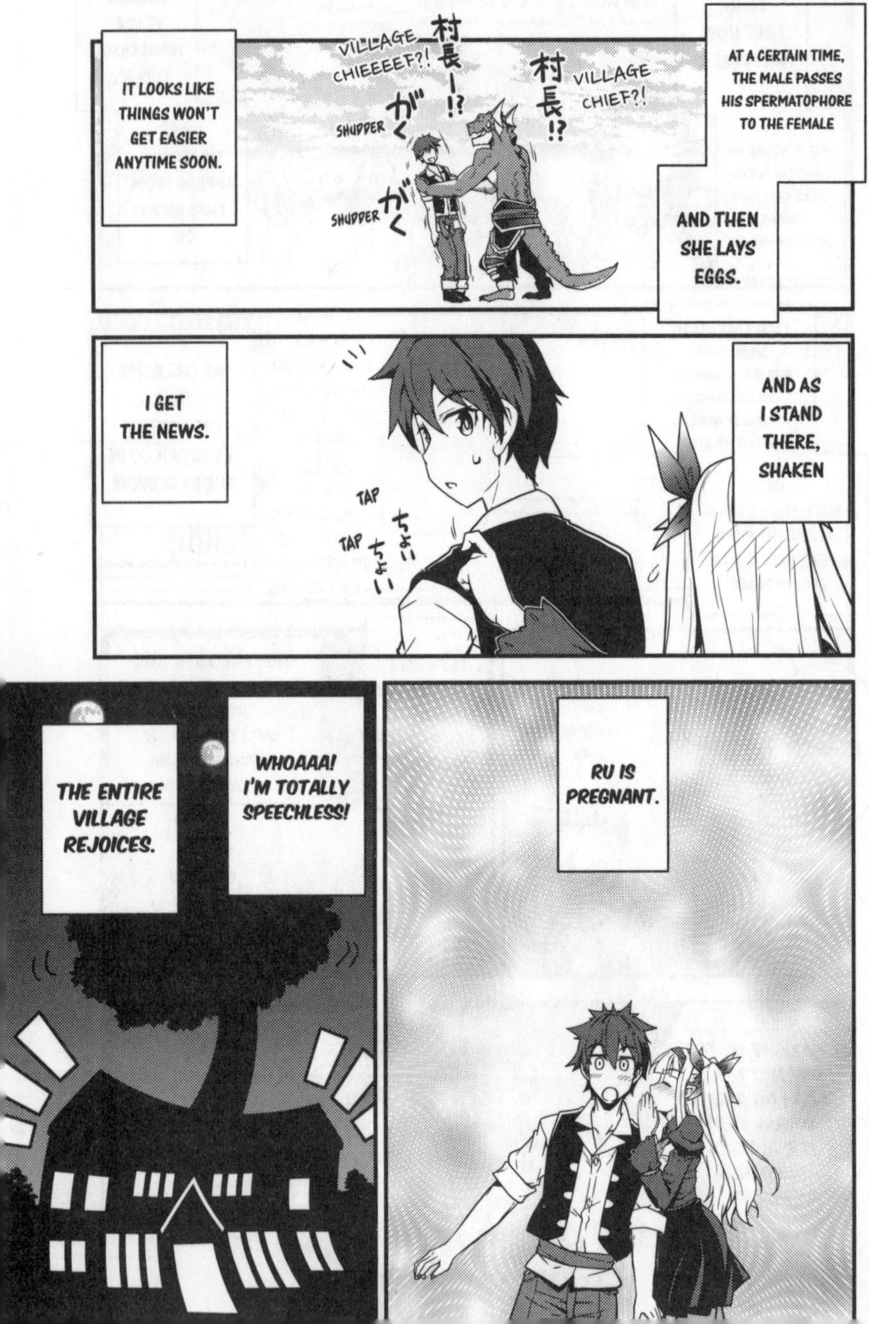
AT A CERTAIN TIME, THE MALE PASSES HIS SPERMATOPHORE TO THE FEMALE
AND THEN SHE LAYS EGGS.
村長ー!?
VILLAGE CHIEF?!
村長ー!?
VILLAGE CHIEEEEF?!
がく
SHUDDER
がく
SHUDDER
IT LOOKS LIKE THINGS WON'T GET EASIER ANYTIME SOON.
AND AS I STAND THERE, SHAKEN
ちょい
TAP
ちょい
TAP
I GET THE NEWS.
RU IS PREGNANT.
WHOAAA! I'M TOTALLY SPEECHLESS!
THE ENTIRE VILLAGE REJOICES.

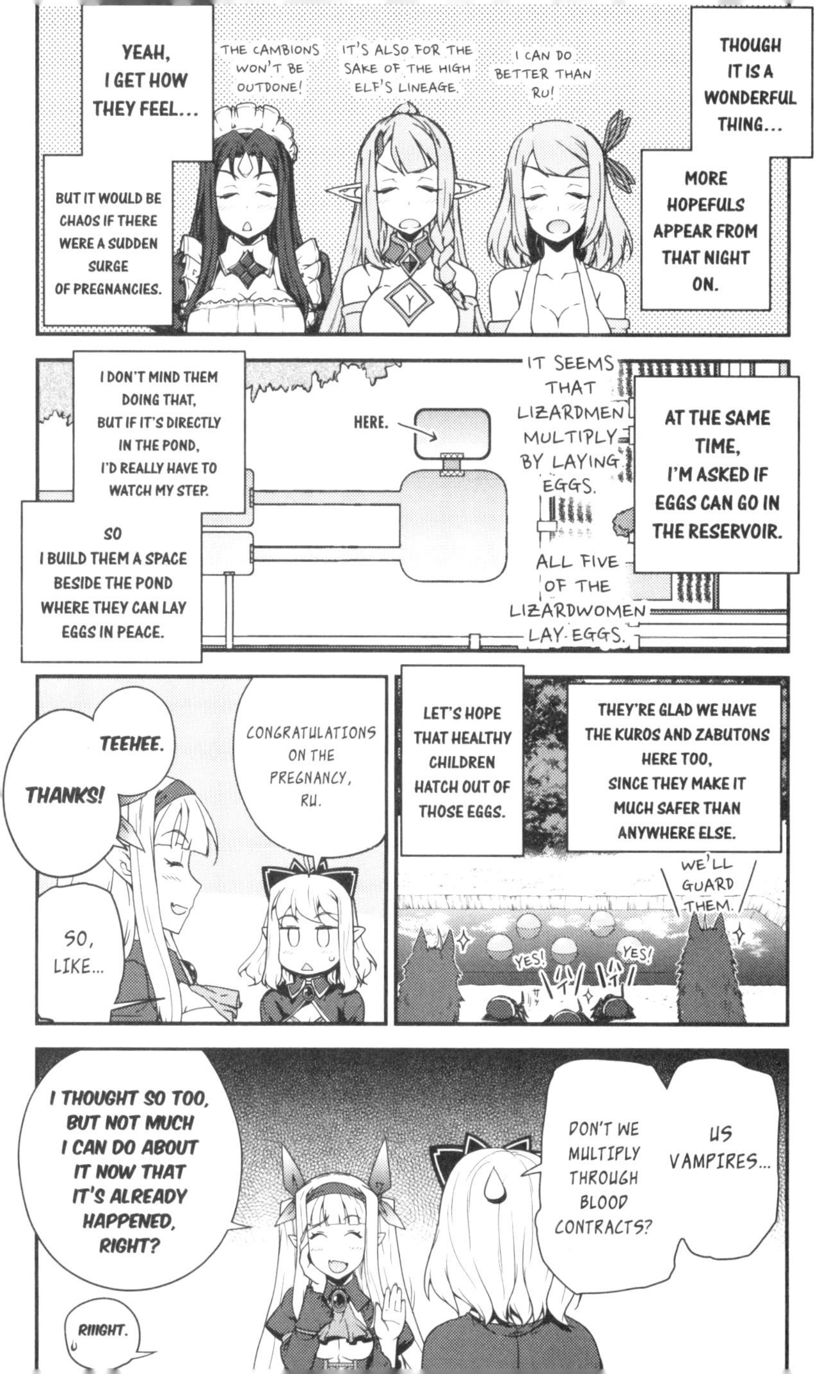
THOUGH IT IS A WONDERFUL THING...
MORE HOPEFULS APPEAR FROM THAT NIGHT ON.
I CAN DO BETTER THAN RU!
IT'S ALSO FOR THE SAKE OF THE HIGH ELF'S LINEAGE.
THE CAMBIONS WON'T BE OUTDONE!
YEAH, I GET HOW THEY FEEL...
BUT IT WOULD BE CHAOS IF THERE WERE A SUDDEN SURGE OF PREGNANCIES.
AT THE SAME TIME, I'M ASKED IF EGGS CAN GO IN THE RESERVOIR.
IT SEEMS THAT LIZARDMEN MULTIPLY BY LAYING EGGS.
ALL FIVE OF THE LIZARDWOMEN LAY EGGS.
HERE.
I DON'T MIND THEM DOING THAT, BUT IF IT'S DIRECTLY IN THE POND, I'D REALLY HAVE TO WATCH MY STEP.
SO I BUILD THEM A SPACE BESIDE THE POND WHERE THEY CAN LAY EGGS IN PEACE.
THEY'RE GLAD WE HAVE THE KUROS AND ZABUTONS HERE TOO, SINCE THEY MAKE IT MUCH SAFER THAN ANYWHERE ELSE.
LET'S HOPE THAT HEALTHY CHILDREN HATCH OUT OF THOSE EGGS.
WE'LL GUARD THEM.
YES!
YES!
CONGRATULATIONS ON THE PREGNANCY, RU.
TEEHEE.
THANKS!
SO, LIKE...
US VAMPIRES...
DON'T WE MULTIPLY THROUGH BLOOD CONTRACTS?
I THOUGHT SO TOO, BUT NOT MUCH I CAN DO ABOUT IT NOW THAT IT'S ALREADY HAPPENED, RIGHT?
RIIIGHT.

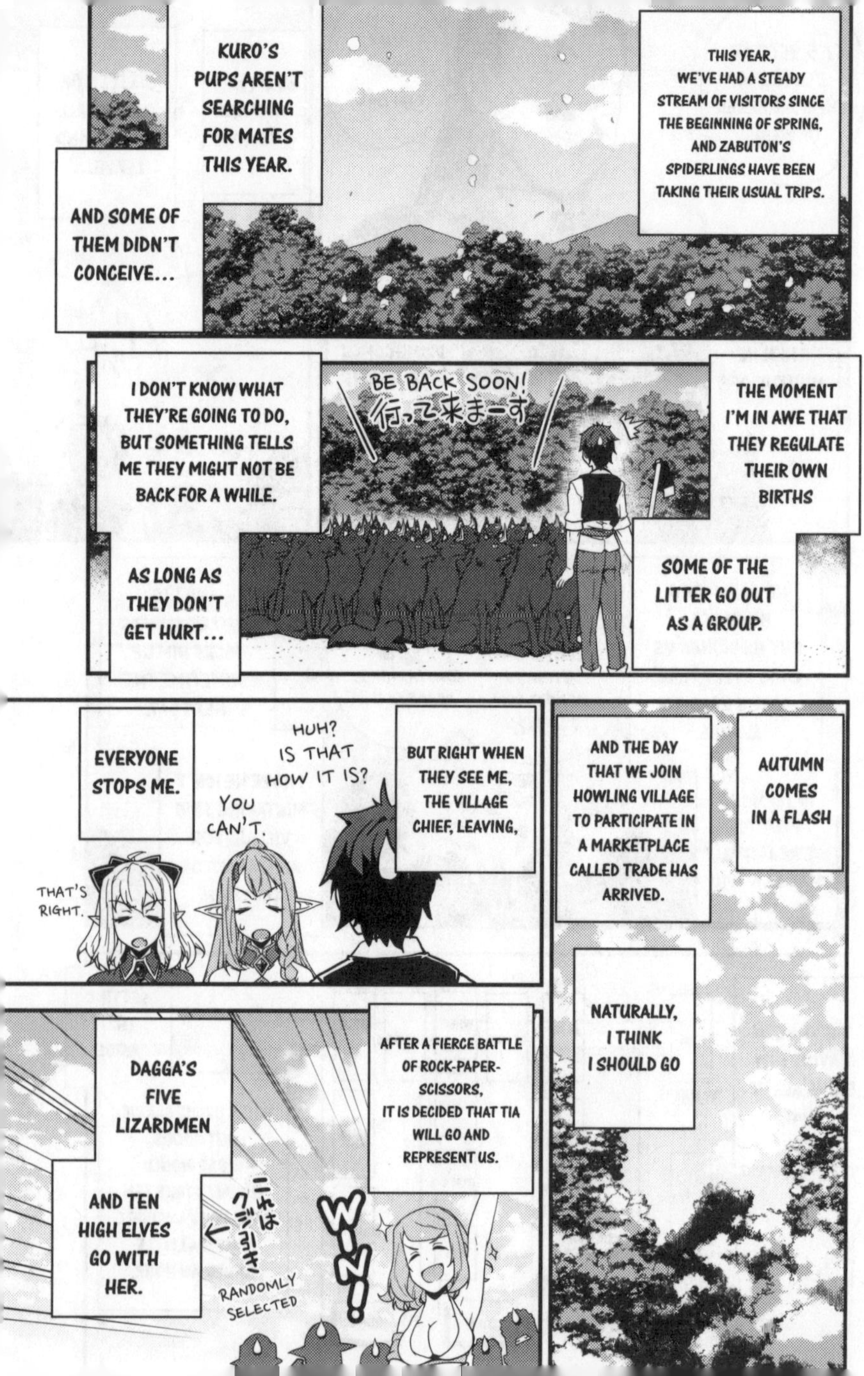

THIS YEAR, WE'VE HAD A STEADY STREAM OF VISITORS SINCE THE BEGINNING OF SPRING, AND ZABUTON'S SPIDERLINGS HAVE BEEN TAKING THEIR USUAL TRIPS.
KURO'S PUPS AREN'T SEARCHING FOR MATES THIS YEAR.
AND SOME OF THEM DIDN'T CONCEIVE...
THE MOMENT I'M IN AWE THAT THEY REGULATE THEIR OWN BIRTHS
SOME OF THE LITTER GO OUT AS A GROUP.
BE BACK SOON!
行って来まーす
I DON'T KNOW WHAT THEY'RE GOING TO DO, BUT SOMETHING TELLS ME THEY MIGHT NOT BE BACK FOR A WHILE.
AS LONG AS THEY DON'T GET HURT...
AUTUMN COMES IN A FLASH
AND THE DAY THAT WE JOIN HOWLING VILLAGE TO PARTICIPATE IN A MARKETPLACE CALLED TRADE HAS ARRIVED.
NATURALLY, I THINK I SHOULD GO
BUT RIGHT WHEN THEY SEE ME, THE VILLAGE CHIEF, LEAVING,
HUH? IS THAT HOW IT IS?
YOU CAN'T.
EVERYONE STOPS ME.
THAT'S RIGHT.
AFTER A FIERCE BATTLE OF ROCK-PAPER-SCISSORS, IT IS DECIDED THAT TIA WILL GO AND REPRESENT US.
WIN!
これはクジ引き
RANDOMLY SELECTED
DAGGA'S FIVE LIZARDMEN
AND TEN HIGH ELVES GO WITH HER.

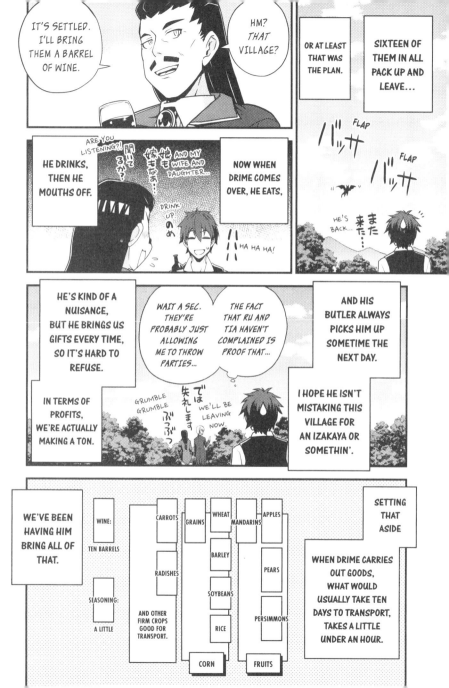

IT'S SETTLED. I'LL BRING THEM A BARREL OF WINE.

HM? *THAT* VILLAGE?

OR AT LEAST THAT WAS THE PLAN.

SIXTEEN OF THEM IN ALL PACK UP AND LEAVE...

FLAP

FLAP

HE DRINKS, THEN HE MOUTHS OFF.

ARE YOU LISTENING?!
聞いてるか?

嫁も娘も...
AND MY WIFE AND DAUGHTER...

NOW WHEN DRIME COMES OVER, HE EATS,

DRINK UP
のめ

HA HA HA!

HE'S BACK.
また来た....

HE'S KIND OF A NUISANCE, BUT HE BRINGS US GIFTS EVERY TIME, SO IT'S HARD TO REFUSE.

WAIT A SEC. THEY'RE PROBABLY JUST ALLOWING ME TO THROW PARTIES...

THE FACT THAT RU AND TIA HAVEN'T COMPLAINED IS PROOF THAT...

AND HIS BUTLER ALWAYS PICKS HIM UP SOMETIME THE NEXT DAY.

IN TERMS OF PROFITS, WE'RE ACTUALLY MAKING A TON.

GRUMBLE GRUMBLE
ぶつぶつ

では失礼します
WE'LL BE LEAVING NOW.

I HOPE HE ISN'T MISTAKING THIS VILLAGE FOR AN IZAKAYA OR SOMETHIN'.

WE'VE BEEN HAVING HIM BRING ALL OF THAT.

WINE:	CARROTS	GRAINS	WHEAT	MANDARINS	APPLES
TEN BARRELS			BARLEY		PEARS
	RADISHES		SOYBEANS		PERSIMMONS
SEASONING:			RICE		
A LITTLE	AND OTHER FIRM CROPS GOOD FOR TRANSPORT.	CORN		FRUITS	

SETTING THAT ASIDE

WHEN DRIME CARRIES OUT GOODS, WHAT WOULD USUALLY TAKE TEN DAYS TO TRANSPORT, TAKES A LITTLE UNDER AN HOUR.

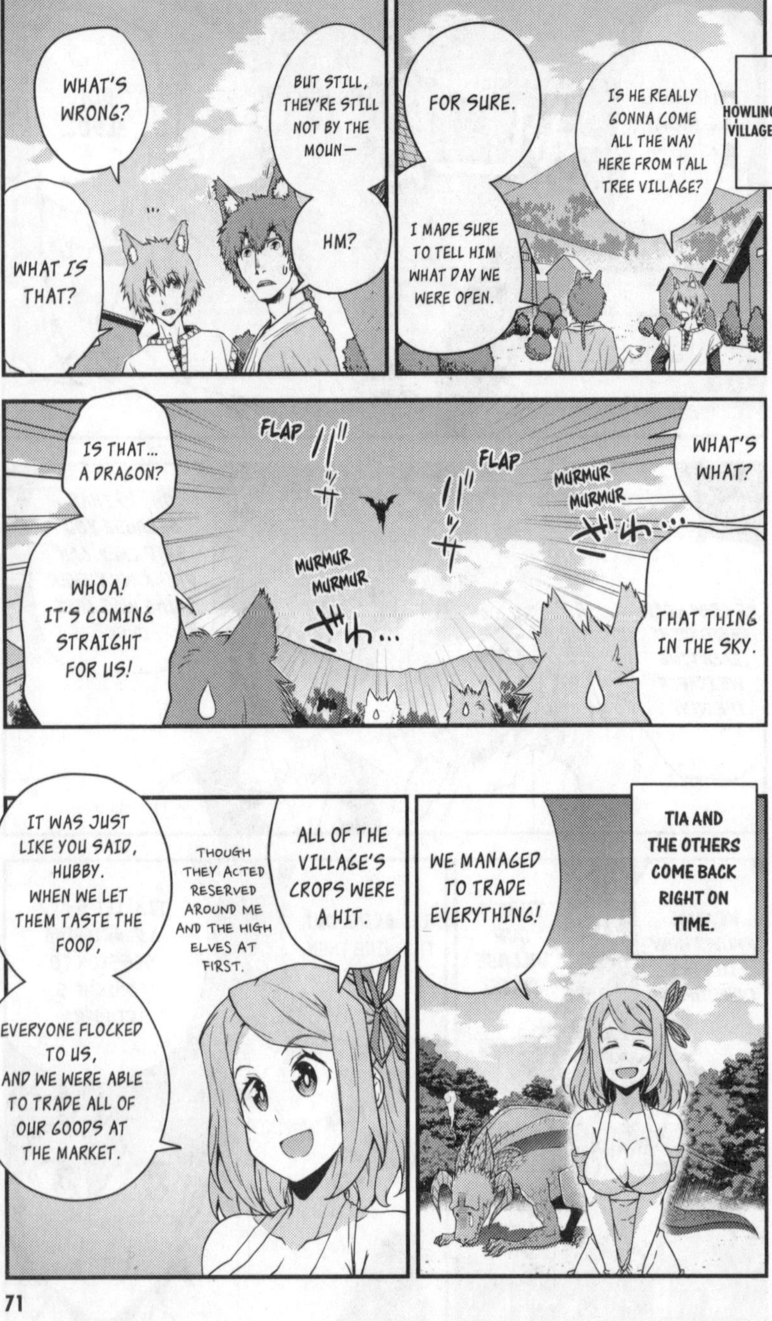
HOWLING VILLAGE
IS HE REALLY GONNA COME ALL THE WAY HERE FROM TALL TREE VILLAGE?
FOR SURE.
I MADE SURE TO TELL HIM WHAT DAY WE WERE OPEN.
BUT STILL, THEY'RE STILL NOT BY THE MOUN—
HM?
WHAT'S WRONG?
...
WHAT *IS* THAT?
WHAT'S WHAT?
THAT THING IN THE SKY.
MURMUR MURMUR
FLAP
FLAP
MURMUR MURMUR
IS THAT... A DRAGON?
WHOA! IT'S COMING STRAIGHT FOR US!
TIA AND THE OTHERS COME BACK RIGHT ON TIME.
WE MANAGED TO TRADE EVERYTHING!
ALL OF THE VILLAGE'S CROPS WERE A HIT.
THOUGH THEY ACTED RESERVED AROUND ME AND THE HIGH ELVES AT FIRST.
IT WAS JUST LIKE YOU SAID, HUBBY. WHEN WE LET THEM TASTE THE FOOD,
EVERYONE FLOCKED TO US, AND WE WERE ABLE TO TRADE ALL OF OUR GOODS AT THE MARKET.

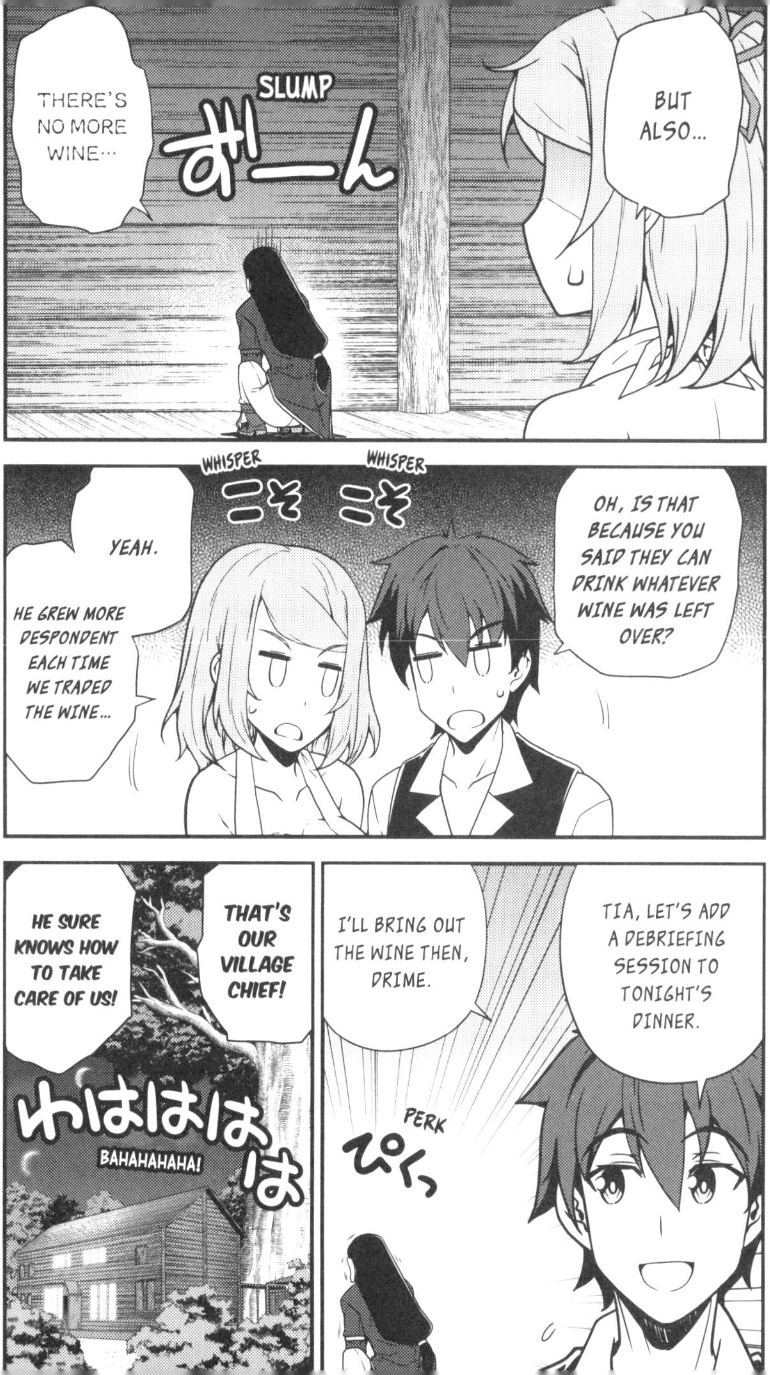
BUT ALSO...
SLUMP
ずーん
THERE'S NO MORE WINE...
OH, IS THAT BECAUSE YOU SAID THEY CAN DRINK WHATEVER WINE WAS LEFT OVER?
WHISPER
こそ
WHISPER
こそ
YEAH.
HE GREW MORE DESPONDENT EACH TIME WE TRADED THE WINE...
TIA, LET'S ADD A DEBRIEFING SESSION TO TONIGHT'S DINNER.
I'LL BRING OUT THE WINE THEN, DRIME.
PERK
ぴくっ
THAT'S OUR VILLAGE CHIEF!
HE SURE KNOWS HOW TO TAKE CARE OF US!
わははははは
BAHAHAHAHA!

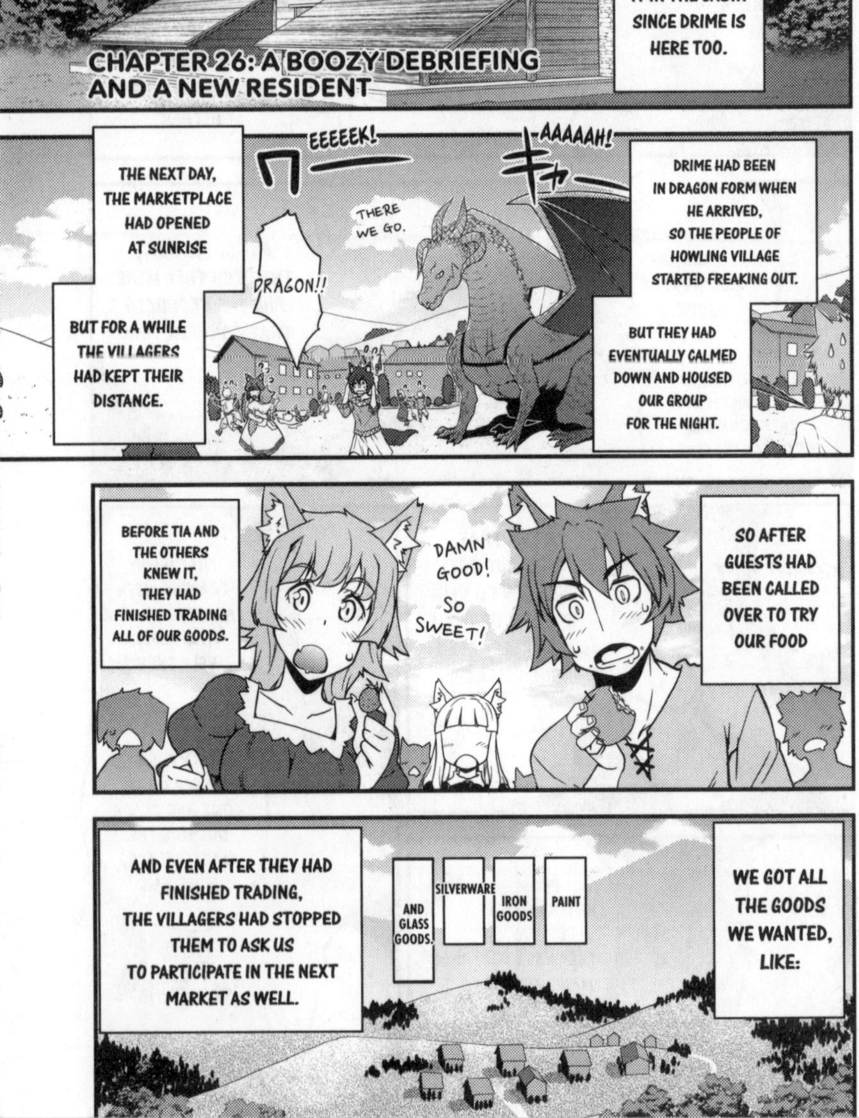
SINCE DRIME IS HERE TOO.
CHAPTER 26: A BOOZY DEBRIEFING AND A NEW RESIDENT
DRIME HAD BEEN IN DRAGON FORM WHEN HE ARRIVED, SO THE PEOPLE OF HOWLING VILLAGE STARTED FREAKING OUT.
BUT THEY HAD EVENTUALLY CALMED DOWN AND HOUSED OUR GROUP FOR THE NIGHT.
AAAAAH!
EEEEEK!
THERE WE GO.
DRAGON!!
THE NEXT DAY, THE MARKETPLACE HAD OPENED AT SUNRISE
BUT FOR A WHILE THE VILLAGERS HAD KEPT THEIR DISTANCE.
SO AFTER GUESTS HAD BEEN CALLED OVER TO TRY OUR FOOD
DAMN GOOD!
SO SWEET!
BEFORE TIA AND THE OTHERS KNEW IT, THEY HAD FINISHED TRADING ALL OF OUR GOODS.
WE GOT ALL THE GOODS WE WANTED, LIKE:
PAINT
IRON GOODS
SILVERWARE
AND GLASS GOODS.
AND EVEN AFTER THEY HAD FINISHED TRADING, THE VILLAGERS HAD STOPPED THEM TO ASK US TO PARTICIPATE IN THE NEXT MARKET AS WELL.

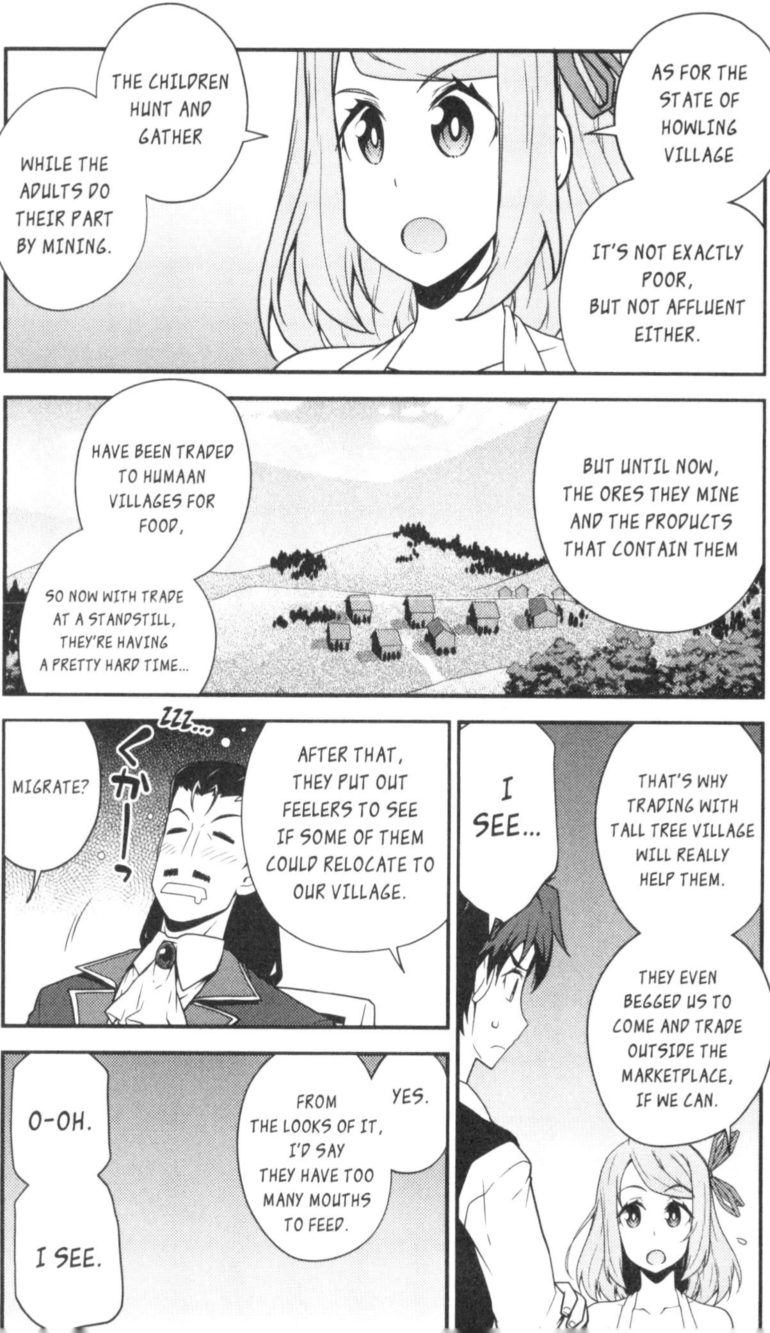
AS FOR THE STATE OF HOWLING VILLAGE
IT'S NOT EXACTLY POOR, BUT NOT AFFLUENT EITHER.
THE CHILDREN HUNT AND GATHER
WHILE THE ADULTS DO THEIR PART BY MINING.
BUT UNTIL NOW, THE ORES THEY MINE AND THE PRODUCTS THAT CONTAIN THEM
HAVE BEEN TRADED TO HUMAAN VILLAGES FOR FOOD,
SO NOW WITH TRADE AT A STANDSTILL, THEY'RE HAVING A PRETTY HARD TIME...
THAT'S WHY TRADING WITH TALL TREE VILLAGE WILL REALLY HELP THEM.
I SEE...
THEY EVEN BEGGED US TO COME AND TRADE OUTSIDE THE MARKETPLACE, IF WE CAN.
AFTER THAT, THEY PUT OUT FEELERS TO SEE IF SOME OF THEM COULD RELOCATE TO OUR VILLAGE.
ZZZ...
MIGRATE?
YES.
FROM THE LOOKS OF IT, I'D SAY THEY HAVE TOO MANY MOUTHS TO FEED.
O-OH.
I SEE.

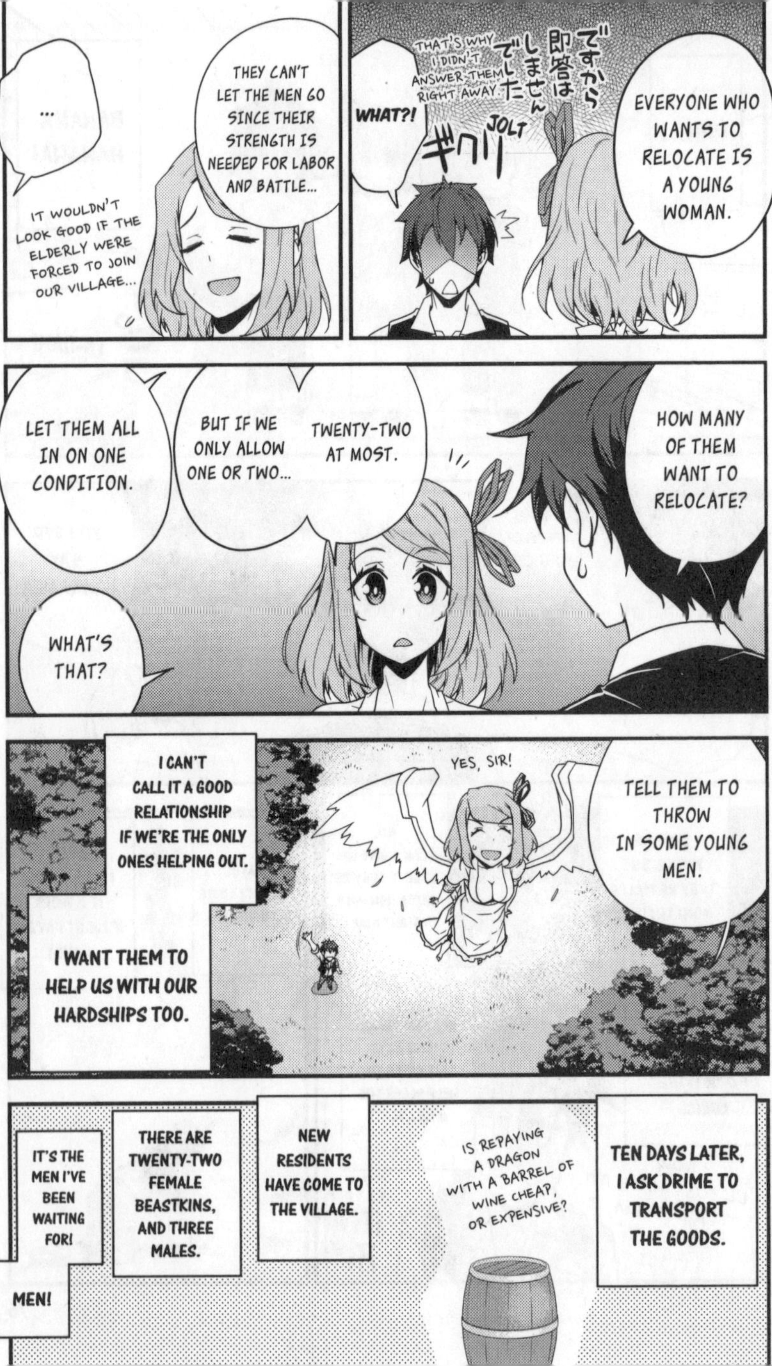
EVERYONE WHO WANTS TO RELOCATE IS A YOUNG WOMAN.
ですから即答はしませんでした
THAT'S WHY I DIDN'T ANSWER THEM RIGHT AWAY
ギクリ
JOLT
WHAT?!
THEY CAN'T LET THE MEN GO SINCE THEIR STRENGTH IS NEEDED FOR LABOR AND BATTLE...
...
IT WOULDN'T LOOK GOOD IF THE ELDERLY WERE FORCED TO JOIN OUR VILLAGE...
HOW MANY OF THEM WANT TO RELOCATE?
TWENTY-TWO AT MOST.
BUT IF WE ONLY ALLOW ONE OR TWO...
LET THEM ALL IN ON ONE CONDITION.
WHAT'S THAT?
TELL THEM TO THROW IN SOME YOUNG MEN.
YES, SIR!
I CAN'T CALL IT A GOOD RELATIONSHIP IF WE'RE THE ONLY ONES HELPING OUT.
I WANT THEM TO HELP US WITH OUR HARDSHIPS TOO.
TEN DAYS LATER, I ASK DRIME TO TRANSPORT THE GOODS.
IS REPAYING A DRAGON WITH A BARREL OF WINE CHEAP, OR EXPENSIVE?
NEW RESIDENTS HAVE COME TO THE VILLAGE.
THERE ARE TWENTY-TWO FEMALE BEASTKINS, AND THREE MALES.
IT'S THE MEN I'VE BEEN WAITING FOR!
MEN!

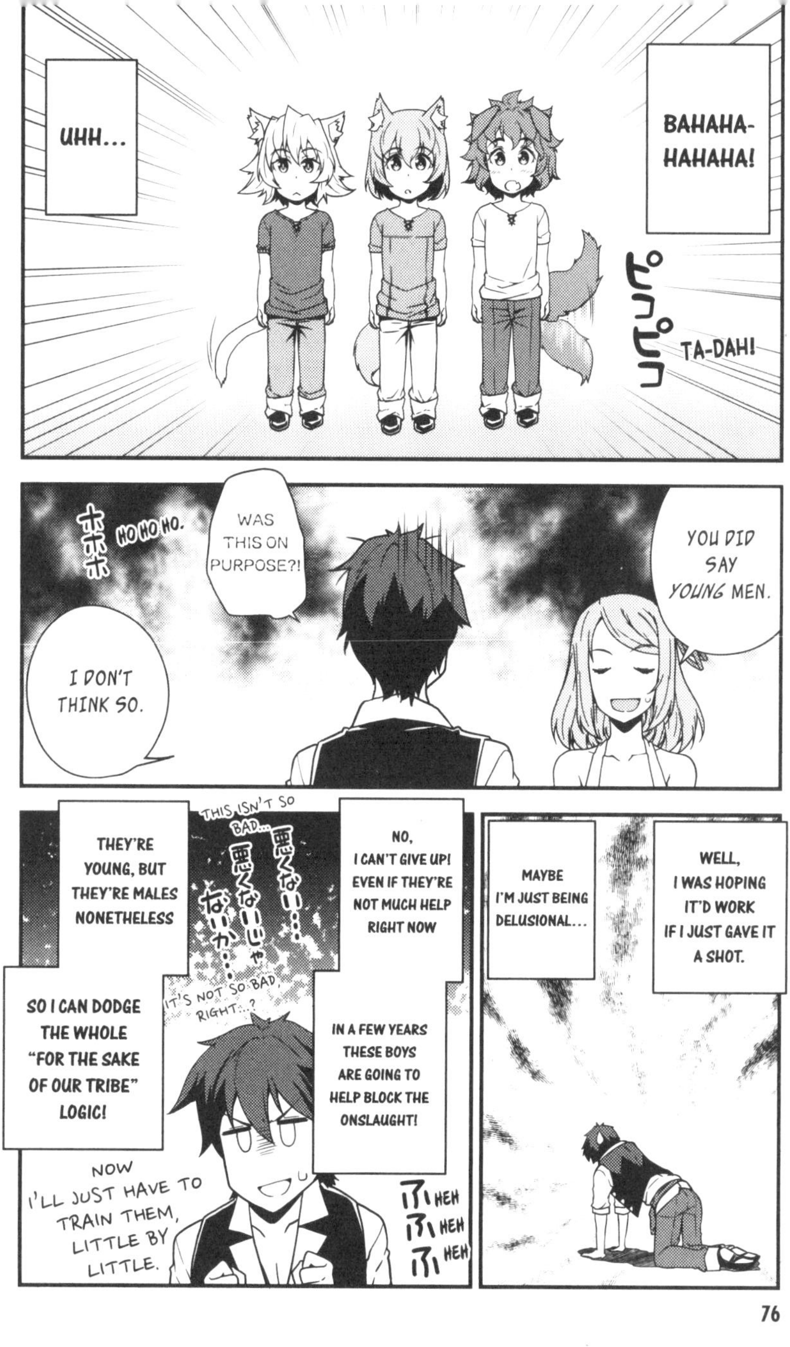
BAHAHA-HAHAHA!
ピコピコ
TA-DAH!
UHH...
YOU DID SAY YOUNG MEN.
WAS THIS ON PURPOSE?!
ホホホ
HO HO HO.
I DON'T THINK SO.
WELL, I WAS HOPING IT'D WORK IF I JUST GAVE IT A SHOT.
MAYBE I'M JUST BEING DELUSIONAL...
NO, I CAN'T GIVE UP! EVEN IF THEY'RE NOT MUCH HELP RIGHT NOW
IN A FEW YEARS THESE BOYS ARE GOING TO HELP BLOCK THE ONSLAUGHT!
悪くない…悪くないじゃないか…
THIS ISN'T SO BAD...
IT'S NOT SO BAD, RIGHT...?
THEY'RE YOUNG, BUT THEY'RE MALES NONETHELESS
SO I CAN DODGE THE WHOLE "FOR THE SAKE OF OUR TRIBE" LOGIC!
ふふふ
HEH HEH HEH
NOW I'LL JUST HAVE TO TRAIN THEM, LITTLE BY LITTLE.

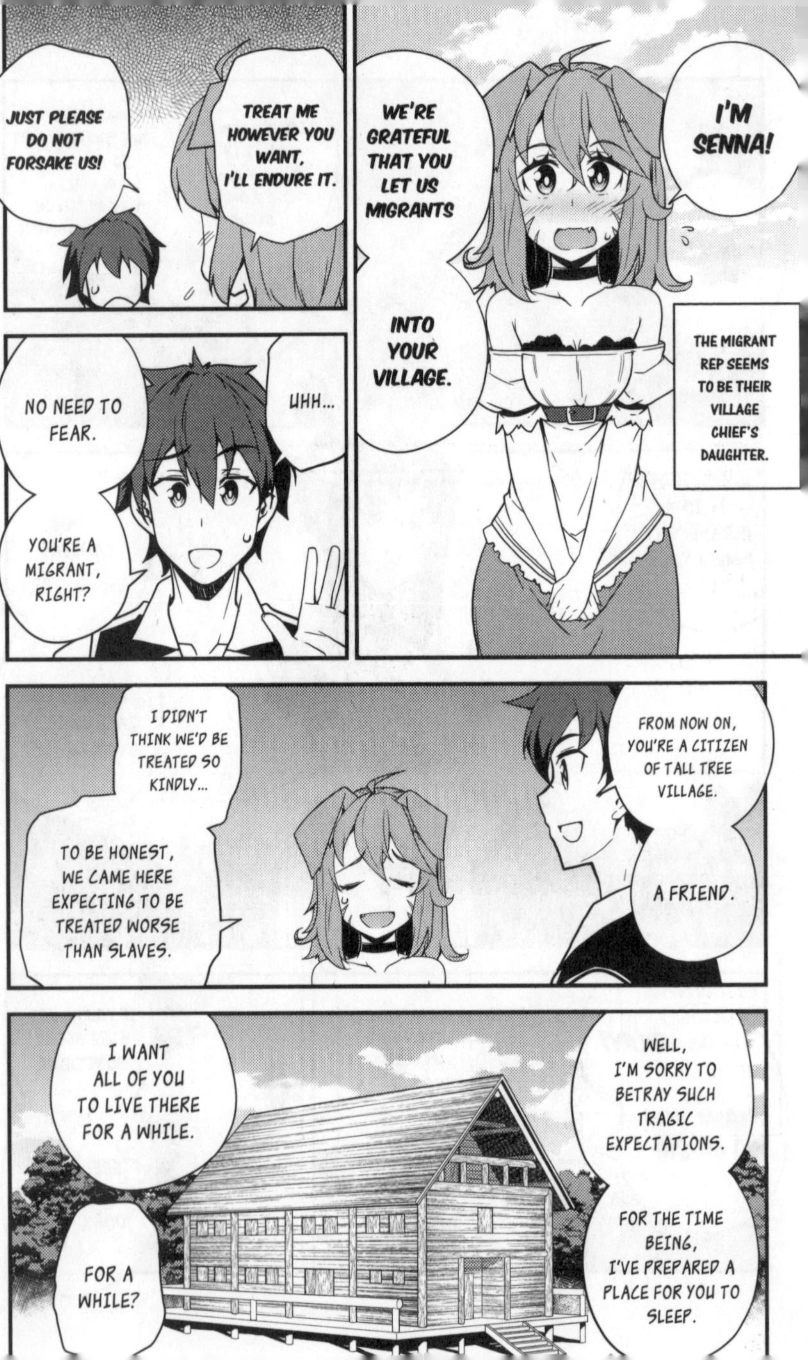
I'M SENNA!
WE'RE GRATEFUL THAT YOU LET US MIGRANTS
INTO YOUR VILLAGE.
THE MIGRANT REP SEEMS TO BE THEIR VILLAGE CHIEF'S DAUGHTER.
TREAT ME HOWEVER YOU WANT, I'LL ENDURE IT.
JUST PLEASE DO NOT FORSAKE US!
UHH...
NO NEED TO FEAR.
YOU'RE A MIGRANT, RIGHT?
FROM NOW ON, YOU'RE A CITIZEN OF TALL TREE VILLAGE.
A FRIEND.
I DIDN'T THINK WE'D BE TREATED SO KINDLY...
TO BE HONEST, WE CAME HERE EXPECTING TO BE TREATED WORSE THAN SLAVES.
WELL, I'M SORRY TO BETRAY SUCH TRAGIC EXPECTATIONS.
FOR THE TIME BEING, I'VE PREPARED A PLACE FOR YOU TO SLEEP.
I WANT ALL OF YOU TO LIVE THERE FOR A WHILE.
FOR A WHILE?

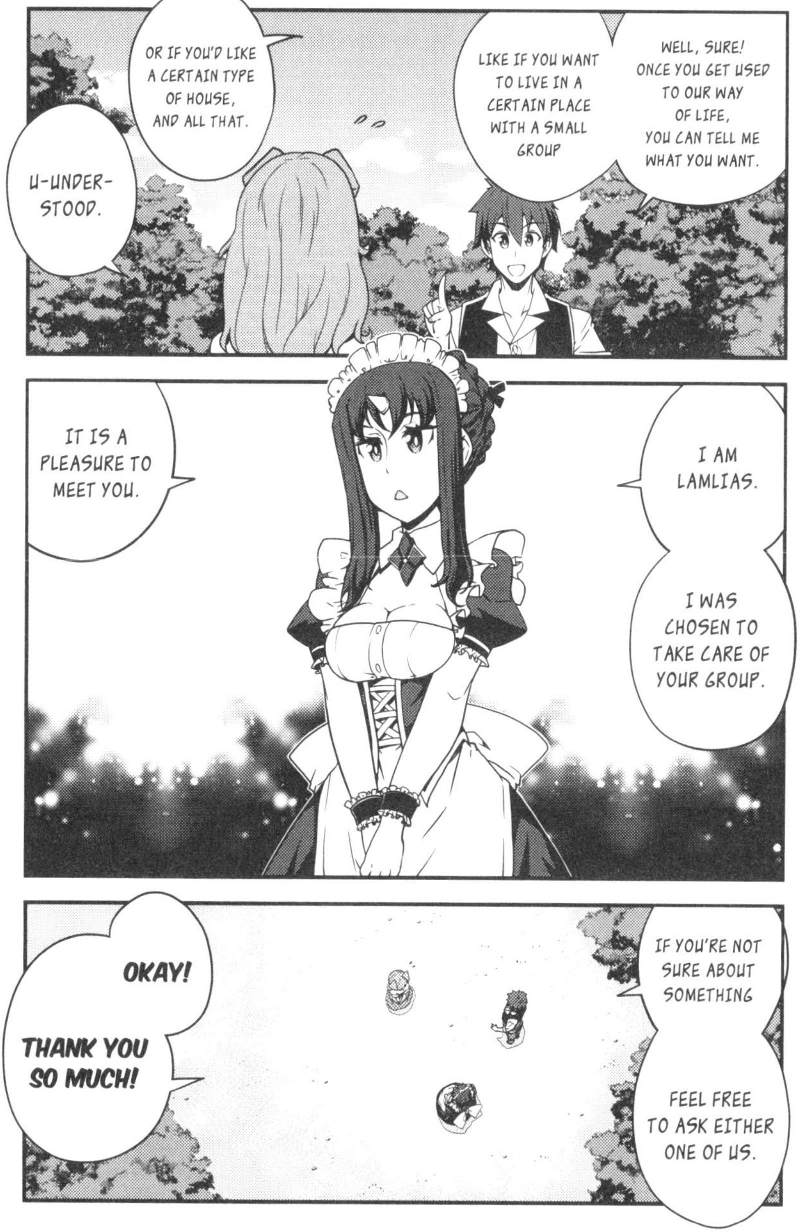
WELL, SURE! ONCE YOU GET USED TO OUR WAY OF LIFE, YOU CAN TELL ME WHAT YOU WANT.
LIKE IF YOU WANT TO LIVE IN A CERTAIN PLACE WITH A SMALL GROUP
OR IF YOU'D LIKE A CERTAIN TYPE OF HOUSE, AND ALL THAT.
U-UNDER-STOOD.
I AM LAMLIAS.
I WAS CHOSEN TO TAKE CARE OF YOUR GROUP.
IT IS A PLEASURE TO MEET YOU.
IF YOU'RE NOT SURE ABOUT SOMETHING
FEEL FREE TO ASK EITHER ONE OF US.
OKAY!
THANK YOU SO MUCH!

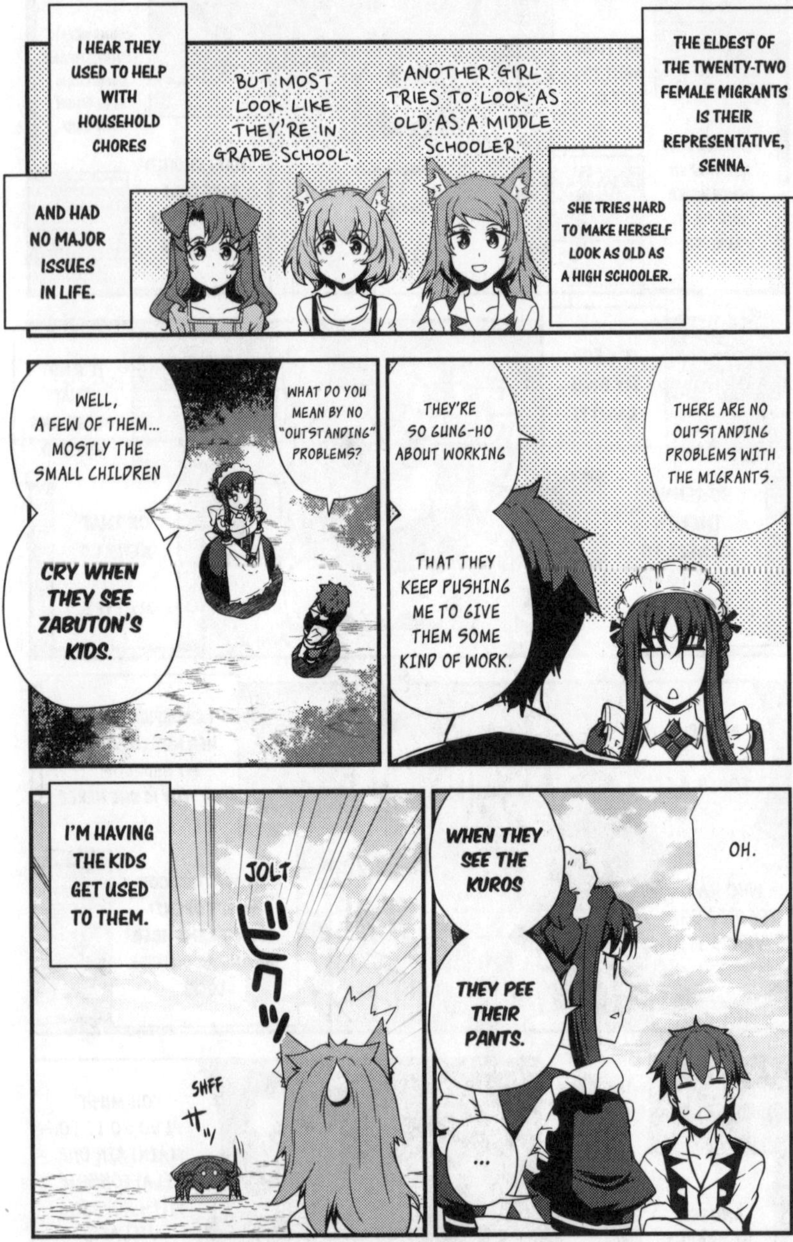

THE ELDEST OF THE TWENTY-TWO FEMALE MIGRANTS IS THEIR REPRESENTATIVE, SENNA.
SHE TRIES HARD TO MAKE HERSELF LOOK AS OLD AS A HIGH SCHOOLER.
ANOTHER GIRL TRIES TO LOOK AS OLD AS A MIDDLE SCHOOLER.
BUT MOST LOOK LIKE THEY'RE IN GRADE SCHOOL.
I HEAR THEY USED TO HELP WITH HOUSEHOLD CHORES
AND HAD NO MAJOR ISSUES IN LIFE.
THERE ARE NO OUTSTANDING PROBLEMS WITH THE MIGRANTS.
THEY'RE SO GUNG-HO ABOUT WORKING
THAT THEY KEEP PUSHING ME TO GIVE THEM SOME KIND OF WORK.
WHAT DO YOU MEAN BY NO "OUTSTANDING" PROBLEMS?
WELL, A FEW OF THEM... MOSTLY THE SMALL CHILDREN
CRY WHEN THEY SEE ZABUTON'S KIDS.
OH.
WHEN THEY SEE THE KUROS
THEY PEE THEIR PANTS.
...
I'M HAVING THE KIDS GET USED TO THEM.
JOLT
ビクッ
SHFF
サッ

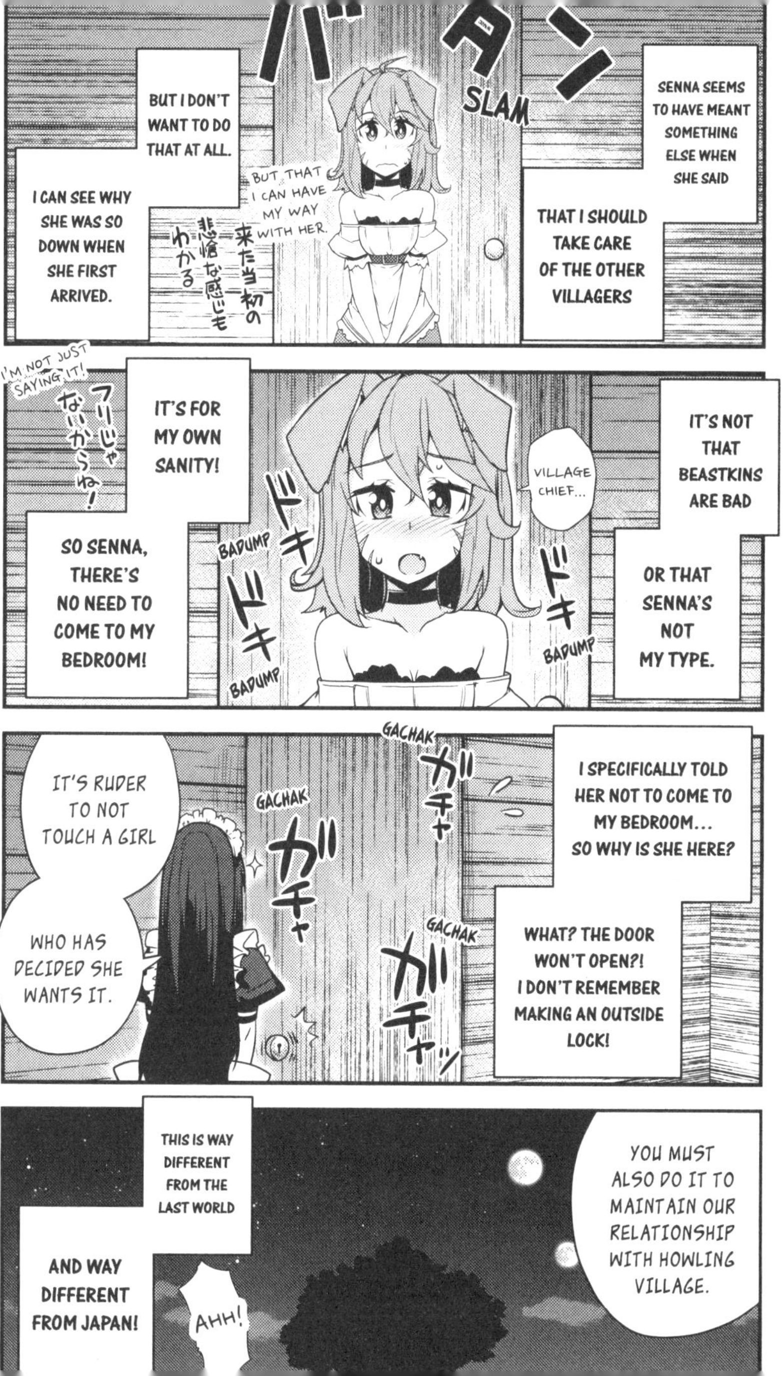
SENNA SEEMS TO HAVE MEANT SOMETHING ELSE WHEN SHE SAID
THAT I SHOULD TAKE CARE OF THE OTHER VILLAGERS
バタン
SLAM
BUT I DON'T WANT TO DO THAT AT ALL.
来た当初の悲惨な感じもわかる
BUT THAT I CAN HAVE MY WAY WITH HER.
I CAN SEE WHY SHE WAS SO DOWN WHEN SHE FIRST ARRIVED.
IT'S NOT THAT BEASTKINS ARE BAD
OR THAT SENNA'S NOT MY TYPE.
ドキ
BADUMP
VILLAGE CHIEF...
ドキドキ
BADUMP BADUMP
IT'S FOR MY OWN SANITY!
SO SENNA, THERE'S NO NEED TO COME TO MY BEDROOM!
フリじゃないからね!
I'M NOT JUST SAYING IT!
I SPECIFICALLY TOLD HER NOT TO COME TO MY BEDROOM... SO WHY IS SHE HERE?
WHAT? THE DOOR WON'T OPEN?! I DON'T REMEMBER MAKING AN OUTSIDE LOCK!
ガチャ
GACHAK
ガチャ
GACHAK
ガチャッ
GACHAK
IT'S RUDER TO NOT TOUCH A GIRL
WHO HAS DECIDED SHE WANTS IT.
YOU MUST ALSO DO IT TO MAINTAIN OUR RELATIONSHIP WITH HOWLING VILLAGE.
AHH!
THIS IS WAY DIFFERENT FROM THE LAST WORLD
AND WAY DIFFERENT FROM JAPAN!

CHAPTER 27: TAX COLLECTION

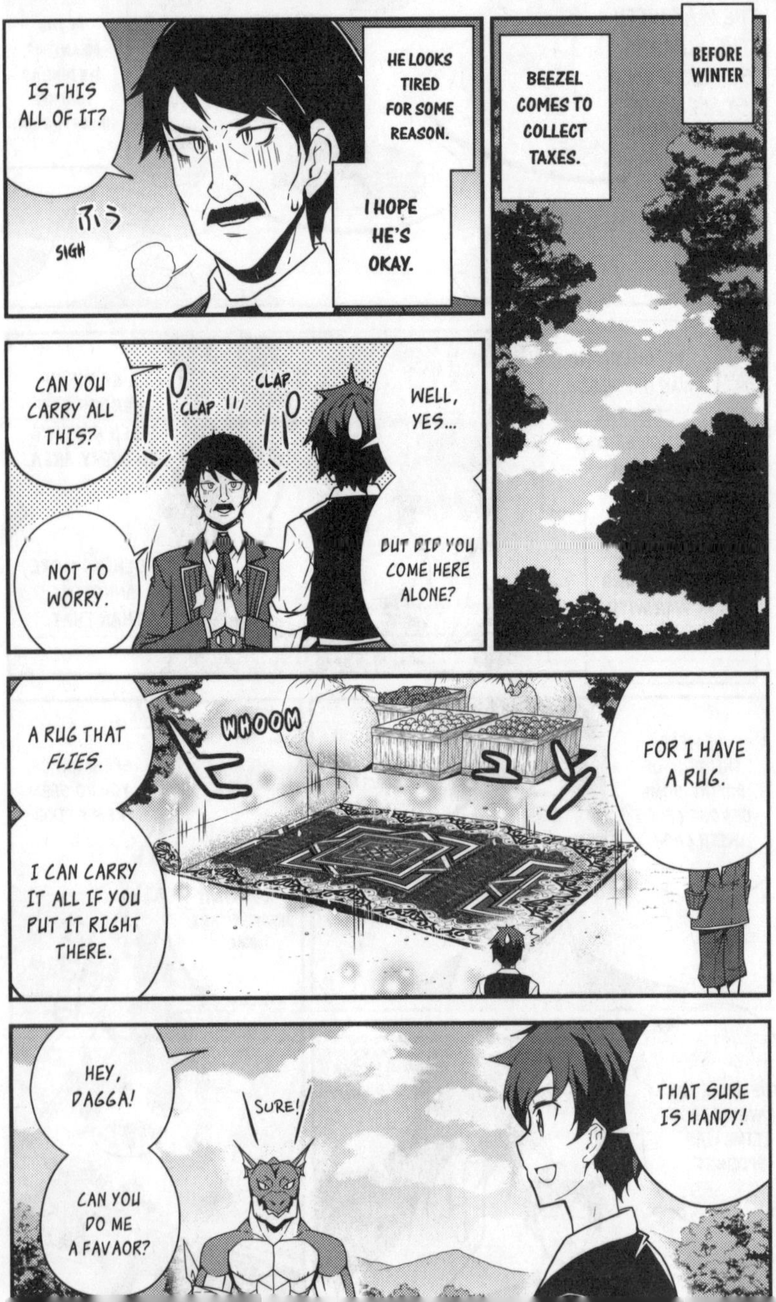
BEFORE WINTER
BEEZEL COMES TO COLLECT TAXES.
HE LOOKS TIRED FOR SOME REASON.
I HOPE HE'S OKAY.
IS THIS ALL OF IT?
ふう
SIGH
WELL, YES...
BUT DID YOU COME HERE ALONE?
CLAP
CLAP
CAN YOU CARRY ALL THIS?
NOT TO WORRY.
FOR I HAVE A RUG.
WHOOM
A RUG THAT *FLIES*.
I CAN CARRY IT ALL IF YOU PUT IT RIGHT THERE.
THAT SURE IS HANDY!
SURE!
HEY, DAGGA!
CAN YOU DO ME A FAVAOR?

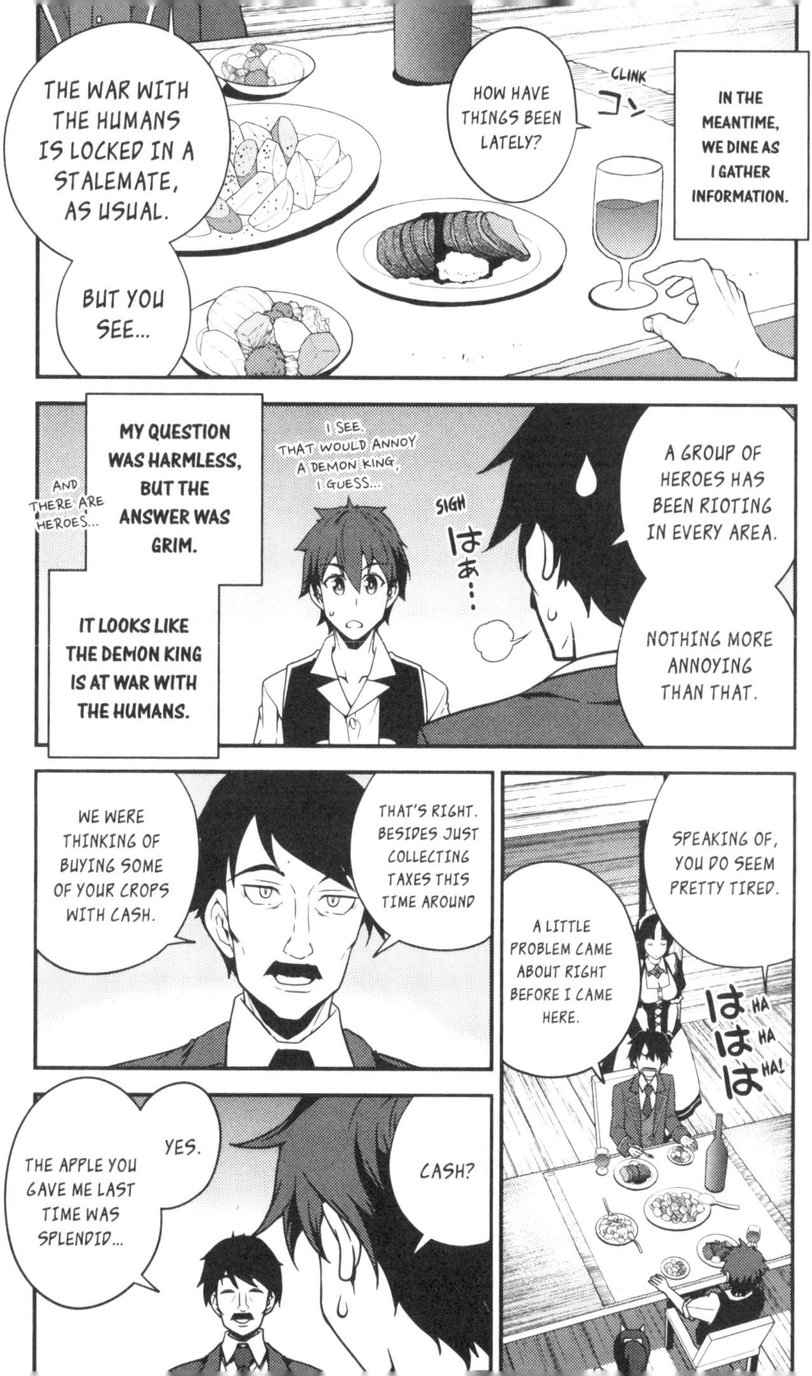
IN THE MEANTIME, WE DINE AS I GATHER INFORMATION.
CLINK
コン
HOW HAVE THINGS BEEN LATELY?
THE WAR WITH THE HUMANS IS LOCKED IN A STALEMATE, AS USUAL.
BUT YOU SEE...
A GROUP OF HEROES HAS BEEN RIOTING IN EVERY AREA.
NOTHING MORE ANNOYING THAN THAT.
SIGH
はぁ…
I SEE. THAT WOULD ANNOY A DEMON KING, I GUESS...
MY QUESTION WAS HARMLESS, BUT THE ANSWER WAS GRIM.
AND THERE ARE HEROES...
IT LOOKS LIKE THE DEMON KING IS AT WAR WITH THE HUMANS.
SPEAKING OF, YOU DO SEEM PRETTY TIRED.
A LITTLE PROBLEM CAME ABOUT RIGHT BEFORE I CAME HERE.
ははは
HA HA HA!
THAT'S RIGHT. BESIDES JUST COLLECTING TAXES THIS TIME AROUND
WE WERE THINKING OF BUYING SOME OF YOUR CROPS WITH CASH.
CASH?
YES.
THE APPLE YOU GAVE ME LAST TIME WAS SPLENDID...

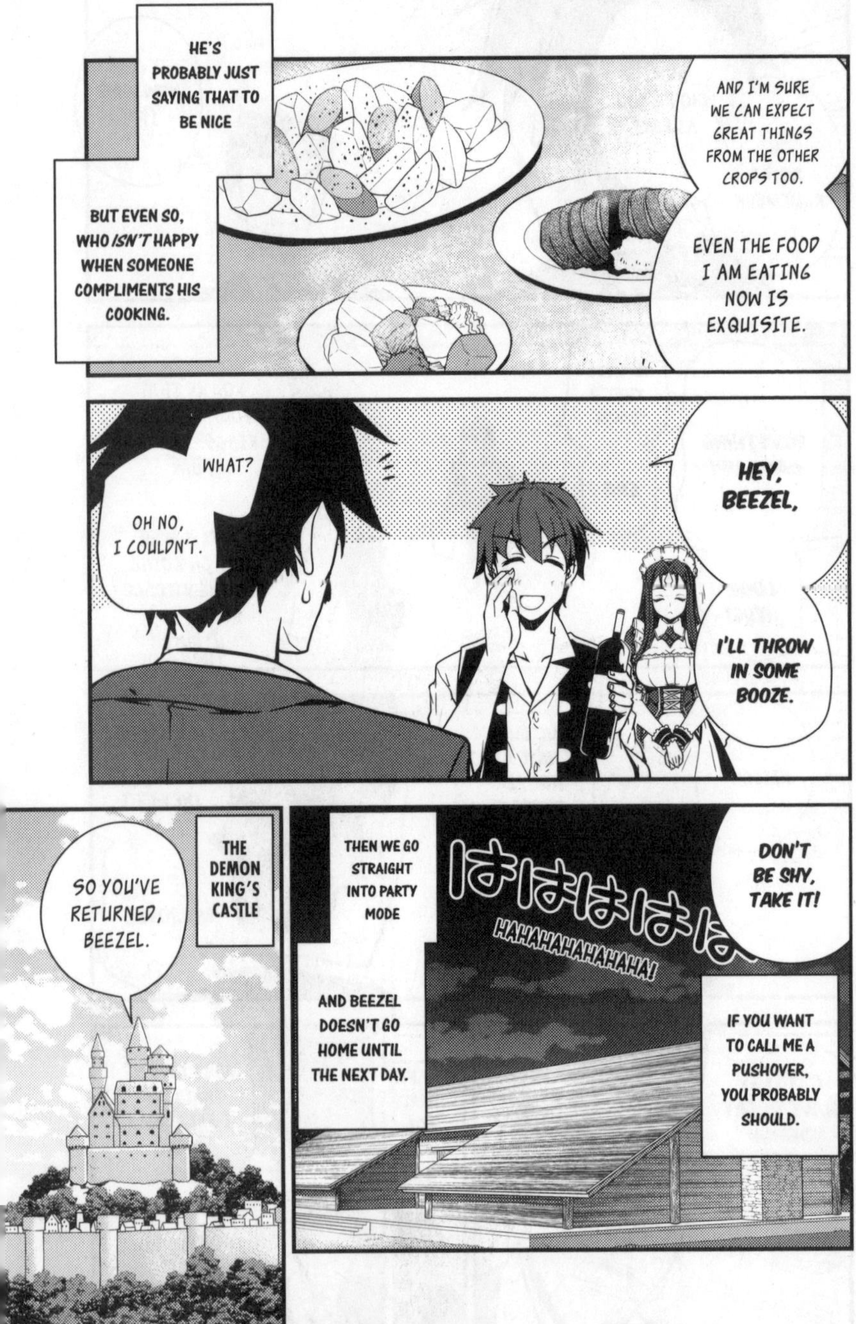
AND I'M SURE WE CAN EXPECT GREAT THINGS FROM THE OTHER CROPS TOO.
EVEN THE FOOD I AM EATING NOW IS EXQUISITE.
HE'S PROBABLY JUST SAYING THAT TO BE NICE
BUT EVEN SO, WHO *ISN'T* HAPPY WHEN SOMEONE COMPLIMENTS HIS COOKING.
HEY, BEEZEL,
I'LL THROW IN SOME BOOZE.
WHAT?
OH NO, I COULDN'T.
DON'T BE SHY, TAKE IT!
ははははは
HAHAHAHAHAHAHA!
THEN WE GO STRAIGHT INTO PARTY MODE
IF YOU WANT TO CALL ME A PUSHOVER, YOU PROBABLY SHOULD.
AND BEEZEL DOESN'T GO HOME UNTIL THE NEXT DAY.
THE DEMON KING'S CASTLE
SO YOU'VE RETURNED, BEEZEL.

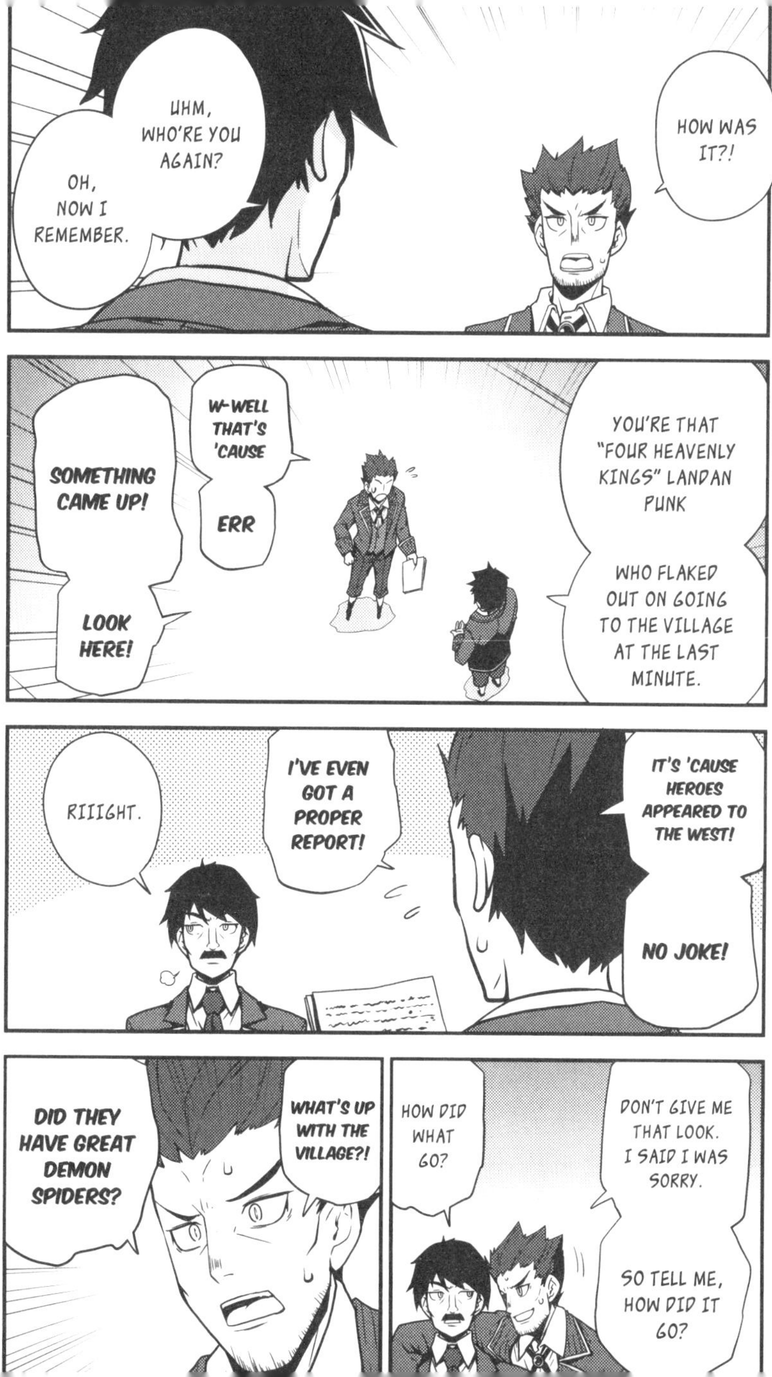
HOW WAS IT?!
UHM, WHO'RE YOU AGAIN?
OH, NOW I REMEMBER.
YOU'RE THAT "FOUR HEAVENLY KINGS" LANDAN PUNK
WHO FLAKED OUT ON GOING TO THE VILLAGE AT THE LAST MINUTE.
W-WELL THAT'S 'CAUSE
ERR
SOMETHING CAME UP!
LOOK HERE!
IT'S 'CAUSE HEROES APPEARED TO THE WEST!
NO JOKE!
I'VE EVEN GOT A PROPER REPORT!
RIIIGHT.
DON'T GIVE ME THAT LOOK. I SAID I WAS SORRY.
SO TELL ME, HOW DID IT GO?
HOW DID WHAT GO?
WHAT'S UP WITH THE VILLAGE?!
DID THEY HAVE GREAT DEMON SPIDERS?

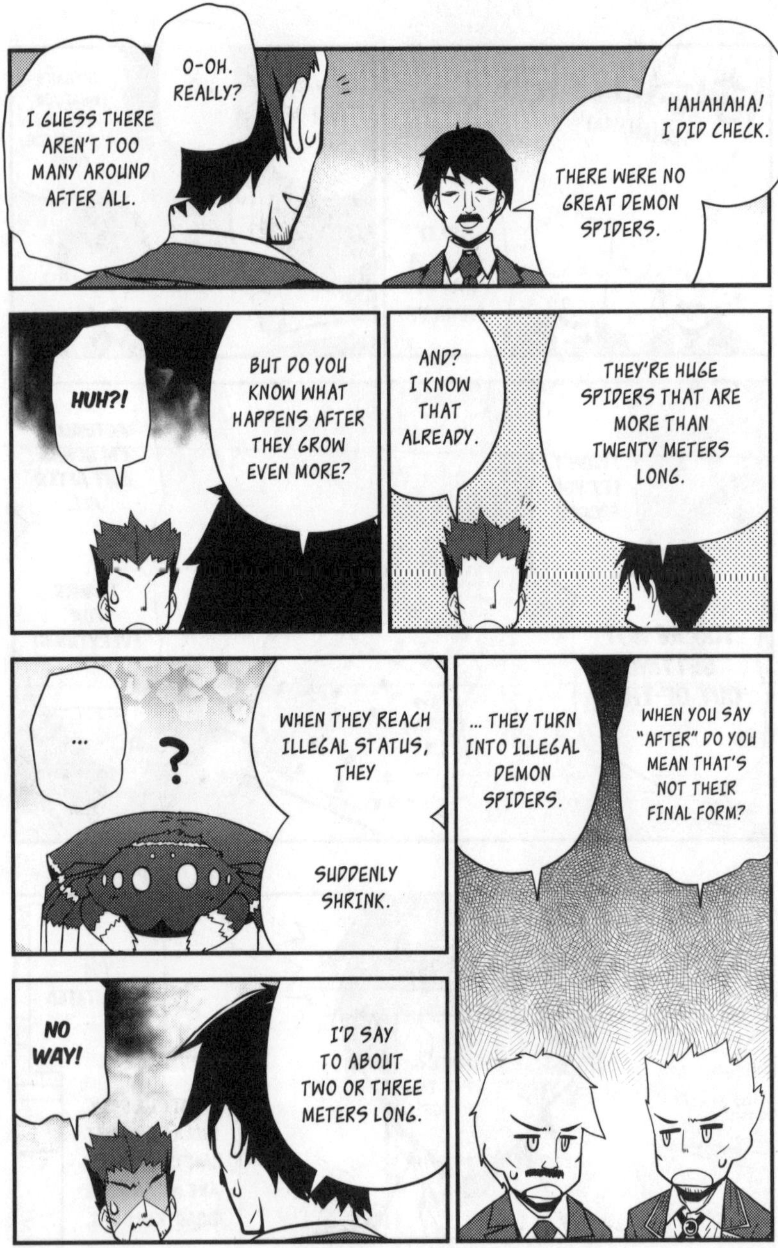
HAHAHAHA! I DID CHECK.
THERE WERE NO GREAT DEMON SPIDERS.
O-OH. REALLY?
I GUESS THERE AREN'T TOO MANY AROUND AFTER ALL.
THEY'RE HUGE SPIDERS THAT ARE MORE THAN TWENTY METERS LONG.
AND? I KNOW THAT ALREADY.
BUT DO YOU KNOW WHAT HAPPENS AFTER THEY GROW EVEN MORE?
HUH?!
WHEN YOU SAY "AFTER" DO YOU MEAN THAT'S NOT THEIR FINAL FORM?
... THEY TURN INTO ILLEGAL DEMON SPIDERS.
WHEN THEY REACH ILLEGAL STATUS, THEY
SUDDENLY SHRINK.
...
?
I'D SAY TO ABOUT TWO OR THREE METERS LONG.
NO WAY!

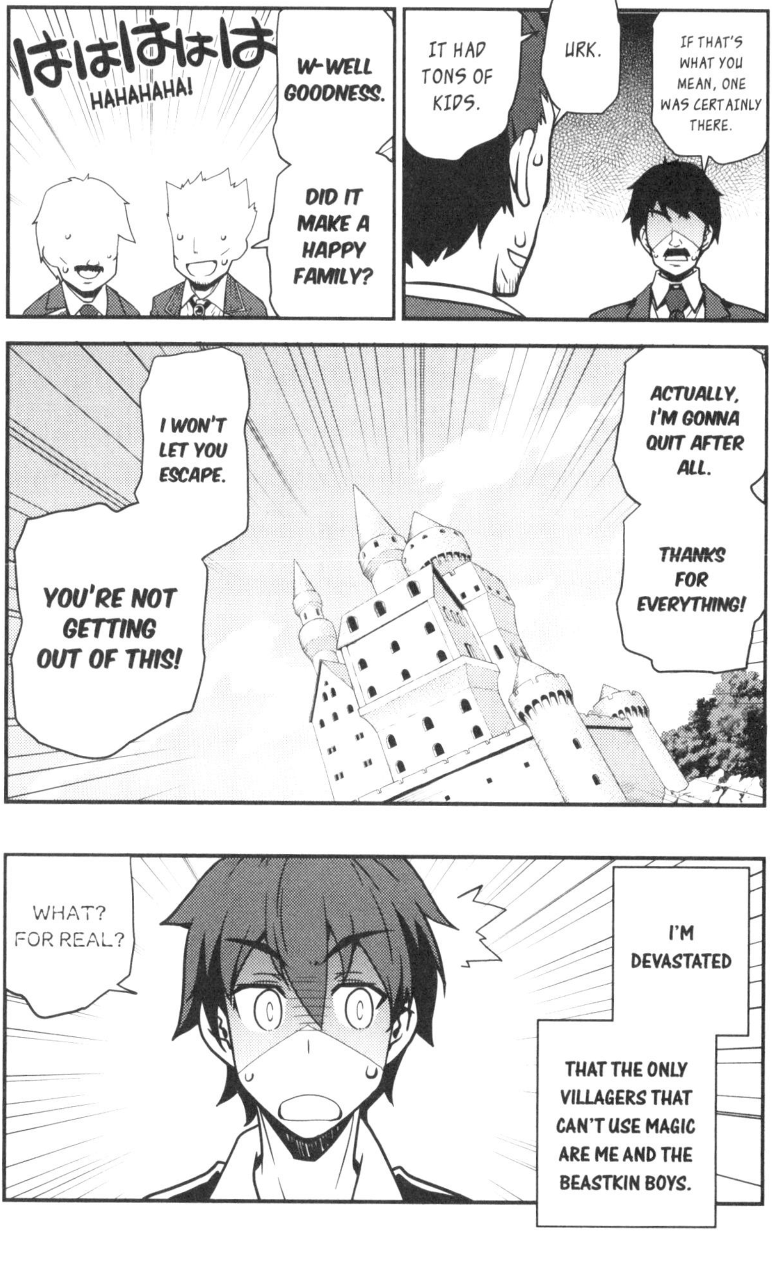
IF THAT'S WHAT YOU MEAN, ONE WAS CERTAINLY THERE.
URK.
IT HAD TONS OF KIDS.
W-WELL GOODNESS.
DID IT MAKE A HAPPY FAMILY?
ははははは
HAHAHAHA!
ACTUALLY, I'M GONNA QUIT AFTER ALL.
THANKS FOR EVERYTHING!
I WON'T LET YOU ESCAPE.
YOU'RE NOT GETTING OUT OF THIS!
I'M DEVASTATED
THAT THE ONLY VILLAGERS THAT CAN'T USE MAGIC ARE ME AND THE BEASTKIN BOYS.
WHAT? FOR REAL?

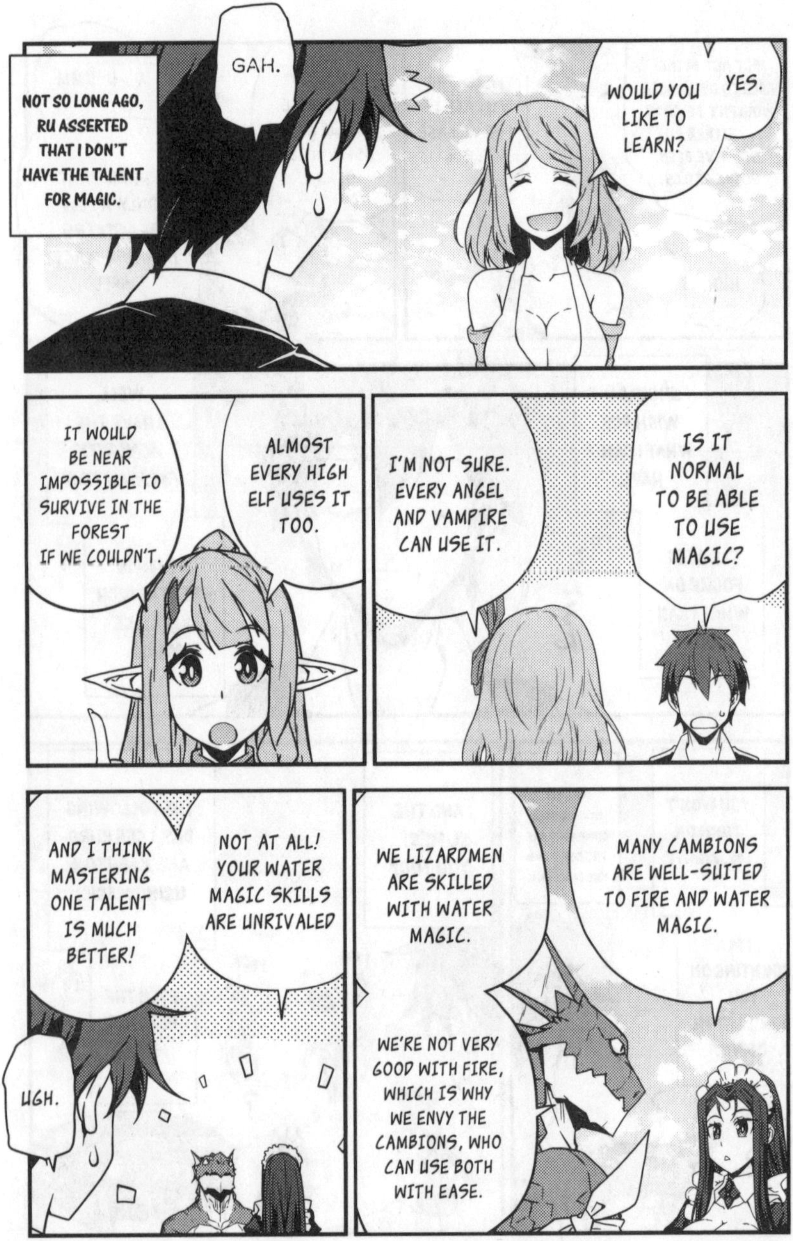
YES.
WOULD YOU LIKE TO LEARN?
GAH.
NOT SO LONG AGO, RU ASSERTED THAT I DON'T HAVE THE TALENT FOR MAGIC.
IS IT NORMAL TO BE ABLE TO USE MAGIC?
I'M NOT SURE. EVERY ANGEL AND VAMPIRE CAN USE IT.
ALMOST EVERY HIGH ELF USES IT TOO.
IT WOULD BE NEAR IMPOSSIBLE TO SURVIVE IN THE FOREST IF WE COULDN'T.
MANY CAMBIONS ARE WELL-SUITED TO FIRE AND WATER MAGIC.
WE LIZARDMEN ARE SKILLED WITH WATER MAGIC.
WE'RE NOT VERY GOOD WITH FIRE, WHICH IS WHY WE ENVY THE CAMBIONS, WHO CAN USE BOTH WITH EASE.
NOT AT ALL! YOUR WATER MAGIC SKILLS ARE UNRIVALED
AND I THINK MASTERING ONE TALENT IS MUCH BETTER!
UGH.

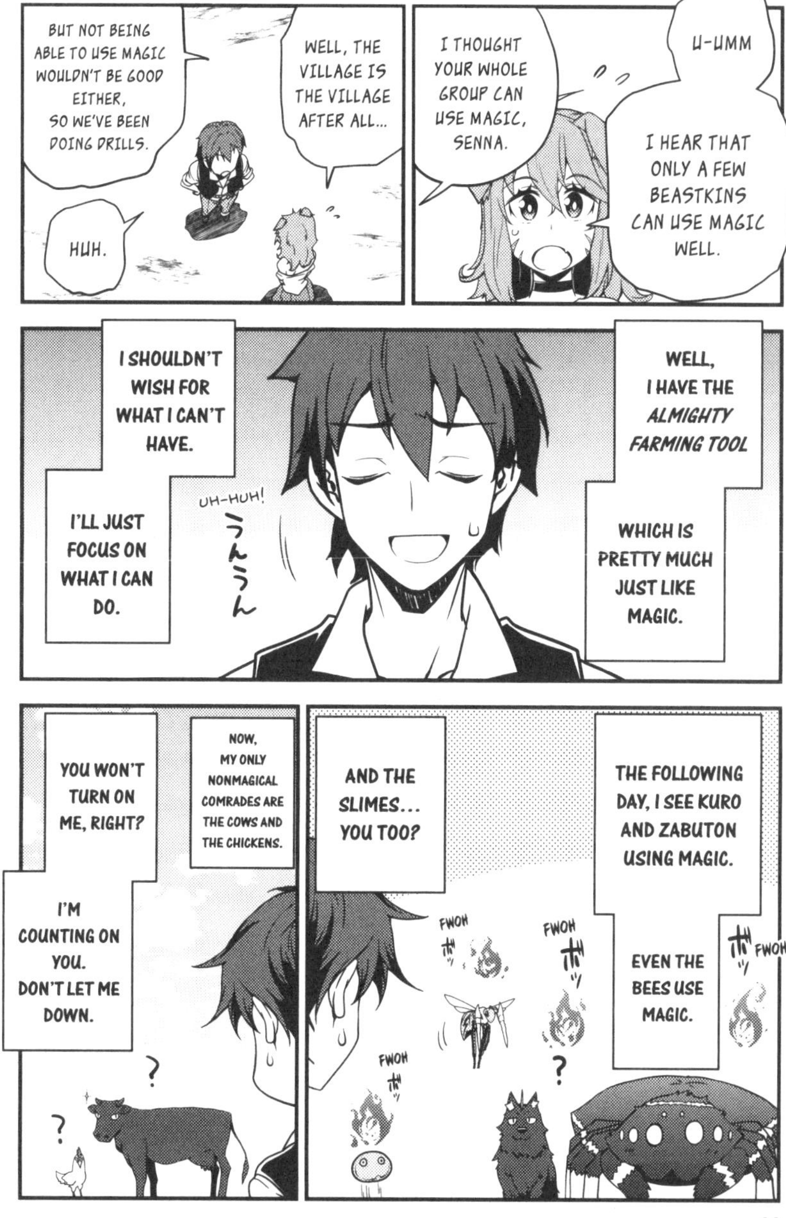
I THOUGHT YOUR WHOLE GROUP CAN USE MAGIC, SENNA.
U-UMM
I HEAR THAT ONLY A FEW BEASTKINS CAN USE MAGIC WELL.
WELL, THE VILLAGE IS THE VILLAGE AFTER ALL...
BUT NOT BEING ABLE TO USE MAGIC WOULDN'T BE GOOD EITHER, SO WE'VE BEEN DOING DRILLS.
HUH.
WELL, I HAVE THE *ALMIGHTY FARMING TOOL*
WHICH IS PRETTY MUCH JUST LIKE MAGIC.
UH-HUH!
うんうん
I SHOULDN'T WISH FOR WHAT I CAN'T HAVE.
I'LL JUST FOCUS ON WHAT I CAN DO.
THE FOLLOWING DAY, I SEE KURO AND ZABUTON USING MAGIC.
EVEN THE BEES USE MAGIC.
FWOH
FWOH
FWOH
AND THE SLIMES... YOU TOO?
FWOH
?
NOW, MY ONLY NONMAGICAL COMRADES ARE THE COWS AND THE CHICKENS.
YOU WON'T TURN ON ME, RIGHT?
I'M COUNTING ON YOU. DON'T LET ME DOWN.
?
?

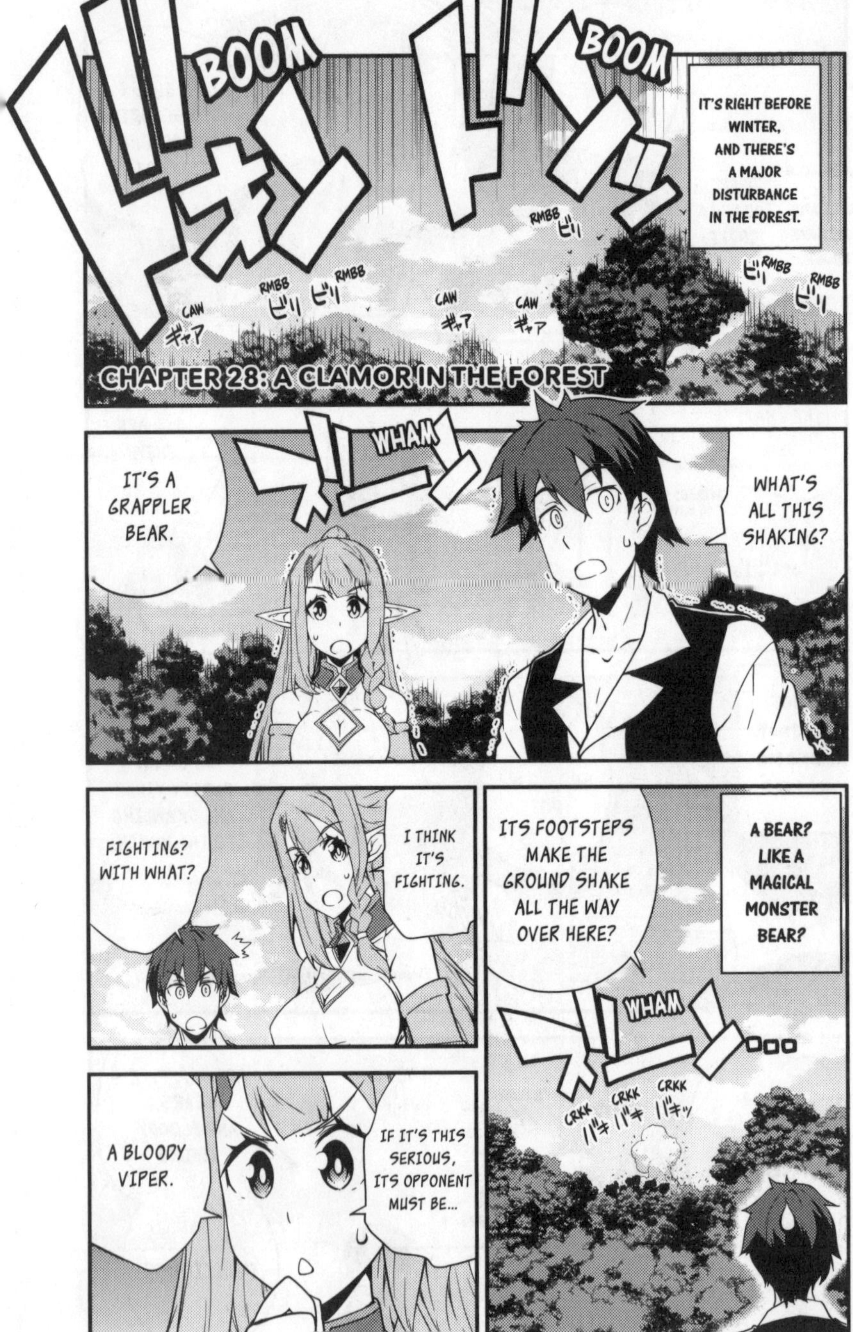
BOOM
IT'S RIGHT BEFORE WINTER, AND THERE'S A MAJOR DISTURBANCE IN THE FOREST.
BOOM
RMBB
RMBB
RMBB
RMBB
RMBB
CAW
CAW
CAW
CHAPTER 28: A CLAMOR IN THE FOREST
WHAT'S ALL THIS SHAKING?
WHAM
IT'S A GRAPPLER BEAR.
A BEAR? LIKE A MAGICAL MONSTER BEAR?
ITS FOOTSTEPS MAKE THE GROUND SHAKE ALL THE WAY OVER HERE?
WHAM
CRKK
CRKK
CRKK
I THINK IT'S FIGHTING.
FIGHTING? WITH WHAT?
IF IT'S THIS SERIOUS, ITS OPPONENT MUST BE...
A BLOODY VIPER.

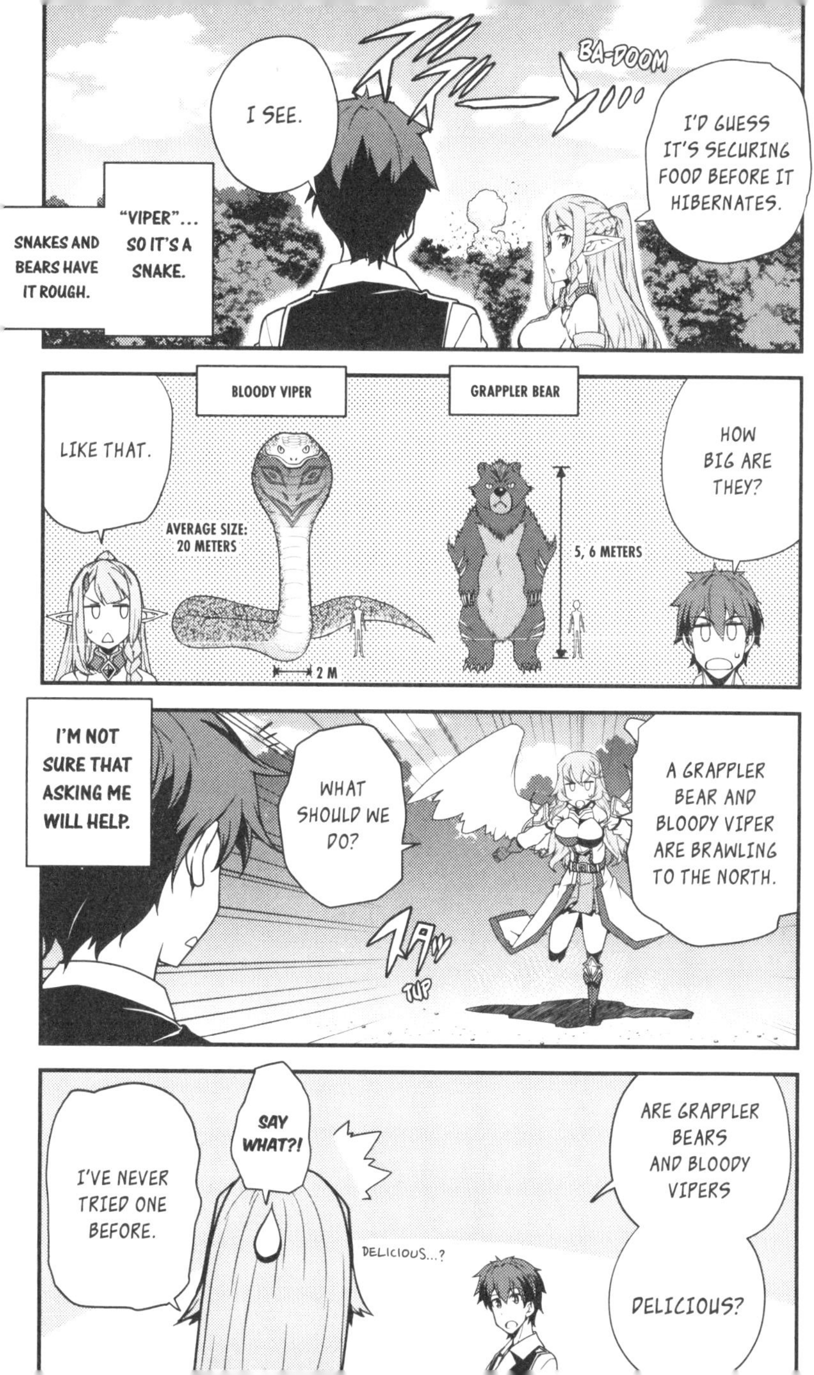
BA-DOOM
I'D GUESS IT'S SECURING FOOD BEFORE IT HIBERNATES.
I SEE.
"VIPER"... SO IT'S A SNAKE.
SNAKES AND BEARS HAVE IT ROUGH.
HOW BIG ARE THEY?
GRAPPLER BEAR
5, 6 METERS
BLOODY VIPER
AVERAGE SIZE: 20 METERS
2 M
LIKE THAT.
A GRAPPLER BEAR AND BLOODY VIPER ARE BRAWLING TO THE NORTH.
TUP
WHAT SHOULD WE DO?
I'M NOT SURE THAT ASKING ME WILL HELP.
ARE GRAPPLER BEARS AND BLOODY VIPERS DELICIOUS?
DELICIOUS...?
SAY WHAT?!
I'VE NEVER TRIED ONE BEFORE.

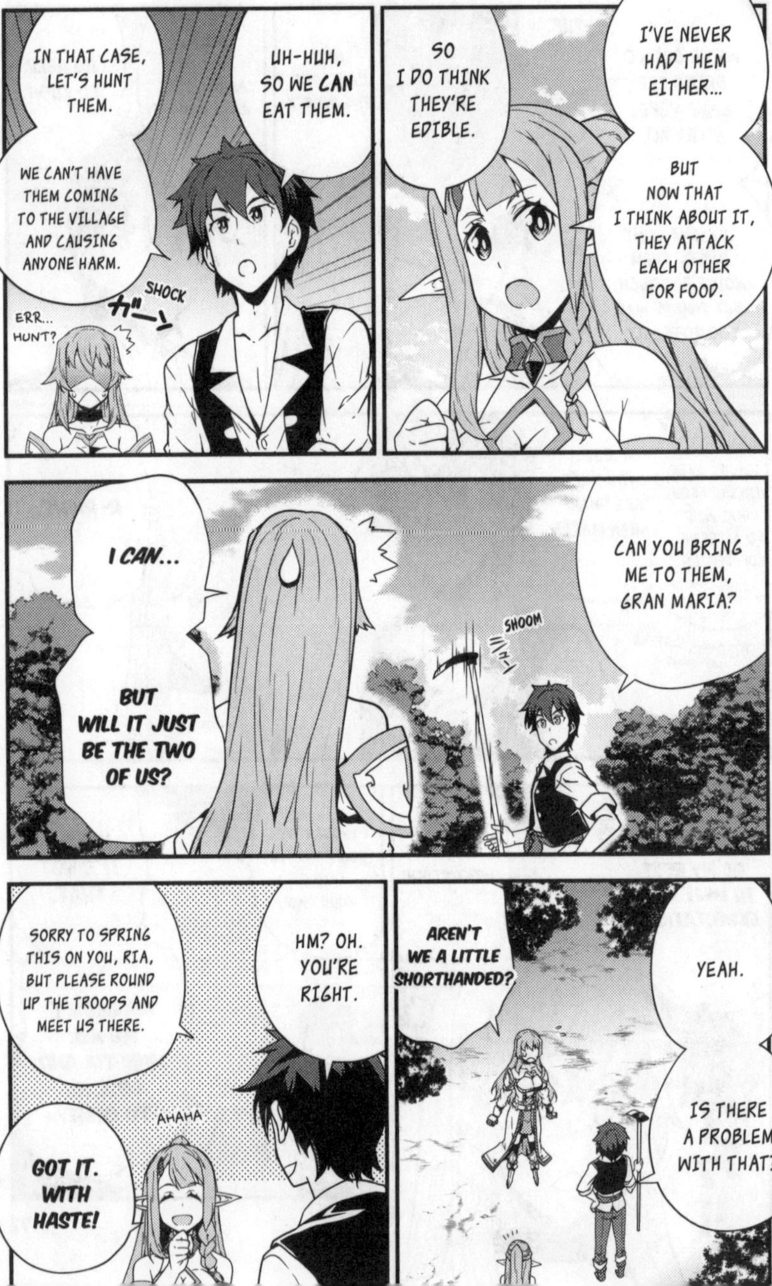
I'VE NEVER HAD THEM EITHER...
BUT NOW THAT I THINK ABOUT IT, THEY ATTACK EACH OTHER FOR FOOD.
SO I DO THINK THEY'RE EDIBLE.
UH-HUH, SO WE CAN EAT THEM.
IN THAT CASE, LET'S HUNT THEM.
WE CAN'T HAVE THEM COMING TO THE VILLAGE AND CAUSING ANYONE HARM.
SHOCK
ERR... HUNT?
CAN YOU BRING ME TO THEM, GRAN MARIA?
SHOOM
I CAN...
BUT WILL IT JUST BE THE TWO OF US?
YEAH.
IS THERE A PROBLEM WITH THAT?
AREN'T WE A LITTLE SHORTHANDED?
HM? OH. YOU'RE RIGHT.
SORRY TO SPRING THIS ON YOU, RIA, BUT PLEASE ROUND UP THE TROOPS AND MEET US THERE.
AHAHA
GOT IT. WITH HASTE!

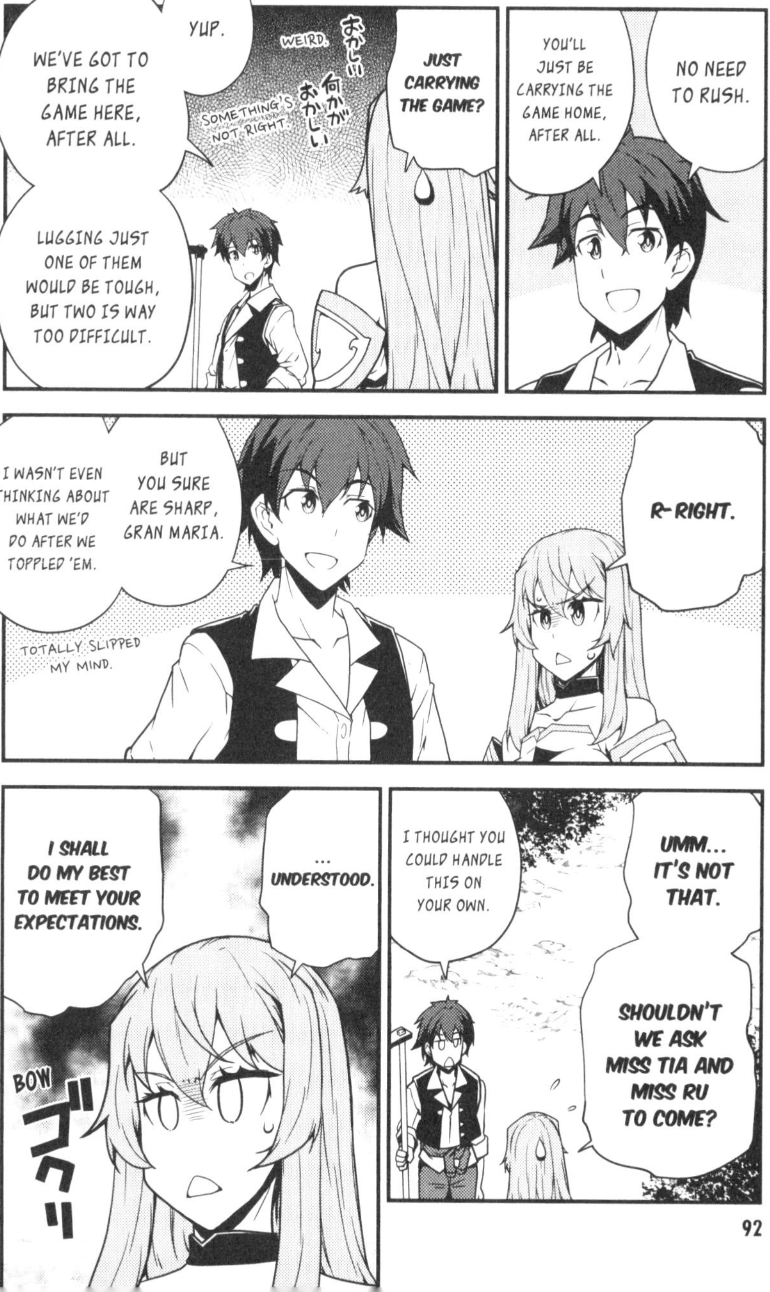

NO NEED TO RUSH.
YOU'LL JUST BE CARRYING THE GAME HOME, AFTER ALL.
JUST CARRYING THE GAME?
おかしい
WEIRD.
何かがおかしい
SOMETHING'S NOT RIGHT.
YUP.
WE'VE GOT TO BRING THE GAME HERE, AFTER ALL.
LUGGING JUST ONE OF THEM WOULD BE TOUGH, BUT TWO IS WAY TOO DIFFICULT.
R-RIGHT.
BUT YOU SURE ARE SHARP, GRAN MARIA.
I WASN'T EVEN THINKING ABOUT WHAT WE'D DO AFTER WE TOPPLED 'EM.
TOTALLY SLIPPED MY MIND.
UMM... IT'S NOT THAT.
I THOUGHT YOU COULD HANDLE THIS ON YOUR OWN.
SHOULDN'T WE ASK MISS TIA AND MISS RU TO COME?
... UNDERSTOOD.
I SHALL DO MY BEST TO MEET YOUR EXPECTATIONS.
BOW
ゴクリ

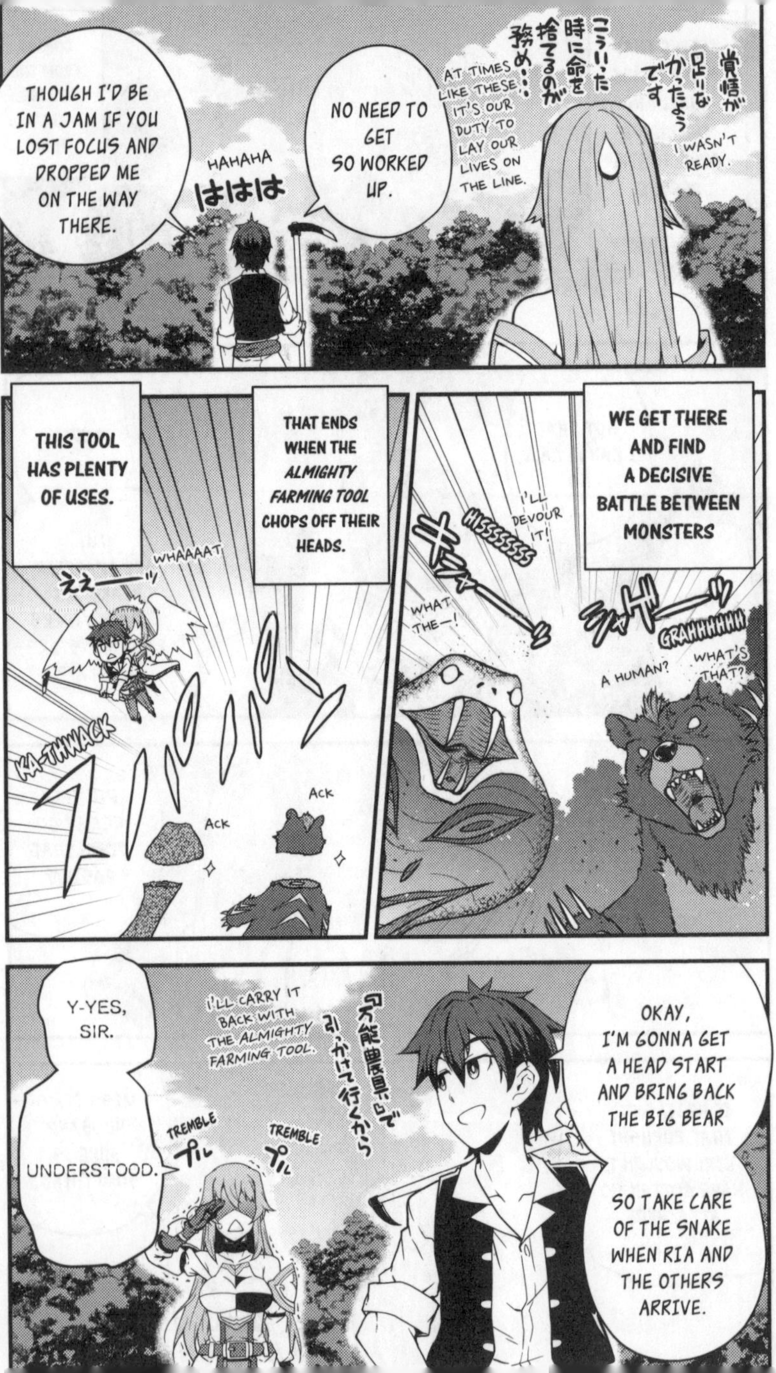
覚悟が足りなかったようです
I WASN'T READY.
こういった時に命を捨てるのが務め…
AT TIMES LIKE THESE IT'S OUR DUTY TO LAY OUR LIVES ON THE LINE.
NO NEED TO GET SO WORKED UP.
ははは
HAHAHA
THOUGH I'D BE IN A JAM IF YOU LOST FOCUS AND DROPPED ME ON THE WAY THERE.
WE GET THERE AND FIND A DECISIVE BATTLE BETWEEN MONSTERS
GRAHHHHHH
I'LL DEVOUR IT!
HISSSSSSSS
WHAT THE—!
WHAT'S THAT?
A HUMAN?
THAT ENDS WHEN THE *ALMIGHTY FARMING TOOL* CHOPS OFF THEIR HEADS.
THIS TOOL HAS PLENTY OF USES.
ええーーッ
WHAAAAT
KA-THWACK
ACK
ACK
OKAY, I'M GONNA GET A HEAD START AND BRING BACK THE BIG BEAR
SO TAKE CARE OF THE SNAKE WHEN RIA AND THE OTHERS ARRIVE.
『万能農具』で引っかけて行くから
I'LL CARRY IT BACK WITH THE ALMIGHTY FARMING TOOL.
TREMBLE
プル
TREMBLE
プル
Y-YES, SIR.
UNDERSTOOD.

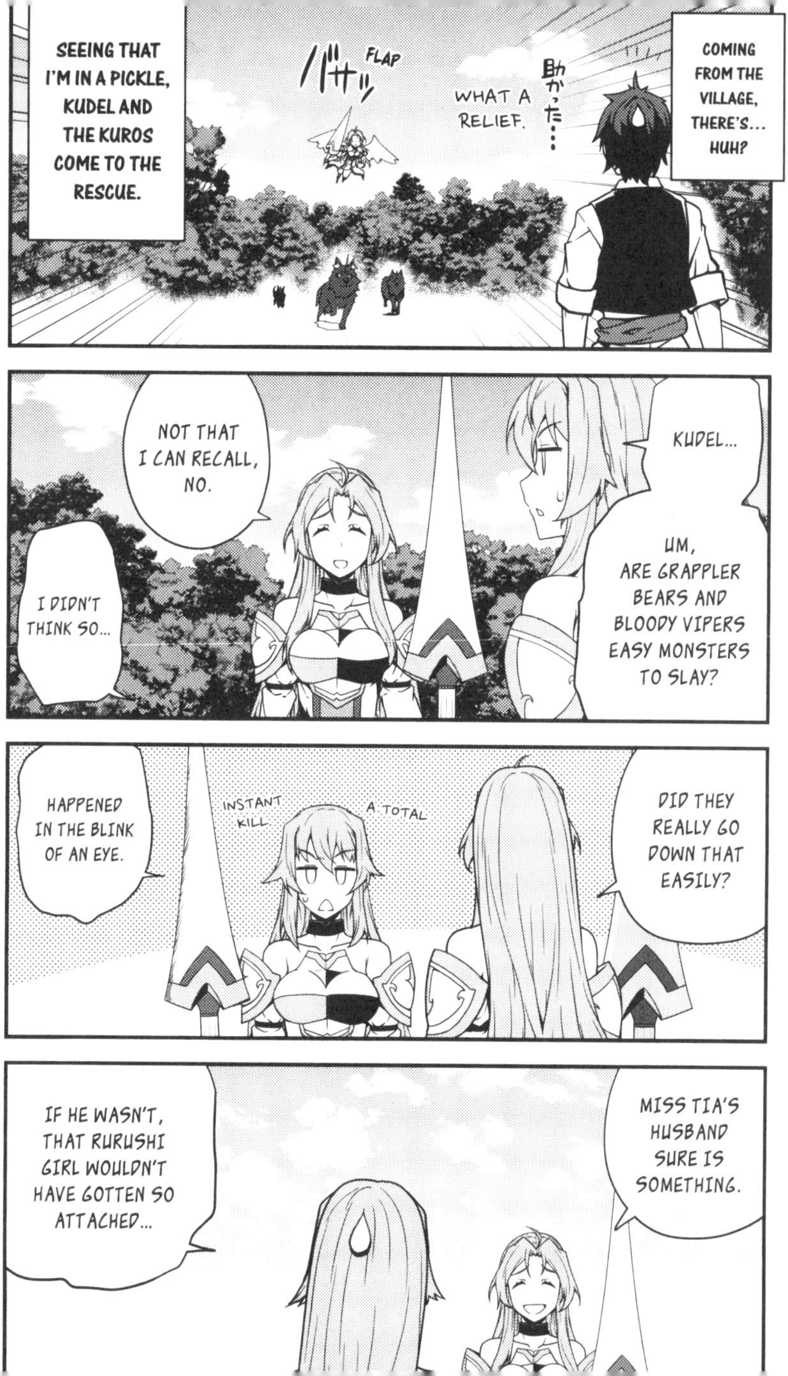
COMING FROM THE VILLAGE, THERE'S... HUH?
助かった…
WHAT A RELIEF.
バサッ
FLAP
SEEING THAT I'M IN A PICKLE, KUDEL AND THE KUROS COME TO THE RESCUE.
KUDEL...
UM, ARE GRAPPLER BEARS AND BLOODY VIPERS EASY MONSTERS TO SLAY?
NOT THAT I CAN RECALL, NO.
I DIDN'T THINK SO...
DID THEY REALLY GO DOWN THAT EASILY?
A TOTAL
INSTANT KILL
HAPPENED IN THE BLINK OF AN EYE.
MISS TIA'S HUSBAND SURE IS SOMETHING.
IF HE WASN'T, THAT RURUSHI GIRL WOULDN'T HAVE GOTTEN SO ATTACHED...

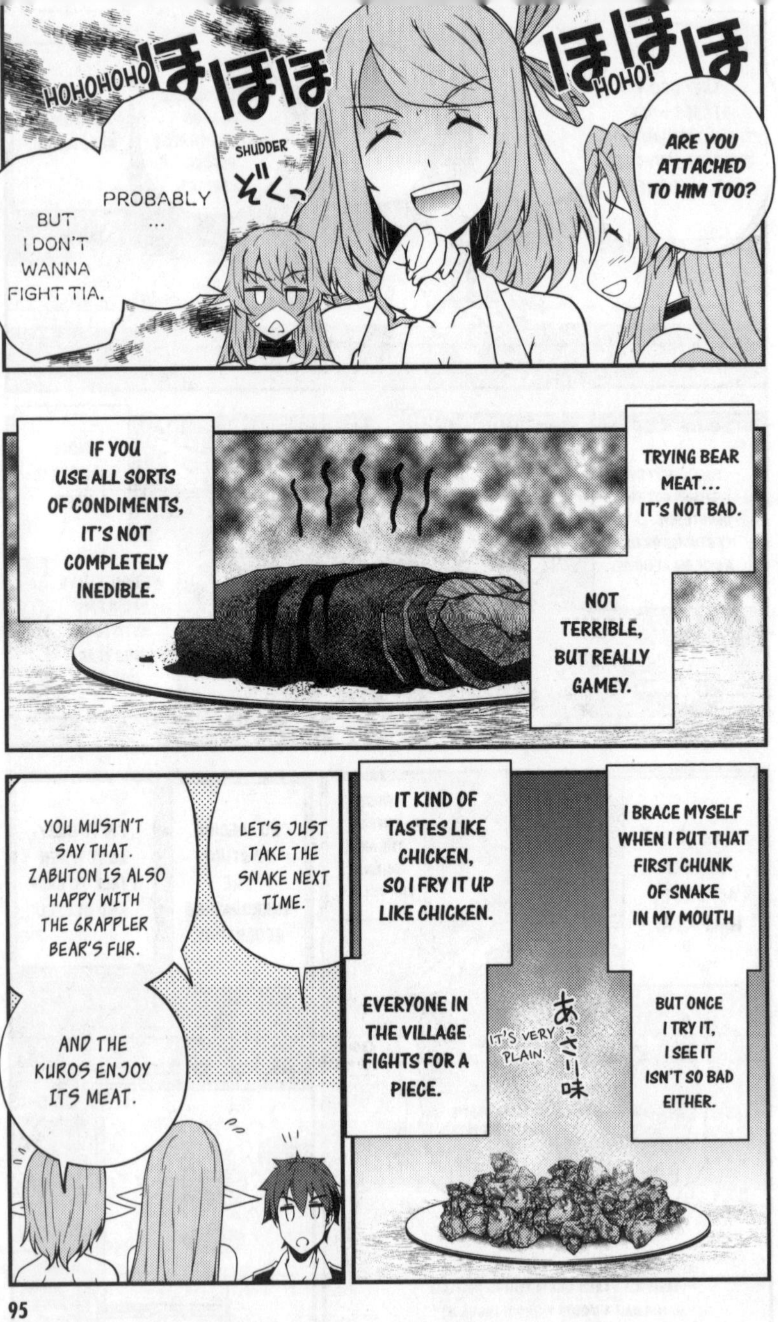

ほほほ
HOHO!
ARE YOU ATTACHED TO HIM TOO?
ほほほ
HOHOHOHO
ぞくっ
SHUDDER
PROBABLY... BUT I DON'T WANNA FIGHT TIA.
TRYING BEAR MEAT... IT'S NOT BAD.
NOT TERRIBLE, BUT REALLY GAMEY.
IF YOU USE ALL SORTS OF CONDIMENTS, IT'S NOT COMPLETELY INEDIBLE.
I BRACE MYSELF WHEN I PUT THAT FIRST CHUNK OF SNAKE IN MY MOUTH
BUT ONCE I TRY IT, I SEE IT ISN'T SO BAD EITHER.
IT KIND OF TASTES LIKE CHICKEN, SO I FRY IT UP LIKE CHICKEN.
あっさー味
IT'S VERY PLAIN.
EVERYONE IN THE VILLAGE FIGHTS FOR A PIECE.
LET'S JUST TAKE THE SNAKE NEXT TIME.
YOU MUSTN'T SAY THAT. ZABUTON IS ALSO HAPPY WITH THE GRAPPLER BEAR'S FUR.
AND THE KUROS ENJOY ITS MEAT.

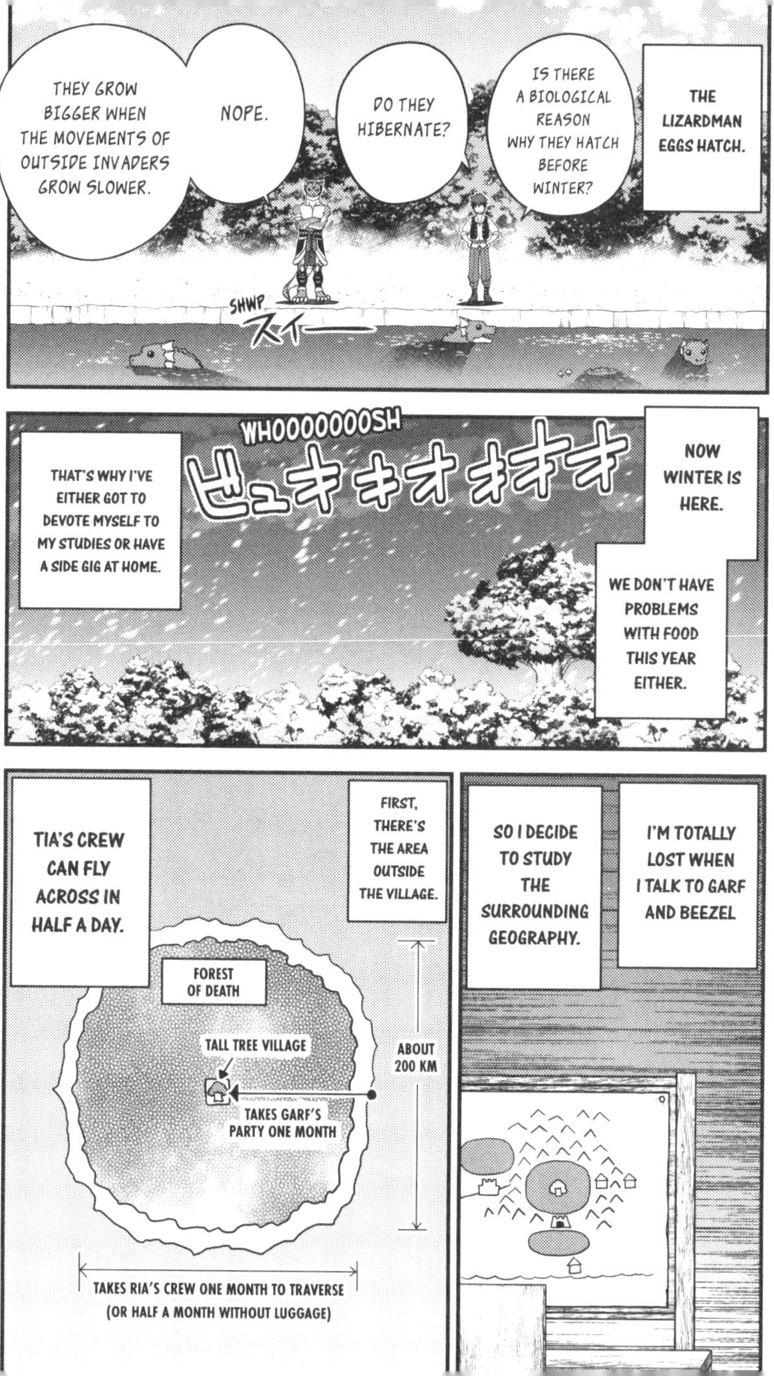
THE LIZARDMAN EGGS HATCH.
IS THERE A BIOLOGICAL REASON WHY THEY HATCH BEFORE WINTER?
DO THEY HIBERNATE?
NOPE.
THEY GROW BIGGER WHEN THE MOVEMENTS OF OUTSIDE INVADERS GROW SLOWER.
SHWP
スイー
NOW WINTER IS HERE.
WE DON'T HAVE PROBLEMS WITH FOOD THIS YEAR EITHER.
WHOOOOOOOSH
THAT'S WHY I'VE EITHER GOT TO DEVOTE MYSELF TO MY STUDIES OR HAVE A SIDE GIG AT HOME.
I'M TOTALLY LOST WHEN I TALK TO GARF AND BEEZEL
SO I DECIDE TO STUDY THE SURROUNDING GEOGRAPHY.
FIRST, THERE'S THE AREA OUTSIDE THE VILLAGE.
TIA'S CREW CAN FLY ACROSS IN HALF A DAY.
FOREST OF DEATH
TALL TREE VILLAGE
TAKES GARF'S PARTY ONE MONTH
ABOUT 200 KM
TAKES RIA'S CREW ONE MONTH TO TRAVERSE (OR HALF A MONTH WITHOUT LUGGAGE)

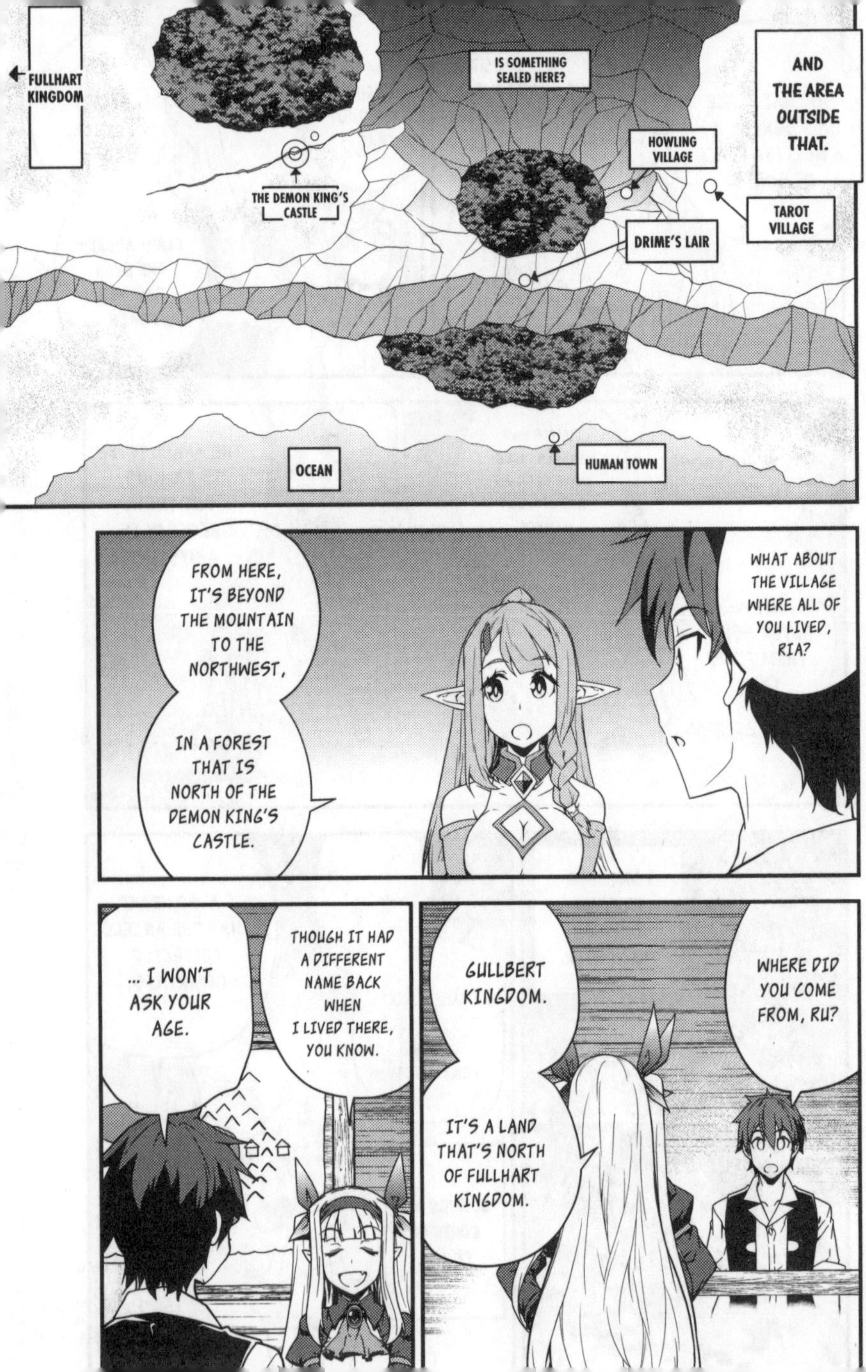
AND THE AREA OUTSIDE THAT.
IS SOMETHING SEALED HERE?
← FULLHART KINGDOM
HOWLING VILLAGE
TAROT VILLAGE
THE DEMON KING'S CASTLE
DRIME'S LAIR
HUMAN TOWN
OCEAN
WHAT ABOUT THE VILLAGE WHERE ALL OF YOU LIVED, RIA?
FROM HERE, IT'S BEYOND THE MOUNTAIN TO THE NORTHWEST,
IN A FOREST THAT IS NORTH OF THE DEMON KING'S CASTLE.
WHERE DID YOU COME FROM, RU?
GULLBERT KINGDOM.
IT'S A LAND THAT'S NORTH OF FULLHART KINGDOM.
THOUGH IT HAD A DIFFERENT NAME BACK WHEN I LIVED THERE, YOU KNOW.
... I WON'T ASK YOUR AGE.

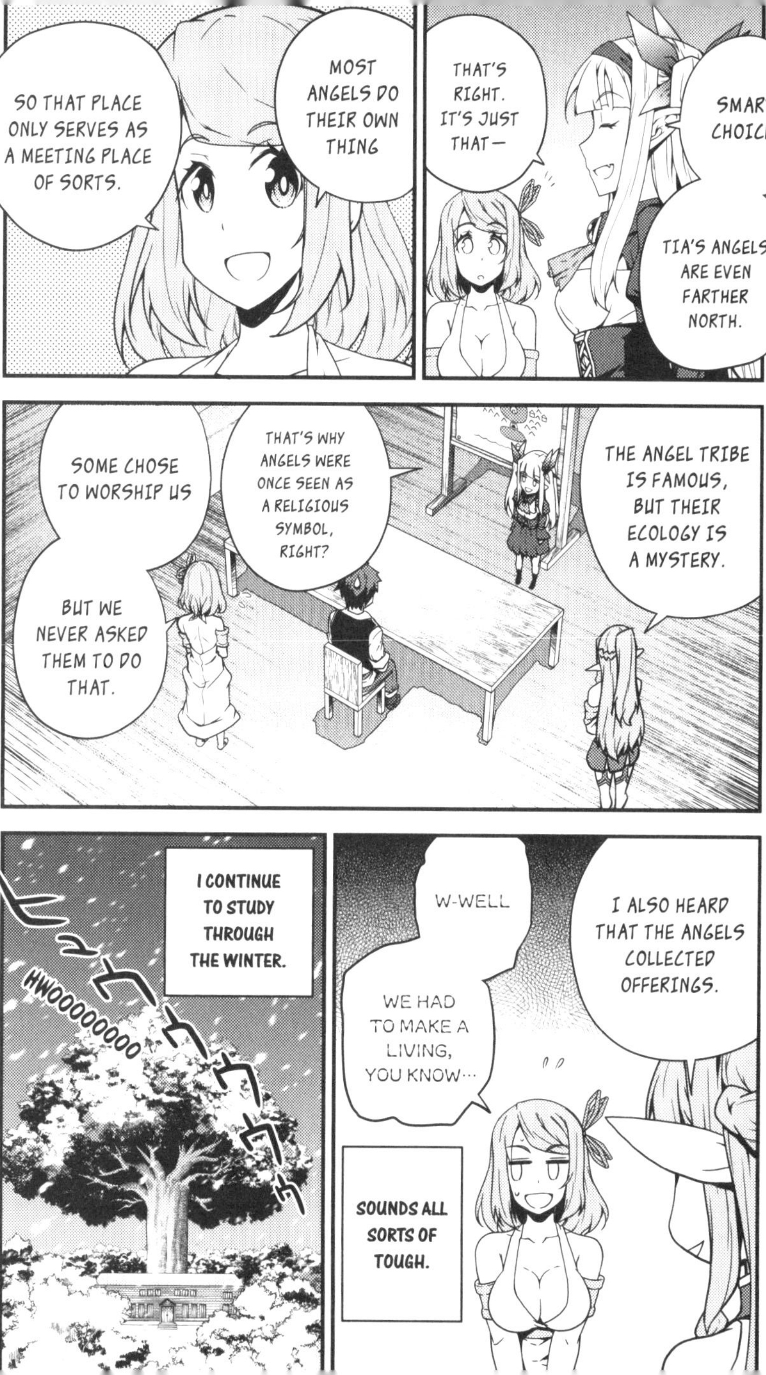
SMART CHOICE.
THAT'S RIGHT. IT'S JUST THAT—
TIA'S ANGELS ARE EVEN FARTHER NORTH.
MOST ANGELS DO THEIR OWN THING
SO THAT PLACE ONLY SERVES AS A MEETING PLACE OF SORTS.
THE ANGEL TRIBE IS FAMOUS, BUT THEIR ECOLOGY IS A MYSTERY.
THAT'S WHY ANGELS WERE ONCE SEEN AS A RELIGIOUS SYMBOL, RIGHT?
SOME CHOSE TO WORSHIP US
BUT WE NEVER ASKED THEM TO DO THAT.
I ALSO HEARD THAT THE ANGELS COLLECTED OFFERINGS.
W-WELL
WE HAD TO MAKE A LIVING, YOU KNOW…
SOUNDS ALL SORTS OF TOUGH.
I CONTINUE TO STUDY THROUGH THE WINTER.
HWOOOOOOOOO

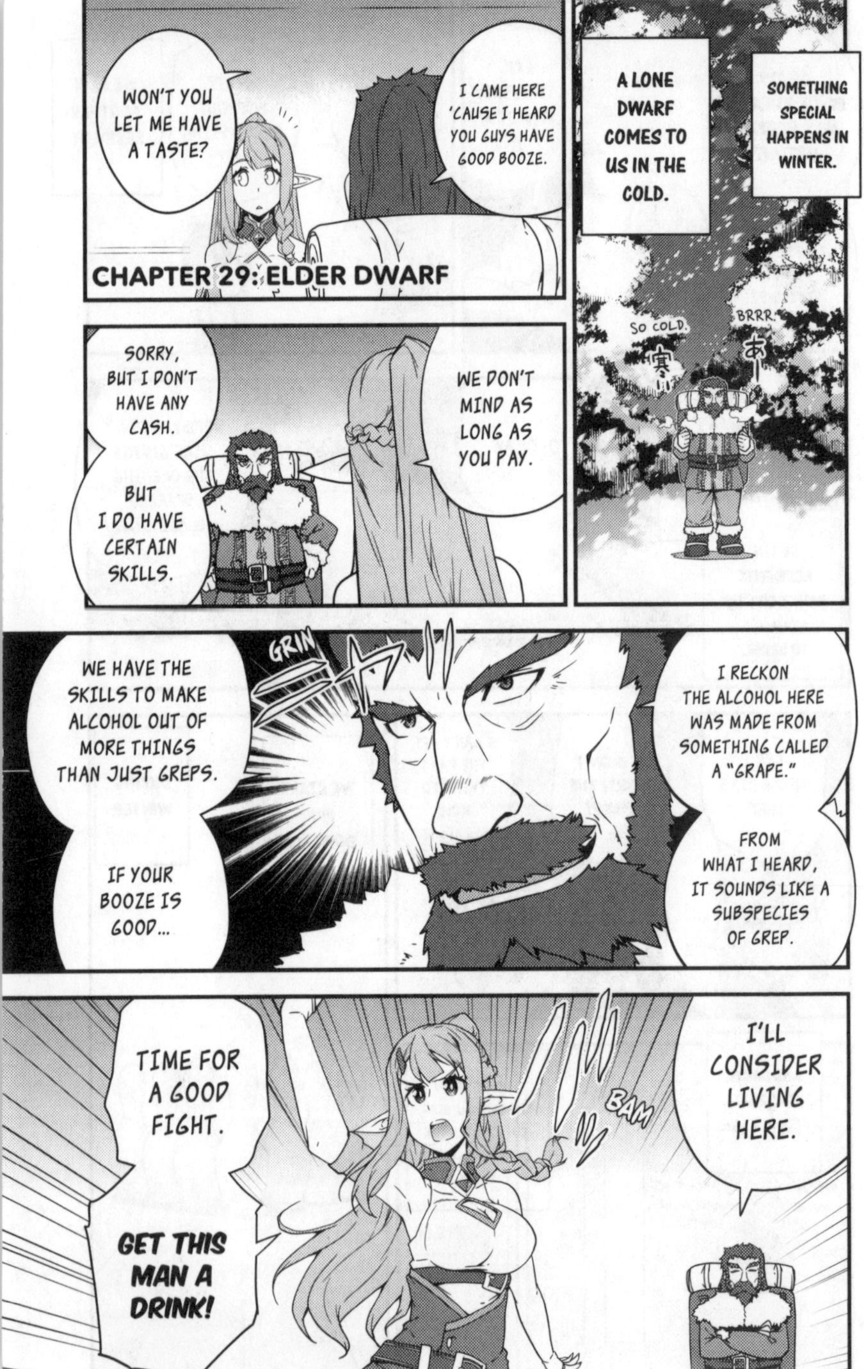
SOMETHING SPECIAL HAPPENS IN WINTER.
A LONE DWARF COMES TO US IN THE COLD.
BRRR.
あー
SO COLD.
寒い
I CAME HERE 'CAUSE I HEARD YOU GUYS HAVE GOOD BOOZE.
WON'T YOU LET ME HAVE A TASTE?
CHAPTER 29: ELDER DWARF
WE DON'T MIND AS LONG AS YOU PAY.
SORRY, BUT I DON'T HAVE ANY CASH.
BUT I DO HAVE CERTAIN SKILLS.
I RECKON THE ALCOHOL HERE WAS MADE FROM SOMETHING CALLED A "GRAPE."
FROM WHAT I HEARD, IT SOUNDS LIKE A SUBSPECIES OF GREP.
GRIN
WE HAVE THE SKILLS TO MAKE ALCOHOL OUT OF MORE THINGS THAN JUST GREPS.
IF YOUR BOOZE IS GOOD...
I'LL CONSIDER LIVING HERE.
BAM
TIME FOR A GOOD FIGHT.
GET THIS MAN A DRINK!

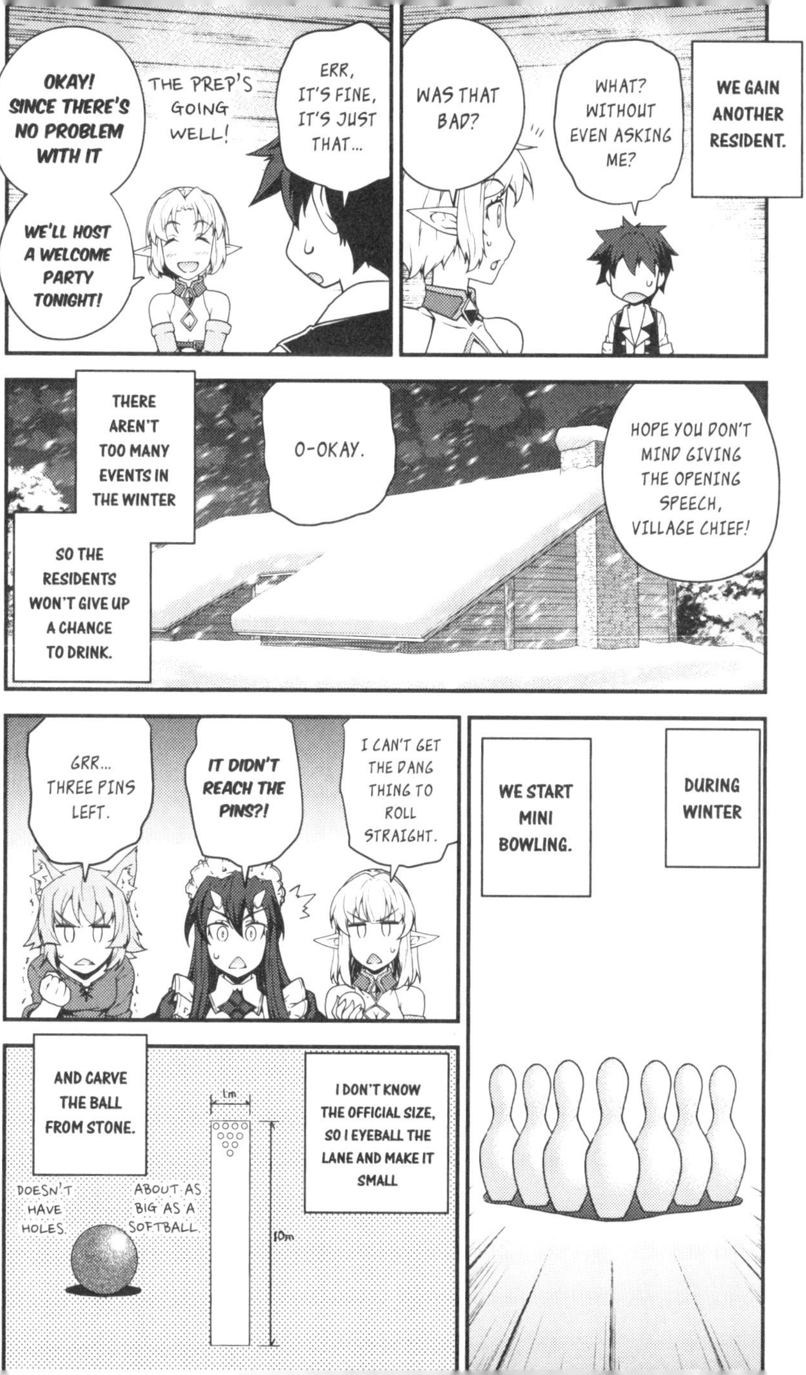
WE GAIN ANOTHER RESIDENT.
WHAT? WITHOUT EVEN ASKING ME?
WAS THAT BAD?
ERR, IT'S FINE, IT'S JUST THAT...
THE PREP'S GOING WELL!
OKAY! SINCE THERE'S NO PROBLEM WITH IT
WE'LL HOST A WELCOME PARTY TONIGHT!
HOPE YOU DON'T MIND GIVING THE OPENING SPEECH, VILLAGE CHIEF!
O-OKAY.
THERE AREN'T TOO MANY EVENTS IN THE WINTER
SO THE RESIDENTS WON'T GIVE UP A CHANCE TO DRINK.
DURING WINTER
WE START MINI BOWLING.
I CAN'T GET THE DANG THING TO ROLL STRAIGHT.
IT DIDN'T REACH THE PINS?!
GRR... THREE PINS LEFT.
I DON'T KNOW THE OFFICIAL SIZE, SO I EYEBALL THE LANE AND MAKE IT SMALL
AND CARVE THE BALL FROM STONE.
1m
10m
ABOUT AS BIG AS A SOFTBALL
DOESN'T HAVE HOLES.

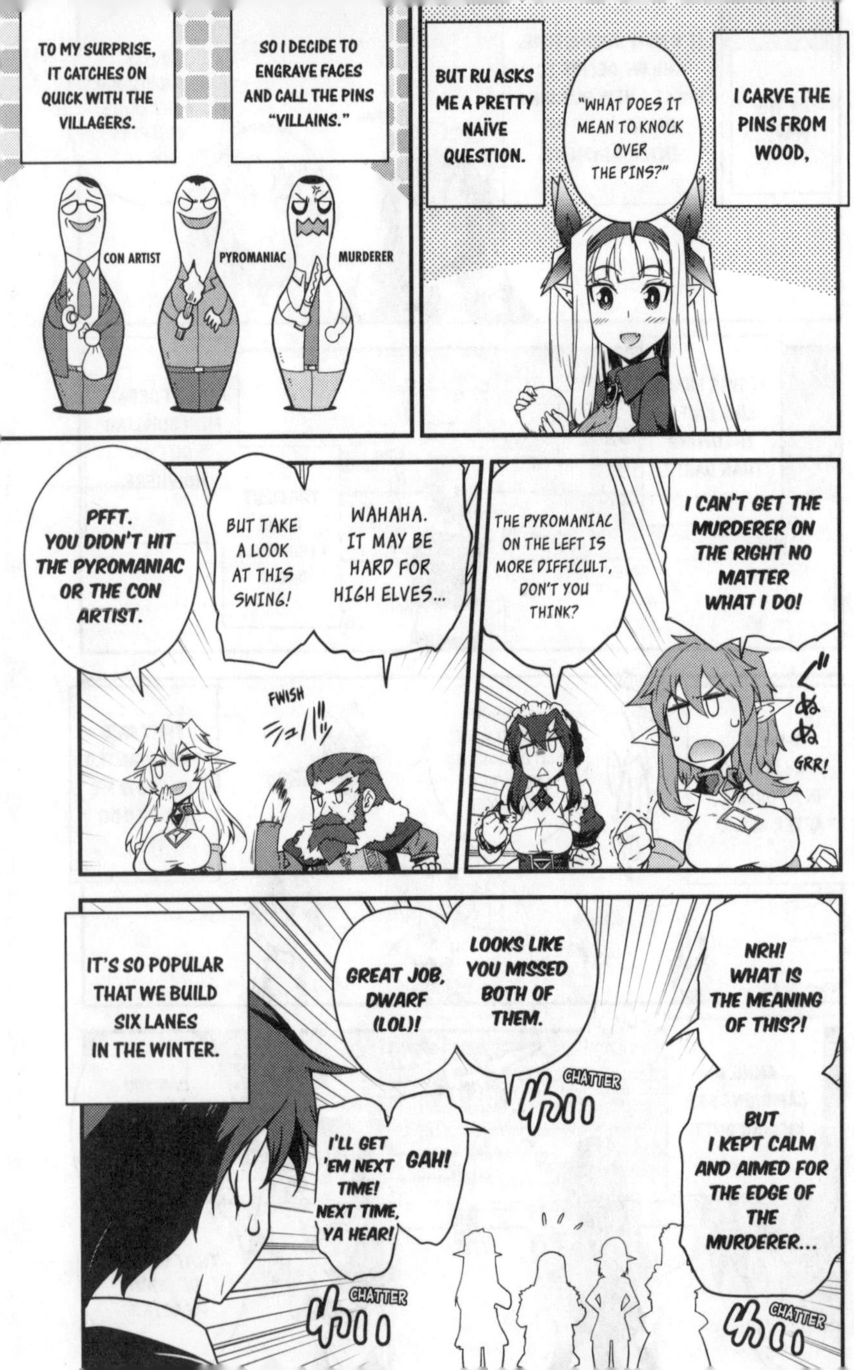
I CARVE THE PINS FROM WOOD,
BUT RU ASKS ME A PRETTY NAÏVE QUESTION.
"WHAT DOES IT MEAN TO KNOCK OVER THE PINS?"
SO I DECIDE TO ENGRAVE FACES AND CALL THE PINS "VILLAINS."
TO MY SURPRISE, IT CATCHES ON QUICK WITH THE VILLAGERS.
MURDERER
PYROMANIAC
CON ARTIST
I CAN'T GET THE MURDERER ON THE RIGHT NO MATTER WHAT I DO!
ぐぬぬ
GRR!
THE PYROMANIAC ON THE LEFT IS MORE DIFFICULT, DON'T YOU THINK?
WAHAHA. IT MAY BE HARD FOR HIGH ELVES...
BUT TAKE A LOOK AT THIS SWING!
シュバッ
FWISH
PFFT. YOU DIDN'T HIT THE PYROMANIAC OR THE CON ARTIST.
NRH! WHAT IS THE MEANING OF THIS?!
BUT I KEPT CALM AND AIMED FOR THE EDGE OF THE MURDERER...
CHATTER
LOOKS LIKE YOU MISSED BOTH OF THEM.
GREAT JOB, DWARF (LOL)!
CHATTER
GAH!
I'LL GET 'EM NEXT TIME! NEXT TIME, YA HEAR!
CHATTER
IT'S SO POPULAR THAT WE BUILD SIX LANES IN THE WINTER.

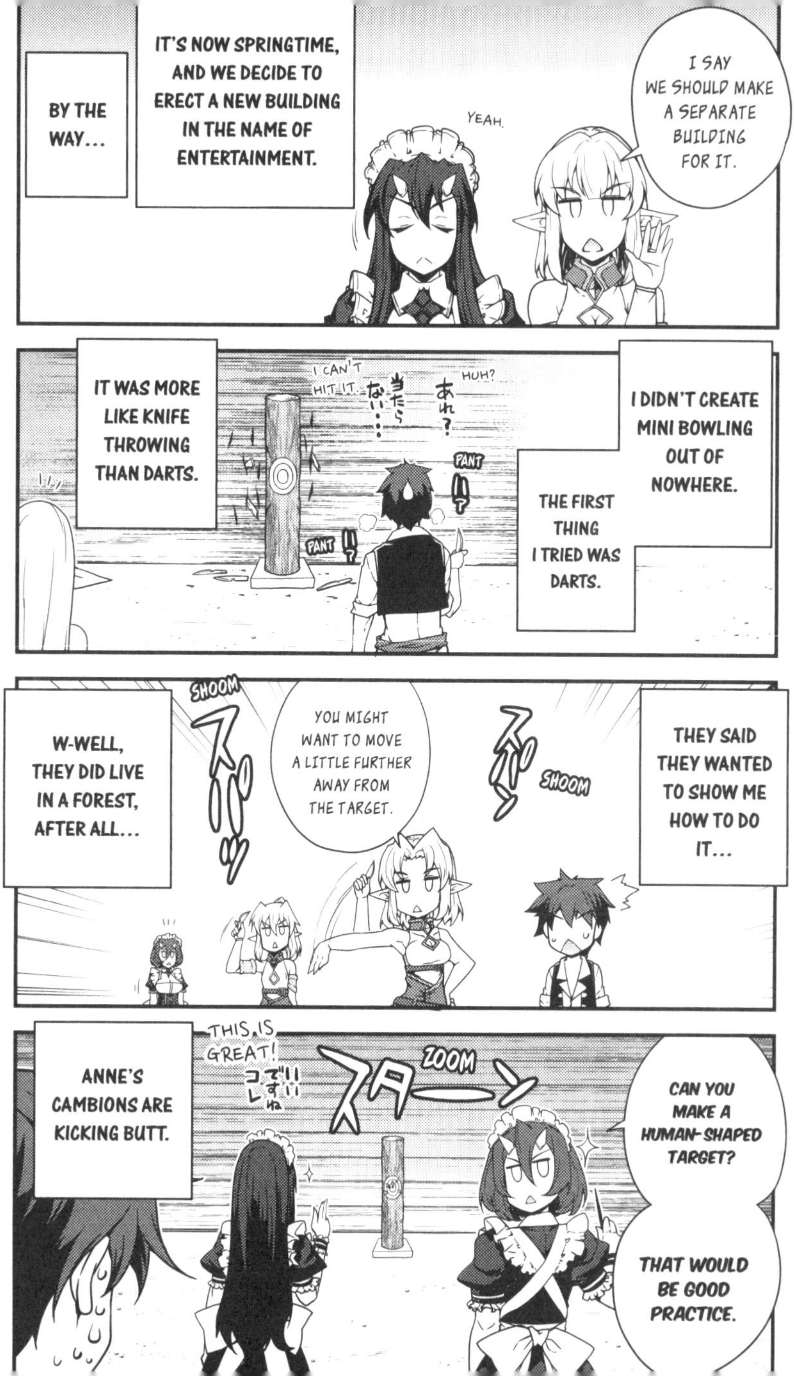

I SAY WE SHOULD MAKE A SEPARATE BUILDING FOR IT.
YEAH.
IT'S NOW SPRINGTIME, AND WE DECIDE TO ERECT A NEW BUILDING IN THE NAME OF ENTERTAINMENT.
BY THE WAY...
I DIDN'T CREATE MINI BOWLING OUT OF NOWHERE.
THE FIRST THING I TRIED WAS DARTS.
HUH?
あれ？
PANT
PANT
I CAN'T HIT IT.
当たらない・・・
IT WAS MORE LIKE KNIFE THROWING THAN DARTS.
THEY SAID THEY WANTED TO SHOW ME HOW TO DO IT...
SHOOM
YOU MIGHT WANT TO MOVE A LITTLE FURTHER AWAY FROM THE TARGET.
SHOOM
W-WELL, THEY DID LIVE IN A FOREST, AFTER ALL...
CAN YOU MAKE A HUMAN-SHAPED TARGET?
THAT WOULD BE GOOD PRACTICE.
ZOOM
THIS IS GREAT!
いいですねコレ
ANNE'S CAMBIONS ARE KICKING BUTT.

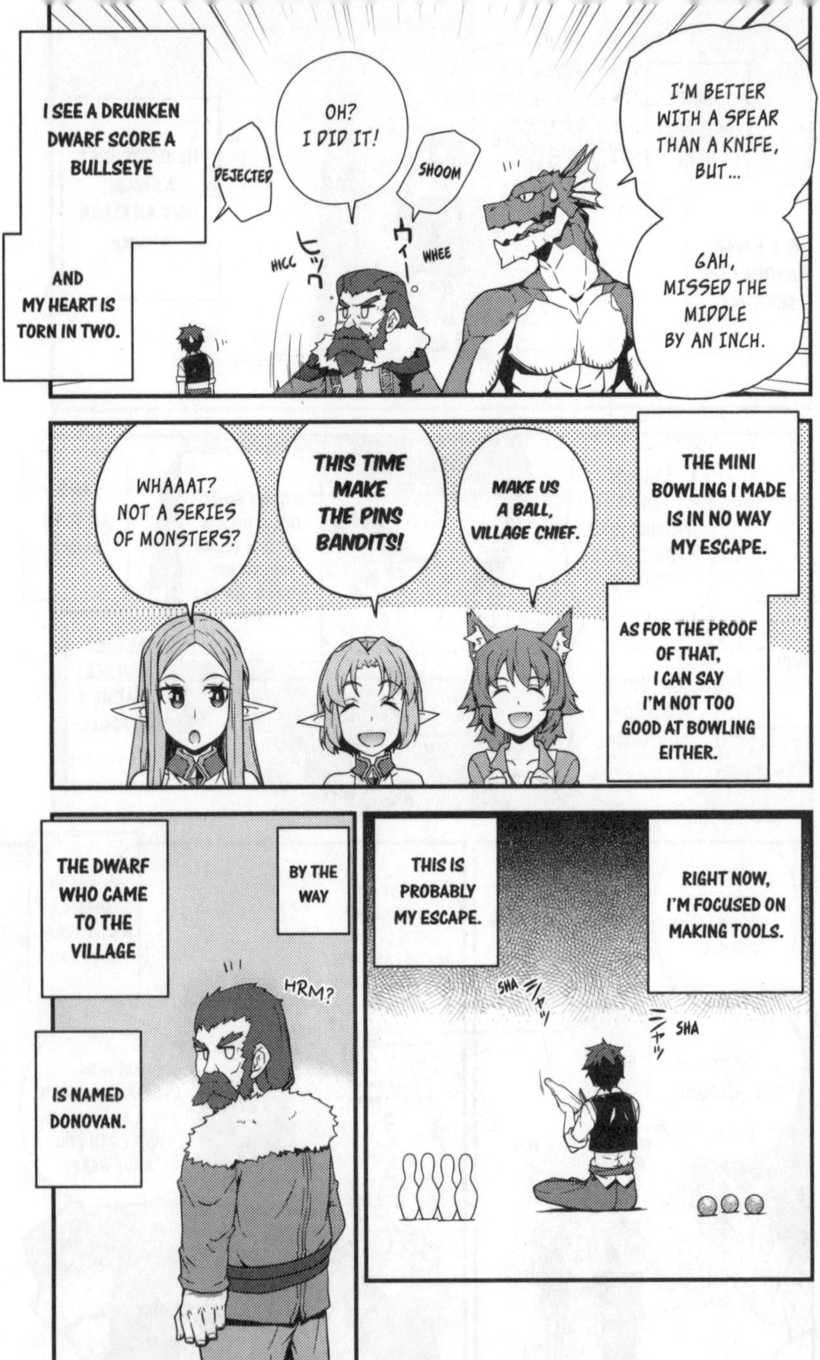

I'M BETTER WITH A SPEAR THAN A KNIFE, BUT...
GAH, MISSED THE MIDDLE BY AN INCH.
SHOOM
WHEE
OH? I DID IT!
HICC
DEJECTED
I SEE A DRUNKEN DWARF SCORE A BULLSEYE
AND MY HEART IS TORN IN TWO.
THE MINI BOWLING I MADE IS IN NO WAY MY ESCAPE.
AS FOR THE PROOF OF THAT, I CAN SAY I'M NOT TOO GOOD AT BOWLING EITHER.
MAKE US A BALL, VILLAGE CHIEF.
THIS TIME MAKE THE PINS BANDITS!
WHAAAT? NOT A SERIES OF MONSTERS?
RIGHT NOW, I'M FOCUSED ON MAKING TOOLS.
THIS IS PROBABLY MY ESCAPE.
SHA
SHA
BY THE WAY
THE DWARF WHO CAME TO THE VILLAGE
HRM?
IS NAMED DONOVAN.

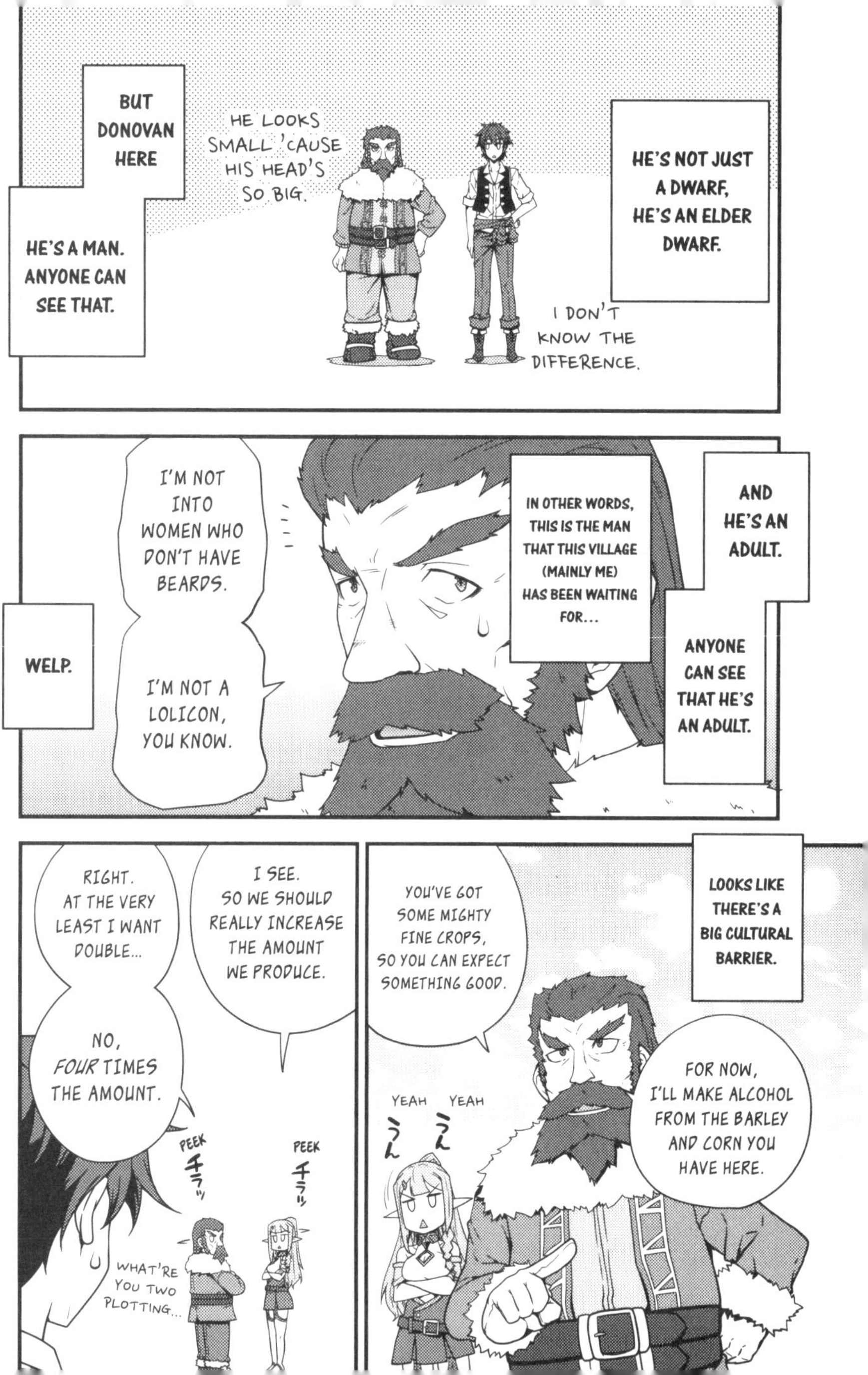
HE'S NOT JUST A DWARF, HE'S AN ELDER DWARF.
I DON'T KNOW THE DIFFERENCE.
HE LOOKS SMALL 'CAUSE HIS HEAD'S SO BIG.
BUT DONOVAN HERE
HE'S A MAN. ANYONE CAN SEE THAT.
AND HE'S AN ADULT.
ANYONE CAN SEE THAT HE'S AN ADULT.
IN OTHER WORDS, THIS IS THE MAN THAT THIS VILLAGE (MAINLY ME) HAS BEEN WAITING FOR...
I'M NOT INTO WOMEN WHO DON'T HAVE BEARDS.
I'M NOT A LOLICON, YOU KNOW.
WELP.
LOOKS LIKE THERE'S A BIG CULTURAL BARRIER.
FOR NOW, I'LL MAKE ALCOHOL FROM THE BARLEY AND CORN YOU HAVE HERE.
YOU'VE GOT SOME MIGHTY FINE CROPS, SO YOU CAN EXPECT SOMETHING GOOD.
YEAH うん
YEAH うん
I SEE. SO WE SHOULD REALLY INCREASE THE AMOUNT WE PRODUCE.
RIGHT. AT THE VERY LEAST I WANT DOUBLE...
NO, *FOUR* TIMES THE AMOUNT.
PEEK チラッ
PEEK チラッ
WHAT'RE YOU TWO PLOTTING...

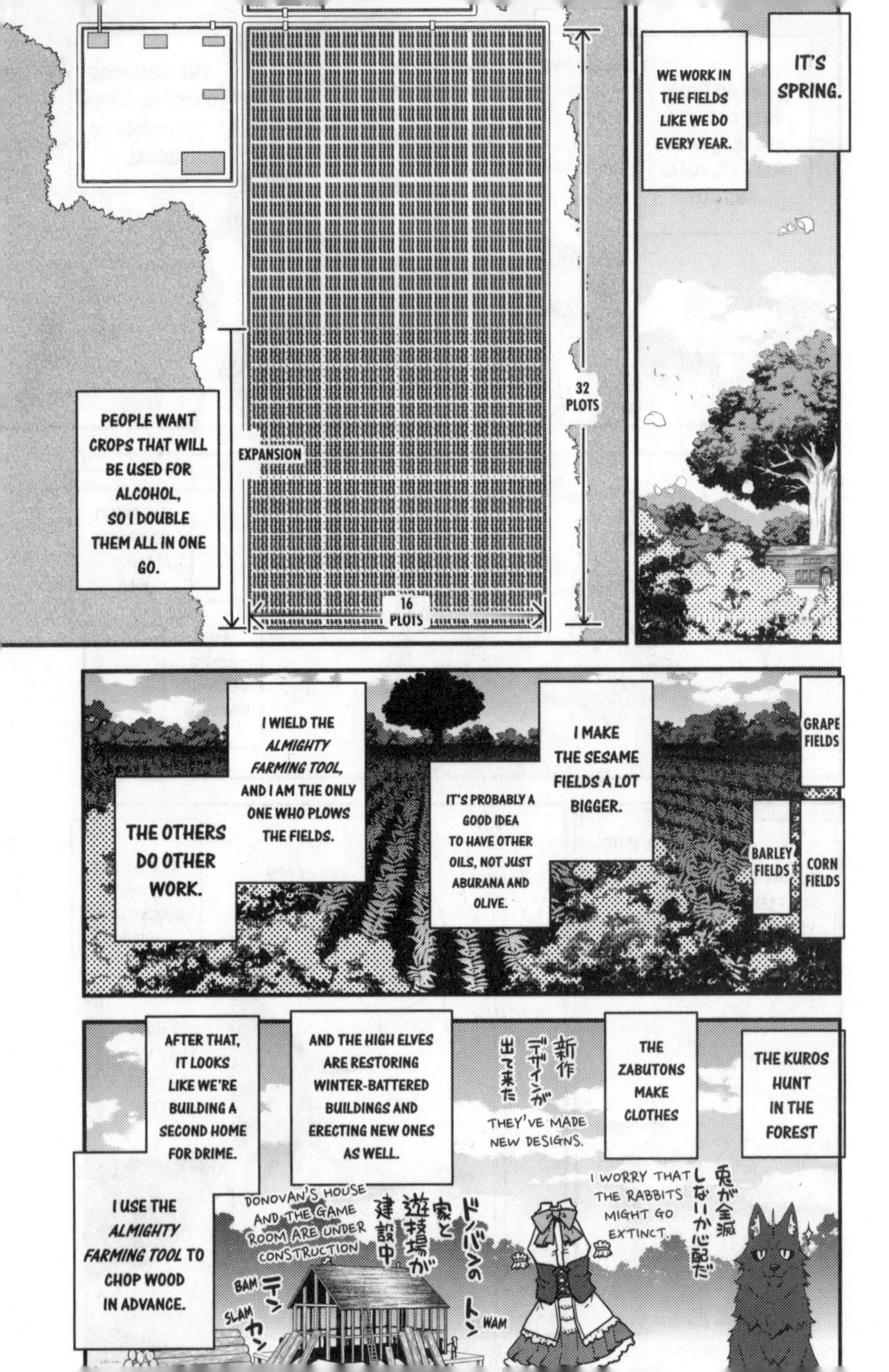
IT'S SPRING.
WE WORK IN THE FIELDS LIKE WE DO EVERY YEAR.
32 PLOTS
EXPANSION
16 PLOTS
PEOPLE WANT CROPS THAT WILL BE USED FOR ALCOHOL, SO I DOUBLE THEM ALL IN ONE GO.
GRAPE FIELDS
CORN FIELDS
BARLEY FIELDS
I MAKE THE SESAME FIELDS A LOT BIGGER.
IT'S PROBABLY A GOOD IDEA TO HAVE OTHER OILS, NOT JUST ABURANA AND OLIVE.
I WIELD THE ALMIGHTY FARMING TOOL, AND I AM THE ONLY ONE WHO PLOWS THE FIELDS.
THE OTHERS DO OTHER WORK.
THE KUROS HUNT IN THE FOREST
兎が全滅しないか心配だ
I WORRY THAT THE RABBITS MIGHT GO EXTINCT
THE ZABUTONS MAKE CLOTHES
新作デザインが出て来た
THEY'VE MADE NEW DESIGNS.
AND THE HIGH ELVES ARE RESTORING WINTER-BATTERED BUILDINGS AND ERECTING NEW ONES AS WELL.
ドノバンの家と遊技場が建設中
DONOVAN'S HOUSE AND THE GAME ROOM ARE UNDER CONSTRUCTION
トン
WAM
AFTER THAT, IT LOOKS LIKE WE'RE BUILDING A SECOND HOME FOR DRIME.
テン
BAM
カン
SLAM
I USE THE ALMIGHTY FARMING TOOL TO CHOP WOOD IN ADVANCE.

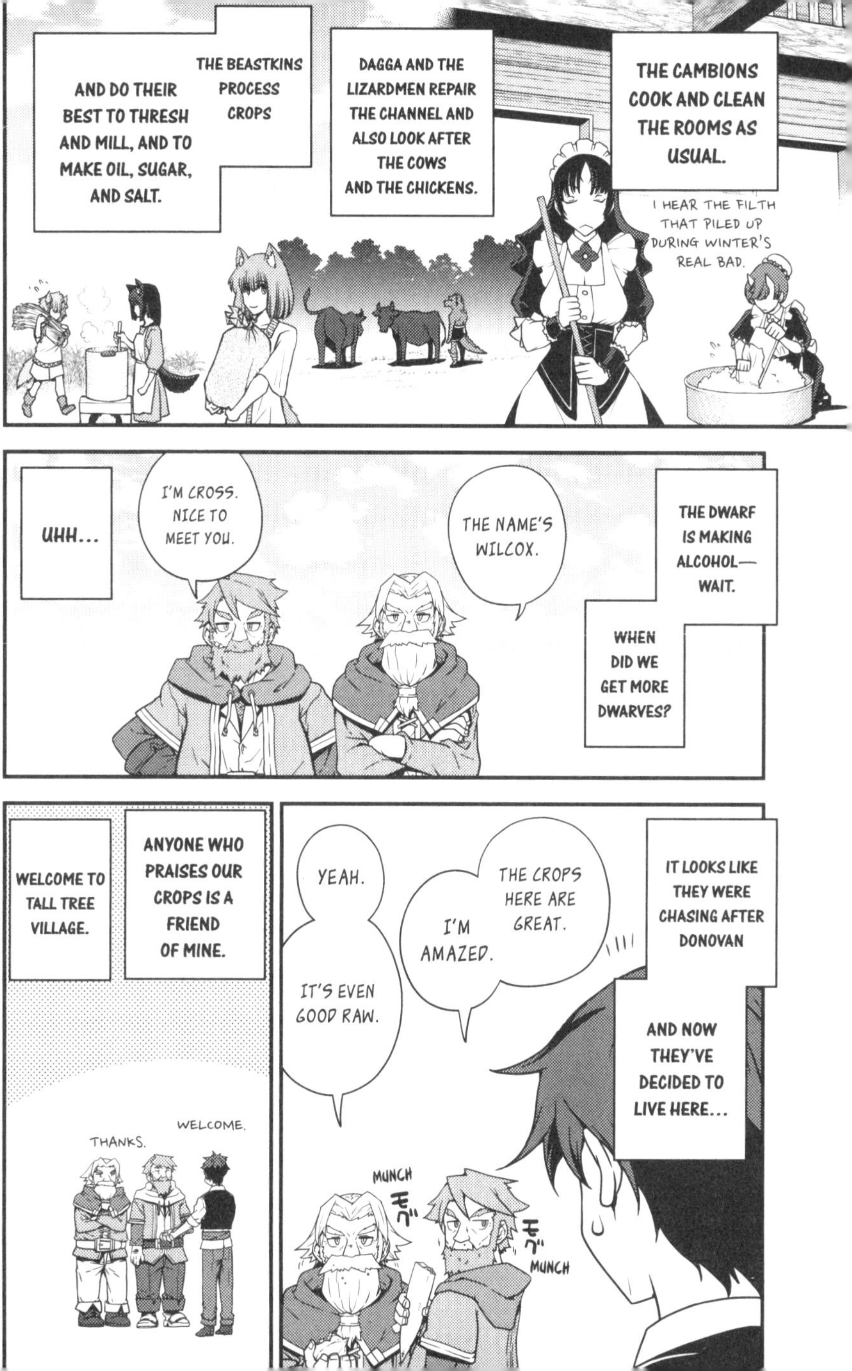
THE CAMBIONS COOK AND CLEAN THE ROOMS AS USUAL.
I HEAR THE FILTH THAT PILED UP DURING WINTER'S REAL BAD.
DAGGA AND THE LIZARDMEN REPAIR THE CHANNEL AND ALSO LOOK AFTER THE COWS AND THE CHICKENS.
THE BEASTKINS PROCESS CROPS
AND DO THEIR BEST TO THRESH AND MILL, AND TO MAKE OIL, SUGAR, AND SALT.
THE DWARF IS MAKING ALCOHOL— WAIT.
WHEN DID WE GET MORE DWARVES?
THE NAME'S WILCOX.
I'M CROSS. NICE TO MEET YOU.
UHH...
IT LOOKS LIKE THEY WERE CHASING AFTER DONOVAN
AND NOW THEY'VE DECIDED TO LIVE HERE...
THE CROPS HERE ARE GREAT.
I'M AMAZED.
YEAH.
IT'S EVEN GOOD RAW.
モグ MUNCH
モグ MUNCH
ANYONE WHO PRAISES OUR CROPS IS A FRIEND OF MINE.
WELCOME TO TALL TREE VILLAGE.
WELCOME.
THANKS.

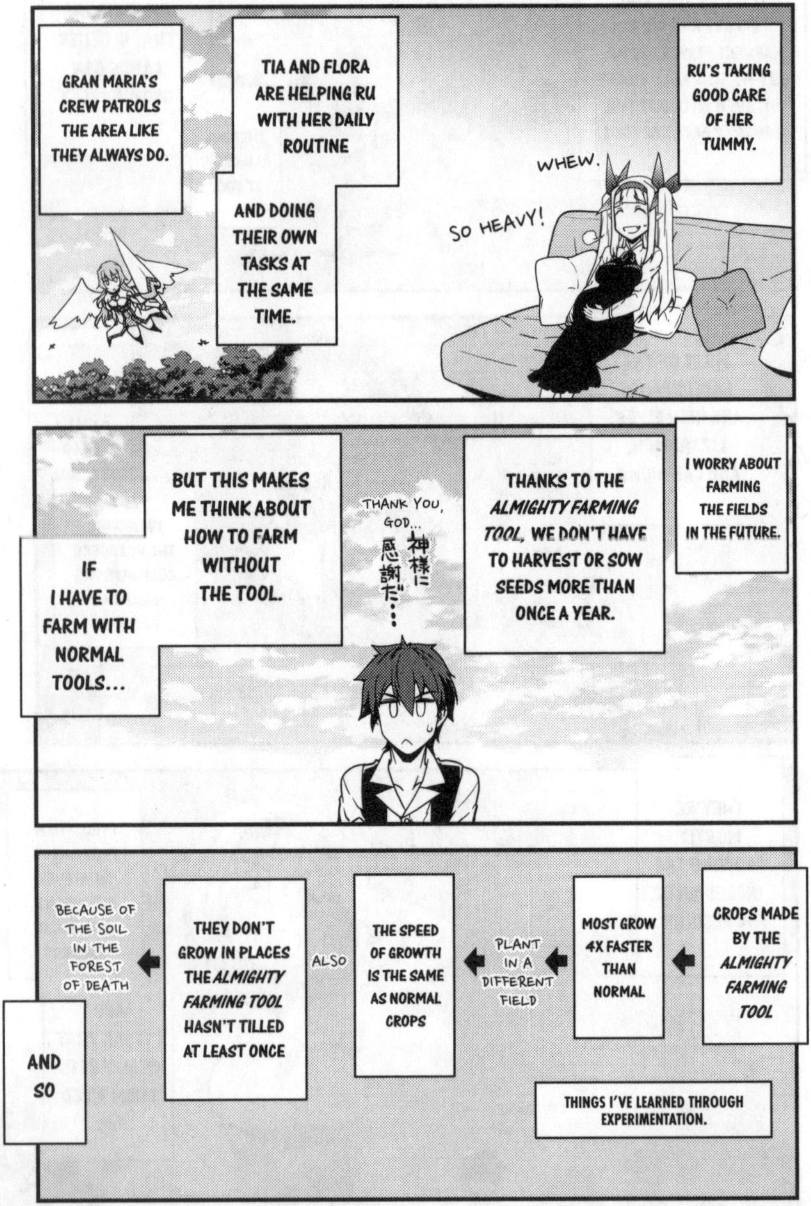
RU'S TAKING GOOD CARE OF HER TUMMY.
WHEW.
SO HEAVY!
TIA AND FLORA ARE HELPING RU WITH HER DAILY ROUTINE
AND DOING THEIR OWN TASKS AT THE SAME TIME.
GRAN MARIA'S CREW PATROLS THE AREA LIKE THEY ALWAYS DO.
I WORRY ABOUT FARMING THE FIELDS IN THE FUTURE.
THANKS TO THE ALMIGHTY FARMING TOOL, WE DON'T HAVE TO HARVEST OR SOW SEEDS MORE THAN ONCE A YEAR.
THANK YOU, GOD...
神様に感謝だ…
BUT THIS MAKES ME THINK ABOUT HOW TO FARM WITHOUT THE TOOL.
IF I HAVE TO FARM WITH NORMAL TOOLS...
THINGS I'VE LEARNED THROUGH EXPERIMENTATION.
CROPS MADE BY THE ALMIGHTY FARMING TOOL
MOST GROW 4X FASTER THAN NORMAL
PLANT IN A DIFFERENT FIELD
THE SPEED OF GROWTH IS THE SAME AS NORMAL CROPS
ALSO
THEY DON'T GROW IN PLACES THE ALMIGHTY FARMING TOOL HASN'T TILLED AT LEAST ONCE
BECAUSE OF THE SOIL IN THE FOREST OF DEATH
AND SO

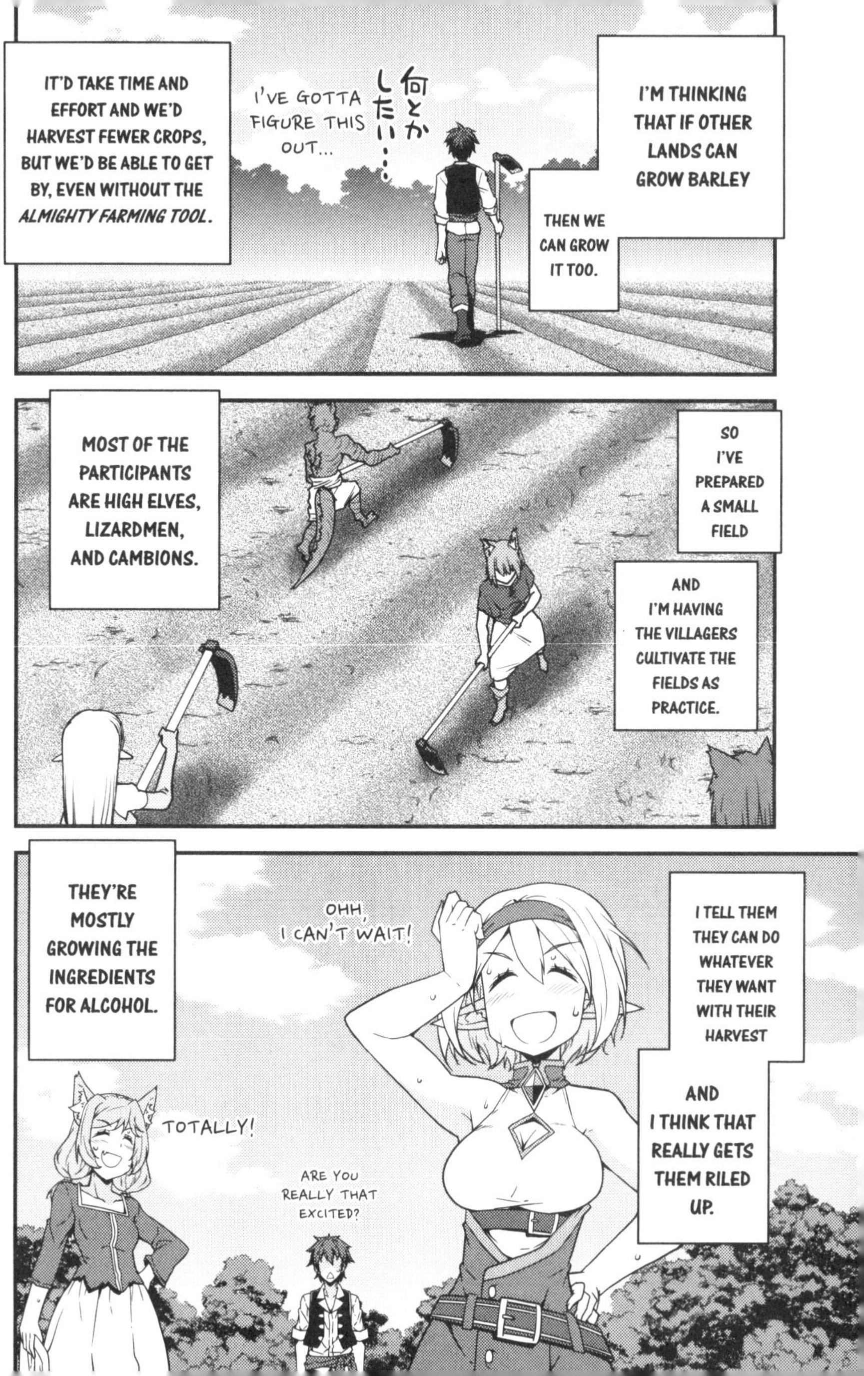
I'M THINKING THAT IF OTHER LANDS CAN GROW BARLEY
THEN WE CAN GROW IT TOO.
何とかしたい…
I'VE GOTTA FIGURE THIS OUT...
IT'D TAKE TIME AND EFFORT AND WE'D HARVEST FEWER CROPS, BUT WE'D BE ABLE TO GET BY, EVEN WITHOUT THE *ALMIGHTY FARMING TOOL*.
SO I'VE PREPARED A SMALL FIELD
AND I'M HAVING THE VILLAGERS CULTIVATE THE FIELDS AS PRACTICE.
MOST OF THE PARTICIPANTS ARE HIGH ELVES, LIZARDMEN, AND CAMBIONS.
I TELL THEM THEY CAN DO WHATEVER THEY WANT WITH THEIR HARVEST
AND I THINK THAT REALLY GETS THEM RILED UP.
OHH, I CAN'T WAIT!
THEY'RE MOSTLY GROWING THE INGREDIENTS FOR ALCOHOL.
TOTALLY!
ARE YOU REALLY THAT EXCITED?

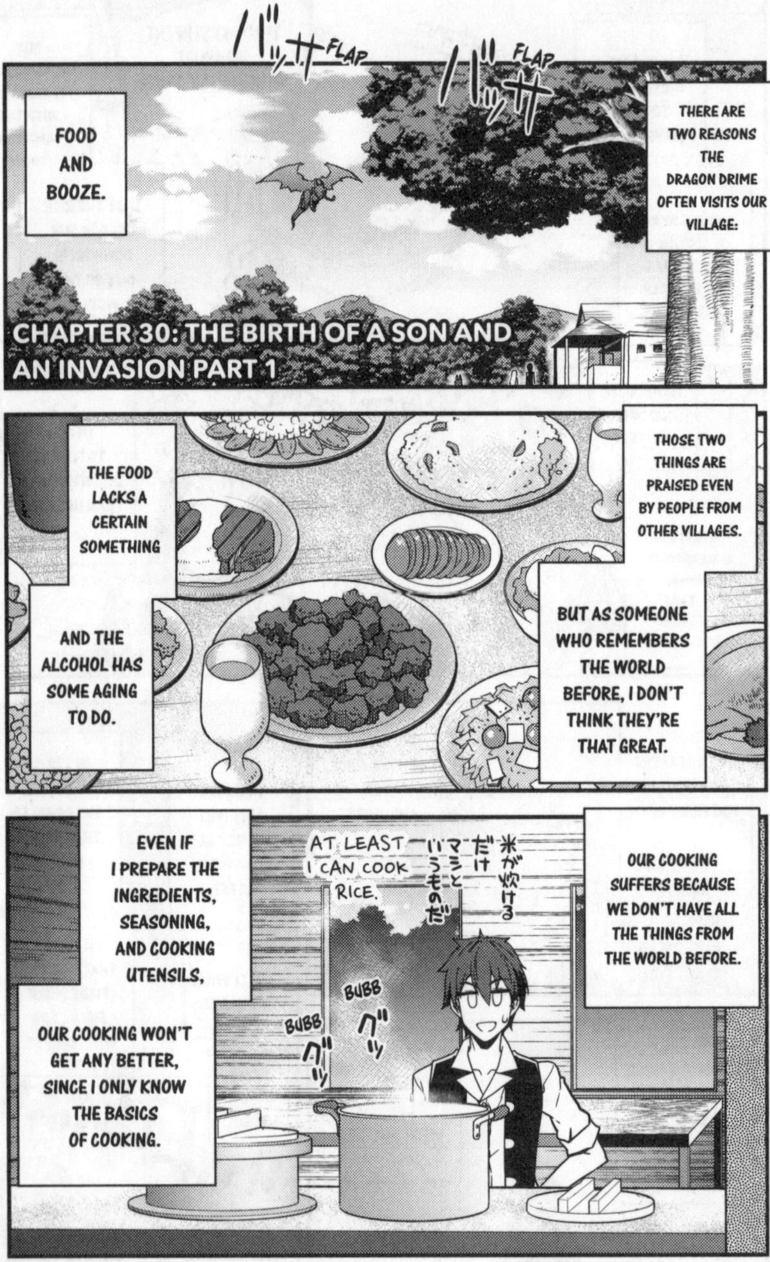
FLAP バッサ
FLAP バッサ
THERE ARE TWO REASONS THE DRAGON DRIME OFTEN VISITS OUR VILLAGE:
FOOD AND BOOZE.
CHAPTER 30: THE BIRTH OF A SON AND AN INVASION PART 1
THOSE TWO THINGS ARE PRAISED EVEN BY PEOPLE FROM OTHER VILLAGES.
BUT AS SOMEONE WHO REMEMBERS THE WORLD BEFORE, I DON'T THINK THEY'RE THAT GREAT.
THE FOOD LACKS A CERTAIN SOMETHING
AND THE ALCOHOL HAS SOME AGING TO DO.
OUR COOKING SUFFERS BECAUSE WE DON'T HAVE ALL THE THINGS FROM THE WORLD BEFORE.
米が炊けるだけマシというものだ
AT LEAST I CAN COOK RICE.
EVEN IF I PREPARE THE INGREDIENTS, SEASONING, AND COOKING UTENSILS,
BUBB グツ
BUBB グツ
OUR COOKING WON'T GET ANY BETTER, SINCE I ONLY KNOW THE BASICS OF COOKING.

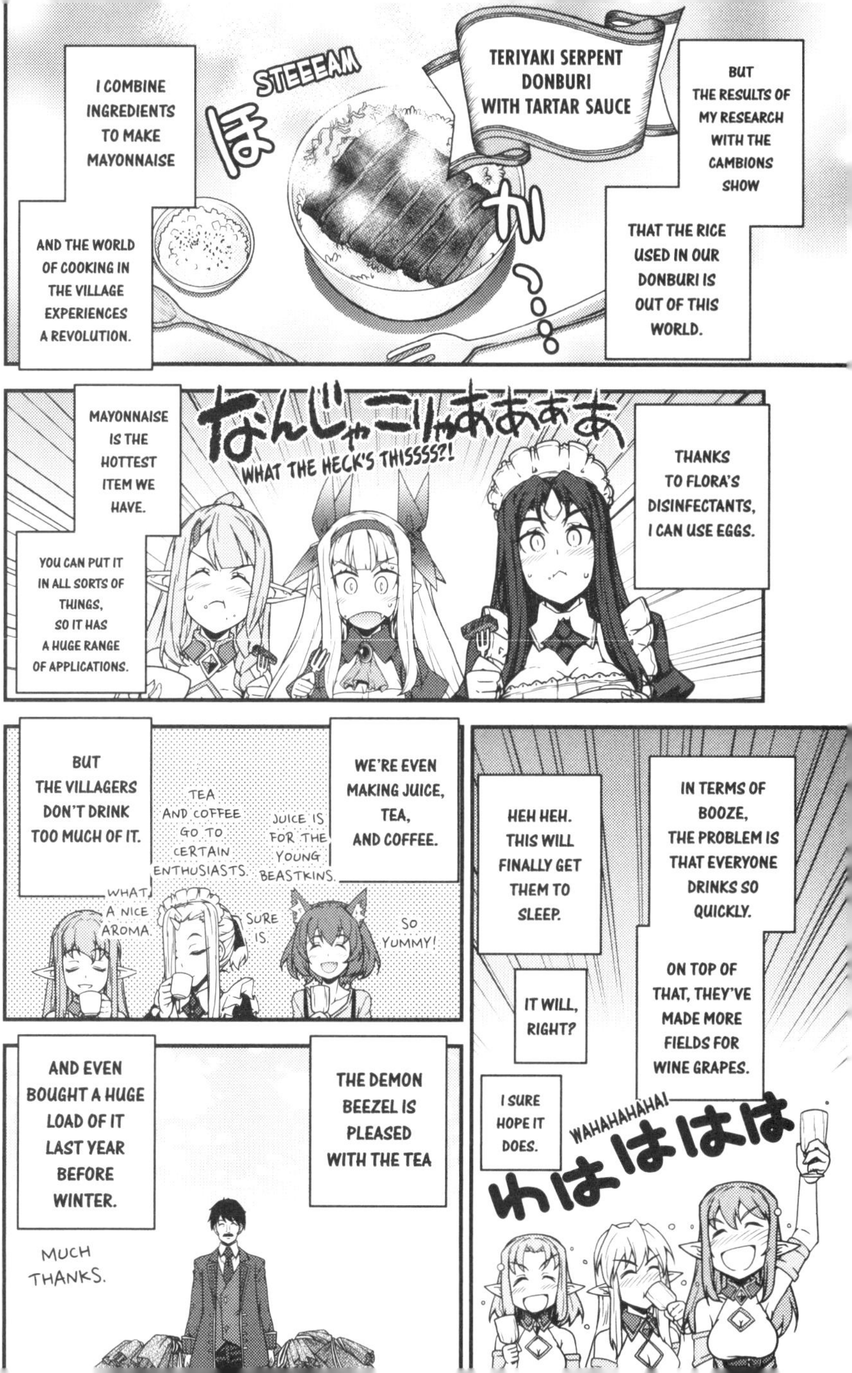
BUT THE RESULTS OF MY RESEARCH WITH THE CAMBIONS SHOW
THAT THE RICE USED IN OUR DONBURI IS OUT OF THIS WORLD.
TERIYAKI SERPENT DONBURI WITH TARTAR SAUCE
かっ
ほ
STEEEAM
I COMBINE INGREDIENTS TO MAKE MAYONNAISE
AND THE WORLD OF COOKING IN THE VILLAGE EXPERIENCES A REVOLUTION.
THANKS TO FLORA'S DISINFECTANTS, I CAN USE EGGS.
なんじゃこりゃあああああ
WHAT THE HECK'S THISSSS?!
MAYONNAISE IS THE HOTTEST ITEM WE HAVE.
YOU CAN PUT IT IN ALL SORTS OF THINGS, SO IT HAS A HUGE RANGE OF APPLICATIONS.
IN TERMS OF BOOZE, THE PROBLEM IS THAT EVERYONE DRINKS SO QUICKLY.
HEH HEH. THIS WILL FINALLY GET THEM TO SLEEP.
ON TOP OF THAT, THEY'VE MADE MORE FIELDS FOR WINE GRAPES.
IT WILL, RIGHT?
I SURE HOPE IT DOES.
わははははは
WAHAHAHAHA!
WE'RE EVEN MAKING JUICE, TEA, AND COFFEE.
JUICE IS FOR THE YOUNG BEASTKINS.
TEA AND COFFEE GO TO CERTAIN ENTHUSIASTS.
BUT THE VILLAGERS DON'T DRINK TOO MUCH OF IT.
SO YUMMY!
SURE IS.
WHAT A NICE AROMA.
THE DEMON BEEZEL IS PLEASED WITH THE TEA
AND EVEN BOUGHT A HUGE LOAD OF IT LAST YEAR BEFORE WINTER.
MUCH THANKS.

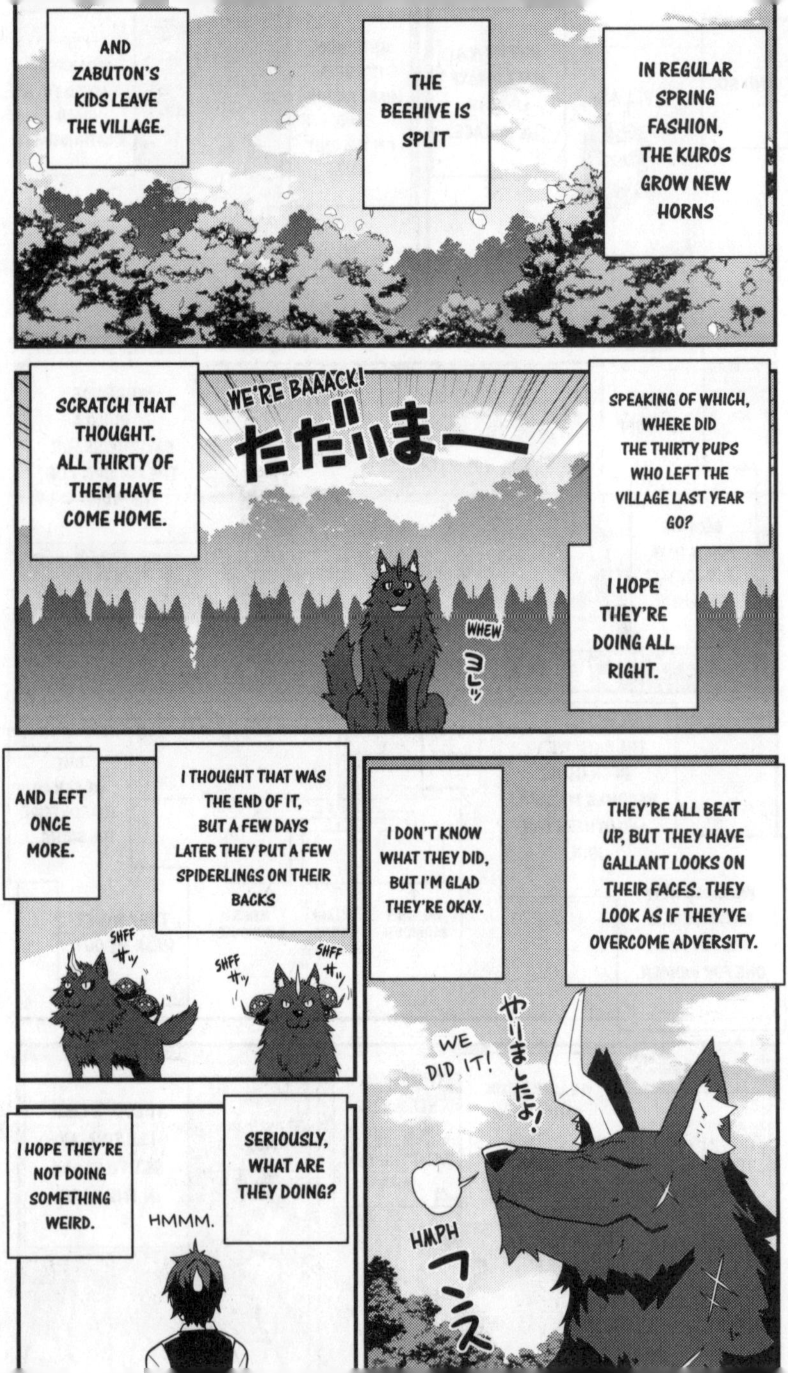
IN REGULAR SPRING FASHION, THE KUROS GROW NEW HORNS
THE BEEHIVE IS SPLIT
AND ZABUTON'S KIDS LEAVE THE VILLAGE.
SPEAKING OF WHICH, WHERE DID THE THIRTY PUPS WHO LEFT THE VILLAGE LAST YEAR GO?
I HOPE THEY'RE DOING ALL RIGHT.
WE'RE BAAACK!
ただいまー
WHEW
ヨレッ
SCRATCH THAT THOUGHT. ALL THIRTY OF THEM HAVE COME HOME.
THEY'RE ALL BEAT UP, BUT THEY HAVE GALLANT LOOKS ON THEIR FACES. THEY LOOK AS IF THEY'VE OVERCOME ADVERSITY.
I DON'T KNOW WHAT THEY DID, BUT I'M GLAD THEY'RE OKAY.
WE DID IT!
やりましたよ!
HMPH
フンス
I THOUGHT THAT WAS THE END OF IT, BUT A FEW DAYS LATER THEY PUT A FEW SPIDERLINGS ON THEIR BACKS
AND LEFT ONCE MORE.
SHFF
サッ
SHFF
サッ
SHFF
サッ
SERIOUSLY, WHAT ARE THEY DOING?
I HOPE THEY'RE NOT DOING SOMETHING WEIRD.
HMMM.

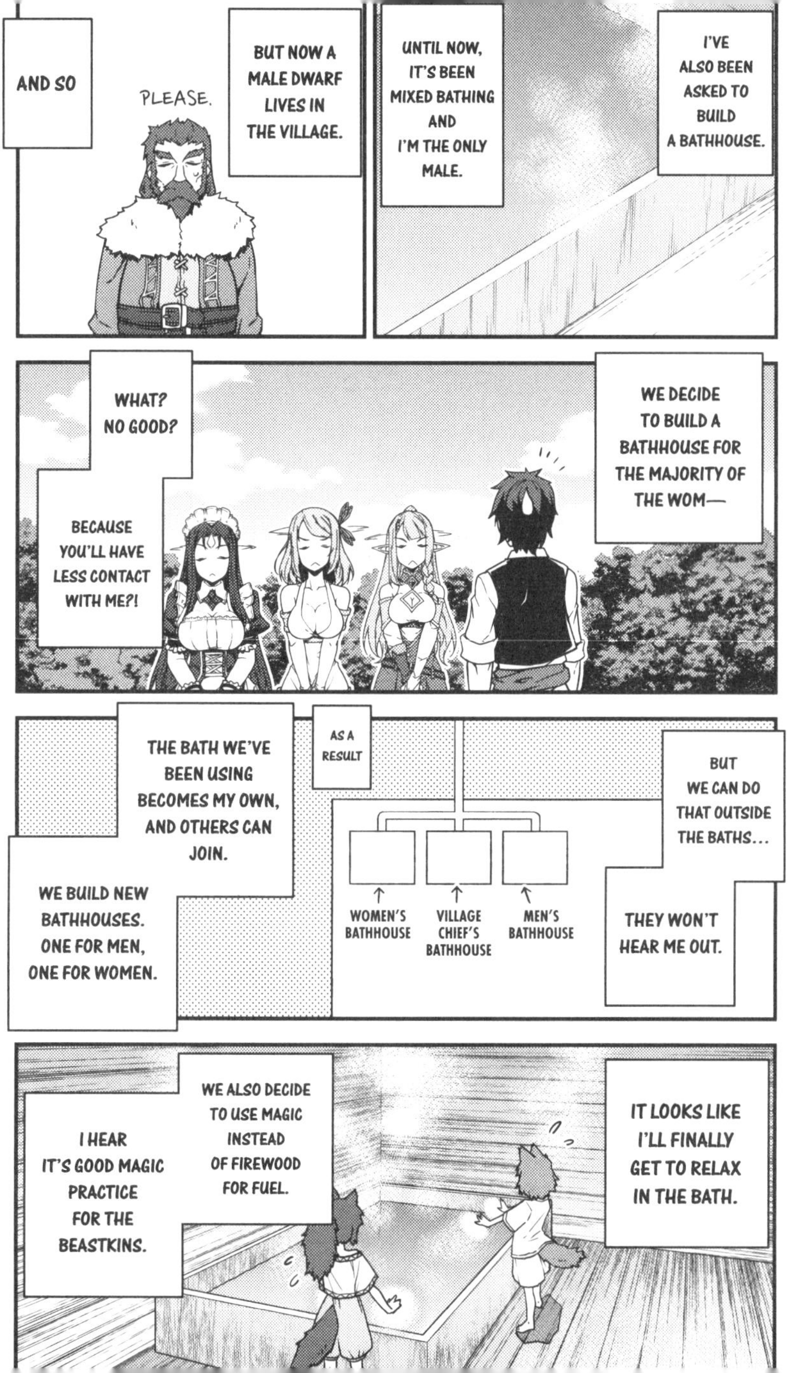

I'VE ALSO BEEN ASKED TO BUILD A BATHHOUSE.
UNTIL NOW, IT'S BEEN MIXED BATHING AND I'M THE ONLY MALE.
BUT NOW A MALE DWARF LIVES IN THE VILLAGE.
PLEASE.
AND SO
WE DECIDE TO BUILD A BATHHOUSE FOR THE MAJORITY OF THE WOM—
WHAT? NO GOOD?
BECAUSE YOU'LL HAVE LESS CONTACT WITH ME?!
BUT WE CAN DO THAT OUTSIDE THE BATHS...
THEY WON'T HEAR ME OUT.
AS A RESULT
MEN'S BATHHOUSE
VILLAGE CHIEF'S BATHHOUSE
WOMEN'S BATHHOUSE
THE BATH WE'VE BEEN USING BECOMES MY OWN, AND OTHERS CAN JOIN.
WE BUILD NEW BATHHOUSES. ONE FOR MEN, ONE FOR WOMEN.
IT LOOKS LIKE I'LL FINALLY GET TO RELAX IN THE BATH.
WE ALSO DECIDE TO USE MAGIC INSTEAD OF FIREWOOD FOR FUEL.
I HEAR IT'S GOOD MAGIC PRACTICE FOR THE BEASTKINS.

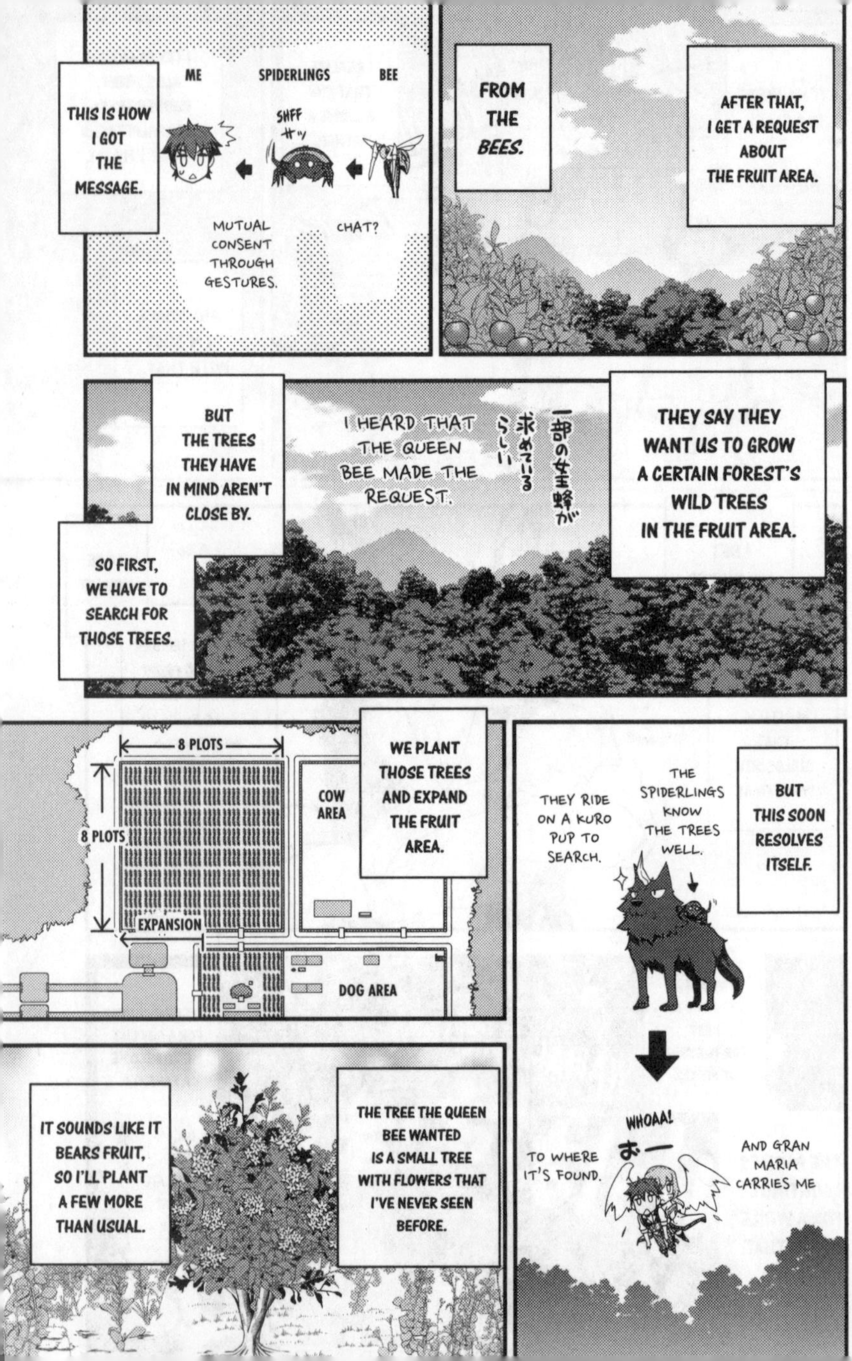
AFTER THAT, I GET A REQUEST ABOUT THE FRUIT AREA.
FROM THE BEES.
BEE
SPIDERLINGS
ME
SHFF
ガッ
CHAT?
MUTUAL CONSENT THROUGH GESTURES.
THIS IS HOW I GOT THE MESSAGE.
THEY SAY THEY WANT US TO GROW A CERTAIN FOREST'S WILD TREES IN THE FRUIT AREA.
一部の女王蜂が求めているらしい
I HEARD THAT THE QUEEN BEE MADE THE REQUEST.
BUT THE TREES THEY HAVE IN MIND AREN'T CLOSE BY.
SO FIRST, WE HAVE TO SEARCH FOR THOSE TREES.
BUT THIS SOON RESOLVES ITSELF.
THE SPIDERLINGS KNOW THE TREES WELL.
THEY RIDE ON A KURO PUP TO SEARCH.
AND GRAN MARIA CARRIES ME
WHOAA!
おー
TO WHERE IT'S FOUND.
WE PLANT THOSE TREES AND EXPAND THE FRUIT AREA.
8 PLOTS
8 PLOTS
COW AREA
EXPANSION
DOG AREA
THE TREE THE QUEEN BEE WANTED IS A SMALL TREE WITH FLOWERS THAT I'VE NEVER SEEN BEFORE.
IT SOUNDS LIKE IT BEARS FRUIT, SO I'LL PLANT A FEW MORE THAN USUAL.

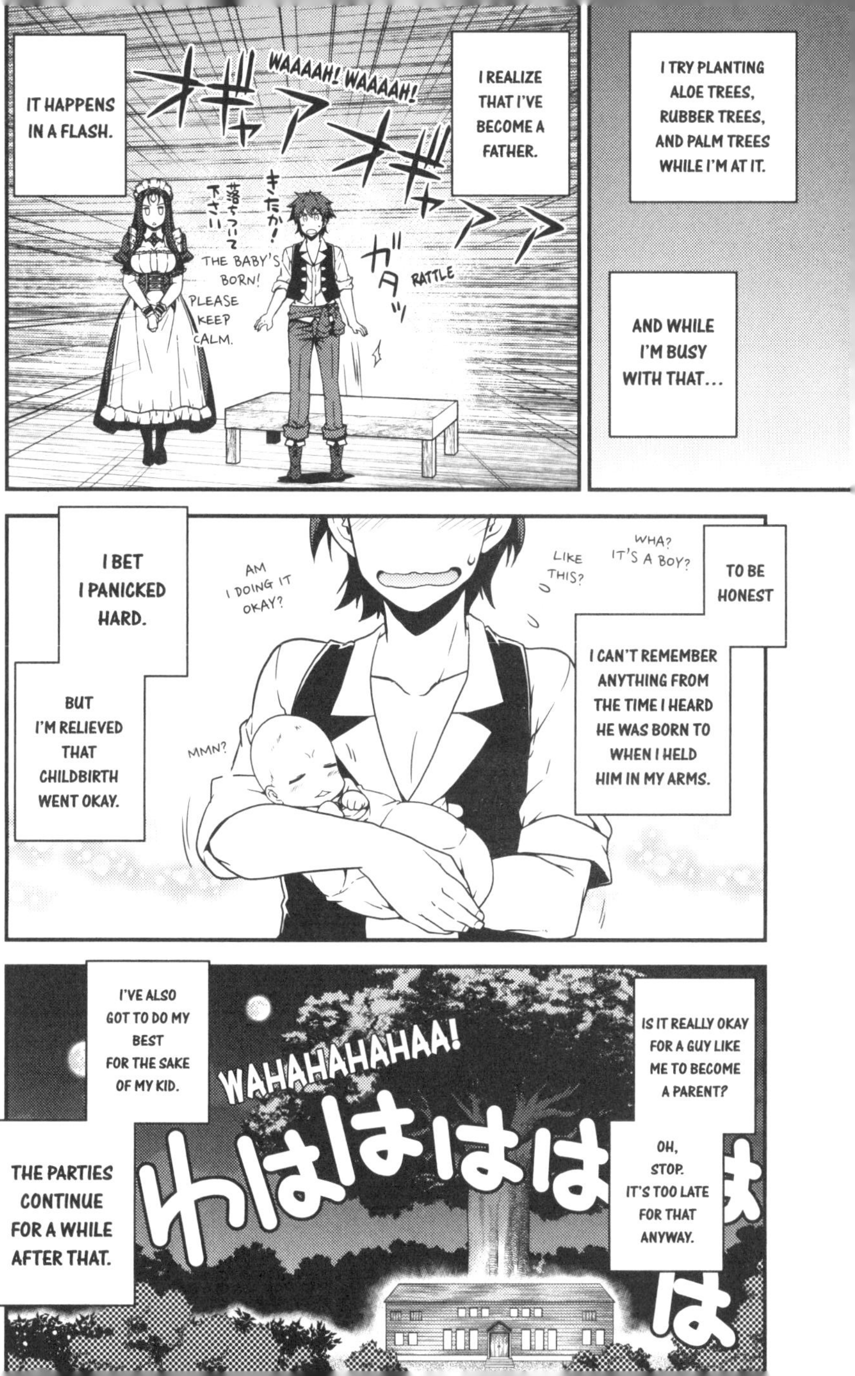

I TRY PLANTING ALOE TREES, RUBBER TREES, AND PALM TREES WHILE I'M AT IT.
AND WHILE I'M BUSY WITH THAT...
I REALIZE THAT I'VE BECOME A FATHER.
オギャアオギャアア
WAAAAH! WAAAAH!
ガタッ
RATTLE
きたか！
THE BABY'S BORN!
落ちついて下さい
PLEASE KEEP CALM.
IT HAPPENS IN A FLASH.
TO BE HONEST
I CAN'T REMEMBER ANYTHING FROM THE TIME I HEARD HE WAS BORN TO WHEN I HELD HIM IN MY ARMS.
WHA? IT'S A BOY?
LIKE THIS?
AM I DOING IT OKAY?
MMN?
I BET I PANICKED HARD.
BUT I'M RELIEVED THAT CHILDBIRTH WENT OKAY.
IS IT REALLY OKAY FOR A GUY LIKE ME TO BECOME A PARENT?
OH, STOP. IT'S TOO LATE FOR THAT ANYWAY.
わはははははは
WAHAHAHAHAA!
I'VE ALSO GOT TO DO MY BEST FOR THE SAKE OF MY KID.
THE PARTIES CONTINUE FOR A WHILE AFTER THAT.

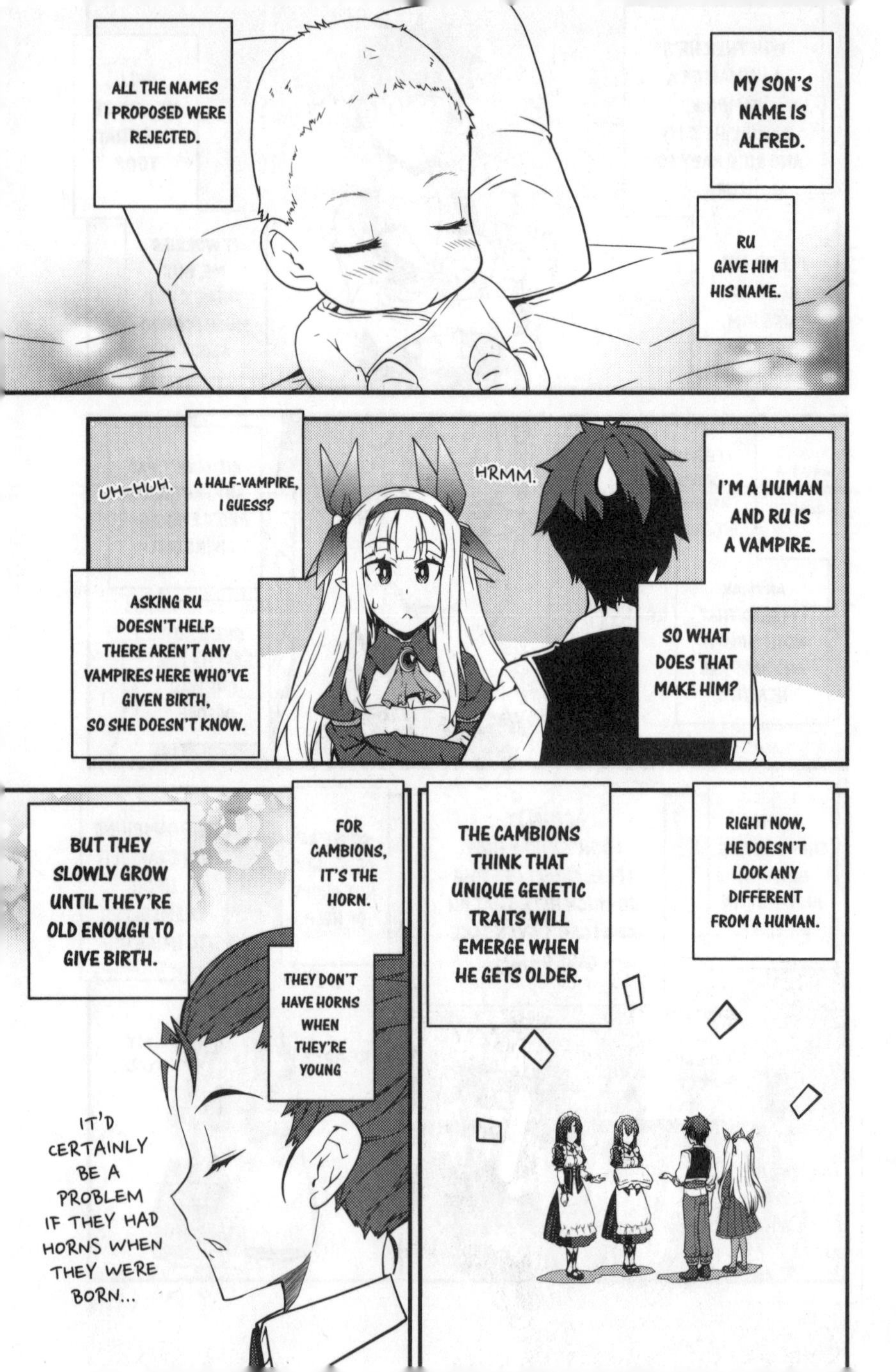
MY SON'S NAME IS ALFRED.
RU GAVE HIM HIS NAME.
ALL THE NAMES I PROPOSED WERE REJECTED.
I'M A HUMAN AND RU IS A VAMPIRE.
SO WHAT DOES THAT MAKE HIM?
HRMM.
A HALF-VAMPIRE, I GUESS?
UH-HUH.
ASKING RU DOESN'T HELP. THERE AREN'T ANY VAMPIRES HERE WHO'VE GIVEN BIRTH, SO SHE DOESN'T KNOW.
RIGHT NOW, HE DOESN'T LOOK ANY DIFFERENT FROM A HUMAN.
THE CAMBIONS THINK THAT UNIQUE GENETIC TRAITS WILL EMERGE WHEN HE GETS OLDER.
FOR CAMBIONS, IT'S THE HORN.
THEY DON'T HAVE HORNS WHEN THEY'RE YOUNG
BUT THEY SLOWLY GROW UNTIL THEY'RE OLD ENOUGH TO GIVE BIRTH.
IT'D CERTAINLY BE A PROBLEM IF THEY HAD HORNS WHEN THEY WERE BORN...

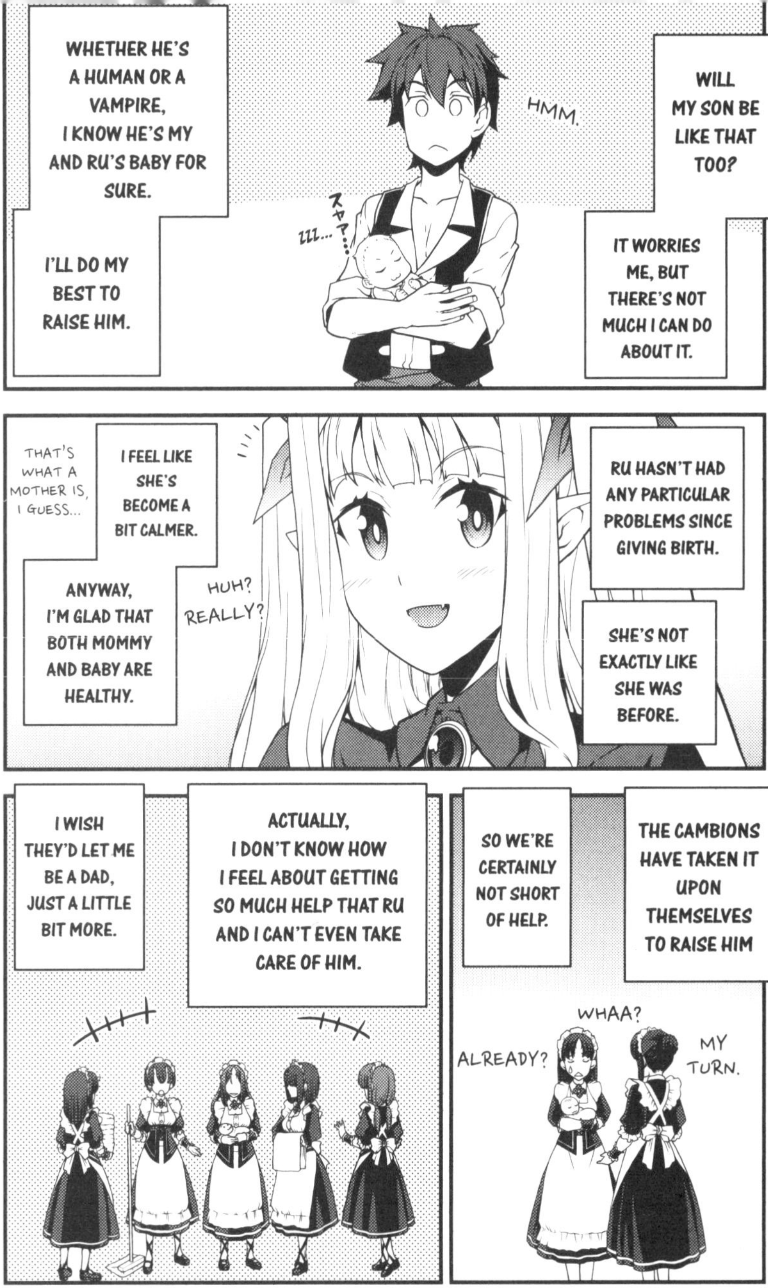
WILL MY SON BE LIKE THAT TOO?
HMM.
IT WORRIES ME, BUT THERE'S NOT MUCH I CAN DO ABOUT IT.
WHETHER HE'S A HUMAN OR A VAMPIRE, I KNOW HE'S MY AND RU'S BABY FOR SURE.
スヤァ…
ZZZ...
I'LL DO MY BEST TO RAISE HIM.
RU HASN'T HAD ANY PARTICULAR PROBLEMS SINCE GIVING BIRTH.
SHE'S NOT EXACTLY LIKE SHE WAS BEFORE.
HUH? REALLY?
I FEEL LIKE SHE'S BECOME A BIT CALMER.
THAT'S WHAT A MOTHER IS, I GUESS...
ANYWAY, I'M GLAD THAT BOTH MOMMY AND BABY ARE HEALTHY.
THE CAMBIONS HAVE TAKEN IT UPON THEMSELVES TO RAISE HIM
SO WE'RE CERTAINLY NOT SHORT OF HELP.
MY TURN.
WHAA?
ALREADY?
ACTUALLY, I DON'T KNOW HOW I FEEL ABOUT GETTING SO MUCH HELP THAT RU AND I CAN'T EVEN TAKE CARE OF HIM.
I WISH THEY'D LET ME BE A DAD, JUST A LITTLE BIT MORE.

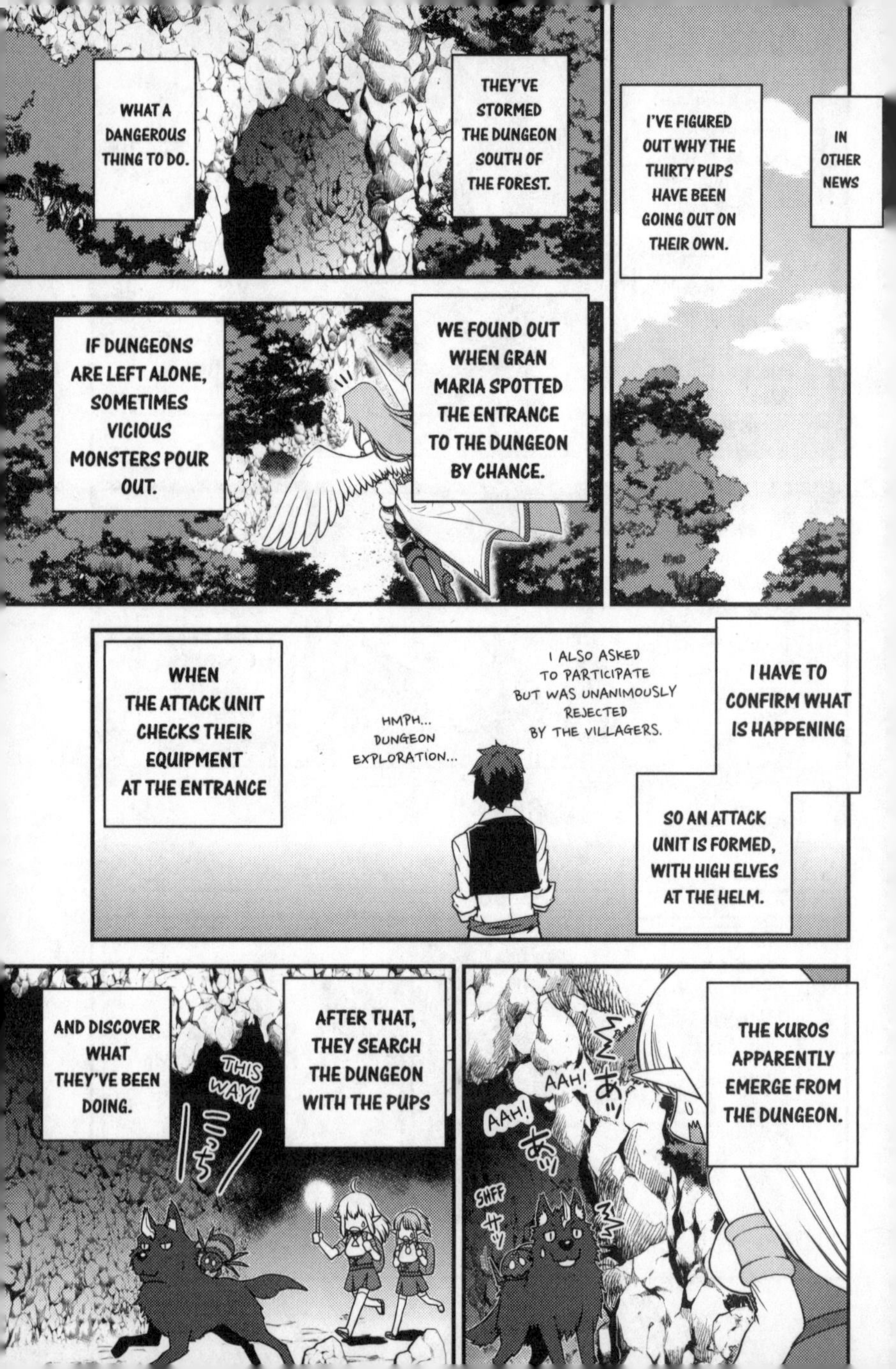

IN OTHER NEWS
I'VE FIGURED OUT WHY THE THIRTY PUPS HAVE BEEN GOING OUT ON THEIR OWN.
THEY'VE STORMED THE DUNGEON SOUTH OF THE FOREST.
WHAT A DANGEROUS THING TO DO.
WE FOUND OUT WHEN GRAN MARIA SPOTTED THE ENTRANCE TO THE DUNGEON BY CHANCE.
IF DUNGEONS ARE LEFT ALONE, SOMETIMES VICIOUS MONSTERS POUR OUT.
I HAVE TO CONFIRM WHAT IS HAPPENING
SO AN ATTACK UNIT IS FORMED, WITH HIGH ELVES AT THE HELM.
I ALSO ASKED TO PARTICIPATE BUT WAS UNANIMOUSLY REJECTED BY THE VILLAGERS.
HMPH... DUNGEON EXPLORATION...
WHEN THE ATTACK UNIT CHECKS THEIR EQUIPMENT AT THE ENTRANCE
THE KUROS APPARENTLY EMERGE FROM THE DUNGEON.
AAH! あッ
AAH! あッ
SHFF サッ
AFTER THAT, THEY SEARCH THE DUNGEON WITH THE PUPS
AND DISCOVER WHAT THEY'VE BEEN DOING.
THIS WAY! こっち

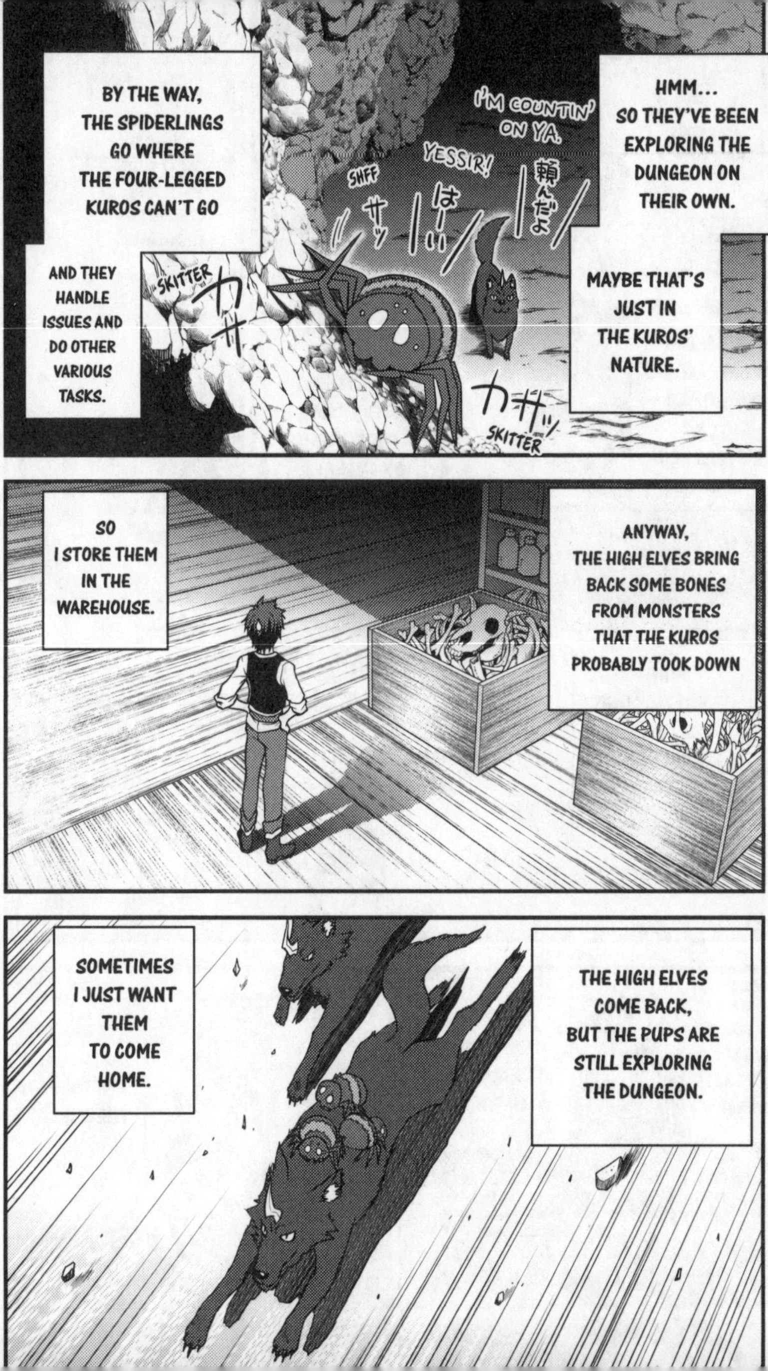
HMM... SO THEY'VE BEEN EXPLORING THE DUNGEON ON THEIR OWN.
MAYBE THAT'S JUST IN THE KUROS' NATURE.
I'M COUNTIN' ON YA.
頼んだよ
YESSIR!
はーい
SHFF
サッ
BY THE WAY, THE SPIDERLINGS GO WHERE THE FOUR-LEGGED KUROS CAN'T GO
AND THEY HANDLE ISSUES AND DO OTHER VARIOUS TASKS.
SKITTER
カサ
カサッ
SKITTER
ANYWAY, THE HIGH ELVES BRING BACK SOME BONES FROM MONSTERS THAT THE KUROS PROBABLY TOOK DOWN
SO I STORE THEM IN THE WAREHOUSE.
THE HIGH ELVES COME BACK, BUT THE PUPS ARE STILL EXPLORING THE DUNGEON.
SOMETIMES I JUST WANT THEM TO COME HOME.

CHAPTER 31: THE BIRTH OF A SON AND AN INVASION PART 2

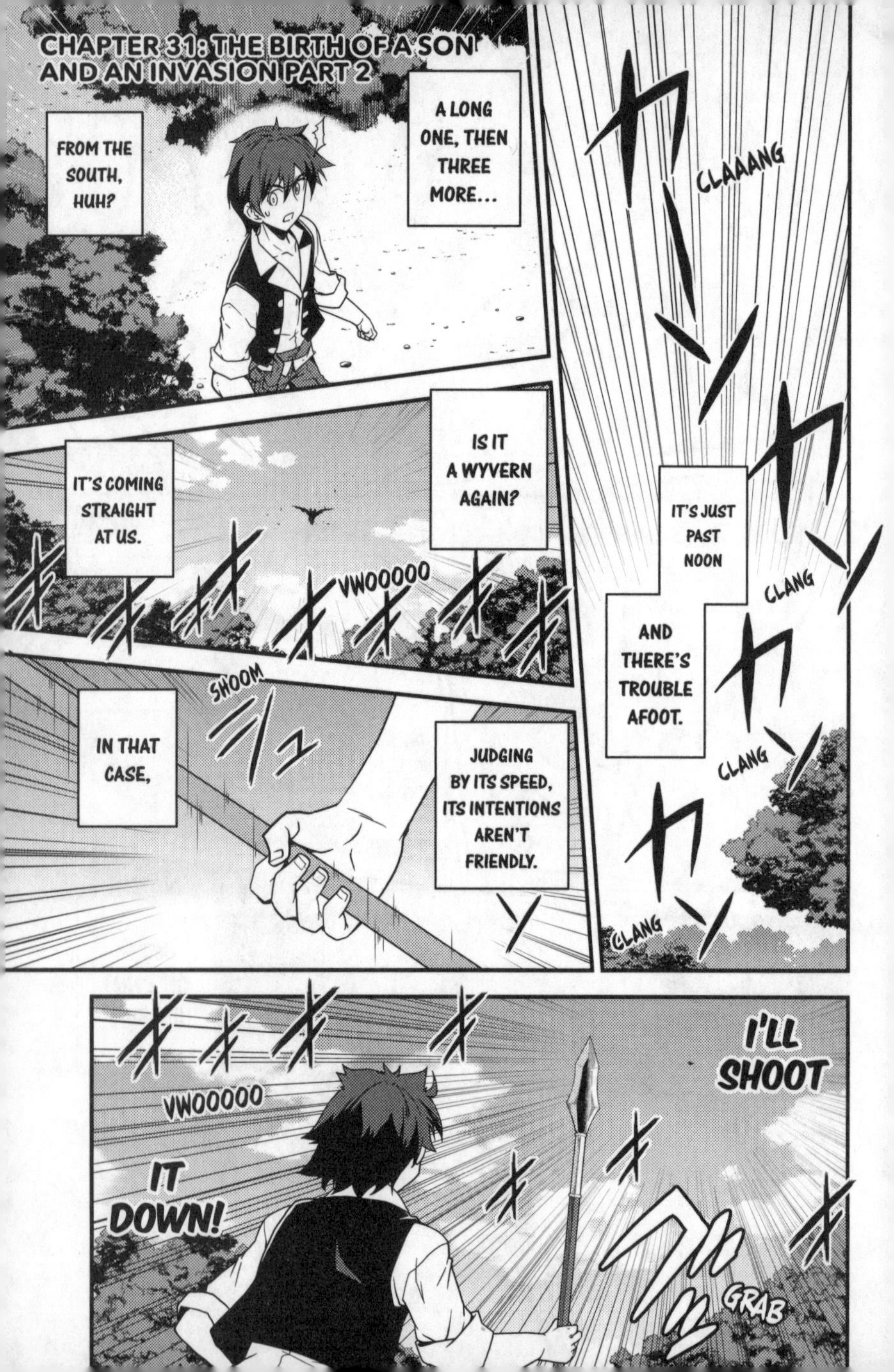
CLAAANG
IT'S JUST PAST NOON
CLANG
AND THERE'S TROUBLE AFOOT.
CLANG
CLANG
A LONG ONE, THEN THREE MORE...
FROM THE SOUTH, HUH?
IS IT A WYVERN AGAIN?
VWOOOOO
IT'S COMING STRAIGHT AT US.
JUDGING BY ITS SPEED, ITS INTENTIONS AREN'T FRIENDLY.
SHOOM
IN THAT CASE,
I'LL SHOOT
GRAB
VWOOOOO
IT DOWN!

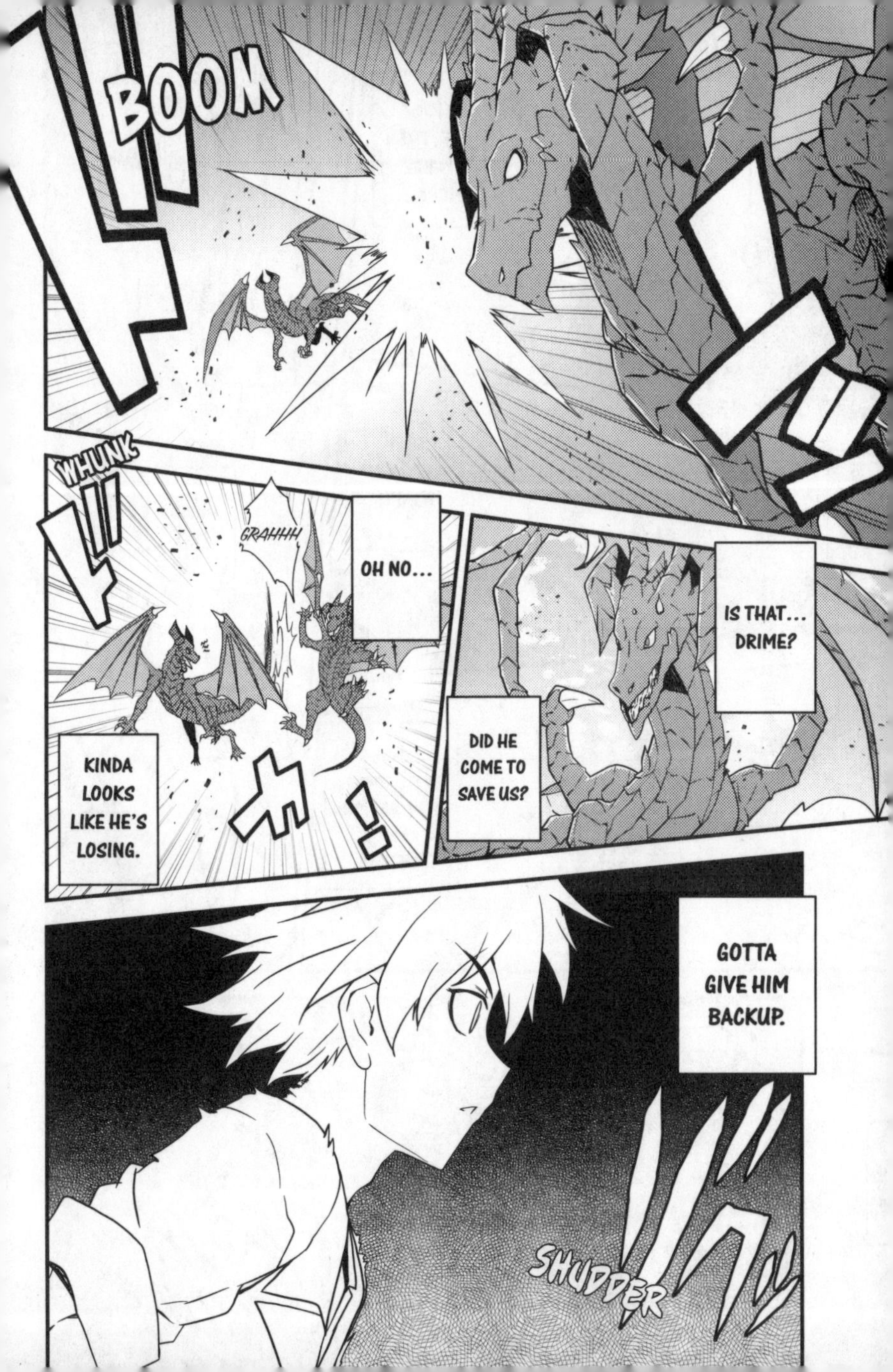
BOOM
IS THAT... DRIME?
DID HE COME TO SAVE US?
OH NO...
GRAHHH
WHUNK
KINDA LOOKS LIKE HE'S LOSING.
GOTTA GIVE HIM BACKUP.
SHUDDER

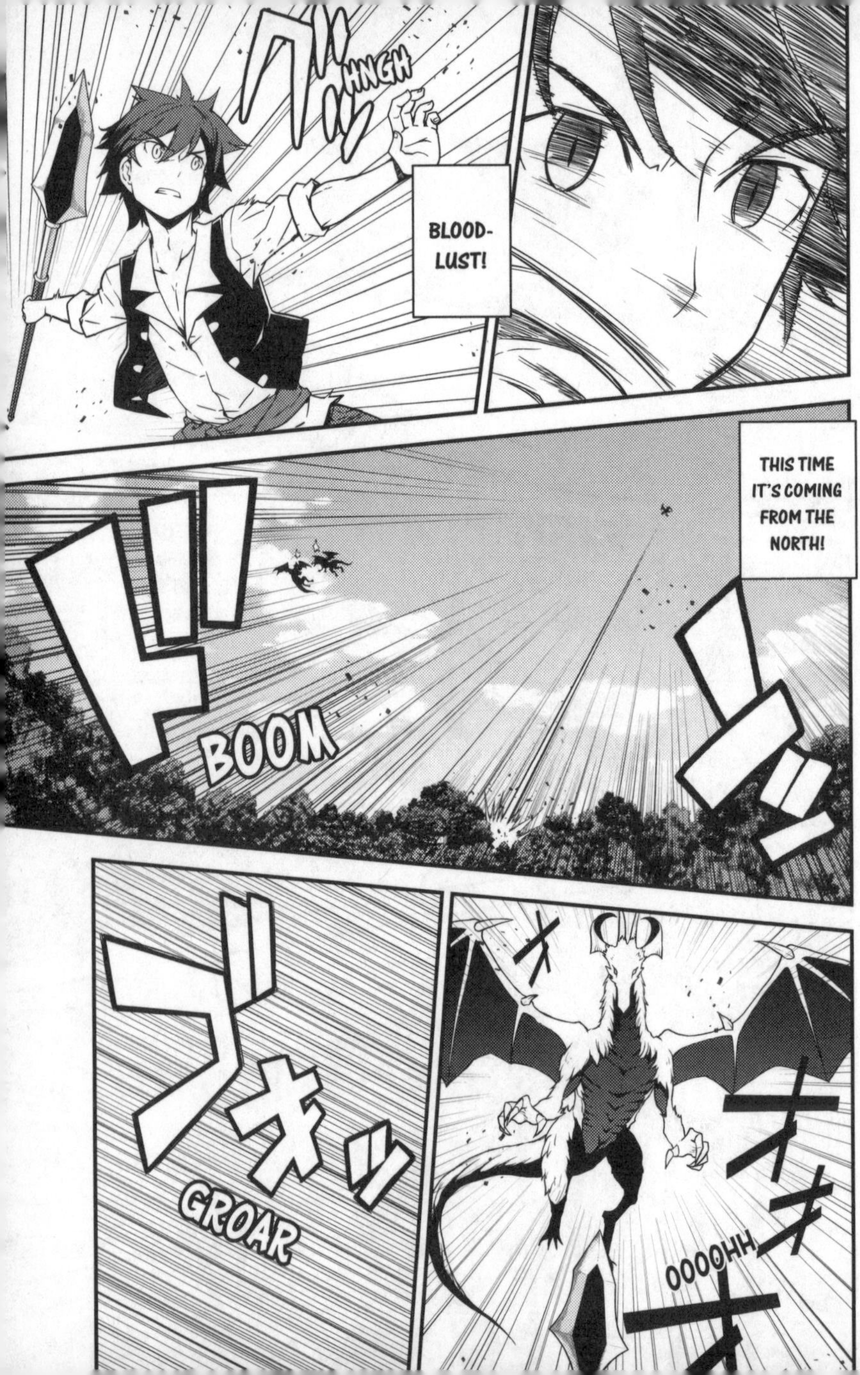
BLOOD-
LUST!
HNGH
THIS TIME IT'S COMING FROM THE NORTH!
BOOM
OOOOHH
GROAR

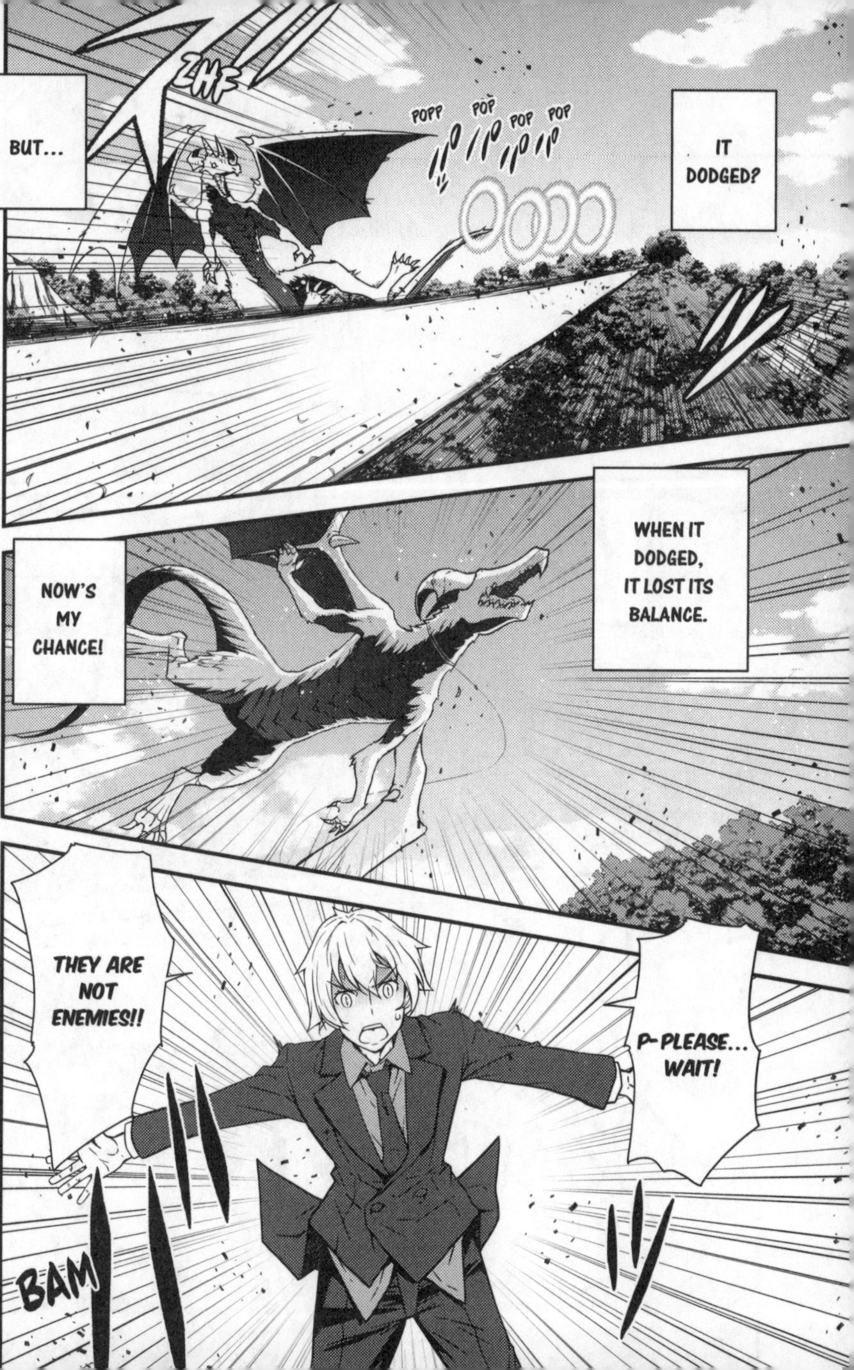
IT DODGED?
POP POP POP POPP
ZHF
BUT…
WHEN IT DODGED, IT LOST ITS BALANCE.
NOW'S MY CHANCE!
P-PLEASE… WAIT!
THEY ARE NOT ENEMIES!!
BAM

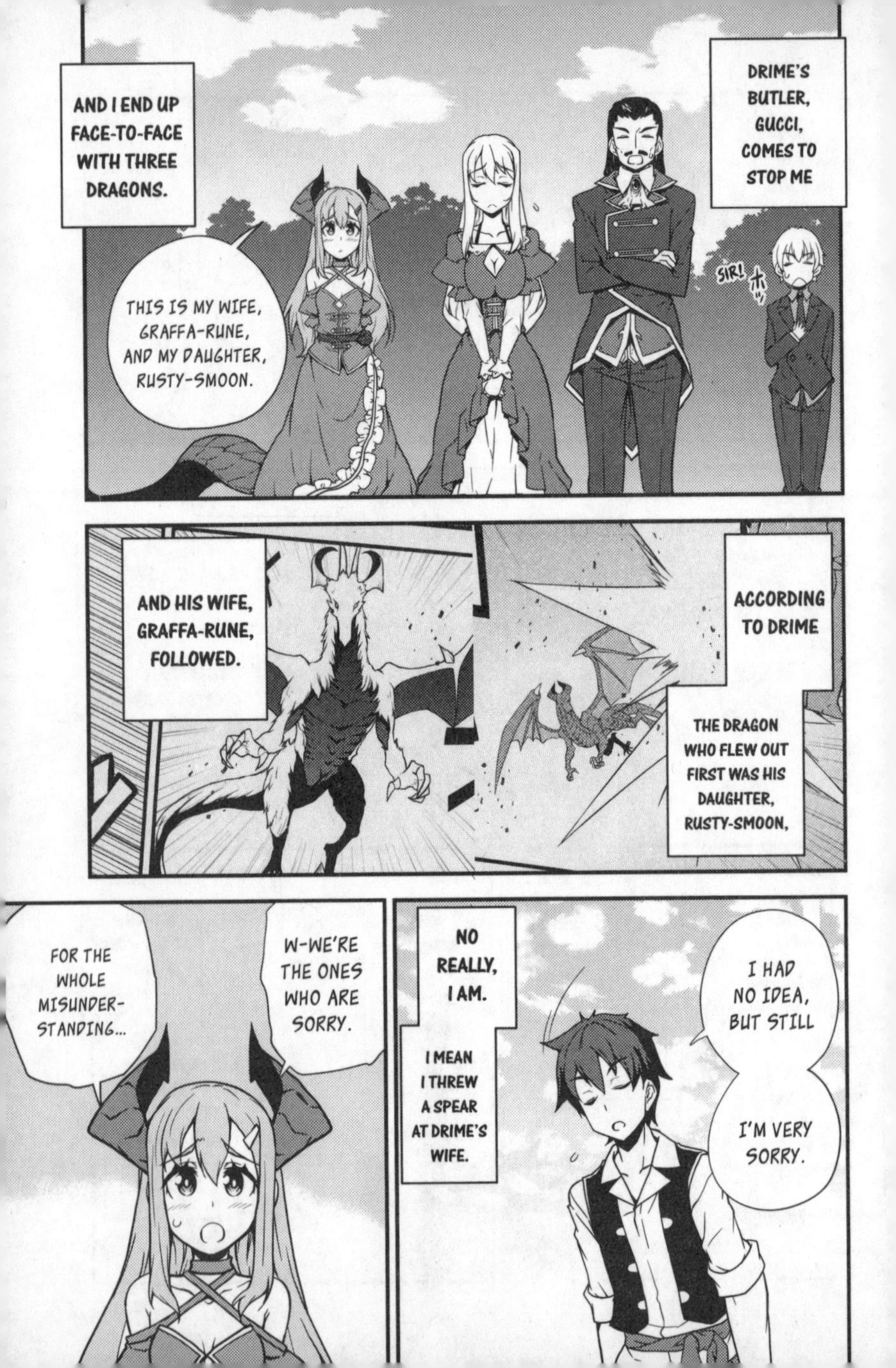
DRIME'S BUTLER, GUCCI, COMES TO STOP ME
SIR!
ホッ
AND I END UP FACE-TO-FACE WITH THREE DRAGONS.
THIS IS MY WIFE, GRAFFA-RUNE, AND MY DAUGHTER, RUSTY-SMOON.
ACCORDING TO DRIME
THE DRAGON WHO FLEW OUT FIRST WAS HIS DAUGHTER, RUSTY-SMOON,
AND HIS WIFE, GRAFFA-RUNE, FOLLOWED.
I HAD NO IDEA, BUT STILL
I'M VERY SORRY.
NO REALLY, I AM.
I MEAN I THREW A SPEAR AT DRIME'S WIFE.
W-WE'RE THE ONES WHO ARE SORRY.
FOR THE WHOLE MISUNDERSTANDING...

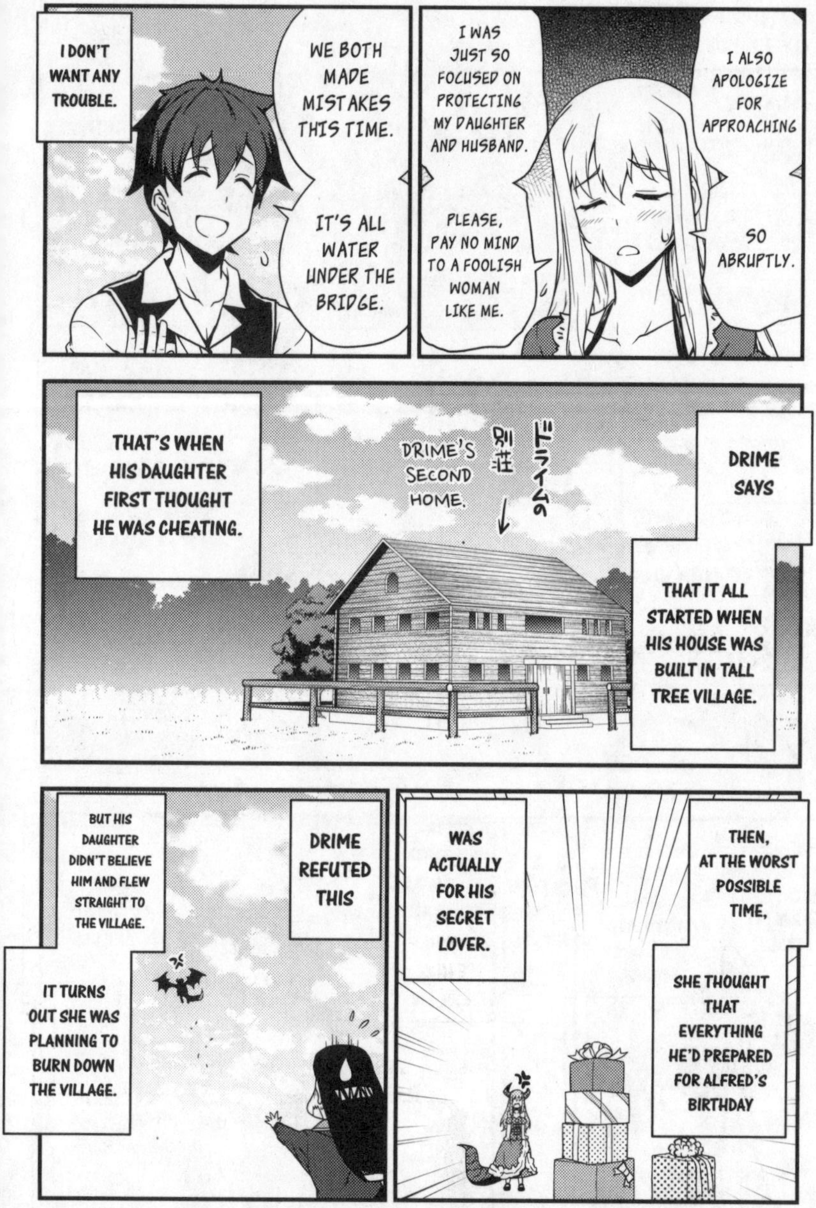
I ALSO APOLOGIZE FOR APPROACHING
SO ABRUPTLY.
I WAS JUST SO FOCUSED ON PROTECTING MY DAUGHTER AND HUSBAND.
PLEASE, PAY NO MIND TO A FOOLISH WOMAN LIKE ME.
WE BOTH MADE MISTAKES THIS TIME.
IT'S ALL WATER UNDER THE BRIDGE.
I DON'T WANT ANY TROUBLE.
DRIME SAYS
THAT IT ALL STARTED WHEN HIS HOUSE WAS BUILT IN TALL TREE VILLAGE.
ドライムの別荘
DRIME'S SECOND HOME.
THAT'S WHEN HIS DAUGHTER FIRST THOUGHT HE WAS CHEATING.
THEN, AT THE WORST POSSIBLE TIME,
SHE THOUGHT THAT EVERYTHING HE'D PREPARED FOR ALFRED'S BIRTHDAY
WAS ACTUALLY FOR HIS SECRET LOVER.
DRIME REFUTED THIS
BUT HIS DAUGHTER DIDN'T BELIEVE HIM AND FLEW STRAIGHT TO THE VILLAGE.
IT TURNS OUT SHE WAS PLANNING TO BURN DOWN THE VILLAGE.

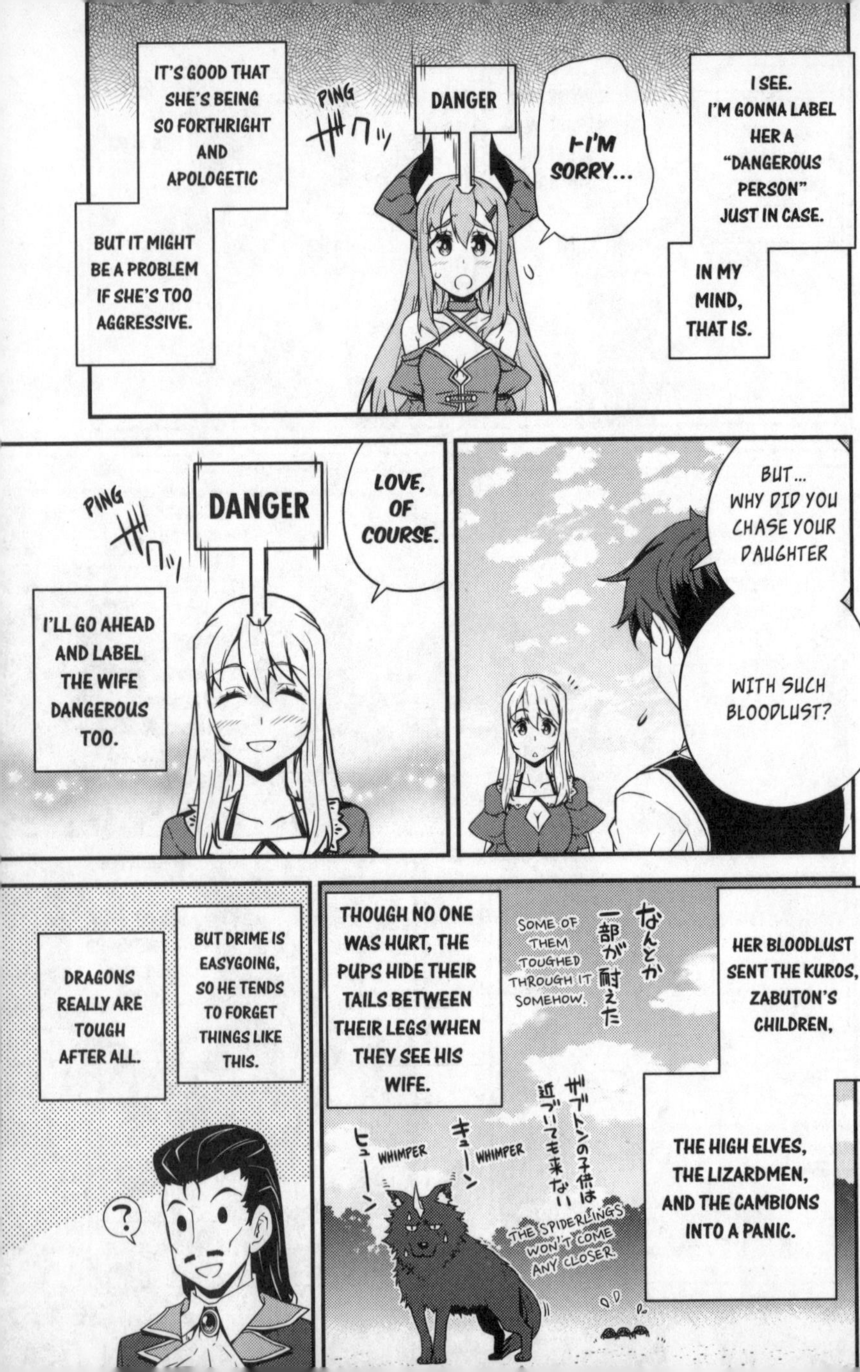
I SEE. I'M GONNA LABEL HER A "DANGEROUS PERSON" JUST IN CASE.
IN MY MIND, THAT IS.
I-I'M SORRY...
DANGER
PING
IT'S GOOD THAT SHE'S BEING SO FORTHRIGHT AND APOLOGETIC
BUT IT MIGHT BE A PROBLEM IF SHE'S TOO AGGRESSIVE.
BUT... WHY DID YOU CHASE YOUR DAUGHTER
WITH SUCH BLOODLUST?
LOVE, OF COURSE.
DANGER
PING
I'LL GO AHEAD AND LABEL THE WIFE DANGEROUS TOO.
HER BLOODLUST SENT THE KUROS, ZABUTON'S CHILDREN,
THE HIGH ELVES, THE LIZARDMEN, AND THE CAMBIONS INTO A PANIC.
なんとか一部が耐えた
SOME OF THEM TOUGHED THROUGH IT SOMEHOW.
THOUGH NO ONE WAS HURT, THE PUPS HIDE THEIR TAILS BETWEEN THEIR LEGS WHEN THEY SEE HIS WIFE.
ザブトンの子供は近づいても来ない
THE SPIDERLINGS WON'T COME ANY CLOSER.
キューン
WHIMPER
ヒューン
WHIMPER
BUT DRIME IS EASYGOING, SO HE TENDS TO FORGET THINGS LIKE THIS.
DRAGONS REALLY ARE TOUGH AFTER ALL.
?

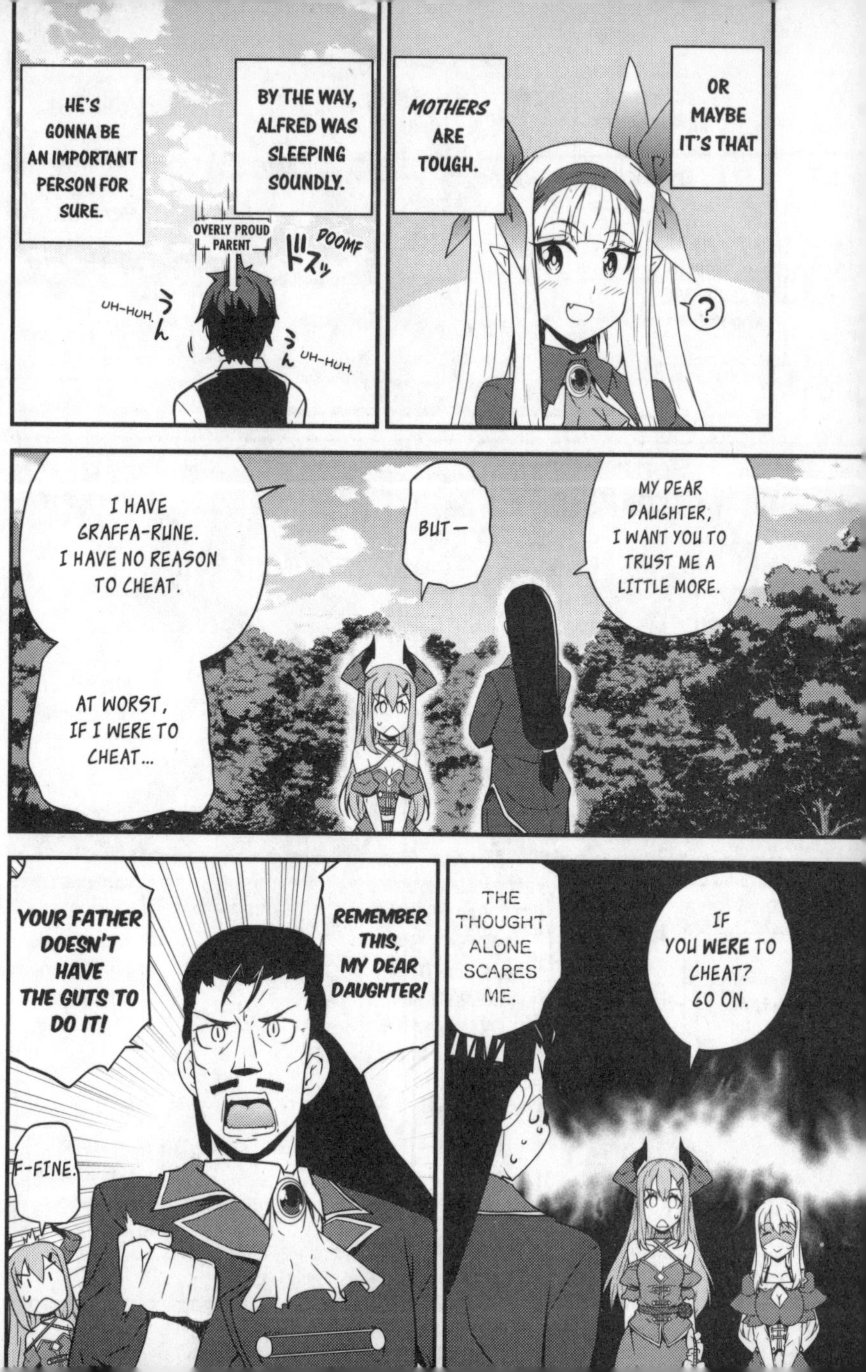
OR MAYBE IT'S THAT
MOTHERS ARE TOUGH.
?
BY THE WAY, ALFRED WAS SLEEPING SOUNDLY.
HE'S GONNA BE AN IMPORTANT PERSON FOR SURE.
OVERLY PROUD PARENT
ドスッ DOOMF
うん UH-HUH.
うん UH-HUH.
MY DEAR DAUGHTER, I WANT YOU TO TRUST ME A LITTLE MORE.
BUT—
I HAVE GRAFFA-RUNE. I HAVE NO REASON TO CHEAT.
AT WORST, IF I WERE TO CHEAT...
IF YOU WERE TO CHEAT? GO ON.
THE THOUGHT ALONE SCARES ME.
REMEMBER THIS, MY DEAR DAUGHTER!
YOUR FATHER DOESN'T HAVE THE GUTS TO DO IT!
F-FINE.

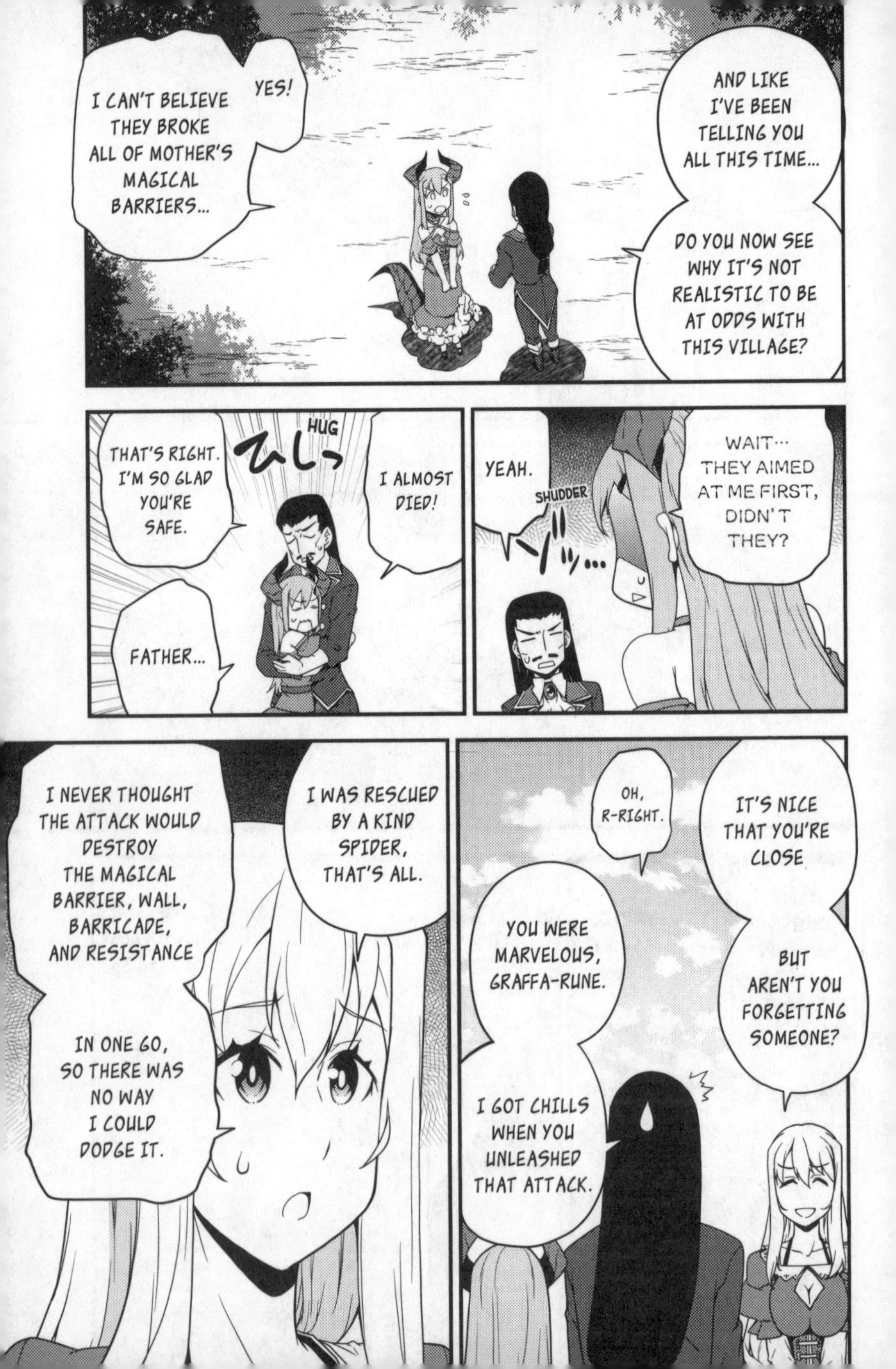
AND LIKE I'VE BEEN TELLING YOU ALL THIS TIME...
DO YOU NOW SEE WHY IT'S NOT REALISTIC TO BE AT ODDS WITH THIS VILLAGE?
YES!
I CAN'T BELIEVE THEY BROKE ALL OF MOTHER'S MAGICAL BARRIERS...
WAIT... THEY AIMED AT ME FIRST, DIDN'T THEY?
SHUDDER
YEAH.
I ALMOST DIED!
HUG
THAT'S RIGHT. I'M SO GLAD YOU'RE SAFE.
FATHER...
IT'S NICE THAT YOU'RE CLOSE
BUT AREN'T YOU FORGETTING SOMEONE?
OH, R-RIGHT.
YOU WERE MARVELOUS, GRAFFA-RUNE.
I GOT CHILLS WHEN YOU UNLEASHED THAT ATTACK.
I WAS RESCUED BY A KIND SPIDER, THAT'S ALL.
I NEVER THOUGHT THE ATTACK WOULD DESTROY THE MAGICAL BARRIER, WALL, BARRICADE, AND RESISTANCE
IN ONE GO, SO THERE WAS NO WAY I COULD DODGE IT.

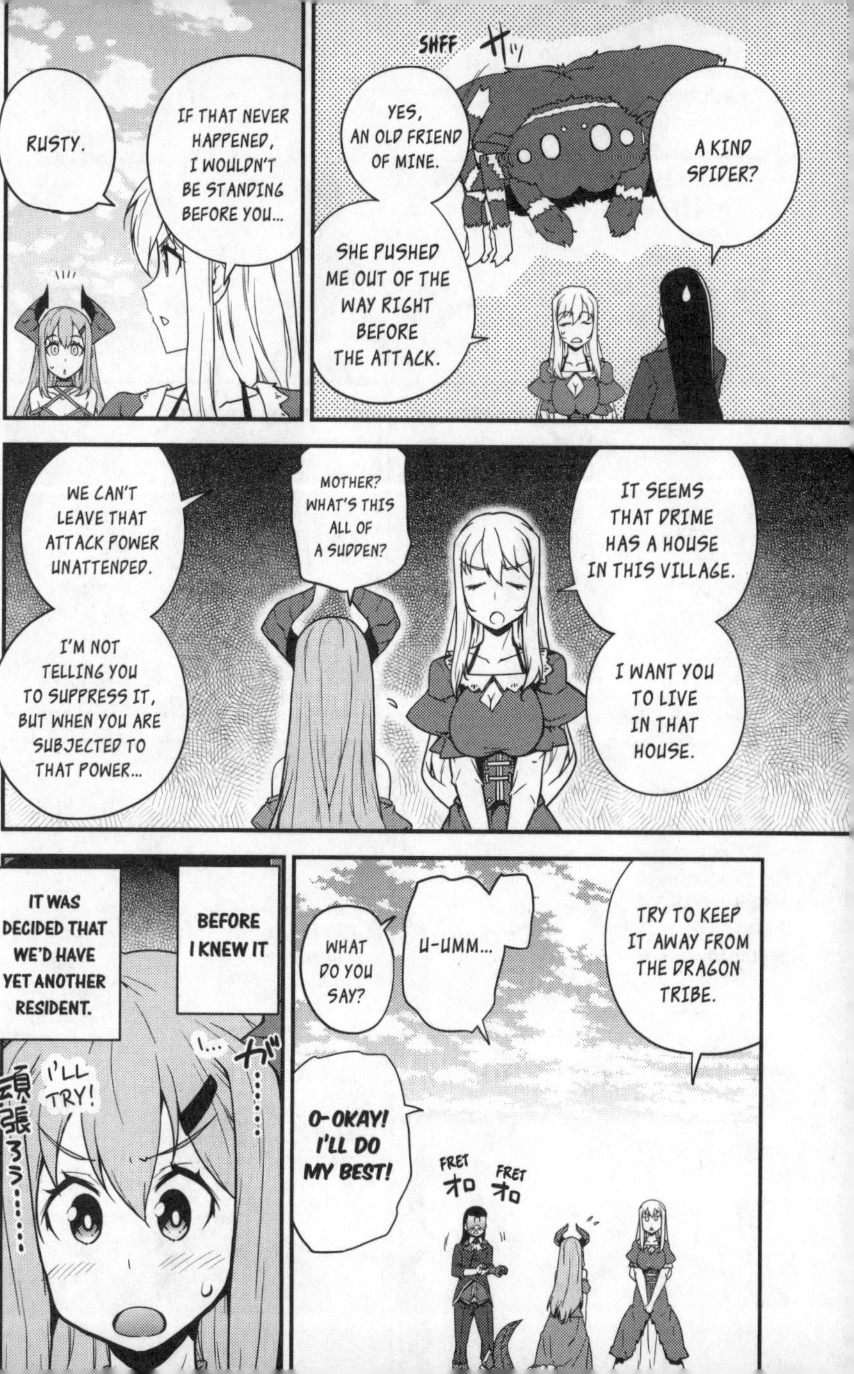
SHFF
A KIND SPIDER?
YES, AN OLD FRIEND OF MINE.
SHE PUSHED ME OUT OF THE WAY RIGHT BEFORE THE ATTACK.
IF THAT NEVER HAPPENED, I WOULDN'T BE STANDING BEFORE YOU...
RUSTY.
IT SEEMS THAT DRIME HAS A HOUSE IN THIS VILLAGE.
I WANT YOU TO LIVE IN THAT HOUSE.
MOTHER? WHAT'S THIS ALL OF A SUDDEN?
WE CAN'T LEAVE THAT ATTACK POWER UNATTENDED.
I'M NOT TELLING YOU TO SUPPRESS IT, BUT WHEN YOU ARE SUBJECTED TO THAT POWER...
TRY TO KEEP IT AWAY FROM THE DRAGON TRIBE.
U-UMM...
WHAT DO YOU SAY?
O-OKAY! I'LL DO MY BEST!
FRET FRET
BEFORE I KNEW IT
IT WAS DECIDED THAT WE'D HAVE YET ANOTHER RESIDENT.
I...
I'LL TRY!

CHAPTER 32: RUSTY

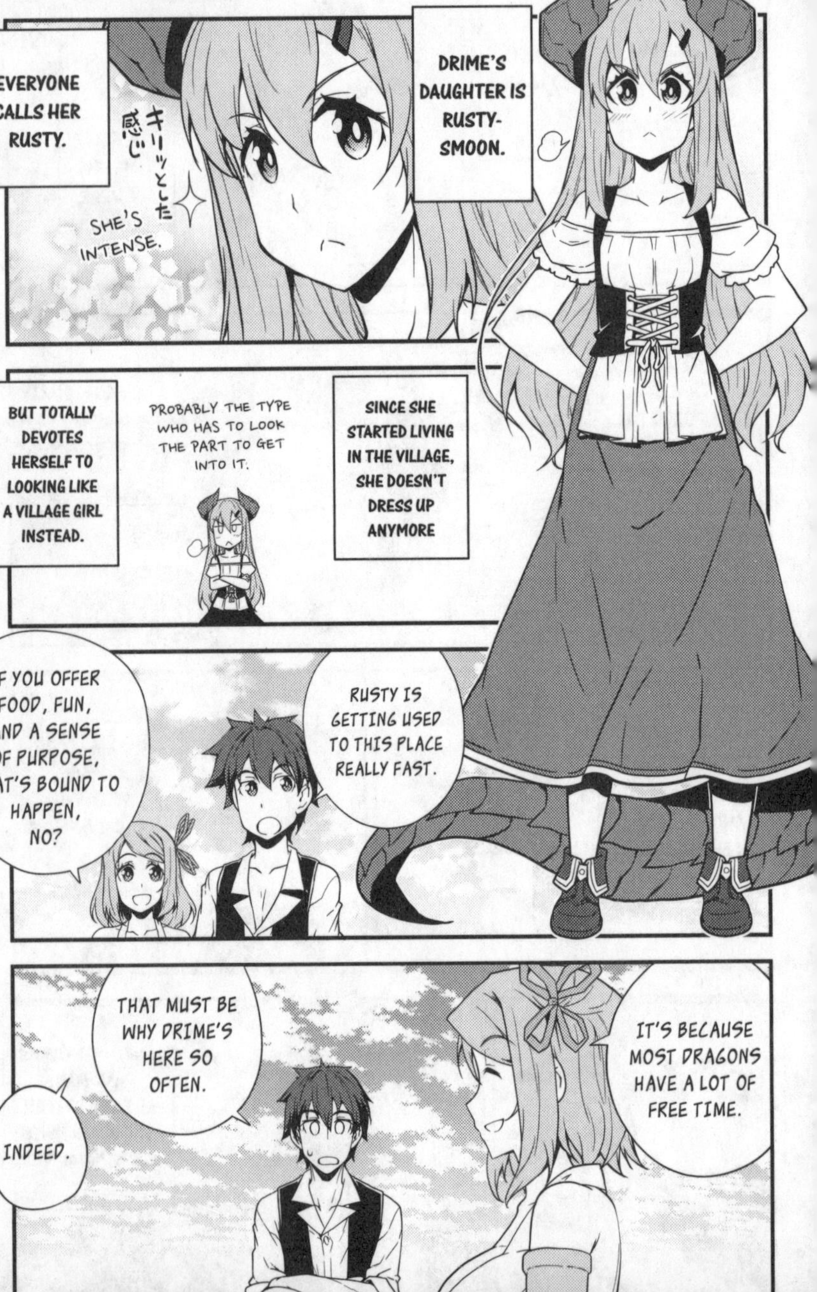
DRIME'S DAUGHTER IS RUSTY-SMOON.
EVERYONE CALLS HER RUSTY.
キリッとした感じ
SHE'S INTENSE.
SINCE SHE STARTED LIVING IN THE VILLAGE, SHE DOESN'T DRESS UP ANYMORE
PROBABLY THE TYPE WHO HAS TO LOOK THE PART TO GET INTO IT.
BUT TOTALLY DEVOTES HERSELF TO LOOKING LIKE A VILLAGE GIRL INSTEAD.
RUSTY IS GETTING USED TO THIS PLACE REALLY FAST.
IF YOU OFFER FOOD, FUN, AND A SENSE OF PURPOSE, THAT'S BOUND TO HAPPEN, NO?
IT'S BECAUSE MOST DRAGONS HAVE A LOT OF FREE TIME.
THAT MUST BE WHY DRIME'S HERE SO OFTEN.
INDEED.

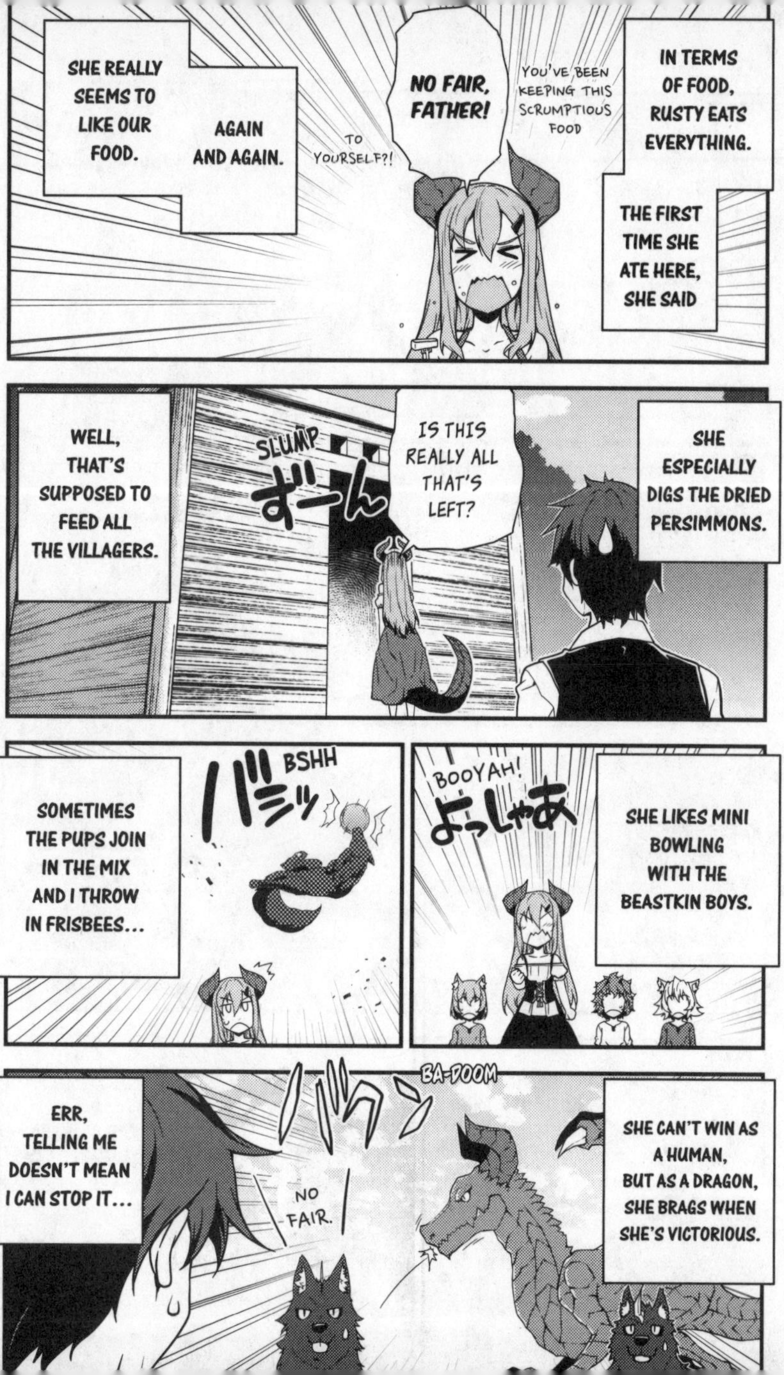
IN TERMS OF FOOD, RUSTY EATS EVERYTHING.
THE FIRST TIME SHE ATE HERE, SHE SAID
NO FAIR, FATHER!
YOU'VE BEEN KEEPING THIS SCRUMPTIOUS FOOD
TO YOURSELF?!
AGAIN AND AGAIN.
SHE REALLY SEEMS TO LIKE OUR FOOD.
SHE ESPECIALLY DIGS THE DRIED PERSIMMONS.
IS THIS REALLY ALL THAT'S LEFT?
SLUMP
ずーん
WELL, THAT'S SUPPOSED TO FEED ALL THE VILLAGERS.
SHE LIKES MINI BOWLING WITH THE BEASTKIN BOYS.
BOOYAH!
よっしゃあ
BSHH
バシッ
SOMETIMES THE PUPS JOIN IN THE MIX AND I THROW IN FRISBEES...
SHE CAN'T WIN AS A HUMAN, BUT AS A DRAGON, SHE BRAGS WHEN SHE'S VICTORIOUS.
BA-DOOM
NO FAIR.
ERR, TELLING ME DOESN'T MEAN I CAN STOP IT...

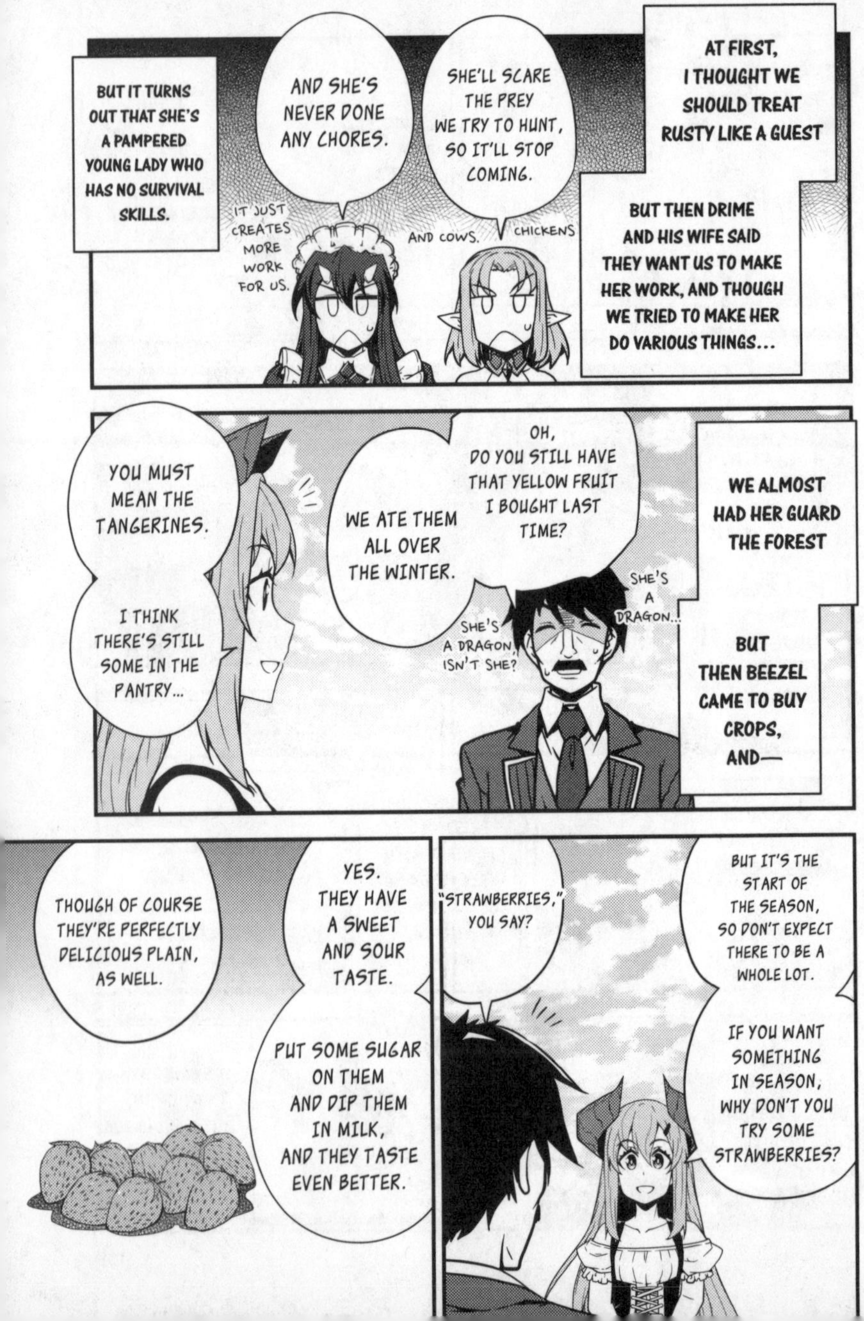
AT FIRST, I THOUGHT WE SHOULD TREAT RUSTY LIKE A GUEST
BUT THEN DRIME AND HIS WIFE SAID THEY WANT US TO MAKE HER WORK, AND THOUGH WE TRIED TO MAKE HER DO VARIOUS THINGS...
SHE'LL SCARE THE PREY WE TRY TO HUNT, SO IT'LL STOP COMING.
CHICKENS
AND COWS.
AND SHE'S NEVER DONE ANY CHORES.
IT JUST CREATES MORE WORK FOR US.
BUT IT TURNS OUT THAT SHE'S A PAMPERED YOUNG LADY WHO HAS NO SURVIVAL SKILLS.
WE ALMOST HAD HER GUARD THE FOREST
BUT THEN BEEZEL CAME TO BUY CROPS, AND—
OH, DO YOU STILL HAVE THAT YELLOW FRUIT I BOUGHT LAST TIME?
SHE'S A DRAGON...
SHE'S A DRAGON, ISN'T SHE?
WE ATE THEM ALL OVER THE WINTER.
YOU MUST MEAN THE TANGERINES.
I THINK THERE'S STILL SOME IN THE PANTRY...
BUT IT'S THE START OF THE SEASON, SO DON'T EXPECT THERE TO BE A WHOLE LOT.
IF YOU WANT SOMETHING IN SEASON, WHY DON'T YOU TRY SOME STRAWBERRIES?
"STRAWBERRIES," YOU SAY?
YES. THEY HAVE A SWEET AND SOUR TASTE.
PUT SOME SUGAR ON THEM AND DIP THEM IN MILK, AND THEY TASTE EVEN BETTER.
THOUGH OF COURSE THEY'RE PERFECTLY DELICIOUS PLAIN, AS WELL.

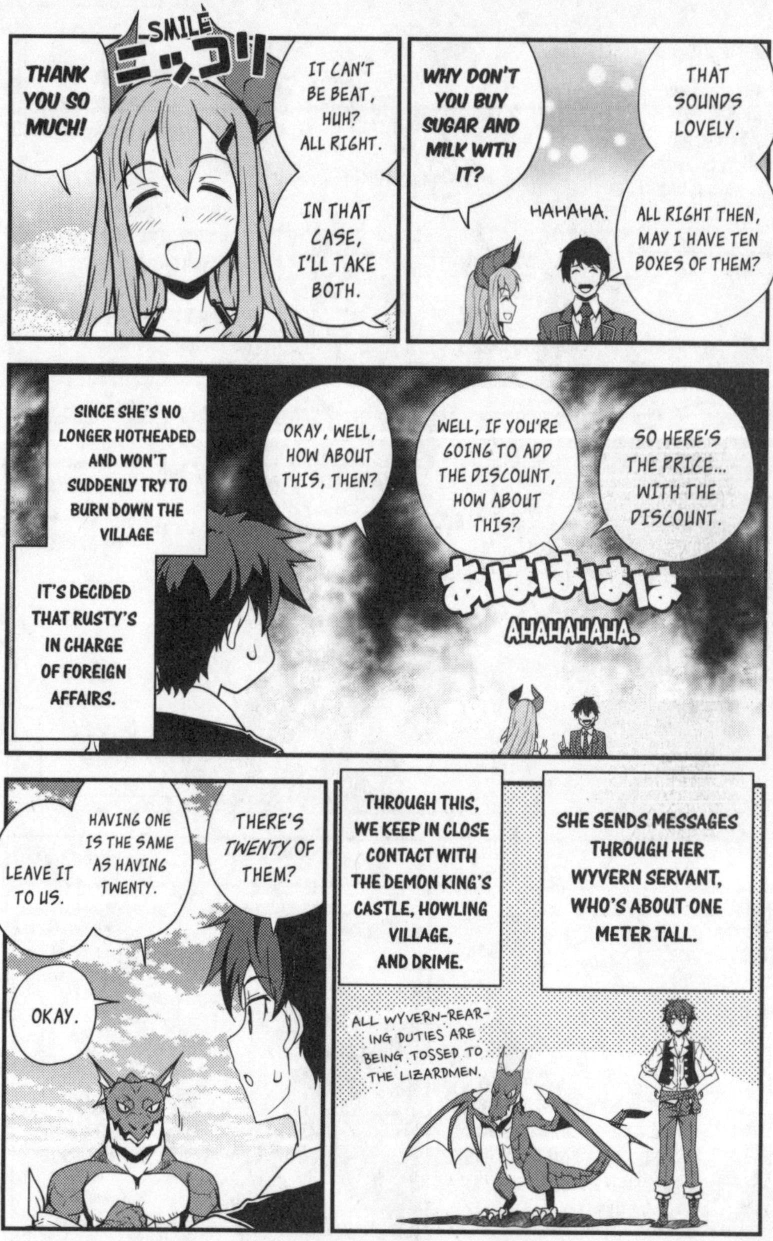
THAT SOUNDS LOVELY.
WHY DON'T YOU BUY SUGAR AND MILK WITH IT?
ALL RIGHT THEN, MAY I HAVE TEN BOXES OF THEM?
HAHAHA.
IT CAN'T BE BEAT, HUH? ALL RIGHT.
IN THAT CASE, I'LL TAKE BOTH.
ニッコリ
SMILE
THANK YOU SO MUCH!
SO HERE'S THE PRICE... WITH THE DISCOUNT.
WELL, IF YOU'RE GOING TO ADD THE DISCOUNT, HOW ABOUT THIS?
OKAY, WELL, HOW ABOUT THIS, THEN?
あははははは
AHAHAHAHA.
SINCE SHE'S NO LONGER HOTHEADED AND WON'T SUDDENLY TRY TO BURN DOWN THE VILLAGE
IT'S DECIDED THAT RUSTY'S IN CHARGE OF FOREIGN AFFAIRS.
SHE SENDS MESSAGES THROUGH HER WYVERN SERVANT, WHO'S ABOUT ONE METER TALL.
THROUGH THIS, WE KEEP IN CLOSE CONTACT WITH THE DEMON KING'S CASTLE, HOWLING VILLAGE, AND DRIME.
ALL WYVERN-REARING DUTIES ARE BEING TOSSED TO THE LIZARDMEN.
THERE'S *TWENTY* OF THEM?
HAVING ONE IS THE SAME AS HAVING TWENTY.
LEAVE IT TO US.
OKAY.

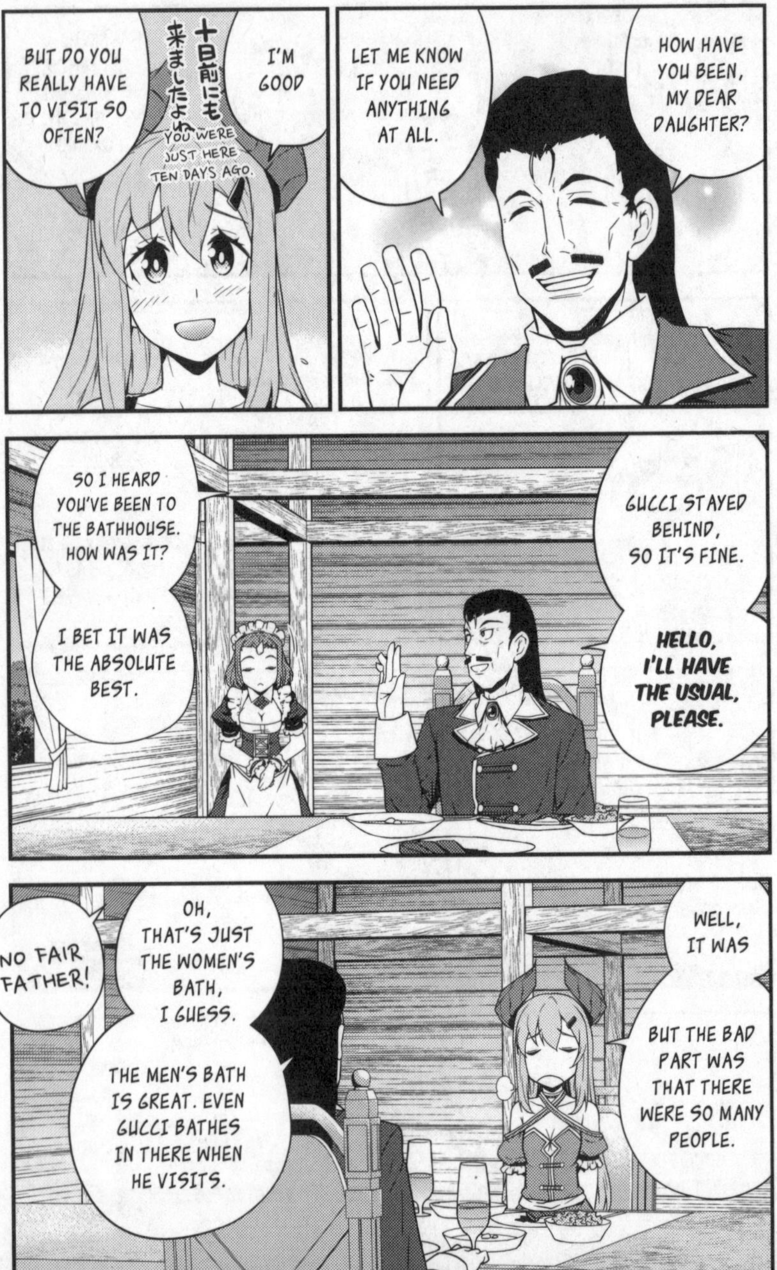
HOW HAVE YOU BEEN, MY DEAR DAUGHTER?
LET ME KNOW IF YOU NEED ANYTHING AT ALL.
I'M GOOD
十日前にも来ましたよね
YOU WERE JUST HERE TEN DAYS AGO.
BUT DO YOU REALLY HAVE TO VISIT SO OFTEN?
GUCCI STAYED BEHIND, SO IT'S FINE.
HELLO, I'LL HAVE THE USUAL, PLEASE.
SO I HEARD YOU'VE BEEN TO THE BATHHOUSE. HOW WAS IT?
I BET IT WAS THE ABSOLUTE BEST.
WELL, IT WAS
BUT THE BAD PART WAS THAT THERE WERE SO MANY PEOPLE.
OH, THAT'S JUST THE WOMEN'S BATH, I GUESS.
THE MEN'S BATH IS GREAT. EVEN GUCCI BATHES IN THERE WHEN HE VISITS.
NO FAIR FATHER!

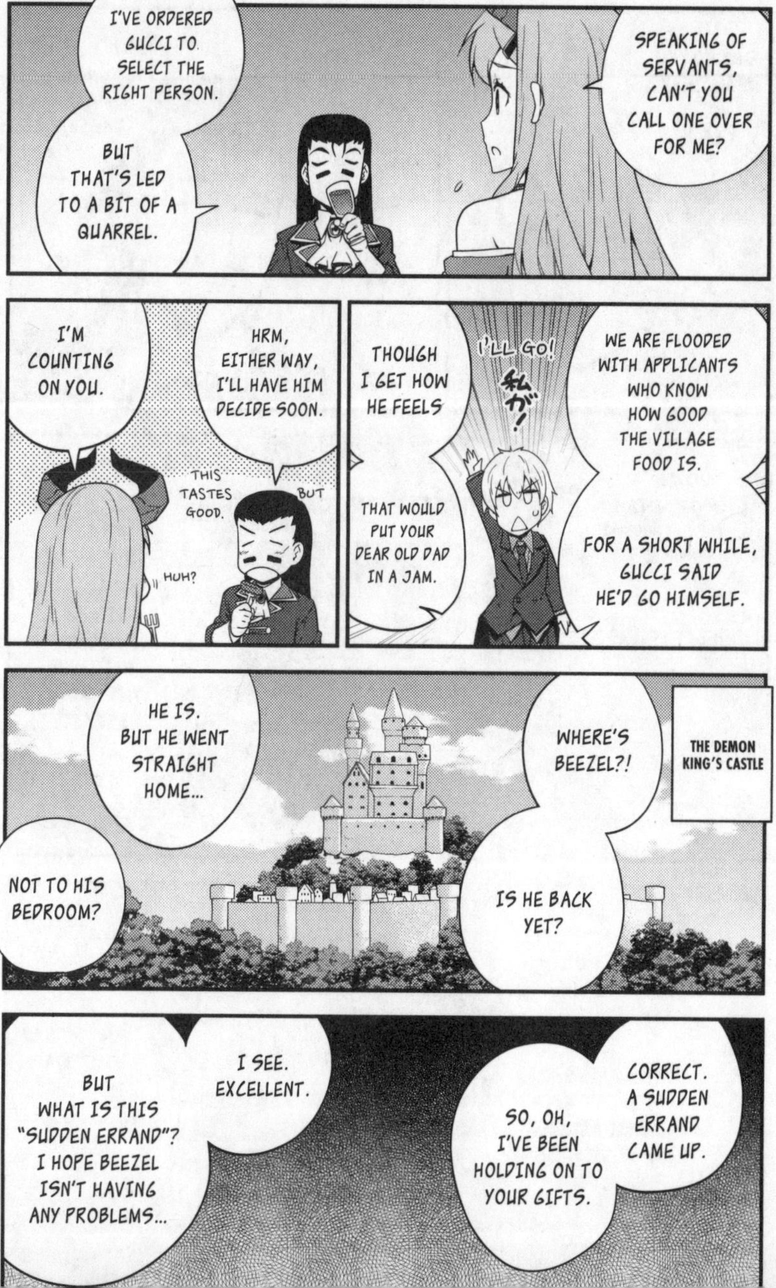
SPEAKING OF SERVANTS, CAN'T YOU CALL ONE OVER FOR ME?
I'VE ORDERED GUCCI TO SELECT THE RIGHT PERSON.
BUT THAT'S LED TO A BIT OF A QUARREL.
WE ARE FLOODED WITH APPLICANTS WHO KNOW HOW GOOD THE VILLAGE FOOD IS.
FOR A SHORT WHILE, GUCCI SAID HE'D GO HIMSELF.
I'LL GO!
私が!
THOUGH I GET HOW HE FEELS
THAT WOULD PUT YOUR DEAR OLD DAD IN A JAM.
HRM, EITHER WAY, I'LL HAVE HIM DECIDE SOON.
BUT
THIS TASTES GOOD.
I'M COUNTING ON YOU.
HUH?
THE DEMON KING'S CASTLE
WHERE'S BEEZEL?!
IS HE BACK YET?
HE IS. BUT HE WENT STRAIGHT HOME...
NOT TO HIS BEDROOM?
CORRECT. A SUDDEN ERRAND CAME UP.
SO, OH, I'VE BEEN HOLDING ON TO YOUR GIFTS.
I SEE. EXCELLENT.
BUT WHAT IS THIS "SUDDEN ERRAND"? I HOPE BEEZEL ISN'T HAVING ANY PROBLEMS...

CHAPTER 33: BEEZEL'S DAUGHTER

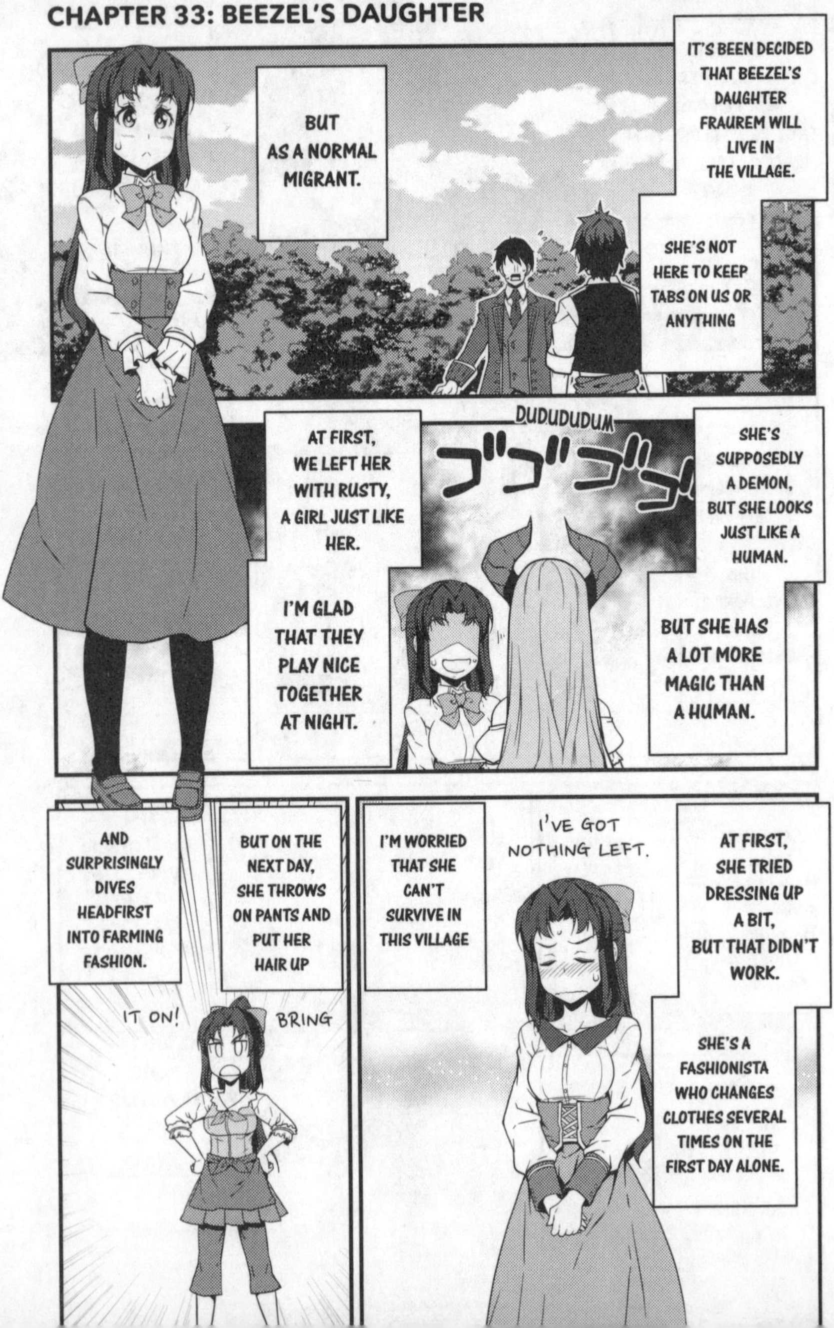
IT'S BEEN DECIDED THAT BEEZEL'S DAUGHTER FRAUREM WILL LIVE IN THE VILLAGE.
SHE'S NOT HERE TO KEEP TABS ON US OR ANYTHING
BUT AS A NORMAL MIGRANT.
SHE'S SUPPOSEDLY A DEMON, BUT SHE LOOKS JUST LIKE A HUMAN.
BUT SHE HAS A LOT MORE MAGIC THAN A HUMAN.
DUDUDUDUM
ゴゴゴゴ
AT FIRST, WE LEFT HER WITH RUSTY, A GIRL JUST LIKE HER.
I'M GLAD THAT THEY PLAY NICE TOGETHER AT NIGHT.
AT FIRST, SHE TRIED DRESSING UP A BIT, BUT THAT DIDN'T WORK.
SHE'S A FASHIONISTA WHO CHANGES CLOTHES SEVERAL TIMES ON THE FIRST DAY ALONE.
I'VE GOT NOTHING LEFT.
I'M WORRIED THAT SHE CAN'T SURVIVE IN THIS VILLAGE
BUT ON THE NEXT DAY, SHE THROWS ON PANTS AND PUT HER HAIR UP
AND SURPRISINGLY DIVES HEADFIRST INTO FARMING FASHION.
BRING
IT ON!

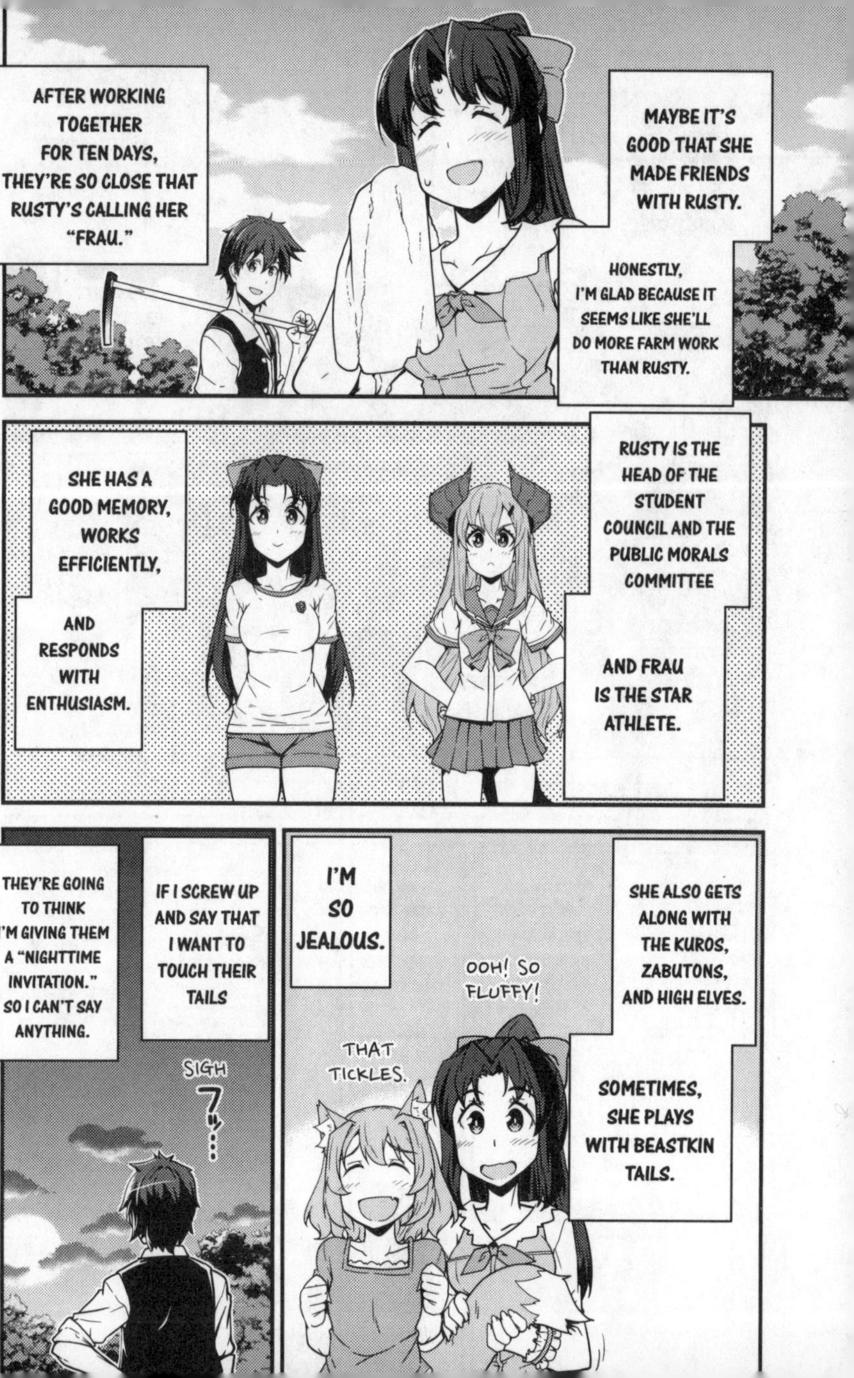
MAYBE IT'S GOOD THAT SHE MADE FRIENDS WITH RUSTY.
HONESTLY, I'M GLAD BECAUSE IT SEEMS LIKE SHE'LL DO MORE FARM WORK THAN RUSTY.
AFTER WORKING TOGETHER FOR TEN DAYS, THEY'RE SO CLOSE THAT RUSTY'S CALLING HER "FRAU."
RUSTY IS THE HEAD OF THE STUDENT COUNCIL AND THE PUBLIC MORALS COMMITTEE
AND FRAU IS THE STAR ATHLETE.
SHE HAS A GOOD MEMORY, WORKS EFFICIENTLY,
AND RESPONDS WITH ENTHUSIASM.
SHE ALSO GETS ALONG WITH THE KUROS, ZABUTONS, AND HIGH ELVES.
I'M SO JEALOUS.
OOH! SO FLUFFY!
SOMETIMES, SHE PLAYS WITH BEASTKIN TAILS.
THAT TICKLES.
IF I SCREW UP AND SAY THAT I WANT TO TOUCH THEIR TAILS
THEY'RE GOING TO THINK I'M GIVING THEM A "NIGHTTIME INVITATION." SO I CAN'T SAY ANYTHING.
SIGH
フッ…

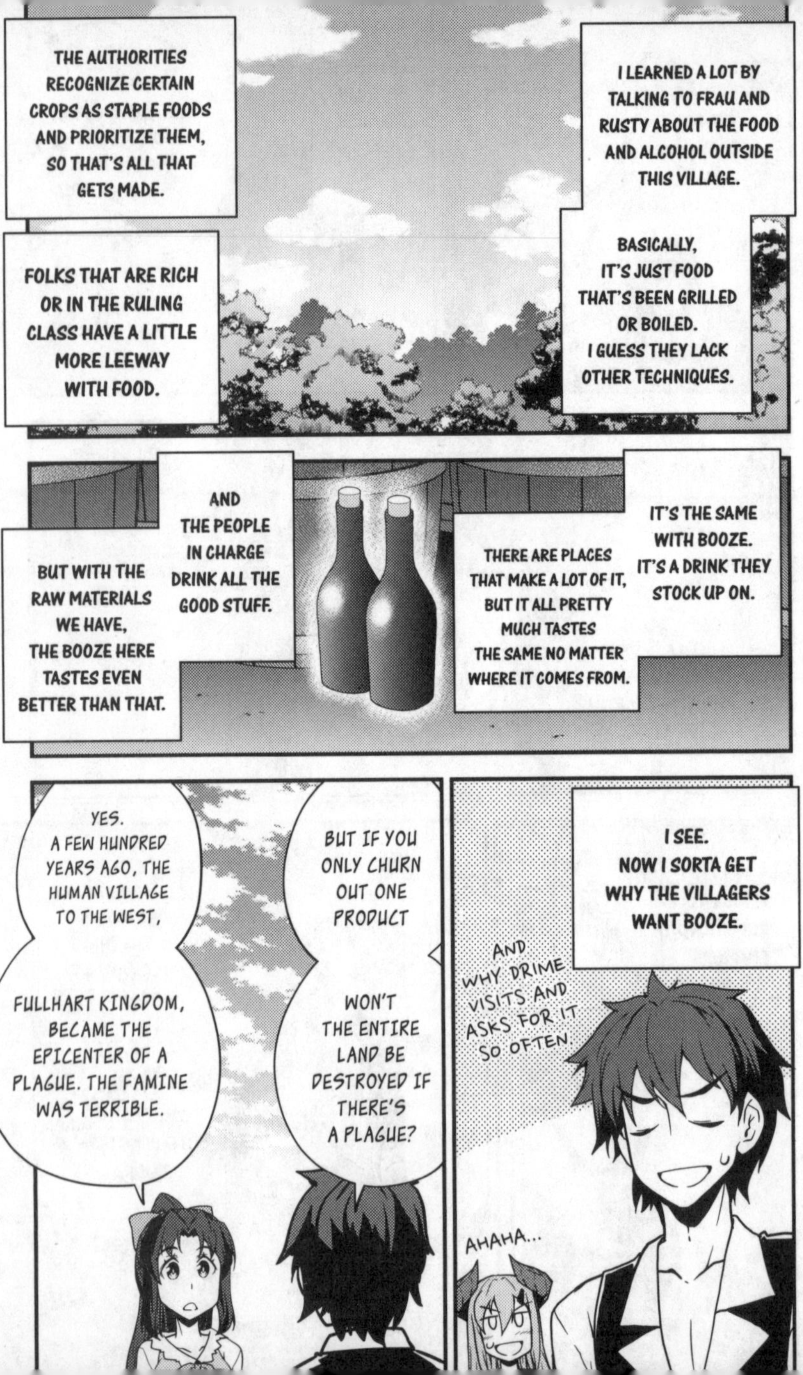
I LEARNED A LOT BY TALKING TO FRAU AND RUSTY ABOUT THE FOOD AND ALCOHOL OUTSIDE THIS VILLAGE.
BASICALLY, IT'S JUST FOOD THAT'S BEEN GRILLED OR BOILED. I GUESS THEY LACK OTHER TECHNIQUES.
THE AUTHORITIES RECOGNIZE CERTAIN CROPS AS STAPLE FOODS AND PRIORITIZE THEM, SO THAT'S ALL THAT GETS MADE.
FOLKS THAT ARE RICH OR IN THE RULING CLASS HAVE A LITTLE MORE LEEWAY WITH FOOD.
IT'S THE SAME WITH BOOZE. IT'S A DRINK THEY STOCK UP ON.
THERE ARE PLACES THAT MAKE A LOT OF IT, BUT IT ALL PRETTY MUCH TASTES THE SAME NO MATTER WHERE IT COMES FROM.
AND THE PEOPLE IN CHARGE DRINK ALL THE GOOD STUFF.
BUT WITH THE RAW MATERIALS WE HAVE, THE BOOZE HERE TASTES EVEN BETTER THAN THAT.
I SEE. NOW I SORTA GET WHY THE VILLAGERS WANT BOOZE.
AND WHY DRIME VISITS AND ASKS FOR IT SO OFTEN.
AHAHA...
BUT IF YOU ONLY CHURN OUT ONE PRODUCT
WON'T THE ENTIRE LAND BE DESTROYED IF THERE'S A PLAGUE?
YES. A FEW HUNDRED YEARS AGO, THE HUMAN VILLAGE TO THE WEST,
FULLHART KINGDOM, BECAME THE EPICENTER OF A PLAGUE. THE FAMINE WAS TERRIBLE.

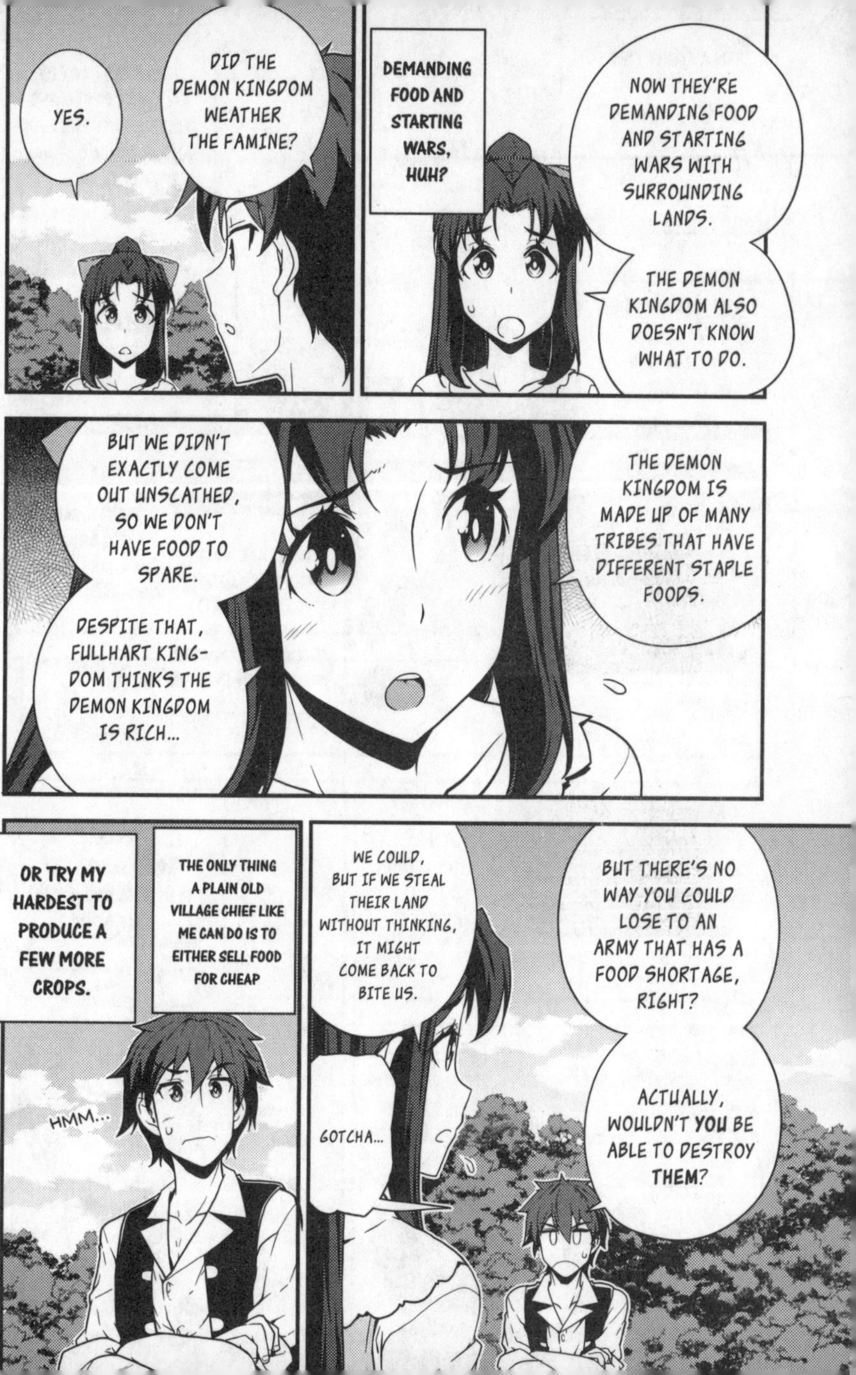
NOW THEY'RE DEMANDING FOOD AND STARTING WARS WITH SURROUNDING LANDS.
THE DEMON KINGDOM ALSO DOESN'T KNOW WHAT TO DO.
DEMANDING FOOD AND STARTING WARS, HUH?
DID THE DEMON KINGDOM WEATHER THE FAMINE?
YES.
THE DEMON KINGDOM IS MADE UP OF MANY TRIBES THAT HAVE DIFFERENT STAPLE FOODS.
BUT WE DIDN'T EXACTLY COME OUT UNSCATHED, SO WE DON'T HAVE FOOD TO SPARE.
DESPITE THAT, FULLHART KING-DOM THINKS THE DEMON KINGDOM IS RICH...
BUT THERE'S NO WAY YOU COULD LOSE TO AN ARMY THAT HAS A FOOD SHORTAGE, RIGHT?
ACTUALLY, WOULDN'T YOU BE ABLE TO DESTROY THEM?
WE COULD, BUT IF WE STEAL THEIR LAND WITHOUT THINKING, IT MIGHT COME BACK TO BITE US.
GOTCHA...
THE ONLY THING A PLAIN OLD VILLAGE CHIEF LIKE ME CAN DO IS TO EITHER SELL FOOD FOR CHEAP
OR TRY MY HARDEST TO PRODUCE A FEW MORE CROPS.
HMM...

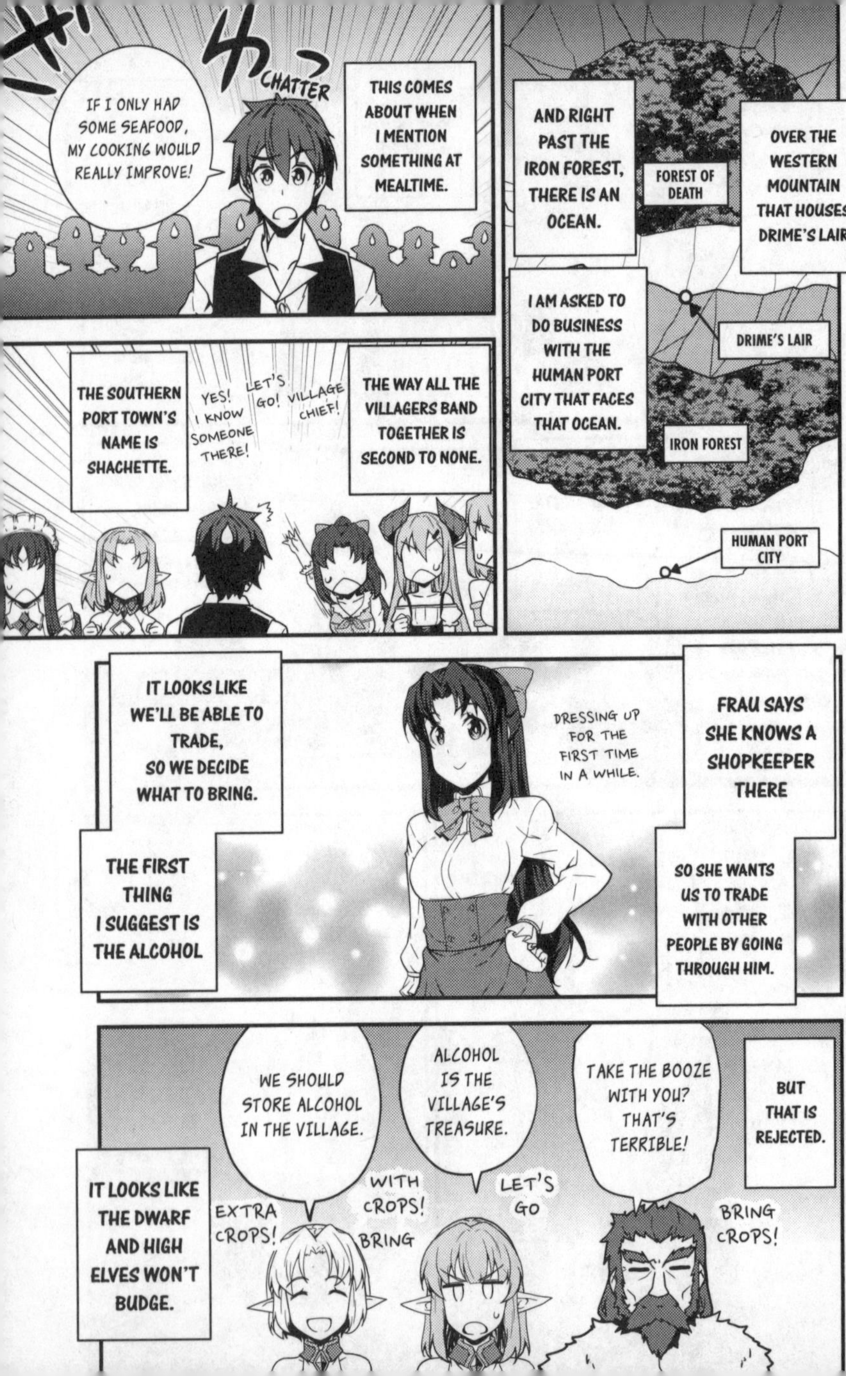
OVER THE WESTERN MOUNTAIN THAT HOUSES DRIME'S LAIR
FOREST OF DEATH
AND RIGHT PAST THE IRON FOREST, THERE IS AN OCEAN.
DRIME'S LAIR
I AM ASKED TO DO BUSINESS WITH THE HUMAN PORT CITY THAT FACES THAT OCEAN.
IRON FOREST
HUMAN PORT CITY
THIS COMES ABOUT WHEN I MENTION SOMETHING AT MEALTIME.
CHATTER
IF I ONLY HAD SOME SEAFOOD, MY COOKING WOULD REALLY IMPROVE!
THE WAY ALL THE VILLAGERS BAND TOGETHER IS SECOND TO NONE.
LET'S GO! VILLAGE CHIEF!
YES! I KNOW SOMEONE THERE!
THE SOUTHERN PORT TOWN'S NAME IS SHACHETTE.
FRAU SAYS SHE KNOWS A SHOPKEEPER THERE
SO SHE WANTS US TO TRADE WITH OTHER PEOPLE BY GOING THROUGH HIM.
DRESSING UP FOR THE FIRST TIME IN A WHILE.
IT LOOKS LIKE WE'LL BE ABLE TO TRADE, SO WE DECIDE WHAT TO BRING.
THE FIRST THING I SUGGEST IS THE ALCOHOL
BUT THAT IS REJECTED.
TAKE THE BOOZE WITH YOU? THAT'S TERRIBLE!
BRING CROPS!
ALCOHOL IS THE VILLAGE'S TREASURE.
LET'S GO
WITH CROPS!
BRING
WE SHOULD STORE ALCOHOL IN THE VILLAGE.
EXTRA CROPS!
IT LOOKS LIKE THE DWARF AND HIGH ELVES WON'T BUDGE.

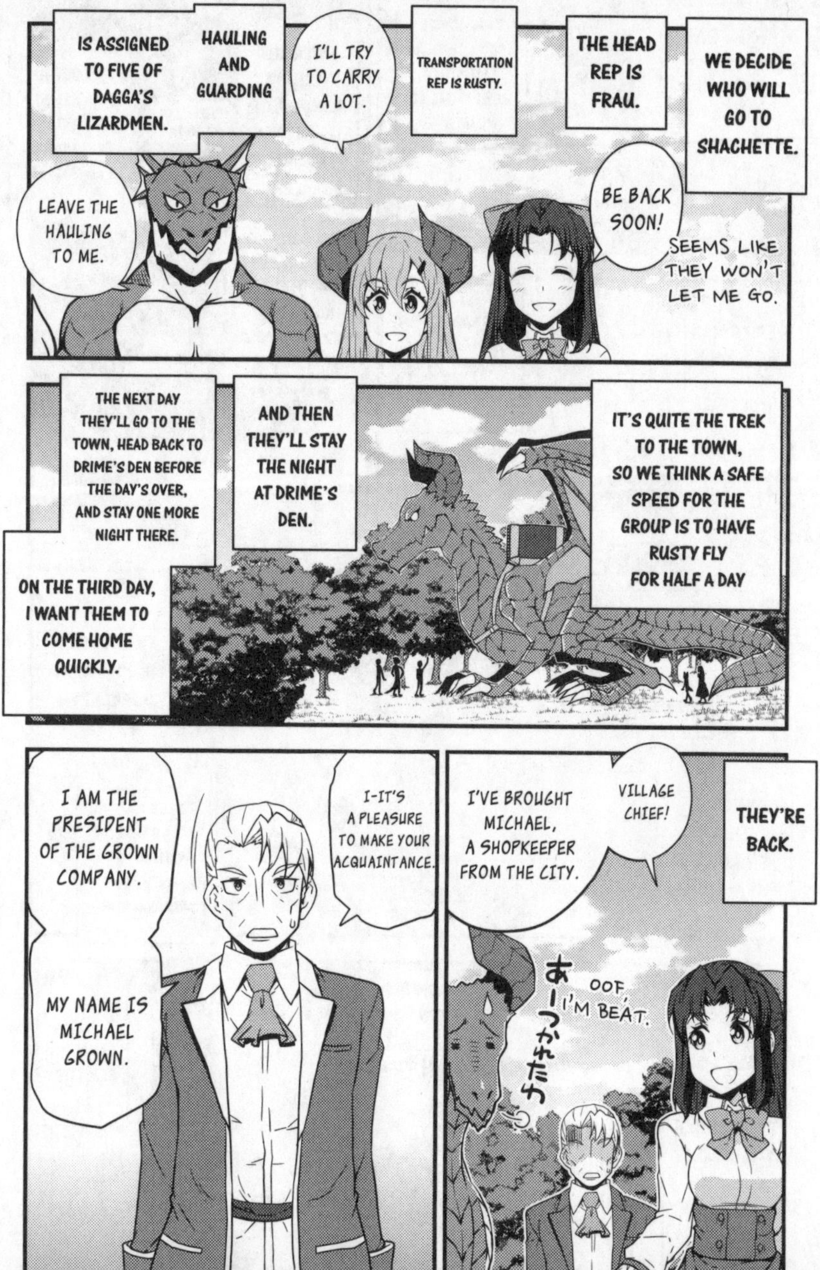
WE DECIDE WHO WILL GO TO SHACHETTE.
THE HEAD REP IS FRAU.
TRANSPORTATION REP IS RUSTY.
I'LL TRY TO CARRY A LOT.
HAULING AND GUARDING
IS ASSIGNED TO FIVE OF DAGGA'S LIZARDMEN.
BE BACK SOON!
SEEMS LIKE THEY WON'T LET ME GO.
LEAVE THE HAULING TO ME.
IT'S QUITE THE TREK TO THE TOWN, SO WE THINK A SAFE SPEED FOR THE GROUP IS TO HAVE RUSTY FLY FOR HALF A DAY
AND THEN THEY'LL STAY THE NIGHT AT DRIME'S DEN.
THE NEXT DAY THEY'LL GO TO THE TOWN, HEAD BACK TO DRIME'S DEN BEFORE THE DAY'S OVER, AND STAY ONE MORE NIGHT THERE.
ON THE THIRD DAY, I WANT THEM TO COME HOME QUICKLY.
THEY'RE BACK.
VILLAGE CHIEF!
I'VE BROUGHT MICHAEL, A SHOPKEEPER FROM THE CITY.
あーつかれたわ
OOF, I'M BEAT.
I-IT'S A PLEASURE TO MAKE YOUR ACQUAINTANCE.
I AM THE PRESIDENT OF THE GROWN COMPANY.
MY NAME IS MICHAEL GROWN.

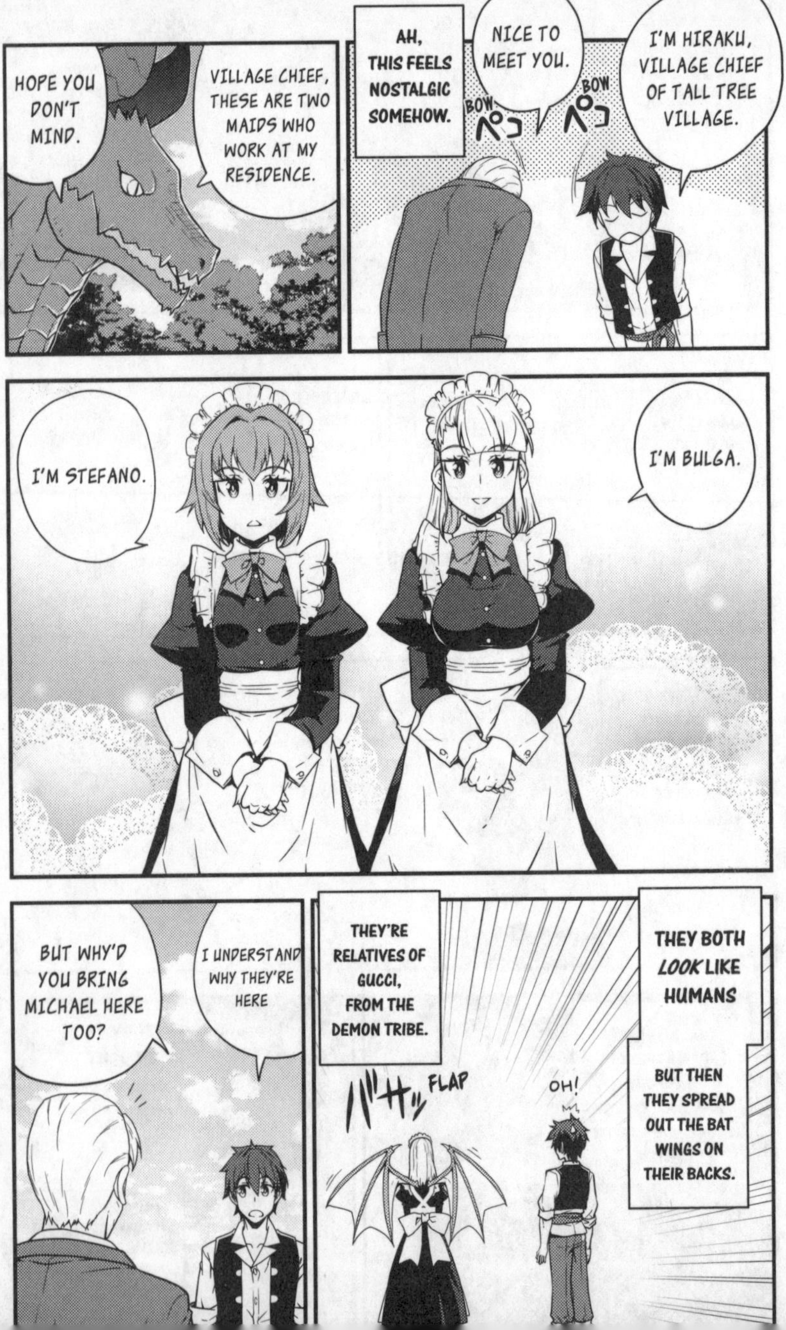
I'M HIRAKU, VILLAGE CHIEF OF TALL TREE VILLAGE.
BOW ペコ
NICE TO MEET YOU.
BOW ペコ
AH, THIS FEELS NOSTALGIC SOMEHOW.
VILLAGE CHIEF, THESE ARE TWO MAIDS WHO WORK AT MY RESIDENCE.
HOPE YOU DON'T MIND.
I'M BULGA.
I'M STEFANO.
THEY BOTH *LOOK* LIKE HUMANS
THEY'RE RELATIVES OF GUCCI, FROM THE DEMON TRIBE.
BUT THEN THEY SPREAD OUT THE BAT WINGS ON THEIR BACKS.
OH!
バサッ FLAP
I UNDERSTAND WHY THEY'RE HERE
BUT WHY'D YOU BRING MICHAEL HERE TOO?

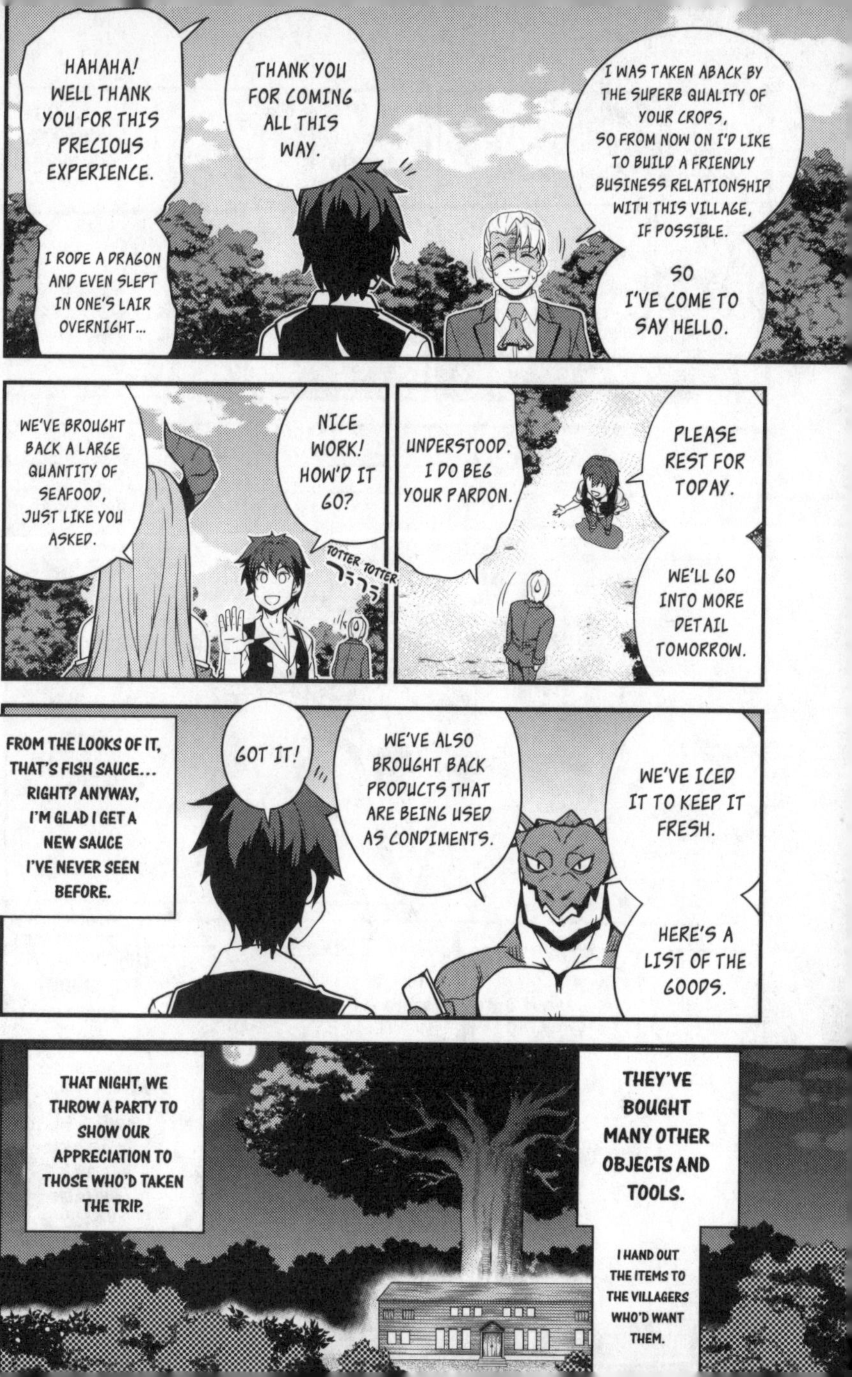
I WAS TAKEN ABACK BY THE SUPERB QUALITY OF YOUR CROPS, SO FROM NOW ON I'D LIKE TO BUILD A FRIENDLY BUSINESS RELATIONSHIP WITH THIS VILLAGE, IF POSSIBLE.
SO I'VE COME TO SAY HELLO.
THANK YOU FOR COMING ALL THIS WAY.
HAHAHA! WELL THANK YOU FOR THIS PRECIOUS EXPERIENCE.
I RODE A DRAGON AND EVEN SLEPT IN ONE'S LAIR OVERNIGHT...
PLEASE REST FOR TODAY.
WE'LL GO INTO MORE DETAIL TOMORROW.
UNDERSTOOD. I DO BEG YOUR PARDON.
NICE WORK! HOW'D IT GO?
TOTTER TOTTER
WE'VE BROUGHT BACK A LARGE QUANTITY OF SEAFOOD, JUST LIKE YOU ASKED.
WE'VE ICED IT TO KEEP IT FRESH.
HERE'S A LIST OF THE GOODS.
WE'VE ALSO BROUGHT BACK PRODUCTS THAT ARE BEING USED AS CONDIMENTS.
GOT IT!
FROM THE LOOKS OF IT, THAT'S FISH SAUCE... RIGHT? ANYWAY, I'M GLAD I GET A NEW SAUCE I'VE NEVER SEEN BEFORE.
THEY'VE BOUGHT MANY OTHER OBJECTS AND TOOLS.
I HAND OUT THE ITEMS TO THE VILLAGERS WHO'D WANT THEM.
THAT NIGHT, WE THROW A PARTY TO SHOW OUR APPRECIATION TO THOSE WHO'D TAKEN THE TRIP.

CHAPTER 34: NEGOTIATIONS?

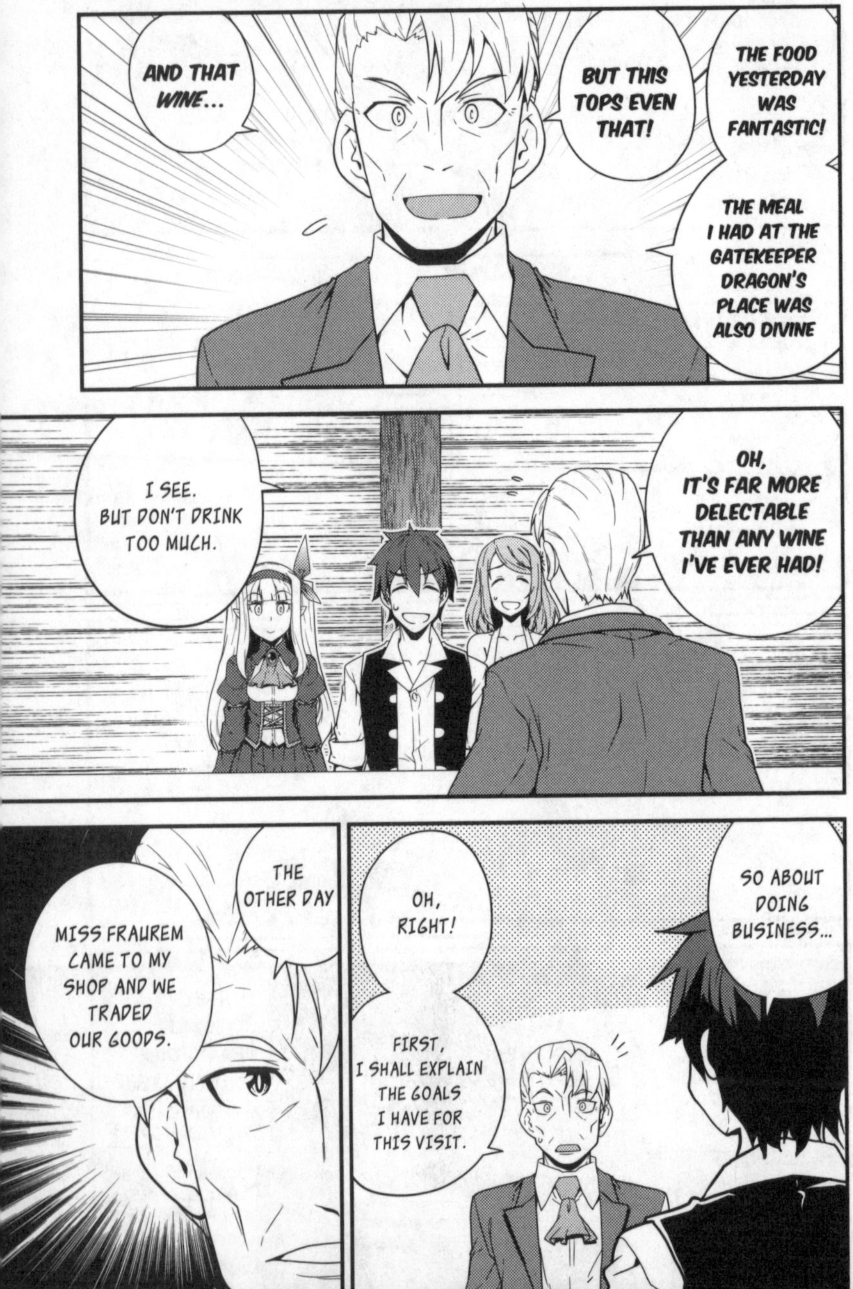
THE FOOD YESTERDAY WAS FANTASTIC!
THE MEAL I HAD AT THE GATEKEEPER DRAGON'S PLACE WAS ALSO DIVINE
BUT THIS TOPS EVEN THAT!
AND THAT WINE...
OH, IT'S FAR MORE DELECTABLE THAN ANY WINE I'VE EVER HAD!
I SEE. BUT DON'T DRINK TOO MUCH.
SO ABOUT DOING BUSINESS...
OH, RIGHT!
FIRST, I SHALL EXPLAIN THE GOALS I HAVE FOR THIS VISIT.
THE OTHER DAY
MISS FRAUREM CAME TO MY SHOP AND WE TRADED OUR GOODS.

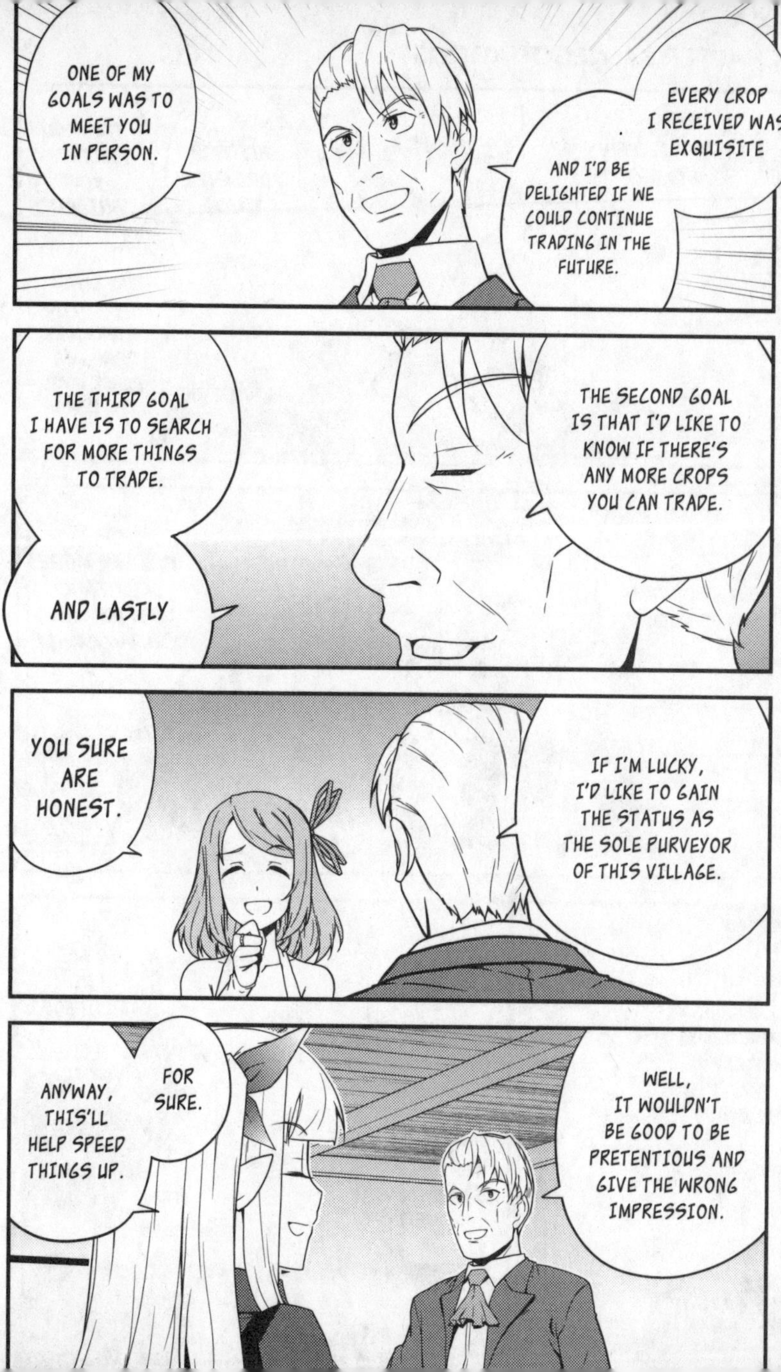
EVERY CROP I RECEIVED WAS EXQUISITE
AND I'D BE DELIGHTED IF WE COULD CONTINUE TRADING IN THE FUTURE.
ONE OF MY GOALS WAS TO MEET YOU IN PERSON.
THE SECOND GOAL IS THAT I'D LIKE TO KNOW IF THERE'S ANY MORE CROPS YOU CAN TRADE.
THE THIRD GOAL I HAVE IS TO SEARCH FOR MORE THINGS TO TRADE.
AND LASTLY
IF I'M LUCKY, I'D LIKE TO GAIN THE STATUS AS THE SOLE PURVEYOR OF THIS VILLAGE.
YOU SURE ARE HONEST.
WELL, IT WOULDN'T BE GOOD TO BE PRETENTIOUS AND GIVE THE WRONG IMPRESSION.
FOR SURE.
ANYWAY, THIS'LL HELP SPEED THINGS UP.

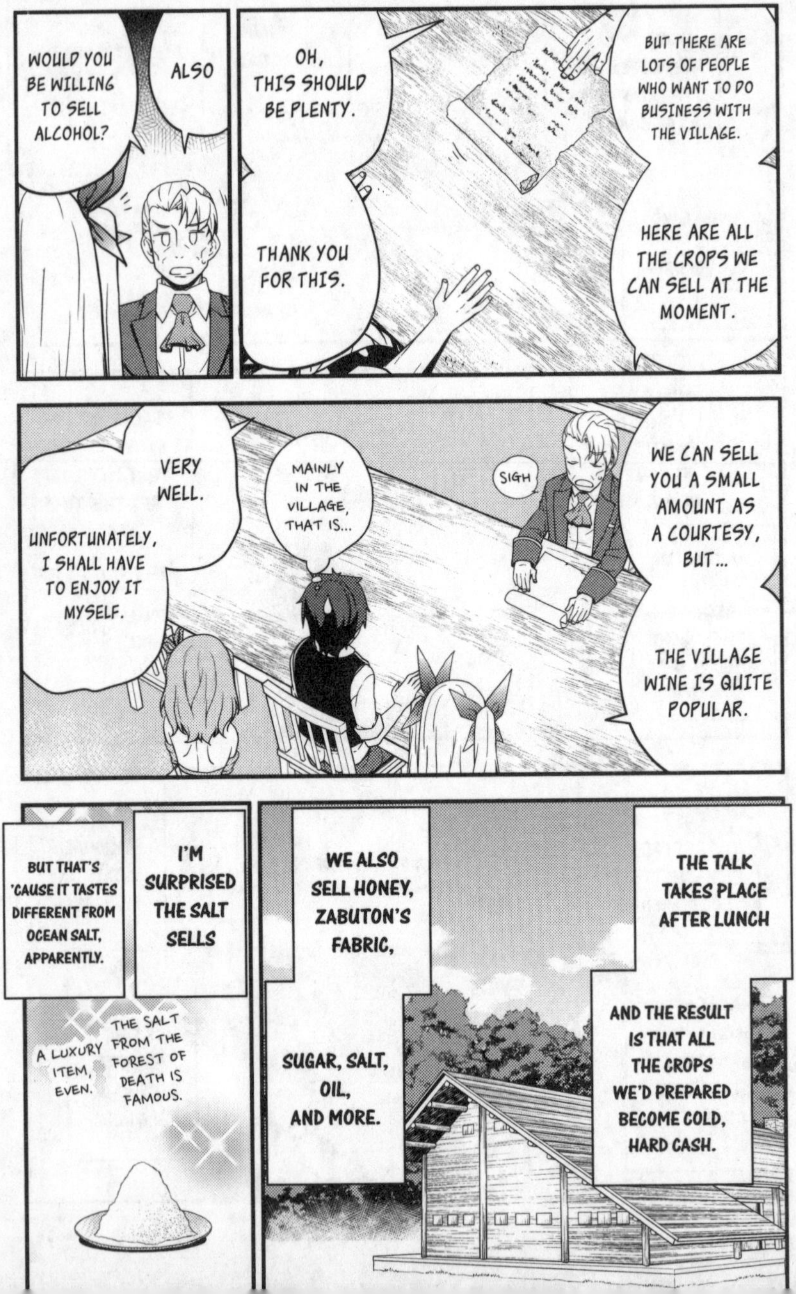
BUT THERE ARE LOTS OF PEOPLE WHO WANT TO DO BUSINESS WITH THE VILLAGE.
HERE ARE ALL THE CROPS WE CAN SELL AT THE MOMENT.
OH, THIS SHOULD BE PLENTY.
THANK YOU FOR THIS.
ALSO
WOULD YOU BE WILLING TO SELL ALCOHOL?
WE CAN SELL YOU A SMALL AMOUNT AS A COURTESY, BUT...
THE VILLAGE WINE IS QUITE POPULAR.
SIGH
MAINLY IN THE VILLAGE, THAT IS...
VERY WELL.
UNFORTUNATELY, I SHALL HAVE TO ENJOY IT MYSELF.
THE TALK TAKES PLACE AFTER LUNCH
AND THE RESULT IS THAT ALL THE CROPS WE'D PREPARED BECOME COLD, HARD CASH.
WE ALSO SELL HONEY, ZABUTON'S FABRIC,
SUGAR, SALT, OIL, AND MORE.
I'M SURPRISED THE SALT SELLS
BUT THAT'S 'CAUSE IT TASTES DIFFERENT FROM OCEAN SALT, APPARENTLY.
THE SALT FROM THE FOREST OF DEATH IS FAMOUS.
A LUXURY ITEM, EVEN.

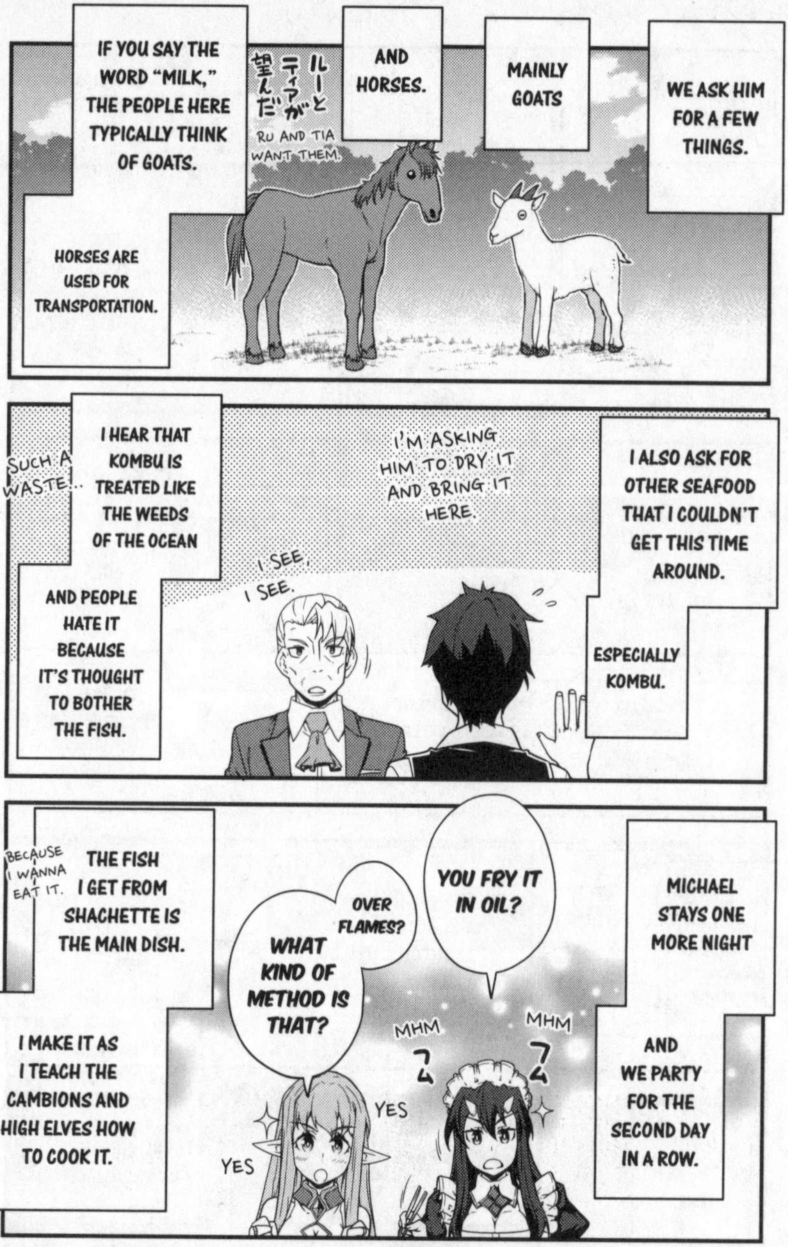
WE ASK HIM FOR A FEW THINGS.
MAINLY GOATS
AND HORSES.
ルーとティアが望んだ
RU AND TIA WANT THEM.
IF YOU SAY THE WORD "MILK," THE PEOPLE HERE TYPICALLY THINK OF GOATS.
HORSES ARE USED FOR TRANSPORTATION.
I ALSO ASK FOR OTHER SEAFOOD THAT I COULDN'T GET THIS TIME AROUND.
ESPECIALLY KOMBU.
I'M ASKING HIM TO DRY IT AND BRING IT HERE.
I SEE, I SEE.
I HEAR THAT KOMBU IS TREATED LIKE THE WEEDS OF THE OCEAN
SUCH A WASTE...
AND PEOPLE HATE IT BECAUSE IT'S THOUGHT TO BOTHER THE FISH.
MICHAEL STAYS ONE MORE NIGHT
AND WE PARTY FOR THE SECOND DAY IN A ROW.
YOU FRY IT IN OIL?
MHM
OVER FLAMES?
WHAT KIND OF METHOD IS THAT?
MHM
YES
YES
THE FISH I GET FROM SHACHETTE IS THE MAIN DISH.
BECAUSE I WANNA EAT IT.
I MAKE IT AS I TEACH THE CAMBIONS AND HIGH ELVES HOW TO COOK IT.

CHAPTER 35: THE FOOD CULTURE

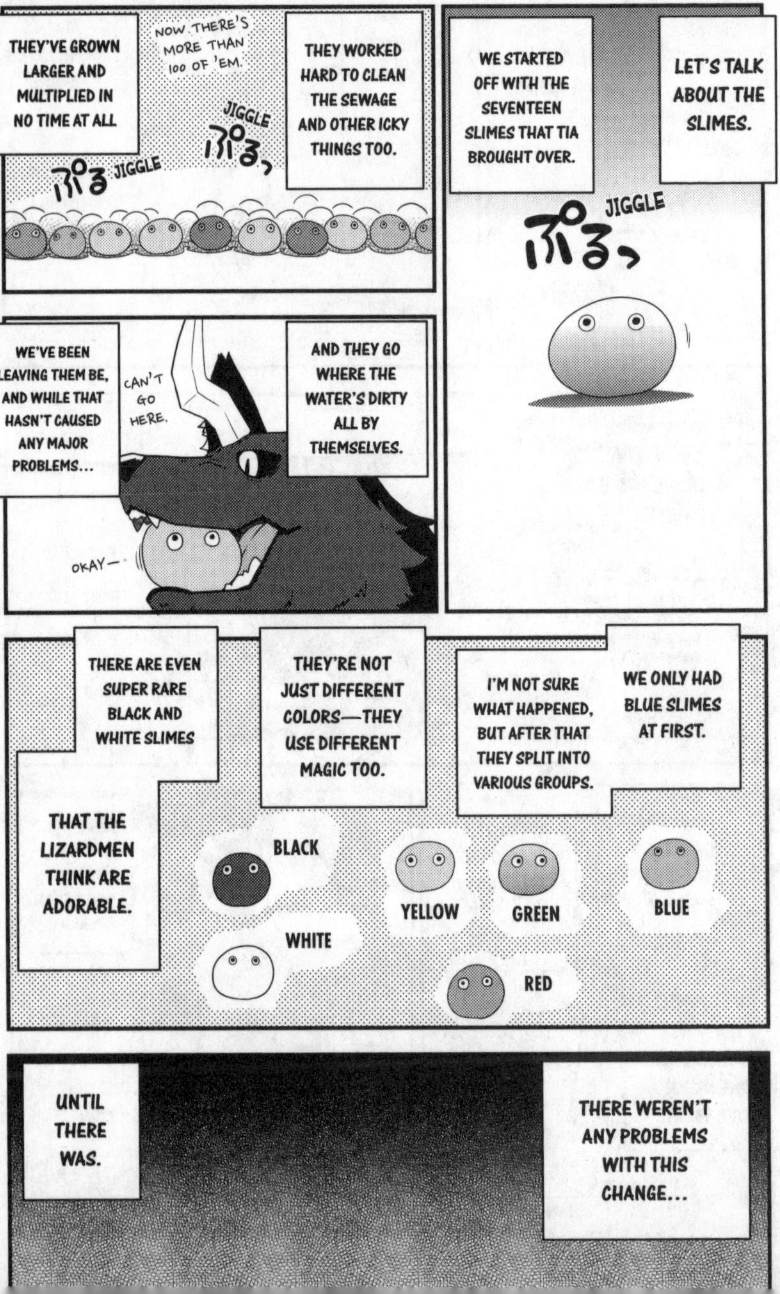
LET'S TALK ABOUT THE SLIMES.
WE STARTED OFF WITH THE SEVENTEEN SLIMES THAT TIA BROUGHT OVER.
ぷるっ JIGGLE
THEY WORKED HARD TO CLEAN THE SEWAGE AND OTHER ICKY THINGS TOO.
NOW THERE'S MORE THAN 100 OF 'EM.
ぷるっ JIGGLE
THEY'VE GROWN LARGER AND MULTIPLIED IN NO TIME AT ALL
ぷる JIGGLE
AND THEY GO WHERE THE WATER'S DIRTY ALL BY THEMSELVES.
CAN'T GO HERE.
WE'VE BEEN LEAVING THEM BE, AND WHILE THAT HASN'T CAUSED ANY MAJOR PROBLEMS...
OKAY—
WE ONLY HAD BLUE SLIMES AT FIRST.
I'M NOT SURE WHAT HAPPENED, BUT AFTER THAT THEY SPLIT INTO VARIOUS GROUPS.
THEY'RE NOT JUST DIFFERENT COLORS—THEY USE DIFFERENT MAGIC TOO.
THERE ARE EVEN SUPER RARE BLACK AND WHITE SLIMES
THAT THE LIZARDMEN THINK ARE ADORABLE.
BLUE
GREEN
YELLOW
BLACK
WHITE
RED
THERE WEREN'T ANY PROBLEMS WITH THIS CHANGE...
UNTIL THERE WAS.

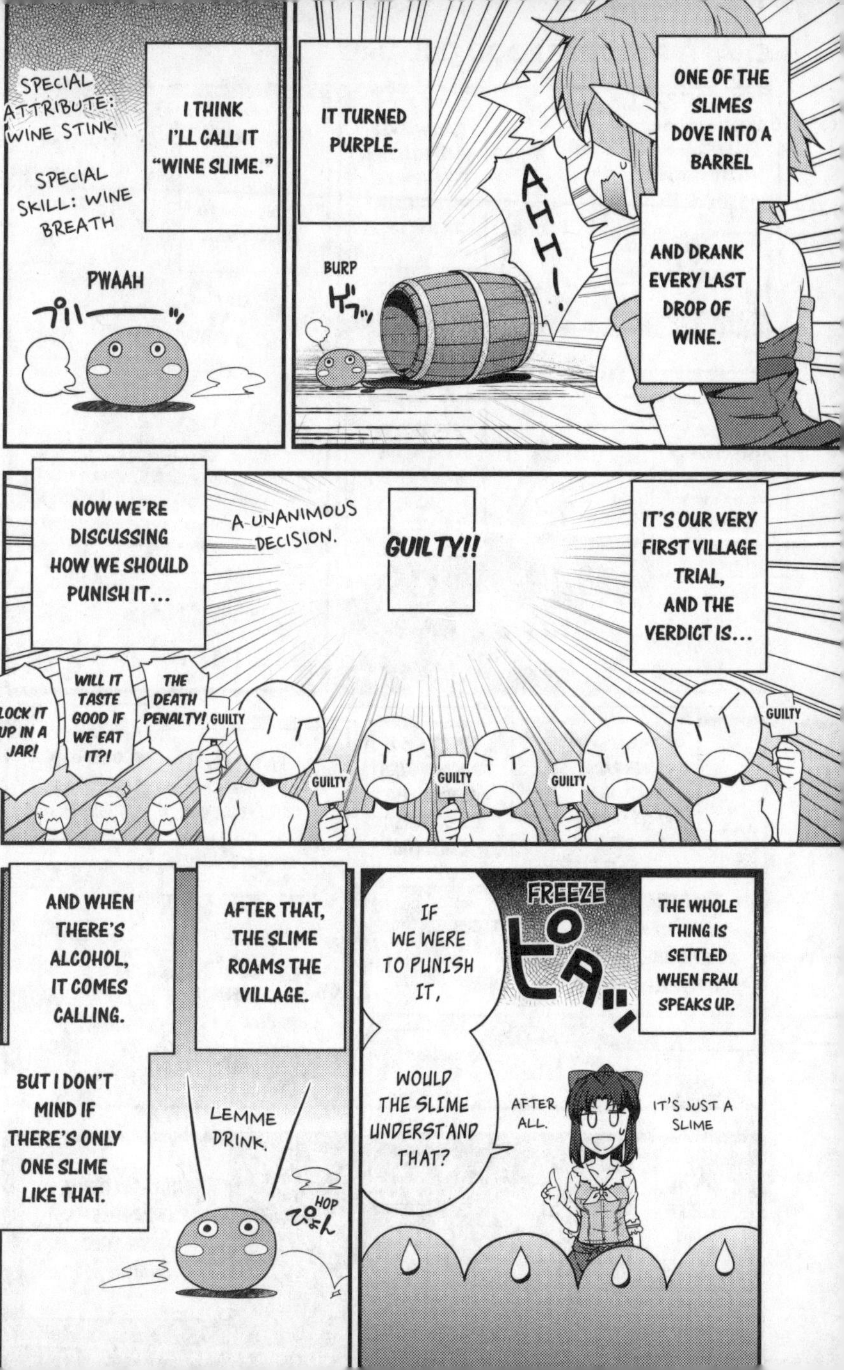

ONE OF THE SLIMES DOVE INTO A BARREL
AND DRANK EVERY LAST DROP OF WINE.
AHH!
BURP
ゲフッ
IT TURNED PURPLE.
I THINK I'LL CALL IT "WINE SLIME."
SPECIAL ATTRIBUTE: WINE STINK
SPECIAL SKILL: WINE BREATH
PWAAH
プハーーーッ
IT'S OUR VERY FIRST VILLAGE TRIAL, AND THE VERDICT IS...
GUILTY!!
A UNANIMOUS DECISION.
NOW WE'RE DISCUSSING HOW WE SHOULD PUNISH IT...
GUILTY
GUILTY
GUILTY
GUILTY
GUILTY
THE DEATH PENALTY!
WILL IT TASTE GOOD IF WE EAT IT?!
LOCK IT UP IN A JAR!
THE WHOLE THING IS SETTLED WHEN FRAU SPEAKS UP.
FREEZE
ピタッ
IF WE WERE TO PUNISH IT,
WOULD THE SLIME UNDERSTAND THAT?
IT'S JUST A SLIME
AFTER ALL.
AFTER THAT, THE SLIME ROAMS THE VILLAGE.
AND WHEN THERE'S ALCOHOL, IT COMES CALLING.
LEMME DRINK.
HOP
ぴょん
BUT I DON'T MIND IF THERE'S ONLY ONE SLIME LIKE THAT.

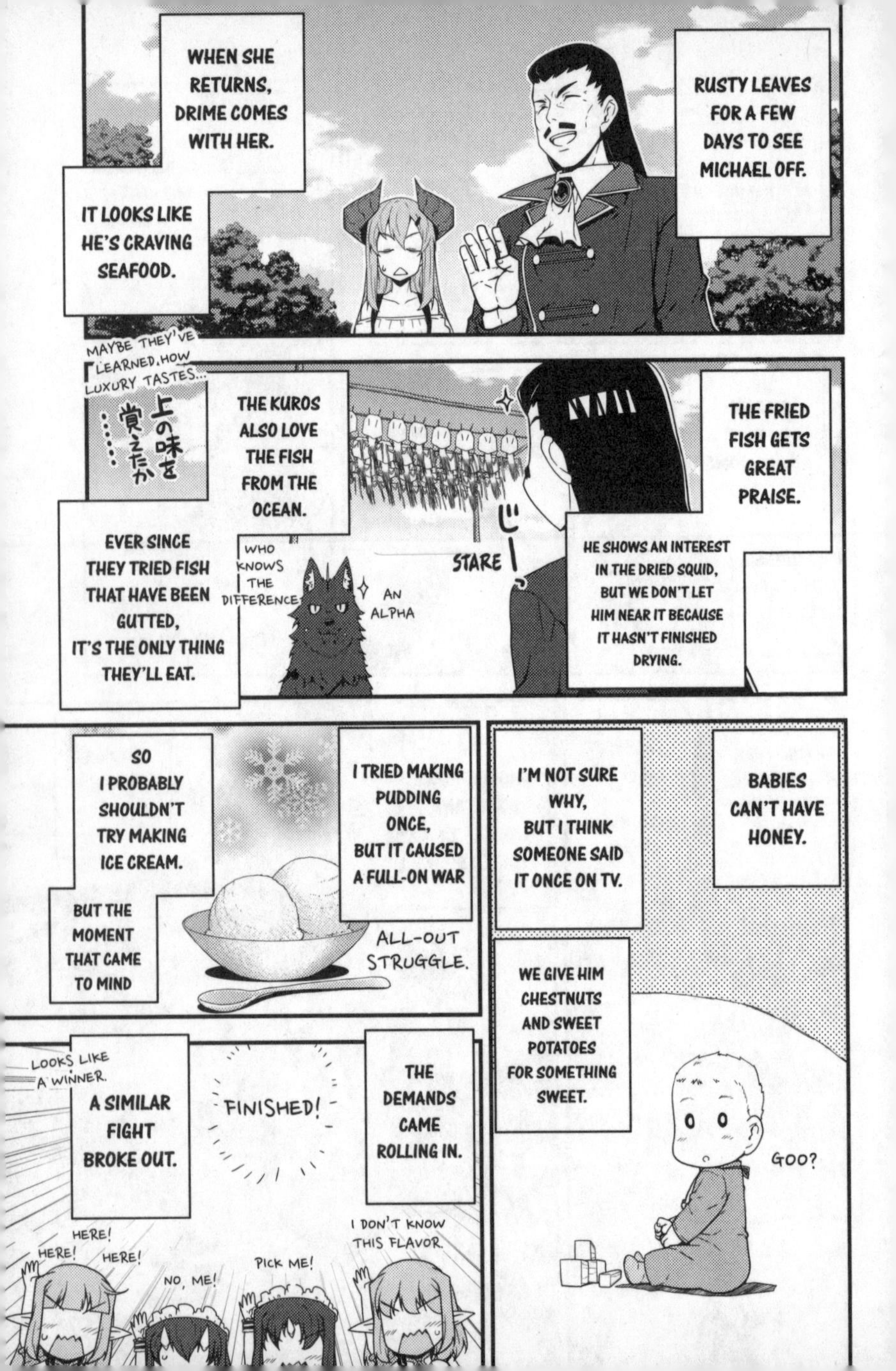
RUSTY LEAVES FOR A FEW DAYS TO SEE MICHAEL OFF.
WHEN SHE RETURNS, DRIME COMES WITH HER.
IT LOOKS LIKE HE'S CRAVING SEAFOOD.
THE FRIED FISH GETS GREAT PRAISE.
HE SHOWS AN INTEREST IN THE DRIED SQUID, BUT WE DON'T LET HIM NEAR IT BECAUSE IT HASN'T FINISHED DRYING.
じー
STARE
THE KUROS ALSO LOVE THE FISH FROM THE OCEAN.
上の味を覚えたか……
MAYBE THEY'VE LEARNED HOW LUXURY TASTES...
EVER SINCE THEY TRIED FISH THAT HAVE BEEN GUTTED, IT'S THE ONLY THING THEY'LL EAT.
AN ALPHA
WHO KNOWS THE DIFFERENCE
BABIES CAN'T HAVE HONEY.
I'M NOT SURE WHY, BUT I THINK SOMEONE SAID IT ONCE ON TV.
WE GIVE HIM CHESTNUTS AND SWEET POTATOES FOR SOMETHING SWEET.
GOO?
I TRIED MAKING PUDDING ONCE, BUT IT CAUSED A FULL-ON WAR
ALL-OUT STRUGGLE.
SO I PROBABLY SHOULDN'T TRY MAKING ICE CREAM.
BUT THE MOMENT THAT CAME TO MIND
THE DEMANDS CAME ROLLING IN.
FINISHED!
A SIMILAR FIGHT BROKE OUT.
LOOKS LIKE A WINNER.
I DON'T KNOW THIS FLAVOR.
PICK ME!
NO, ME!
HERE!
HERE!
HERE!

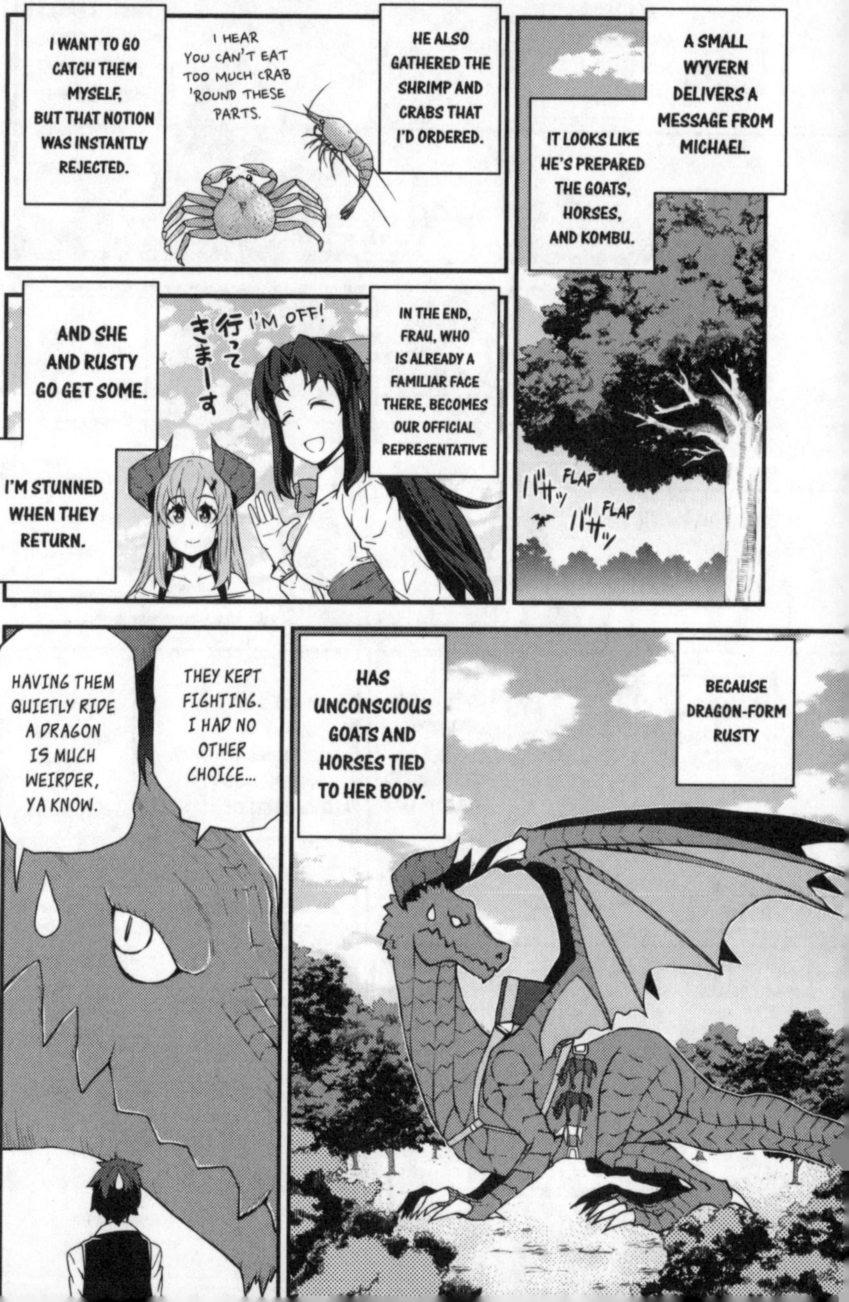
A SMALL WYVERN DELIVERS A MESSAGE FROM MICHAEL.
IT LOOKS LIKE HE'S PREPARED THE GOATS, HORSES, AND KOMBU.
バサッ FLAP
バサッ FLAP
HE ALSO GATHERED THE SHRIMP AND CRABS THAT I'D ORDERED.
I HEAR YOU CAN'T EAT TOO MUCH CRAB 'ROUND THESE PARTS.
I WANT TO GO CATCH THEM MYSELF, BUT THAT NOTION WAS INSTANTLY REJECTED.
IN THE END, FRAU, WHO IS ALREADY A FAMILIAR FACE THERE, BECOMES OUR OFFICIAL REPRESENTATIVE
行ってきまーす I'M OFF!
AND SHE AND RUSTY GO GET SOME.
I'M STUNNED WHEN THEY RETURN.
BECAUSE DRAGON-FORM RUSTY
HAS UNCONSCIOUS GOATS AND HORSES TIED TO HER BODY.
THEY KEPT FIGHTING. I HAD NO OTHER CHOICE...
HAVING THEM QUIETLY RIDE A DRAGON IS MUCH WEIRDER, YA KNOW.

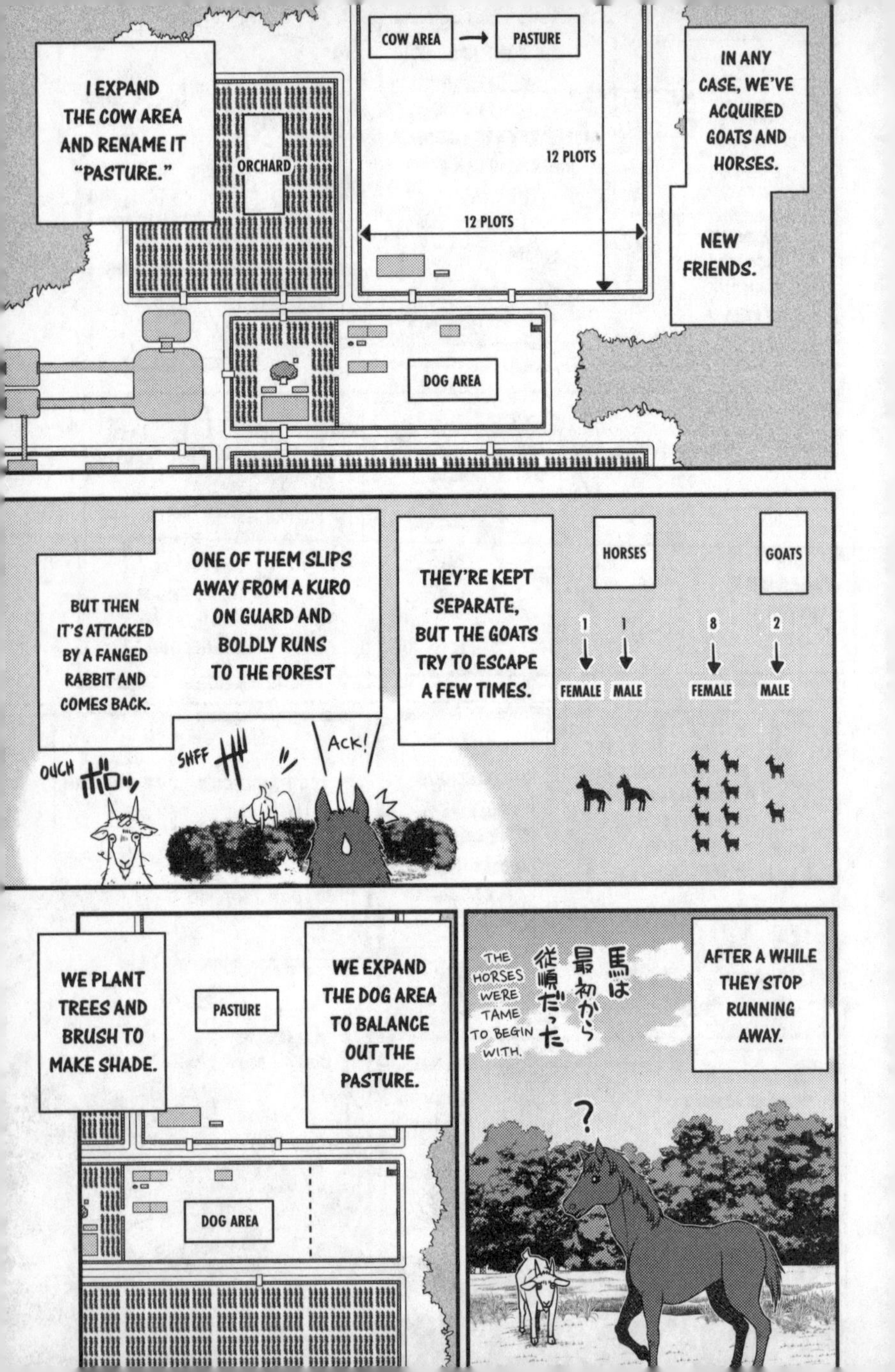

COW AREA → PASTURE

I EXPAND THE COW AREA AND RENAME IT "PASTURE."

ORCHARD

12 PLOTS

12 PLOTS

IN ANY CASE, WE'VE ACQUIRED GOATS AND HORSES.

NEW FRIENDS.

DOG AREA

BUT THEN IT'S ATTACKED BY A FANGED RABBIT AND COMES BACK.

ONE OF THEM SLIPS AWAY FROM A KURO ON GUARD AND BOLDLY RUNS TO THE FOREST

THEY'RE KEPT SEPARATE, BUT THE GOATS TRY TO ESCAPE A FEW TIMES.

HORSES

GOATS

1	1		8	2
FEMALE	MALE		FEMALE	MALE

OUCH ボカッ

SHFF

ACK!

WE PLANT TREES AND BRUSH TO MAKE SHADE.

PASTURE

WE EXPAND THE DOG AREA TO BALANCE OUT THE PASTURE.

THE HORSES WERE TAME TO BEGIN WITH.

馬は最初から従順だった

AFTER A WHILE THEY STOP RUNNING AWAY.

?

DOG AREA

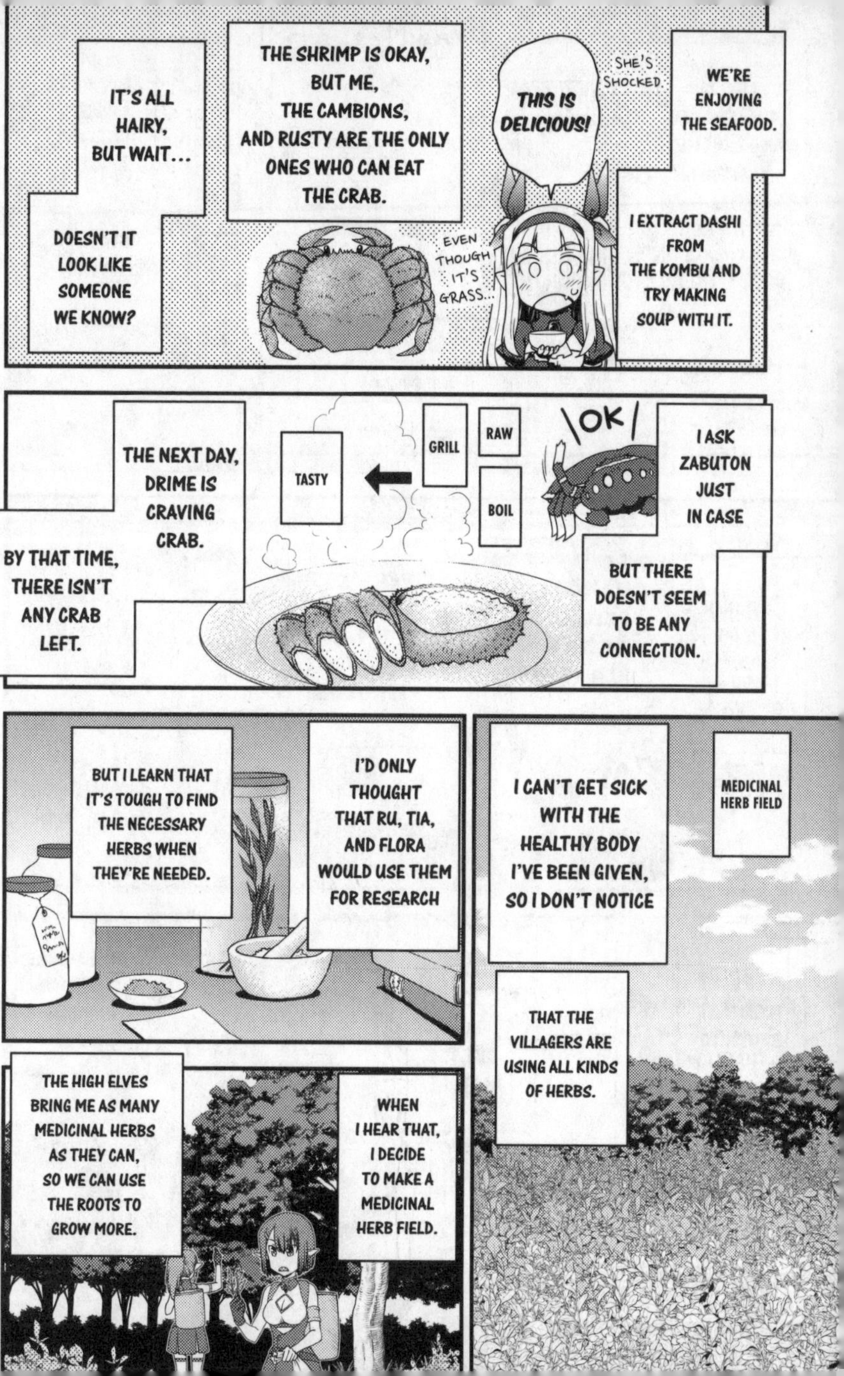
WE'RE ENJOYING THE SEAFOOD.
SHE'S SHOCKED
THIS IS DELICIOUS!
I EXTRACT DASHI FROM THE KOMBU AND TRY MAKING SOUP WITH IT.
EVEN THOUGH IT'S GRASS...
THE SHRIMP IS OKAY, BUT ME, THE CAMBIONS, AND RUSTY ARE THE ONLY ONES WHO CAN EAT THE CRAB.
IT'S ALL HAIRY, BUT WAIT...
DOESN'T IT LOOK LIKE SOMEONE WE KNOW?
I ASK ZABUTON JUST IN CASE
\OK/
BUT THERE DOESN'T SEEM TO BE ANY CONNECTION.
RAW
GRILL
BOIL
TASTY
THE NEXT DAY, DRIME IS CRAVING CRAB.
BY THAT TIME, THERE ISN'T ANY CRAB LEFT.
MEDICINAL HERB FIELD
I CAN'T GET SICK WITH THE HEALTHY BODY I'VE BEEN GIVEN, SO I DON'T NOTICE
THAT THE VILLAGERS ARE USING ALL KINDS OF HERBS.
I'D ONLY THOUGHT THAT RU, TIA, AND FLORA WOULD USE THEM FOR RESEARCH
BUT I LEARN THAT IT'S TOUGH TO FIND THE NECESSARY HERBS WHEN THEY'RE NEEDED.
WHEN I HEAR THAT, I DECIDE TO MAKE A MEDICINAL HERB FIELD.
THE HIGH ELVES BRING ME AS MANY MEDICINAL HERBS AS THEY CAN, SO WE CAN USE THE ROOTS TO GROW MORE.

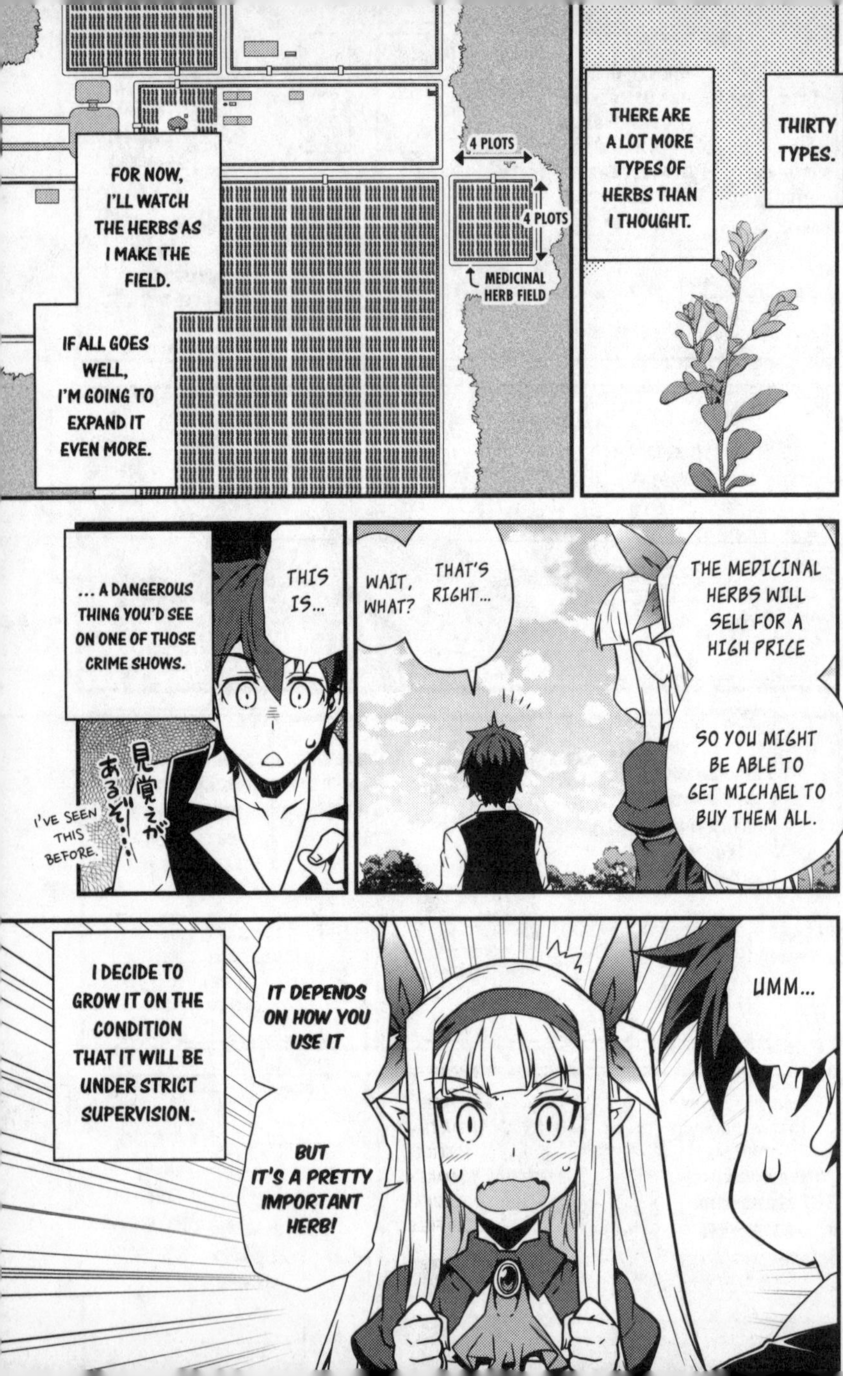
THIRTY TYPES.
THERE ARE A LOT MORE TYPES OF HERBS THAN I THOUGHT.
4 PLOTS
4 PLOTS
MEDICINAL HERB FIELD
FOR NOW, I'LL WATCH THE HERBS AS I MAKE THE FIELD.
IF ALL GOES WELL, I'M GOING TO EXPAND IT EVEN MORE.
THE MEDICINAL HERBS WILL SELL FOR A HIGH PRICE
SO YOU MIGHT BE ABLE TO GET MICHAEL TO BUY THEM ALL.
THAT'S RIGHT...
WAIT, WHAT?
THIS IS...
... A DANGEROUS THING YOU'D SEE ON ONE OF THOSE CRIME SHOWS.
見覚えがあるぞ…
I'VE SEEN THIS BEFORE.
UMM...
IT DEPENDS ON HOW YOU USE IT
BUT IT'S A PRETTY IMPORTANT HERB!
I DECIDE TO GROW IT ON THE CONDITION THAT IT WILL BE UNDER STRICT SUPERVISION.

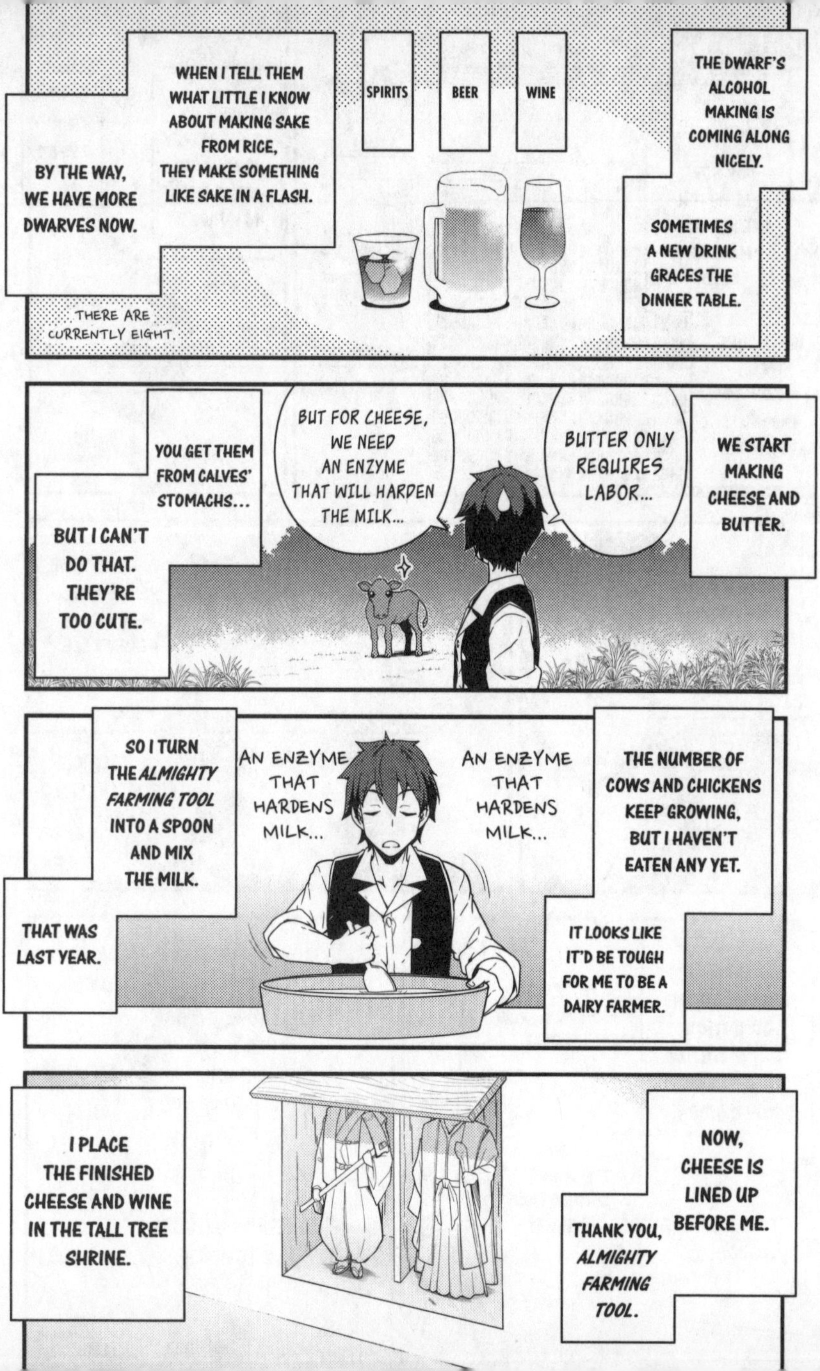
THE DWARF'S ALCOHOL MAKING IS COMING ALONG NICELY.
SOMETIMES A NEW DRINK GRACES THE DINNER TABLE.
WINE
BEER
SPIRITS
WHEN I TELL THEM WHAT LITTLE I KNOW ABOUT MAKING SAKE FROM RICE, THEY MAKE SOMETHING LIKE SAKE IN A FLASH.
BY THE WAY, WE HAVE MORE DWARVES NOW.
THERE ARE CURRENTLY EIGHT.
WE START MAKING CHEESE AND BUTTER.
BUTTER ONLY REQUIRES LABOR...
BUT FOR CHEESE, WE NEED AN ENZYME THAT WILL HARDEN THE MILK...
YOU GET THEM FROM CALVES' STOMACHS...
BUT I CAN'T DO THAT. THEY'RE TOO CUTE.
THE NUMBER OF COWS AND CHICKENS KEEP GROWING, BUT I HAVEN'T EATEN ANY YET.
IT LOOKS LIKE IT'D BE TOUGH FOR ME TO BE A DAIRY FARMER.
AN ENZYME THAT HARDENS MILK...
AN ENZYME THAT HARDENS MILK...
SO I TURN THE *ALMIGHTY FARMING TOOL* INTO A SPOON AND MIX THE MILK.
THAT WAS LAST YEAR.
NOW, CHEESE IS LINED UP BEFORE ME.
THANK YOU, *ALMIGHTY FARMING TOOL*.
I PLACE THE FINISHED CHEESE AND WINE IN THE TALL TREE SHRINE.

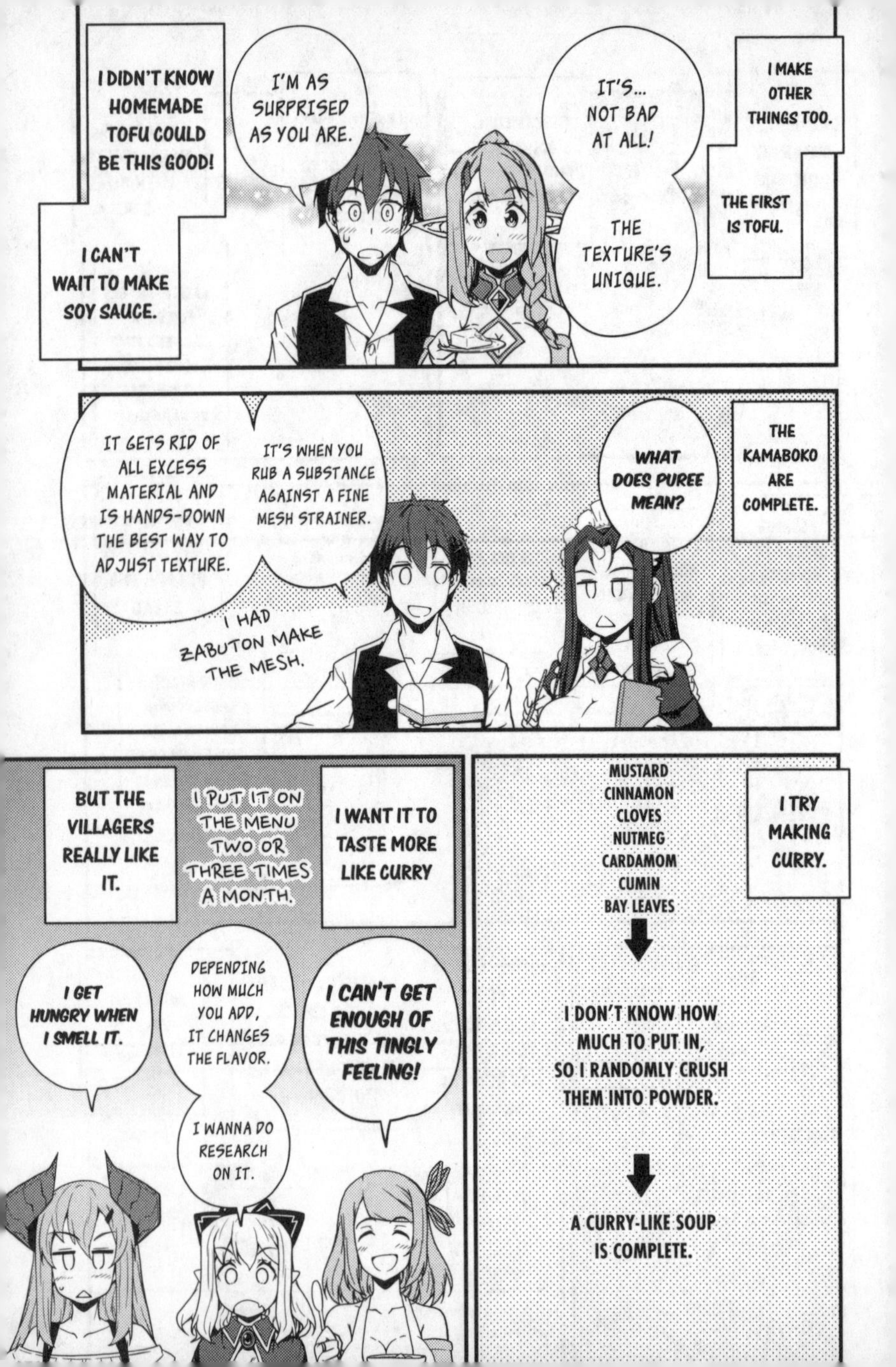
I MAKE OTHER THINGS TOO.
THE FIRST IS TOFU.
IT'S... NOT BAD AT ALL!
THE TEXTURE'S UNIQUE.
I'M AS SURPRISED AS YOU ARE.
I DIDN'T KNOW HOMEMADE TOFU COULD BE THIS GOOD!
I CAN'T WAIT TO MAKE SOY SAUCE.
THE KAMABOKO ARE COMPLETE.
WHAT DOES PUREE MEAN?
IT'S WHEN YOU RUB A SUBSTANCE AGAINST A FINE MESH STRAINER.
IT GETS RID OF ALL EXCESS MATERIAL AND IS HANDS-DOWN THE BEST WAY TO ADJUST TEXTURE.
I HAD ZABUTON MAKE THE MESH.
I TRY MAKING CURRY.
MUSTARD
CINNAMON
CLOVES
NUTMEG
CARDAMOM
CUMIN
BAY LEAVES
I DON'T KNOW HOW MUCH TO PUT IN, SO I RANDOMLY CRUSH THEM INTO POWDER.
A CURRY-LIKE SOUP IS COMPLETE.
I WANT IT TO TASTE MORE LIKE CURRY
I PUT IT ON THE MENU TWO OR THREE TIMES A MONTH.
BUT THE VILLAGERS REALLY LIKE IT.
I CAN'T GET ENOUGH OF THIS TINGLY FEELING!
DEPENDING HOW MUCH YOU ADD, IT CHANGES THE FLAVOR.
I WANNA DO RESEARCH ON IT.
I GET HUNGRY WHEN I SMELL IT.

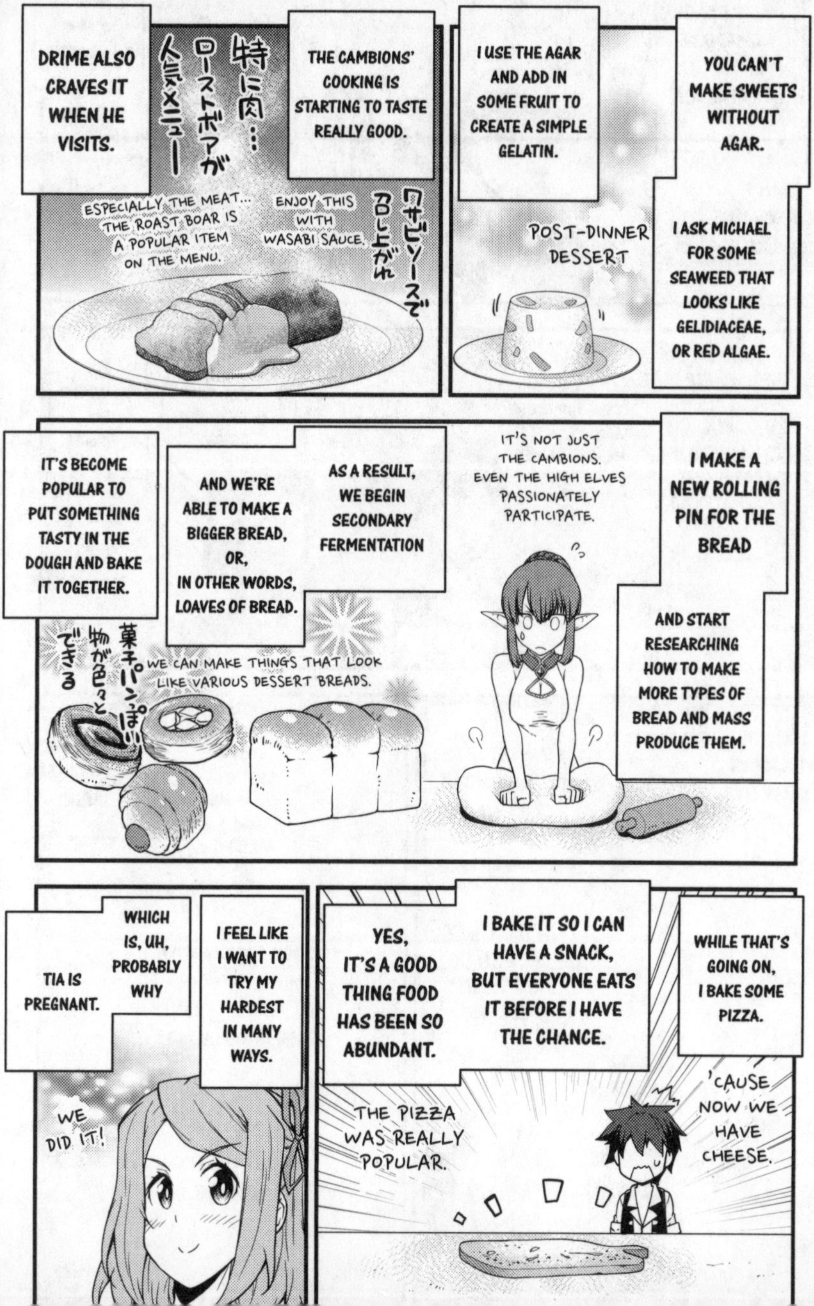
YOU CAN'T MAKE SWEETS WITHOUT AGAR.
I USE THE AGAR AND ADD IN SOME FRUIT TO CREATE A SIMPLE GELATIN.
I ASK MICHAEL FOR SOME SEAWEED THAT LOOKS LIKE GELIDIACEAE, OR RED ALGAE.
POST-DINNER DESSERT
THE CAMBIONS' COOKING IS STARTING TO TASTE REALLY GOOD.
特に肉…ローストボアが人気メニュー
DRIME ALSO CRAVES IT WHEN HE VISITS.
ワサビソースで召し上がれ
ENJOY THIS WITH WASABI SAUCE.
ESPECIALLY THE MEAT... THE ROAST BOAR IS A POPULAR ITEM ON THE MENU.
I MAKE A NEW ROLLING PIN FOR THE BREAD
IT'S NOT JUST THE CAMBIONS. EVEN THE HIGH ELVES PASSIONATELY PARTICIPATE.
AS A RESULT, WE BEGIN SECONDARY FERMENTATION
AND WE'RE ABLE TO MAKE A BIGGER BREAD, OR, IN OTHER WORDS, LOAVES OF BREAD.
IT'S BECOME POPULAR TO PUT SOMETHING TASTY IN THE DOUGH AND BAKE IT TOGETHER.
AND START RESEARCHING HOW TO MAKE MORE TYPES OF BREAD AND MASS PRODUCE THEM.
菓子パンっぽい物が色々とできる
WE CAN MAKE THINGS THAT LOOK LIKE VARIOUS DESSERT BREADS.
WHILE THAT'S GOING ON, I BAKE SOME PIZZA.
I BAKE IT SO I CAN HAVE A SNACK, BUT EVERYONE EATS IT BEFORE I HAVE THE CHANCE.
YES, IT'S A GOOD THING FOOD HAS BEEN SO ABUNDANT.
'CAUSE NOW WE HAVE CHEESE.
THE PIZZA WAS REALLY POPULAR.
I FEEL LIKE I WANT TO TRY MY HARDEST IN MANY WAYS.
WHICH IS, UH, PROBABLY WHY
TIA IS PREGNANT.
WE DID IT!

CHAPTER 36: THE GOVERNOR

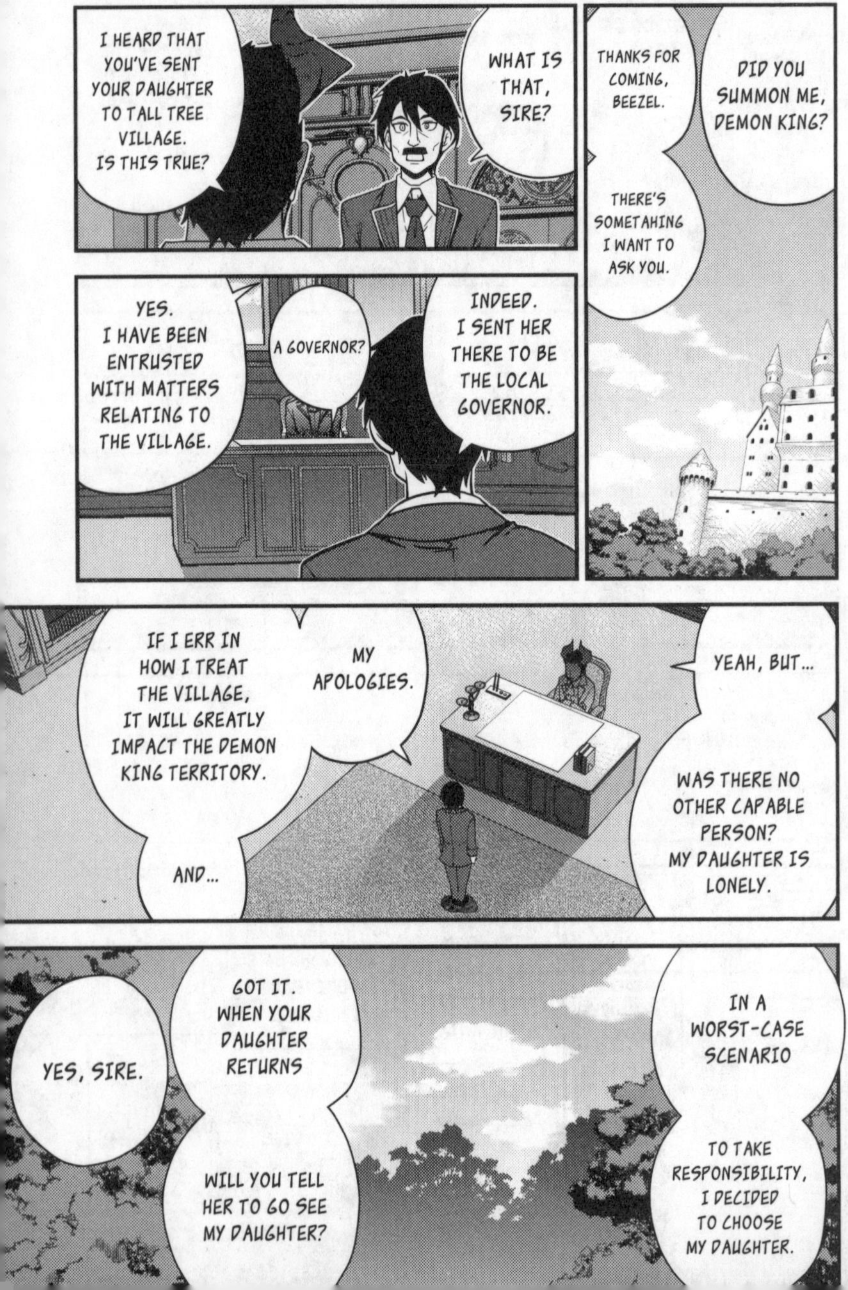
DID YOU SUMMON ME, DEMON KING?
THANKS FOR COMING, BEEZEL.
THERE'S SOMETAHING I WANT TO ASK YOU.
WHAT IS THAT, SIRE?
I HEARD THAT YOU'VE SENT YOUR DAUGHTER TO TALL TREE VILLAGE. IS THIS TRUE?
INDEED. I SENT HER THERE TO BE THE LOCAL GOVERNOR.
A GOVERNOR?
YES. I HAVE BEEN ENTRUSTED WITH MATTERS RELATING TO THE VILLAGE.
YEAH, BUT...
WAS THERE NO OTHER CAPABLE PERSON? MY DAUGHTER IS LONELY.
MY APOLOGIES.
IF I ERR IN HOW I TREAT THE VILLAGE, IT WILL GREATLY IMPACT THE DEMON KING TERRITORY.
AND...
IN A WORST-CASE SCENARIO
TO TAKE RESPONSIBILITY, I DECIDED TO CHOOSE MY DAUGHTER.
GOT IT. WHEN YOUR DAUGHTER RETURNS
WILL YOU TELL HER TO GO SEE MY DAUGHTER?
YES, SIRE.

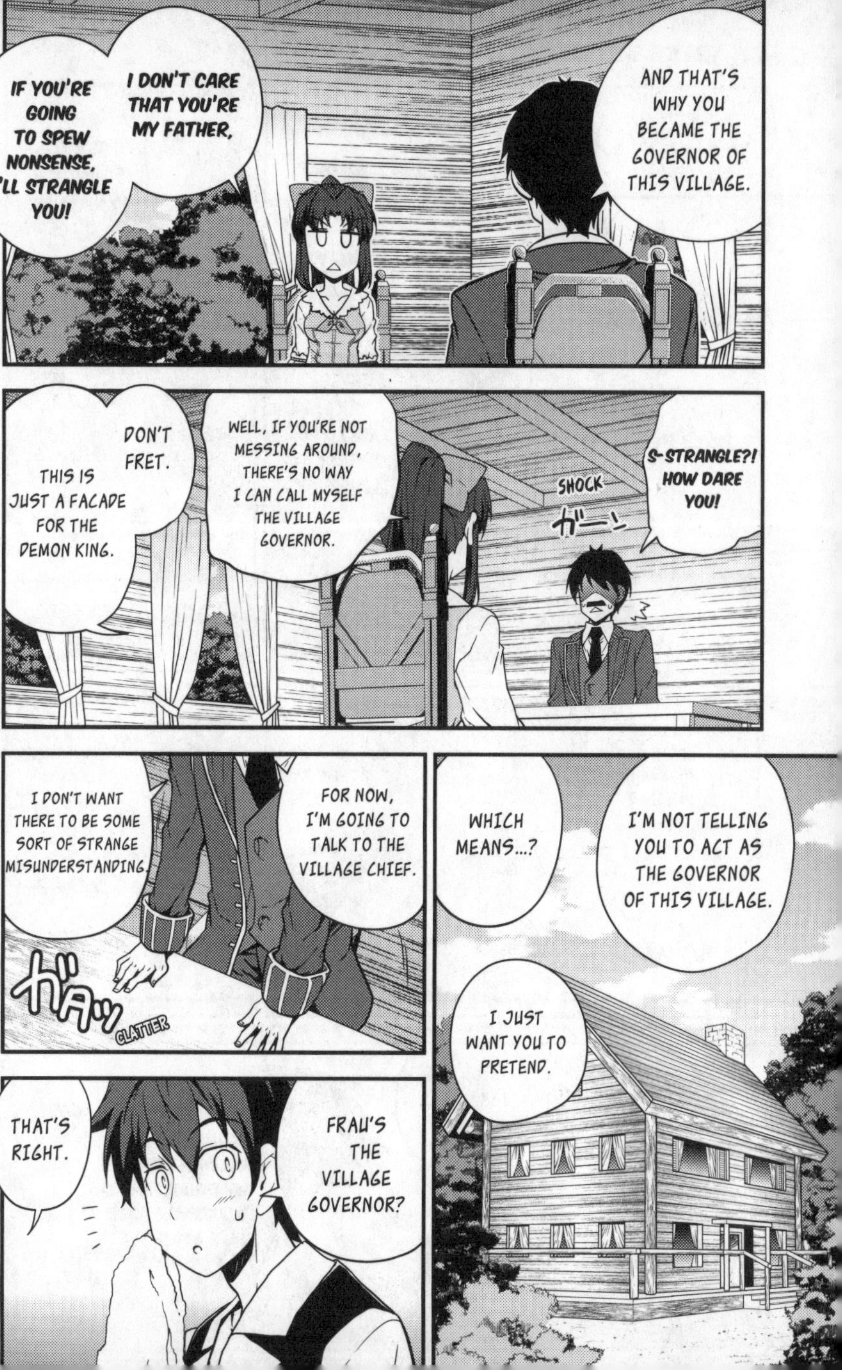
AND THAT'S WHY YOU BECAME THE GOVERNOR OF THIS VILLAGE.
I DON'T CARE THAT YOU'RE MY FATHER,
IF YOU'RE GOING TO SPEW NONSENSE, I'LL STRANGLE YOU!
S-STRANGLE?! HOW DARE YOU!
SHOCK
WELL, IF YOU'RE NOT MESSING AROUND, THERE'S NO WAY I CAN CALL MYSELF THE VILLAGE GOVERNOR.
DON'T FRET.
THIS IS JUST A FACADE FOR THE DEMON KING.
I'M NOT TELLING YOU TO ACT AS THE GOVERNOR OF THIS VILLAGE.
WHICH MEANS...?
I JUST WANT YOU TO PRETEND.
FOR NOW, I'M GOING TO TALK TO THE VILLAGE CHIEF.
I DON'T WANT THERE TO BE SOME SORT OF STRANGE MISUNDERSTANDING.
CLATTER
FRAU'S THE VILLAGE GOVERNOR?
THAT'S RIGHT.

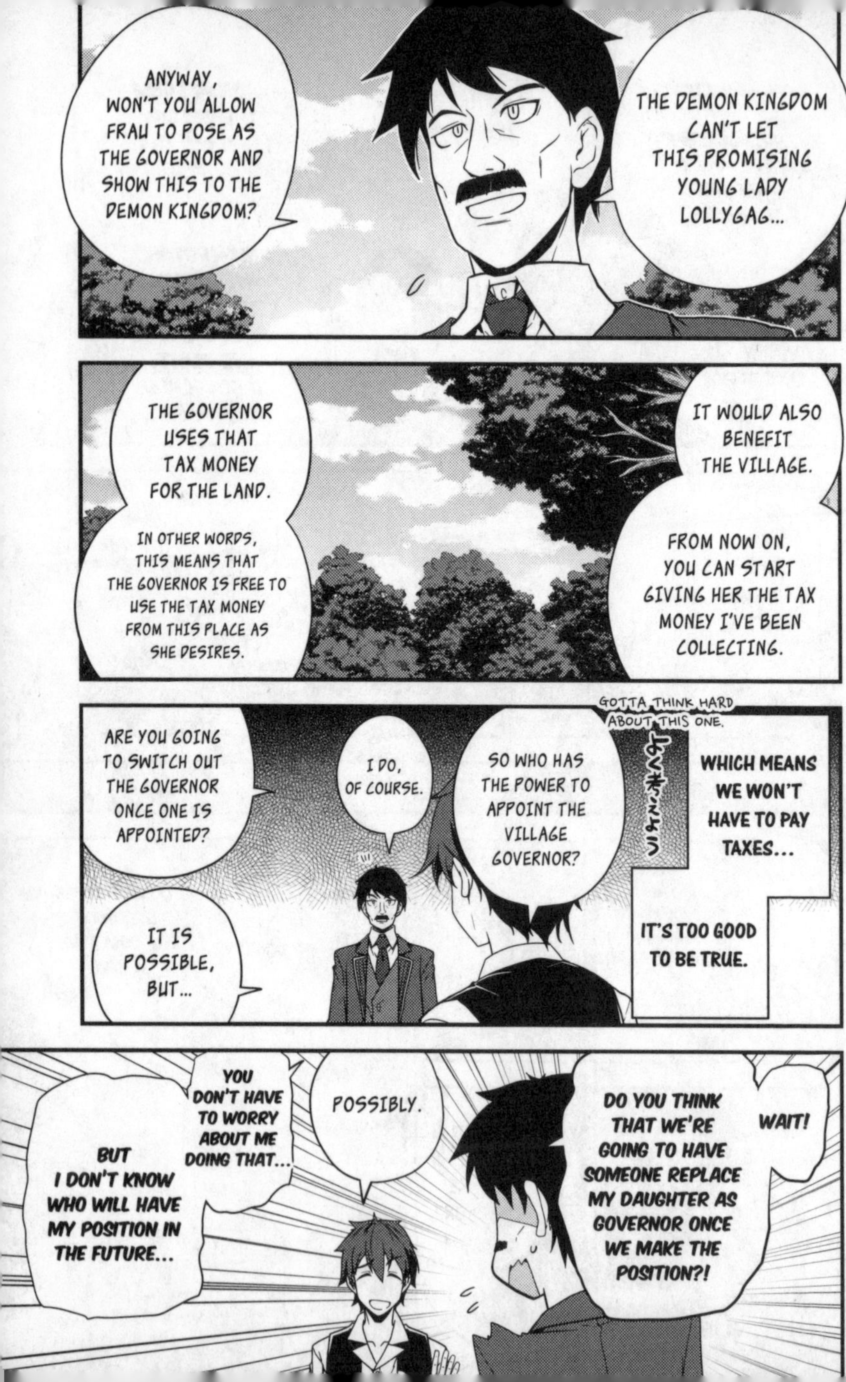
THE DEMON KINGDOM CAN'T LET THIS PROMISING YOUNG LADY LOLLYGAG...
ANYWAY, WON'T YOU ALLOW FRAU TO POSE AS THE GOVERNOR AND SHOW THIS TO THE DEMON KINGDOM?
IT WOULD ALSO BENEFIT THE VILLAGE.
FROM NOW ON, YOU CAN START GIVING HER THE TAX MONEY I'VE BEEN COLLECTING.
THE GOVERNOR USES THAT TAX MONEY FOR THE LAND.
IN OTHER WORDS, THIS MEANS THAT THE GOVERNOR IS FREE TO USE THE TAX MONEY FROM THIS PLACE AS SHE DESIRES.
WHICH MEANS WE WON'T HAVE TO PAY TAXES...
IT'S TOO GOOD TO BE TRUE.
GOTTA THINK HARD ABOUT THIS ONE.
SO WHO HAS THE POWER TO APPOINT THE VILLAGE GOVERNOR?
I DO, OF COURSE.
ARE YOU GOING TO SWITCH OUT THE GOVERNOR ONCE ONE IS APPOINTED?
IT IS POSSIBLE, BUT...
WAIT!
DO YOU THINK THAT WE'RE GOING TO HAVE SOMEONE REPLACE MY DAUGHTER AS GOVERNOR ONCE WE MAKE THE POSITION?!
POSSIBLY.
YOU DON'T HAVE TO WORRY ABOUT ME DOING THAT...
BUT I DON'T KNOW WHO WILL HAVE MY POSITION IN THE FUTURE...

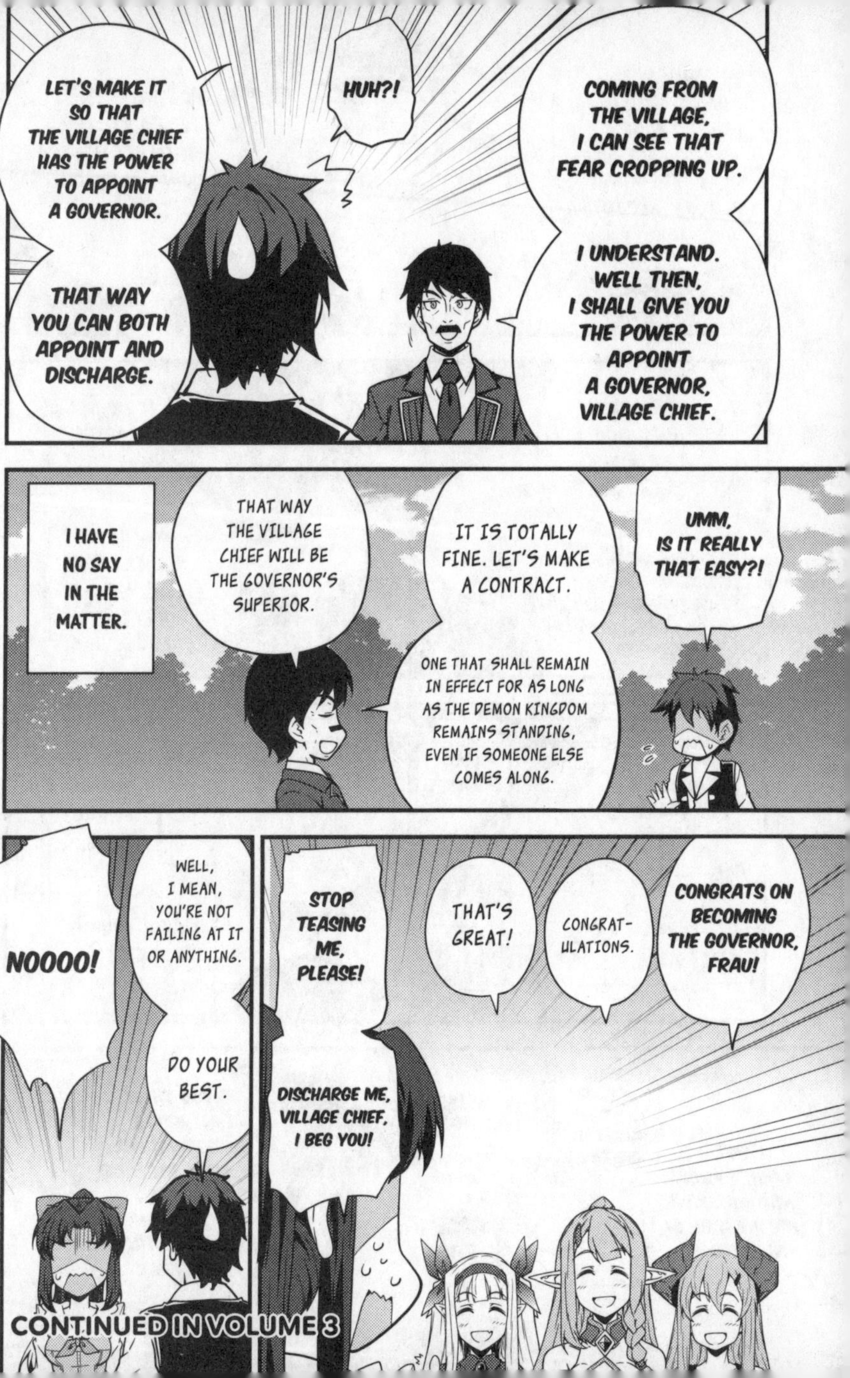
COMING FROM THE VILLAGE, I CAN SEE THAT FEAR CROPPING UP.
I UNDERSTAND. WELL THEN, I SHALL GIVE YOU THE POWER TO APPOINT A GOVERNOR, VILLAGE CHIEF.
HUH?!
LET'S MAKE IT SO THAT THE VILLAGE CHIEF HAS THE POWER TO APPOINT A GOVERNOR.
THAT WAY YOU CAN BOTH APPOINT AND DISCHARGE.
UMM, IS IT REALLY THAT EASY?!
IT IS TOTALLY FINE. LET'S MAKE A CONTRACT.
ONE THAT SHALL REMAIN IN EFFECT FOR AS LONG AS THE DEMON KINGDOM REMAINS STANDING, EVEN IF SOMEONE ELSE COMES ALONG.
THAT WAY THE VILLAGE CHIEF WILL BE THE GOVERNOR'S SUPERIOR.
I HAVE NO SAY IN THE MATTER.
CONGRATS ON BECOMING THE GOVERNOR, FRAU!
CONGRAT-ULATIONS.
THAT'S GREAT!
STOP TEASING ME, PLEASE!
DISCHARGE ME, VILLAGE CHIEF, I BEG YOU!
WELL, I MEAN, YOU'RE NOT FAILING AT IT OR ANYTHING.
DO YOUR BEST.
NOOOO!
CONTINUED IN VOLUME 3

POSTSCRIPT

Hi there. My name is Kinosuke Naito.
I'm so happy that all these new characters appear in the manga.
It makes them so much easier to remember!
What's that? Oh,
I totally remember them.
Yeah. I'm at the point where I sometimes mix up their names.

-Original Author: Kinosuke Naito

I'm Yasumo, the person in charge of the character designs in this manga.
It's so fun to watch the characters I design move around. I even get excited just checking the sketches!
I'll do my best to make great character designs that stand out!

-Original Character Design: Yasumo

"TREE" CONTINUED

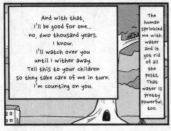

A huge spider's moved innn!!!
SHFF
デーモンスパイダーだぁぁ!
A freaking Demon Spiderrr!!!
Huh? It's okay? It's not doing anything weird? You want to give birth here? Oh, by all means. You got this. I'll protect you from the cold.
1
Wyverns?! Whaaat?! It's no good!
I'll be burned to the ground! It's heading this way! SPEWING FIREEE!!
Wha? The human shot down the wyvern. Hmm.
BOOM
BOOM
BOOM
B-Bang up job. Leave it to the human, I guess. I hope we can always take care of each other.
2
Yup, here comes a strange one. And a dragon. The human somehow handled them all. Okay, I get it now.
You can't disobey this human. In other words, if I weren't helping him ...my fruit would take a lot longer to ripen. I'm gonna do my best to repay him. I'll protect him from sickness.
3
The human sprinkled me with water and it got rid of all the pests. That water is pretty powerful, too.
And with that, I'll be good for one... no, *two* thousand years. I know. I'll watch over you until I wither away. Tell this to your children so they take care of me in turn. I'm counting on you.
4

POSTSCRIPT

Thank you for reading to the end of volume 2!
A lot more characters showed up in this volume, and there's going to be even more!
Expect great things in the next volume!

-In charge of illustrations: Tsurugi -Staff: Nagaji, souer (Suu)

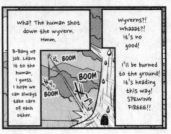

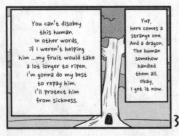

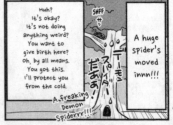

DRIME

I am a most . . . Err, let me to start over. My name is Drime, and I am a dragon.

I shoulder the perilous task of "Dragon Gatekeeper." But it's only because my father Dos is the Dragon Lord, not because I have any actual power. I'm aware.

But as long as I'm not so weak that I'll lose to those dragons, then I am not supremely incompetent.

And I'm not . . . but I'm pretty sure there's no way I can topple that wyvern. You know, the one from the Iron Forest.

I don't know how it got like this, but that wyvern is definitely stronger than any one of those dragons. It's got as many barriers, walls, and barricades as a dragon, so I doubt my attack will actually land.

Hopefully, its attacks won't land either, but now's not the time to let my guard down. If it does turn into a showdown, my chances of winning should be 50/50 . . . oh, who am I kidding? I'd be at a disadvantage for sure.

But even so, there's a reason why the wyvern won't go near my lair: It's scared of my wife and my daughter.

It never told me that, but I can just tell by the way it's acting. In any case, it only flies over the mountain that houses our lair when my wife and daughter aren't home.

My wife and daughter haven't toppled it because of the anti-war pact between the wyverns and dragons.

Most dragons ignore it, but my wife and daughter care, and so do I.

That's why I will not strike a wyvern. It pains me, but I absolutely refuse.

That wyvern was suddenly attacked.

It was a long-range attack too. Unbelievable.

Now that it's been attacked, I'm feeling more fear than joy.

"What do I do if the attacker comes after me next?" I ask my butler, who's standing beside me, and he expounds upon a gruesome future.

Can't you give me a little more hope? No? I see. Would you be able to protect me? You're quite confident in your defensive skills, right? What's that? You could defend against its attack if it only hits once? Incredible! Can you protect me with . . . Oh? You'll use me as a shield to take the hit? Har har. Now I get it.

My butler and I get into a bit of a scuffle.

For now, the actual plan is to not fight the thing that killed the wyvern. While I'm glad this has nothing to do with me, in a worst-case scenario, I might have to form an alliance.

Are you saying I should go greet them now? Hold on—let's do that after we gather information. It's scary because we don't know who we're dealing with here. Not to mention, we've got to prepare the gifts.

Yes, it should be when my wife and daughter aren't around, so we don't bicker.

My wife and daughter don't like when I'm being meek.

So I'm here in Tall Tree Village to form an alliance, but this is a place of refuge.

The food and the drinks are exquisite. And the bathhouse facility is quite pleasant. And the entertainment is second to none.

The hordes of Inferno Wolves and Demon Spiders aren't good for the nerves, but I've already gotten used to them. Once they grow on you, they're really adorable. Hahaha. This is my meat. Not yours.

What?

You're going to bring luggage to the Cambion village? Well then, I shall do it!

I can't have people thinking I'm a dragon who does nothing but eat and sleep.

I've got to show that I can be useful.

Are you asking if my pride will be wounded if a dragon like me has to carry luggage? My pride isn't so fragile that it would shatter over such a small thing.

Hahaha. I'm not really sad so you don't have to comfort me. I'm fine.

There's nothing that a dragon like me can't handle. I do what I can, and that's it.

What's that? I can drink the rest of the wine we don't sell? Well then, I'll carry this with all the vigor I have.

I scared people in the Cambion village.

It's been so long that I've forgotten that even a dragon like me can be threatening.

It's refreshing.

But I don't know how I feel about them trading all of the alcohol. I wish they tried harder to read the room.

I've come here under the direction of the village chief in Tall Tree Village, but I wish they would consider my feelings since I can't intervene. Actually, never mind. It's nothing.

The angel lady glares at me.

I can easily beat her in a fight, but she is of the village chief's wives. I want to avoid a scuffle if I can.

Right. I'll do my best to sell their stuff.

When I get back to the village, the village chief pours me some wine. What a great chief. He really knows how to treat a guy.

Oh, how I'd love to live in this village.

But that's not going to happen. My butler will come to pick me up. I have to go back home tomorrow.

By the way, the reason I don't go home right away is because I know my butler secretly can't wait for the food.

I'm a guy who really cares about his butler. Hahaha.

It's definitely not because I want to stay here for as long as I can.

READ THIS PAGE LAST.

Hm? What's wrong, butler, whom I trust more than anyone? Isn't the fruit in your hand the one that was prepared just for me?
I should have a vacation home here? Not a bad idea.
I can sleep in the room I'm renting, but I'll have to wake up when the maids come in.
My wife and daughter aren't here. I'd like to sleep in a little more.
If it's a second home, I can do what I want.
Yeah, a second home sounds swell.
But in terms of the food . . . I want your tribe to work in my second home.
I see. They're going to learn how to cook? Good. I have no complaints.
I trust you to pick the right personnel.
You're right. When it comes to building a second home, my wife and daughter don't have to . . . nice answer.
All right, that's enough fruit for you. You've already had three.

My name is Drime.
I am a dragon whose daughter accused him of cheating when she found out about his second home.
How did she find out? Did my butler betray me? Oh no, no, I'm not cheating at all. Really. I have no reason to cheat.

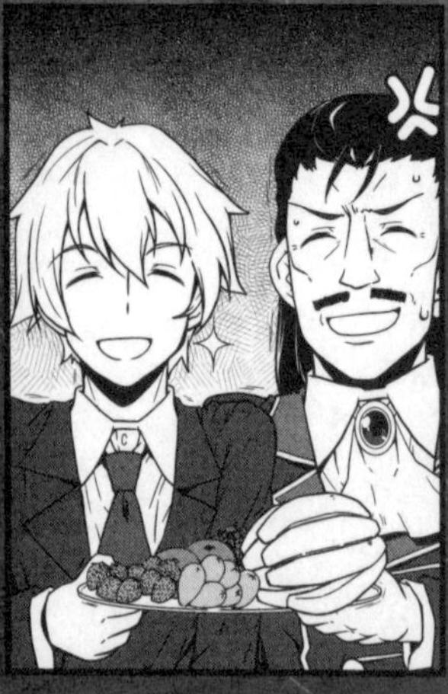

A daughter her age is complicated in various ways.
As I experience this firsthand, I lament my weakness for wanting to go back to the village tomorrow.

End

Illustration
Yasuyuki Tsurugi

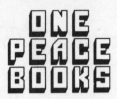

Farming Life in Another World Volume 2
(ISEKAI NONBIRI NOUKA Vol.2)
© Yasuyuki Tsurugi 2018
© Kinosuke Naito, Yasumo 2018
First published in Japan in 2018 by KADOKAWA CORPORATION, Tokyo.
English translation rights arranged with KADOKAWA CORPORATION, Tokyo.

ISBN: 978-1-64273-102-6

Story by Kinosuke Naito
Art by Yasuyuki Tsurugi
Character design by Yasumo
Translated by Kristi Fernandez
English Edition Published by One Peace Books 2021

Printed in Canada
1 2 3 4 5 6 7 8 9 10

One Peace Books
43-32 22nd Street STE 204 Long Island City, New York 11101
www.onepeacebooks.com

D0920841